Fundamentals *of*
PLAY DIRECTING

Fundamentals *of*
PLAY DIRECTING

ALEXANDER DEAN

Late Associate Professor of Play Directing
Yale University

RINEHART & COMPANY, INC.

PUBLISHERS   NEW YORK

First Printing, 1941
Second Printing, 1942
Third Printing, 1943
Fourth Printing, 1945
Fifth Printing, 1946
Sixth Printing, 1947
Seventh Printing, 1948
Eighth Printing, 1950
Ninth Printing, 1951
Tenth Printing, 1952
Eleventh Printing, 1953

Dedication

To those who have been pupils of mine, to those who have loyally supported my approach and without whose interest and enthusiasm this analysis of Play Directing would have been neither developed nor presented in book form, I gratefully dedicate these pages.

Foreword

THIS BOOK on play directing is an expansion of the first third of Alexander Dean's *Syllabus of a Course in Play Directing* and includes the material covered in the first-year class in directing as he gave it at the Department of Drama, Yale University. To the author, play directing was not necessarily either a divine or a mysterious gift but an art in which, just as in other arts, certain principles could be both perceived and taught. Without belittling innate talent or claiming that an artist could be created where there was no inherent flair for the art, the author believed that the knowledge and application of certain principles would avoid costly mistakes and eliminate economic and artistic waste.

Because there is little agreement among schools and teachers of drama as to what can be taught and how it is to be taught, and because professionals in the theater usually deny that the teaching of theater is a possibility, criticism of these methods and of this approach may be expected. The only answer is that the theory of play directing as developed in these pages proved to be workable and successful with a large number of students and casts. In fact it was at the request of many former students who have become teachers and directors that the writing of this material was undertaken. The present volume is the analysis of eighteen years' experience in schools and theaters, with students and actors, with amateurs and professionals.

Since no book for the beginner would fulfill its purpose unless the reader were acquainted with ordinary stage terminology, a glossary in Appendix B is included in which terms relating to the stage, the setting, and stage management are defined.

There was work still to be done on Mr. Dean's manuscript at the time of his death; through the loyalty and devoted industry of several of those who had been his students the following pages have finally been made ready for publication. To

Henry F. Boettcher, Head of the Department of Drama, Carnegie Institute of Technology; to Lawrence Carra, Assistant Professor of Drama and Director of the Experimental Theater, University of Texas; to Wilson Lehr, Instructor and Director of Drama, Packer Collegiate Institute; and to Frank McMullan, Assistant Professor of Play Production, Yale University, belongs the credit for the completion of this volume.

Table of Contents

Contents

Contents

PART IV: PRODUCTION PROCEDURE

Part I

INTRODUCTION

I

Drama as Art

JUST AS the writing of drama is an art, so, too, a dramatic performance is a work of art. Before we can have a basic understanding of the dramatic performance, it is necessary to analyze the purpose and the fundamental principles of art and apply them to the theater.

A. DEFINITION OF ART

Broadly speaking, all art is an imitation of nature. By this we mean that painting, music, sculpture, architecture, literature, and drama are expressions of human ideas which in turn are the product of recalled images. These images are recalled because the creator uses the images of past experience, the recollected forms of life, and through them creates an object that is the result of his own imagination but that fundamentally is nothing but life itself. Art is man's interpretation of life expressed in a way that can be universally recognized and understood.

B. PURPOSE OF ART

The purpose of all art is to arouse the emotions. A great painting like the "Sistine Madonna" or a great building like the Taj Mahal arouses the emotions of the spectators. Beethoven's *Fifth Symphony* and Wagner's *Tristan and Isolde* do the same for the listeners. Dramas like *Oedipus Rex, Hamlet,* and *The Lower Depths* excite intense feeling in an audience. This emotional agitation must not be merely a passing effect; instead, the force of the passion on the individual must be so profound that when he leaves the immediate stimulus there will remain a lasting impression conducive to thought. Unless both of these are aroused, the work cannot be classified as a work of art. The thinking or afterthought is a very necessary part of the reaction. The stimulus given by the work of art

3

has not told the individual what to think, but it has brought to action or consciousness the individual's own experiences, images, or ideas about life. It may stir the individual to a deeper realization of life and man's relationship to it or to such important fundamental forces as God or the universe or nature. More usually, it gives him an insight into man's pitiful helplessness, insignificance, and ineffectuality when confronted with or compared to the greater force that prompts his thoughts and actions. The individual's thought reception need not be uniform to all but may differ as each person's experience and beliefs in life differ from his neighbor's.

If we wish to understand where and how a work of art received the power to stir our emotions deeply or to make us think profoundly, we must return to the artist himself. To convey this power through his artistic expression, the artist or creator must first have had within himself the highly developed gift of being deeply moved emotionally and intellectually by some object in life. In drama this object is usually man in relation to his environment or events and his reaction to these circumstances. Having the greatness to be moved, the artist, then, has in turn to move us. The purpose of art, therefore, is to stir us emotionally and intellectually in the same manner in which the artist was moved when he received his inspiration to create from nature.*

---

*The art of great comedy presents a special problem. If we accept the common explanation that comedy is an intellectual exercise and tragedy an emotional one, it would seem to be denying that comedy is art. A brief explanation may be made as follows: When we are exposed to the predicaments of comic character and comic situation, we are not asked to feel for them, and a sense of pleasure is derived from the relaxation of the emotions. Just as tragedy exercises these emotions, so comedy provides what might be comparable to a rest cure. Actually, the intellect plays a very important role in bringing this about— the emotions are relaxed because they are protected by an intellectual judgment. This judgment makes clear the inferiority and disproportion of the comic character and situation and the futility of ever bothering to worry about them. This is the comic spirit; and notice how under these circumstances we accept much that is impudent and shocking. The moment, however, that such impudence breaks through to arouse feeling, all comic spirit disappears.

Comedy as an art may then be said to have a basis as emotional as that of tragedy. The difference lies only in the way in which our feelings accept the events portrayed, and, of course, in our outward reaction to them. Aroused, the emotions express themselves in tears and indignation; relaxed, there is no choice but laughter.

C. The Creation of a Work of Art

1. CONCEPT

The creative artist must first form in his mind the image of an external object to which he attaches an impression, a thought, or any other product of memory or imagination. This is the concept, the creation, the subject. It will have resulted from a deeply felt emotional experience in his own life—an experience, not peculiar to himself, but one that is universal and, in drama especially, common to a mass of people. The dramatist may conceive a human being or character; he may review an event or story; or he may have an idea. Whatever the concept, it must deal fundamentally with man in relation to greater forces, such as the laws of God and man.

2. TECHNIQUE

Sheer imagination alone, however, is incapable of arousing emotional states in others. The artist, besides feeling his concept, must know his materials in order to produce it. The artist's emotion expressed in whatever material—clay, granite, paint, words, or musical instruments—will, without form, fail completely to fulfill his purpose of stirring the spectator or audience. The pure reproduction of the concept will not make the art product complete. If this were sufficient, all that the playwright need do would be to reproduce nature or a part of life literally, photographically, and minutely. But to do this is not art. Literal reproduction on the stage never succeeds in evoking emotional reactions of a profound sort. The theater artists must rearrange the parts of actual life into a whole that may perhaps seem to be a life reproduction but in reality is not. Art is not nature's creation—it is man's.

Of what does this rearrangement consist? Let us give answer to this by giving it first a name. The rearrangement of the concept or nature is achieved through technique—known in drama as form, or structure. Each art has its own technique based upon fundamental principles. In all writings on the arts, these principles are the most difficult to describe, the most intangible to make clear, the most contradictory ·to arrange in order. Time alone has developed them; trial and error have made them factual. At the beginning of any art there were few principles, if any; artists have added them by degrees and from experience.

We shall now discuss those principles which are generally accepted as being common to all arts: unity, coherence, emphasis and selectivity, proportion, rearrangement, and intensification.

3. UNITY

Unity is one of the principles common to all arts—not the unity of time, place, and mood, as the French later declared, but of adherence to the subject. The earliest literature, like the *Iliad,* the *Odyssey,* and *Beowulf,* as well as the earliest plays of all countries, lacked this quality of unity. In every art it was one of the first signs of technique to be acquired. The rambling, loose, and interrupted putting together of unassociated, irrelevant, and disconnected subjects sifted through time into a treatment of a single subject. This factor of unity in technique has a broader usage than at first seems possible. The "porter scene" in *Macbeth* is not irrelevant, because it is tied up in the technical suspense writing which hinges on whether or not Macbeth will, in his murder of Duncan, be apprehended by Macduff who is knocking to enter.

Several plots in a play do not violate unity if they eventually lead to a unified major situation. The naturalistic style of writing practiced by Chekhov and the Russians in general, by O'Casey in *Juno and the Paycock,* and by the American playwrights of *Street Scene, Dead End,* and *Ah, Wilderness* does, in spite of the first and casual observation, adhere to a definite unity. In any art the violation of unity tires and confuses the spectator.

4. COHERENCE

Coherence is closely related to unity in that each part of the whole should not only bear a relation to but develop or evolve from the previous part. Coherence demands logical and probable relationship of the parts; in a play this might be the psychological relationships of the character to the action or the motivation of character and action.

5. EMPHASIS AND SELECTIVITY

Emphasis is essential in all arts. It is the expression of the kernel, the core, the heart and soul of every concept. In nature there is no emphasis; in man's expression of nature there must be. Through emphasis the artist is able to make the important parts of his creation stand out vividly from their background of lesser parts so that the spectator may recognize their importance more easily and clearly. Emphasis involves *selectivity;* in fact, one of the simplest ways to emphasize is to omit entirely certain elements of its nature. The parts omitted are no longer present to detract from the unity and coherence of the whole and by their very absence help to concentrate the spectator's attention more closely upon the important factor. Selectivity also leads to greater beauty, since confusion and disorder, constantly existing in nature, are discordant with our idea of a pleasing effect.

6. PROPORTION

Closely related to emphasis is proportion. Although emphasis demands certain omissions, it cannot call for the elimination of everything except the important part. In art, accordingly, other elements are included, but these elements are subordinated to the important parts. They take up less space or time. They may occur at the same time as the important part, but they are of less account or in the background.

7. REARRANGEMENT

The emphasis of the important part is conveyed not only by actual size in space or time but by rearrangement so that through its position the important part is readily recognized by the spectator. The placement of the important part becomes emphatic not only by the subordinate placement of the other parts but also by placing the subordinate parts in such a manner that they lead into and toward the important or dominant part.

This consideration of rearrangement is fully discussed in the chapter on Composition.

8. INTENSIFICATION

Rearrangement further produces an intensifying effect. Dramatic or theatrical effect is a result of intensification; in fact the two terms are often used as synonyms. By technical devices of contrast, unexpectedness, movement, events, tone, or vibrancy in color, a reproduction becomes more effective, more compelling, more dynamic, and more climactic.

A simple example of how technique is applied to the actual reproduction of life and the need of it as far as the audience is concerned is illustrated in the following experience in actual production.

Some years ago I was directing a play whose locale was the corner of Forty-second Street and Broadway in New York. The weather was hot, the window was open and there was considerable dialogue in the play about the noise outside. For the outside noise effect, an actual recording of the noise at that corner was made. Those who forgot their knowledge of the theory were delighted with the result of the record. At the first dress rehearsal the record was used without the knowledge of the actors or the audience. No one on stage or in the auditorium knew what the racket backstage was, and the rehearsal was stopped while inquiry was made. The actual reproduction of nature was not recognizable. It had no suggestion of street noises. It was a mad, discordant rumble signifying nothing. Every possible speed in the sound machine was tried, but nothing improved the effect. Finally a crew of eleven worked out the sounds of the dominant or emphatic elements. The sounds were selected, proportioned, and arranged in climactic order. They were timed, contrasted, and varied. In the end it was an orchestra that performed a technicalized arrangement of street noises.

9. MOOD

A concept or idea when it is reproduced has the power to convey a certain amount of feeling to an observer. This same object rearranged in accordance with the principles of art is able to convey or suggest something more than the denoted object; it can convey the essence of itself which is an aggregation of its own attributes. This is the mood. For instance, one person may paint a picture of an open fire in which the observer can recognize the flames, the sticks of wood, and the coals. The real artist, on the other hand, will paint an open fire so that you may not see these things but instead feel warmth, coziness, security, and family affection. In this projection of an object's essence lies the power of art.

If in a painting of a battle scene the details are of horrible slaughter and attack, the spectator will receive a definite impression of what war is like. But if in his treatment of the scene the artist so arranges the spears, axes, helmets, and figures of the combatants that their lines and positions are opposite and in juxtaposition to one another, then a more intense feeling of war will be conveyed to the spectator. In fact we shall see later in our exercises under Composition that excitement, horror, dread, and anguish may be conveyed to the audience in the abstract by using only lines, masses, and the other principles of design. Even if the subject matter is omitted from the picture, the sheer form will give rise to a mood quality that will stir the emotions of a spectator. In the same way the very form, or structure, alone of a play can convey excitement, fear, and pulsating life or repose, introspection, and sadness or brittleness, humor, and superficiality.

10. THE PURPOSE OF TECHNIQUE

The purpose of technique in all the arts is the same, namely, to make the concept, or subject matter, clearer, more effective, more compelling, and more moving and to convey its mood to the spectator or listener by using the elements of art that will coordinate and express its inherent mood qualities.

The word *technique* is used in many different ways. Each art has its own definition of the term; but although they vary in the different arts, on analysis they are fundamentally similar. Furthermore, each art has its own minor technical points to master; these are usually the treatments of detailed rendering that time and experience have shown to be the most direct method of execution or the most effective manner of obtaining emphasis. Sometimes they regulate the control of visual considerations in respect to the audience or the control of timing, of articulation, or of the many other determinants that make for the best expression.

Technique is apt to change from age to age, so that in each art we find methods that have become obsolete. In playwrighting, for instance, the aside and soliloquy are now out of use. In acting, the whole body position in its relation to the audience has changed from facing directly the front row of the balcony to a more turned-in and blended relation with the other actors on the stage. Formerly the scene designer executed his work with painted perspective; now his technique is to deal with architectural masses.

Although technique changes from age to age, the principles of art that technique has gradually established remain fundamental truths; and even as regards technique itself, much of the technique of the past cannot be improved upon. The heritage of the ages is therefore to be valued not only as the great discoverer of fundamental principles of art but also as the greatest teacher of technique and execution.

Technique is often belittled, despised, and considered unnecessary by those who do not know its purpose, its beauty, its power, and its art. Used by an expert, it can do work for him that creation should do. In other words, an artist's creation may be inferior or poor, yet the technique may be so brilliant that it is forced to do both its own work and that of the creation. The reverse of this is also true: A creation can be so moving, so stirring, and so thought provoking, even when the technique is neglected, that the total effect is one of greatness. Few of us do not know plays of mediocre, conventional, and spiritless subjects that by the sheer brilliance of their execution are refreshing, novel, and even convincingly lifelike. Conversely, many plays with noble and overwhelming topics are a mass of inarticulate and confused events.

11. PROPORTION IN CONCEPT AND TECHNIQUE

It is obvious, therefore, that the ideal creation is one in which there is perfect proportion of concept and technique. Nowadays the near attainment of this perfect proportion occurs more frequently, since audiences are demanding more from the creator in drama than they have done for centuries. Twenty-five years ago we were in an era of dramas that were mainly technical achievements based upon some slight concept of fleeting interest. Today the box-office attraction must have vital and moving concepts written in a manner to convey their essence and attributes.

If we briefly survey for a moment the earliest English dramas up to Dryden, we shall see this struggle between creation and technique during the different periods of drama.

In the earliest mystery plays we find the art of dramatic writing to be a completely unhampered creative expression. It existed as a magnificent natural emotional outpouring of a soul which felt something that it wanted others to share. The authors of these plays had no predecessors to tell them how to write, so they relied merely on their feelings. The result was an inspired creation which had no unity, coherence, emphasis, selectivity, proportion, rearrangement, or intensification. These plays are rambling, irrelevant, and undramatic, but they have, in their concept, a sublime beauty.

Because the dramatic in the theater is more compelling for an audience than the uneventful, the writers of dramas who followed these early writers added more technical elements; their incidents had a beginning and an end, and by degrees they developed a middle. Through the conscious desire for effect these later writers put more and more structure and form into their plays until finally their efforts resulted in a technically good play.

With Marlowe we find that we have the introduction of tragic theory. His plays are interspersed with reflections on the themes or ideas of man in relation to other men, to life, and to God. Such plays demanded a more intricate form, a more exacting technique; but the spontaneity of divine inspiration was still present, although pure creation was diminishing as technique improved. Shakespeare, at his best, gave us the perfect proportion: great creation and great form. After Shakespeare, inspiration and imagination waned and gradually disappeared. Technical effects took their place. Critical analysis was carried to greater heights, until reason and theory destroyed imagination. In Dryden we reach the master of pure order and reason—and great drama disappears for many decades.

Such a cycle of concept and technique is observable in general literature as well as in drama. A preponderance of technique will destroy the greatness of spontaneous expression. But, and I repeat this emphatically, neither is of any great value without the other.

D. Art and the Teacher

1. development of the artist

Every art has had its geniuses who created masterpieces without the apparent aid of an instructor or teacher. Drama is no exception. This fact is frequently used as an argument that teachers are unnecessary—that if a person has the ability to create as an actor, a director, a designer, or a playwright, he will create. The great masters have done it in the past and will do it again in the future. This is true, but its corollary—that every gift will find its expression—is not true. Many of those most gifted have perished unknown, because they lacked a consciousness of form and a deductive mind that orders and arranges. This fact is usually overlooked.

Most people believe that merely the feeling is necessary for expression, that an artistic genius is born fully matured and armed, like Pallas Athena from the head of Zeus. These mistaken beliefs arise from the fact that great artists are known for their greatest works and not for their early attempts and their later experiments and mistakes. Further ignorance exists about those creators, usually very good ones, who exercised their craft just before the artistic trend of their age culminated in a great master.

In the theater particularly the predecessors of a great master have contributed highly to his success. And again in the theater particularly have the various steps in the great master's development been very apparent; whether it be Shakespeare, Racine, Calderon, Molière, or Ibsen, their study of their predecessors and their development in their own work show clearly the manner in which they have taught themselves. Their native genius was such that they had not only the divine spark of creation but also the purely deductive mind which pointed out to them the erroneous as well as the successful parts in their plays.

The theater is fortunate in that the audience tells quickly and decisively whether or not the product is successful. The development of a playwright by the study of his failures as well as of his successes is perhaps the most powerful method of learning. This self-instruction is distinctly noticeable in all the masters and is the complete proof of its merit. Sometimes the teaching is merely a consciousness of the writer of his creation and of how it will affect an audience. Each great master in the theater must have these two inherent qualities: the creative impulse and the consciousness of the way and manner of expression.

The creative impulse and imagination and conception of idea are so nearly synonymous that they will be regarded as such in these pages. The manner of expression is generally spoken of as form, structure, or technique.

The genius, although an analysis of his work has constantly shown him to possess a consciousness of form, is likely to be the first to deny the fact, because conception and form are bound so closely together that he creates in form. Nature, moreover, does not produce the two different types of mind—the creative and the critical—simultaneously in one person. Numerous examples have proved that if a person has at the start of his career a good supply of both, the one that he works with most will destroy the other. In other words, if an artist possessed of both faculties works in the creative, his critical and deductive faculty diminishes in value. The converse of this is more frequent: The artist who uses his critical and technical faculties in the arts soon destroys his creative ability. This gives rise constantly to the accusation that the critic and the director, whose work calls for a fuller use of the deductive and conscious

thought processes, are disappointed creative artists. This may
be but is not necessarily true. The fact is that a person may be
attracted to art at an early age when his knowledge of it and
of himself in relation to it is little. He merely feels an emotional impulse toward the art and is drawn to work in some
capacity in that field. Not until he has experimented with himself in the many phases of that art is he able to find in which
particular aspect he excels. Many a playwright has found himself more proficient as an actor and vice versa. But in neither
case should we accuse one or the other of being disappointed.

Following almost every period of great creation there has
arisen a great deductor, or teacher. The most startling example is Aristotle. Greek drama started with natural simplicity
and in a most spontaneous manner. Before there was any written history of this drama, it developed beyond a purely religious rite into a form of its own. The plays of Aeschylus
(our earliest specimens of Greek drama) are magnificent combinations of creation and technique, showing a deliberate attempt on the author's part to utilize whatever of value had
existed before his time and to develop the form with his own
contributions. So marked are these changes of development
within his own work that mere chance cannot account for them.
Sophocles developed the form further than his predecessor, and
in turn Euripides surpassed Sophocles at least in this one respect.
These men have left us no explanation of what they were deliberately attempting; they merely executed their changing
ideas of structure in their successive plays. It was left to
Aristotle, a deductive thinker on many subjects, to write about
the arts and to analyze the form, theory, and technique of his
countrymen's plays.

Shakespeare, too, has left us no written record of his conscious study of dramatic technique, of what carried over to the
audience and what did not, of what moved them and what did
not, of wherein lay his mistakes and his success. Yet a careful
examination of his predecessors and of his plays in chronologi-
cal order is perhaps the greatest instruction that we can find in
the fundamental technique of playwriting even for the present-
day dramatist. This examination has been made by Professor
George Pierce Baker, whose little-known *Development of*

Shakespeare as a Dramatist is as important a textbook on play-writing as his well-known lectures on Dramatic Technique.

Ibsen, on the other hand, in his *Drama Workshop* gives a full account of his struggle to master form. The comparison of the early *Doll's House* with the later and final version is a source of valuable knowledge in itself as well as a final proof of the consciousness of expression that this foremost creative genius possessed.

The following quotation from the memoirs of the composer Tchaikovsky furnishes an excellent example of a serious creator's attitude toward form:

Kamenka, July 7, 1878

". . . Talking with you yesterday about the process of composing, I did not express myself clearly concerning the work that follows the first sketch. The phrase is especially important: What has been written with passion must now be looked upon critically, corrected, extended, and most important of all, condensed to fit the requirements of the form. One must sometimes go against the grain in this, be merciless, and destroy things that were written with love and inspiration. Although I cannot complain of poor inventive powers or imagination, I have always suffered from lack of skill in management of form. Only persistent labor has at last permitted me to achieve a form that in some degree corresponds to the content. In the past I was careless, I did not realize the extreme importance of this critical examination of the preliminary sketch. For this reason, the succeeding episodes were loosely held together and seams were visible. . . . I know also that I am very far from achieving the full maturity of my talent. But I see with joy that I am progressing slowly, and I ardently desire to take myself as far along this road to perfection as I can go. Therefore I was inaccurate yesterday when I said I wrote out my compositions unhesitatingly from the first sketches. It is more than a copy, it is a detailed critical examination of the first plan, corrected, rarely added to and very often cut."*

With men like Tchaikovsky and many others declaring the importance of form and struggling to achieve perfection in it, we still find beginners and even teachers in the arts who believe that the most or even the only important element in successful creation is the artist's conviction of the greatness of the conception, subject, or thought.

*From *Beloved Friend,* the story of Tchaikovsky and Madejda von Meck, by Catherine Dunker Bowen and Barbara von Meck. Random House, Inc., New York, 1937.

2. CREATION AND FORM

The part that consciousness of form should play in the mind
of the creator is open to endless dispute. It is true that the experienced and practiced worker in all arts creates in form—
that is, in the process of imagination the concept appears directly to him in form—but he cannot do this until he has
worked on and learned his technique so thoroughly that actual
thought of it can be dismissed during the process of creation.
The mental processes of concept and form become in reality
only one. This, perhaps, is as responsible as any one factor for
the frequent feeling that the distinguished worker pays little
or no attention to form.

Experience in dealing with the beginner for many years has
forced me to the conclusion that the best process of blending
these two elements into a fused whole is to learn each separately, to practice and use each separately, and to apply one
to the other in separate stages. Time alone will blend the two
parts into one mental process. For an example I should like to
show how this theory applies to the work of a playwright.
(Later, under Picturization, I shall apply it fully to that of
a director.) We shall refer to the factor of the imaginative
concept as "flight" and of the technical execution as "restriction."

The playwright takes for his stimulus, let us say, a certain
character from his observation. The flight consists of absorbing each phase of this person. The playwright then adds a great
deal to the original subject by gathering further qualities from
other people that the original may not have had. A strong
reason, an impelling thought or purpose urges him to place
the character into a play. This character has a fundamental
and universal meaning and relationship. The musing and
imaginative flight of the creator's mind may take months. He
must be completely absorbed in the character and develop in
his mind many sides and phases of characterization, even
though eventually these may not all be used in the play.

The writer then "restricts" this imaginative flight by dividing the development of the character into the emphatic moments. There may be three; there may be eleven. This will

probably mean that certain characteristics or phases of the person will have to be dropped, for those which are used must bear a relation to the thought that the writer wishes to convey. This planning is obviously a technical consideration. He then jots down his notes on paper to arrive at the first draft of form.

The creator's next flight is to see this character in action, in a series of events. This, again, is a long imaginative process; not only must the action fit the character, but it must fit the idea. The choice of action will rest on many different conditions: The action must be interesting; it must be varied; it must be climactic. The creator's inherent nature—his human experience and sense of the dramatic—will aid him in deciding upon the proper action. At this point the story will be vague and formless.

Restriction now compels the ordering of the story. Through pure reasoning he divides his story into a beginning, a middle, and an end; he determines the number of acts and scenes; he arranges the climaxes before the intermissions. On paper he finally creates a definite pattern, a fuller synopsis.

When this has been done, the work of restricting proceeds. The writer divides the story up into "French scenes," that is, the minor situations which lead to the major climaxes. Usually, on the entrance or exit of a character a new thought or turn of events follows. The outline now has a large number of unit events, or "French scenes," through which the character proceeds. Much thought is then given to the order and arrangement of scenes, as it is this sequence that gives greatly heightened dramatic effects. The knowledge of the best moments at which to have disclosures made and events take place is the secret of successful plotting.

A flight again follows as the dramatist plans the psychological reactions of his characters to the situation and to one another. When this is thought out and written down, his synopsis is roughly complete.

The next step is most important; it is a procedure true of any work in the theater. When the form has been sketched and settled, the creator should study it over and over, absorbing the arrangement as much as he did the original subject. This is necessary, because the first draft should be a completely emotional flight. The creator, I believe, should not follow the written outline or synopsis or form when he sits down actually to write out the play, but he should have absorbed the synopsis to such an extent that he writes into his form as he creates. If he deviates from his form for the moment, that is all right, for his writing of the first draft should be done without restriction—without technical hindrance or thought. It should be a fresh torrent of feeling. If the writer is unable to retain the whole skeleton of the play, then he should do his writing by acts.

The next restriction is obvious. It is a cold-blooded critical analysis, a comparison between what has been written and what was the outline. It is a cutting, a molding, and a shaping of that which has been written. This is the restriction that Tchaikovsky speaks of in his memoirs. Often in "what has been written with passion" new twists and turns of plot and unanticipated reactions of characters will have appeared. If so, a deliberate weighing of what had been thought out against what has come out spontaneously should be made. Sometimes the new material is worth keeping; sometimes it has to be scrapped. Some scenes, perhaps, especially the early ones, have been poorly done emotionally, and these must be rewritten.

Restriction after restriction follows: The length and proportion of scenes must be adjusted; the logical thought development within the scene will need to be carefully rearranged; business will have to be inserted or carried through; sentences must be polished, tightened, pointed, or emphasized; comedy lines must be rephrased and spaced at more or less regular intervals. The playwright at this stage must become the severest critic. He must look at his work in cold perspective. He must be a thorough technician.

This brief analysis, of course, is not a formula for writing a play, nor is it in any way complete. Many problems are bound to arise that I have not mentioned. But it is roughly, at least, a process that is workable and that makes clear the relationship between emotional creation and rational technique. It tells why and how in all the arts the creation should be first and the restriction and ordering second, not in importance but in pro-

cedure. It also emphasizes the point already made that with
time and experience the two processes will blend into one so
that the original conception will be executed in form—or
nearly so.

E. Art and Its Appreciation

Our previous use of the phrase "arousing the emotions of
the spectator" makes it necessary at this point to qualify and
explain this effect more fully and to digress for the moment
into giving an account of those who are capable of judging a
work of art.

Although every real creation must arouse an emotional and
intellectual response in the spectator, it does not follow that
every creation that achieves this is a work of art; nor does it
follow that every great creation must achieve this for everyone.

1. TRAINING

The drama more than any other art suffers in these two respects from erroneous thinking on the part of the spectator.
The most ignorant person does not hesitate to pass ultimate
judgment on a play or its performance. Young and old alike
condemn or praise with decisive and final words. The primary
business of the drama is to arouse emotional states of one sort
or another. The most critical of us can go to the theater and
laugh and applaud, even though the play and performance
may be definitely mediocre. This sort of emotional pleasure is
certainly not to be understood as being the sort that I mean.

Some years ago during Christmastime my grocer presented
me with a calendar, at the same time telling me with emotional
warmth how much he admired the colored picture on it. He
gave me a detailed account of the expense and trouble that he
had gone to in obtaining it for his customers. The picture was
of a buxom beauty with red cheeks and dark olive skin, with
an abundance of black hair flowing over her shoulders and a
rose dangling coyly from her scarlet mouth. To the grocer
this colored rotogravure was an object of beauty which aroused
deep emotion in his breast. "A piece of art!" he kept repeating.

"I have the original framed in my parlor." Obviously it was not a "piece of art." Yet he and many of his friends and customers were more moved by it than they would have been by Botticelli's "Venus."

Not in the same category, but similar in regard to the emotional response that it stirred in thousands, myself included, was the excitement created by a mediocre but effective piece of music, Ravel's *Bolero*. To many this was as superb a piece of music as a Beethoven symphony. Yet in cold analysis the *Bolero* is not a very good musical composition—effective, vivid, above all exciting, and yet not for a moment great. Who it is that must be moved by a work of art and what he must have in order to judge its worth we shall see presently. Let us in passing recall the number of artists who never received the acclaim during their lifetime that should have been theirs but who received posthumous recognition in later years when the public had matured sufficiently to appreciate their works.

Appreciation of art is not, for most of us, a spontaneous reaction. Masterpieces of art make no impression on the untrained and unfamiliar eye or ear. It follows, then, that not only the individual but a great mass of individuals as well must be trained to appreciate any single work of art. Hundreds of people view the "Sistine Madonna" at Dresden daily. Hung in its own room—ideally lighted—the majority of visitors look in and pass by; some remain to buy a postal card; but only a few sit before it reverently for an hour and absorb its beauty. Is it art's fault that more do not appreciate? Yet how many people believe it so: "It doesn't move me. So off with its head!"

2. SENSITIVITY

The first requisite for the appreciation of an art by the spectator is an inclination within himself toward the art. There must be an affinity between an art and its appraiser. If a man is tone deaf, he can never appreciate music; if he is color blind, he can never love painting; if he does not like the theater, he does not like the theater. There are, however, many degrees of this sort of insensitivity, and these extreme conditions are not necessary for an indifference to an art or to art in general. But,

without exception, the man who in his maturity is to be a specialist in the field of art must have a marked degree of sensitivity and harmony in his natural make-up.

3. ASSOCIATION AND FAMILIARITY

We often hear that the appreciation of an art is an acquired
taste. The saying is only partially true. You do have to have
contact with an art, the closest contact, before your power of
consuming it to the fullest is reached. Frequency of contact
and association is a necessity—not that one needs to know anything about the art or should study it at this early stage but that
one should experience repeatedly for many years the pure emotional reaction to the art as a spectator.

Nothing is so distressing as the neglect of this requirement
in young people anxious to succeed in the theater. All over this
country there are aspirants in acting, with long tales of woe
about their earnest desire, who have not attended any productions of the theater to which they are applying. The inferior
plays that are submitted in the contests throughout the country
show that what the author needs is to go to the theater, not
once but again and again.

It is unfortunately not feasible for a person living outside
New York City to attend the theater very often, but my repeated experience—in the university theater, in the little
theater, in the professional theater—has been to find that the
people who are most anxious to function in the theater do not
go to the theater. Continuous association with an art is as
important as an inherent predilection for it. The earlier in life
this association with the art begins the better it is for one's
future development.

One of the reasons why the professional theater failed on
the road was the fact that New Yorkers from a long and intensive familiarity with the theater had been educated to appreciate the advances being made in writing and production. The
trend of the drama in New York during the past fifteen years
has been a progressive one. We find deeper concepts, more
fundamental pictures of life, less obvious technique, richer
writing, and broader and more subtle ideas. The New York

stage has reached a high level—too high in many of our greater
pieces of work for those communities who have not had the
opportunity of frequent association with the theater to demand
better plays. The list of plays winning the acclaim of both press
and public in New York and traveling forth to failure in the
provinces is too long to give here.

The reason why frequency of attendance improves the demand for better plays is quite easy to understand. If a person
goes to the theater two or three times a year, he does not
become saturated with the drama: he does not become tired
of timeworn ideas and stereotyped theatricalities. There may
be nothing wrong with the plays; but let a person go to conventional theatrical performances sixteen to twenty times a year
for ten years, and we find that he becomes anticipatory of the
material and aware of the form. For him the play will become
a dead and unexciting product, and he will soon be demanding
something richer and truer, something more vital and more
fundamental. What he demands is given him, and he supports
it. This demand, arising from frequency of association, produces gradual changes in the drama and is one of the most
fundamental causes of its development.

When the little and university theaters were first becoming
the factor that they are now in furnishing dramatic fare to
their respective communities, many prophesied that they would
become the experimental theaters of the country, trying new
subjects and methods of treatment. This has proved an unfulfilled prophecy, mainly because the outer communities were not
cognizant of and familiar with the accepted forms sufficiently
to appreciate the unusual and the experimental in drama. Furthermore, experimentation in the creation of any art demands
a greater knowledge on the part of the artist than creation
along conventional lines. Until the creator has mastered the
accepted form, he cannot express his ideas in an unusual manner. Experimentation without a thorough knowledge of the
past usually amounts to a mere repetition of mistakes that have
been made a thousand times before. The greatest innovators
in the drama as well as in other arts, before they became the
revolutionary figures for which they are famed, first became distinguished in the accepted form. They have first mastered thor-

oughly the fundamentals of their art. A complete study of Shakespeare, Molière, Ibsen, Shaw, and O'Neill in their different stages of development furnishes sufficient proof of this.

The critic, then, as well as those others who would judge a work of art, must possess a thorough knowledge of innumerable plays and the performance methods of the past, because in addition to having a keenly appreciative nature the critic must be able to judge intellectually the value and originality of the subject matter as well as the originality and suitability of the form to express the subject. The knowledge of this relationship has already been mentioned as a necessity for the creator. The critic or real student of an art is required to be even more aware of this inherent relationship and the perfection of execution.

The director, too, must understand the merits of each of these factors and must be able to analyze them in order to handle them in the finished product.

F. The Director as an Interpretative Artist

The work of the director obviously is to convey to the audience every part and quality of a play, to see that his actors not only act their characters but convey the concept and take advantage of the heightened effect made possible by the technical arrangement. Let us understand further the relation of the director to the play.

1. THE CREATIVE AND THE INTERPRETATIVE ARTIST

There are two kinds of artist: the creative and the interpretative. The composer, the sculptor, the painter, the writer of literature are all creative artists. They conceive a subject and through the medium of their respective materials give form to the concept. With most arts the work stands complete when the creative artist has finished. With music and drama, however, other artists are required to give the created product its complete fruition and expression. These artists—conductors, musicians, directors, actors, and other workers in the theater— do not produce their artistic expression out of the void but have the already created product to interpret. In some respects their

powers must be greater than that of the creator. The demands
on their native and trained abilities are more exacting, particularly as regards the technical requirements. Interpretative
artists must know their own technique as well as the creator's.
Their imagination is different but must be no less vivid. They
must sense emotionally and intellectually the creator's emotional and intellectual expression. Frequently they must drive
their imagination beyond his—sensing the creator's imagination and adding to it.

They are, nevertheless, interpretative because they must
bring to life for an audience the particular product given them
and not some other that might be their own or one that the
original reminds them of. Just because he is romantically
minded and has a natural flair for picturization the director
must not direct *The Dark Lady of the Sonnets* as if it were
written by Mr. Shakespeare; he must direct it as written by
Mr. Shaw—as an artificial, arbitrary verbal battle. In the
theater the playwright alone is a creative artist; the director,
the actor, and the designer are interpretative.

2. VERSATILITY IN DIRECTING

Notwithstanding this, many directors, year in and year out,
direct every play in the same manner with identical technique,
forcing their own stamp and mark on every part. As plays vary
in their inherent nature and manner, these directors change the
costumes and scenery (seldom the furniture arrangement) but
continue to stamp the products with their own individual styles.
No matter what particular and individualistic qualities the
plays possess, the directing for them all remains basically similar, and little quality, beyond that of the director's, comes
across the footlights.

Professional New York directors are not above this severe
criticism. Much has been written about versatility in acting;
little or nothing, about versatility in directing. As a matter of
fact, although type casting is frowned upon, type setting of
directors is an acknowledged and accepted fact. If a producer
has a mammoth mob spectacle, he hires one director; if he has
a humorous fast-moving farce, he obtains another. A serious

introspective realistic drama must have a third. Each professional director is catalogued according to type, and he works only within the confines of his typed field. It is not uncommon for such a director actually to boast about his own individual treatment that he brings to plays. If the producer is his own director, we can follow the trail of the rubber stamp with perfect ease.

The reason for this lack of versatility and adaptability in directors is that most of them have a preponderance either of auditory or else of visual imagination. Only a few have or acquire both types. The innate tendency of these directors toward one or the other of these elements in stage directing leads them to emphasize their particular bias. For those who only hear the characters speaking, interpretation becomes their main interest; their directing becomes "a living of every character in every scene." Those who are visually minded "see" the actors in an effective composition. The constant stage picture may be formalized with the result that a static, heavy, and classic quality will predominate even though the play is light or realistic. Others have a vivid visualization or picturizing trend so that realism and informality prevail no matter how intrinsically light or artificial the play may be. Constant and rapid movement constitutes some other director's "feeling" for any play, even though it may have been written by Chekhov. "I imagine each play as a series of ocean waves," says a certain director, "some scenes billowing with might and strength, and others quiet but seething." Forced changes of tempo will make the most sincere and honest character play into a claptrap piece of theater.

3. KNOWLEDGE OF FUNDAMENTALS THE BASIS OF DIRECTING

All these methods are purely instinctive as far as directing goes and will result in hit-or-miss productions. Years of experience along this line of instinctive directing will seldom develop a director who can reproduce a play's inherent quality or one who has variety in his directing ability.

Let me liken the study of the wide field of play directing to the study of medicine. Of a four-year course in medical school, the first three years are devoted to the learning of many facts —sometimes related, sometimes not. The last year is given over to diagnosis which considers a certain given condition in the patient. Because of the nature of the condition the facts of medicine may become modified, restricted, or even contradicted. But before the young doctor can learn to diagnose a case, he must first learn the facts of medicine in the normal ordinary condition of a person, even though in actual diagnosis under different existing conditions he may radically change what he has learned.

So it is with play directing: It is the contradiction that makes the exposition of technique difficult. Many statements that one is forced to write, when read literally, are not true. They are so, and they are not so. Their truthfulness depends on the given condition. In writing, however, it is impossible to stop frequently and explain all the exceptions and restrictions that accompany a diagnosis of a particular case. The following pages, therefore, are concerned with facts that we shall call absolute, that is, true under normal conditions. They are true with all other factors being equal—true if the intellectual concept, the mood, the style, the kind of play, or the physical stage does not restrict, control, or change them. When the facts are known, then comes the time to learn the exceptions and restrictions and how they affect the absolute; then comes the time to learn how to diagnose a play, to learn to a far greater depth and length what we have merely touched upon in this chapter.

The director's task, therefore, as interpretative artist, is to study the interpretation of the qualities of a play. But before we can learn the technique and method of conveying these intangible and evasive factors, we must learn first the rudiments of technique of our own field—play directing. To teach these rudiments is the purpose of the present volume.

II

The Function of the Director

A. THE HISTORY OF DIRECTING

IN THE first year of my teaching I received a postal card from a schoolteacher in a small town in Montana. She was to direct the junior class play, but, being probably a specialist in mathematics, she was in a complete quandary as to how to go about directing a play. The card, written in a very fine hand, was covered with endless questions. If merely the first question after the "Dear Sir" had been answered, 500,000 words would have been none too many. The definition of the duties and required knowledge of a play director would have been made clear. The sentence was simple: "Dear Sir, what do you do with your actors when you get them on the stage?"

The complete ignorance of most people about the function of a director is not, perhaps, surprising, since the rise of the director as an important figure in the theater is comparatively recent. This ignorance is not so startling to one as the incompetence that one feels in explaining to the layman just what a director has to do. The task is a baffling one and is usually given up as hopeless. After one of my early and lengthy explanations, my listener remarked, "Oh, I see, you tell them when to come in and when to sit down." And I, with honor, found myself replying: "And when to go out. Yes, that's it."

The play director is a recent arrival in the theater, because only lately have conditions required his contribution to a dramatic performance. The need for him came with the modern understanding of what a production in the theater of today has to be.

In the entire history of dramatic production we find his nearest counterpart in the *choregeus,* or trainer of the chorus, in the Greek drama. His work consisted not only in teaching the technique of dancing to the individual dancers and in perfecting the synchronization of movement but also in interpreting the subject matter of the strophe and antistrophe in terms of positions, movement, and rhythm. To the verses of battle he had to convey the mood and feeling of battle; to the poems of woe he had to contrive a pattern for his dancers that would arouse in 10,000 people a feeling of grief, even though this audience did not hear every word of the chant that the chorus delivered when dancing. The *choregeus* had to fit the interpretative movement to the spoken word so that the word, besides being reinforced and clarified, might connote a definite mood quality for the spectator. As we understand the term today, the *choregeus* was a play director. What was done for the principal speaking actors is uncertain. Except for pure speech coaching, probably very little was done. Certain conventions developed with time, and these were familiar to actor and audience: Royalty entered by the center large basileus gate and remained in that emphatic position; the less important personages used the rear side entrances and held their distances from the leading actors; the mutes came in by the side openings and for the most part remained beside them. With only three or four speakers at a time on stage, the problem of ensemble playing did not exist. The sight lines and acoustics, furthermore, did not allow much freedom in positions, nor did the buskin and mask allow much opportunity for movement. Usually, performances were static declamations.

For centuries productions continued in this method of direction. The French classical school with revolutionary originality developed from a soliloquy underneath a chandelier to a conversation on two benches. Their direction consisted mostly in speech training, since the power of performance lay in their reading the speeches as if they were operatic arias.

Although Goethe and many others urged the use of greater realism in dramatic performances, Goethe also had rules for his actors that contradict our modern conception of realism. For example, they were fined if they took their eyes off the balcony. As time developed, however, realism was stressed more and more, and gradually instead of two benches we find radical innovations—a bench or sofa on one side of the stage and a table with three chairs on the other. This radical setup has continued for centuries, and our present-day stage setting, although designers sometimes cleverly disguise the setup, remains basically the same. Occasionally, we find more realistic arrangements. Furniture arrangement, as we shall see later, has style and, moreover, forces the director into a corresponding style in his directing. Furthermore, a director can seldom in such a formalized setup of furniture convey a quality totally different from that of his actors.

When Gordon Craig conceived dramatic productions as a unity and looked upon scenery, lighting, and costume not as separate entities but as correlated and related parts of a whole, a revolution in the accepted standards of theatrical production took place. The art of the theater became a reality.

There had been, of course, forerunners of the movement. In 1874 the Duke of Saxe-Meiningen presented in Berlin a company that for the first time stressed the "ensemble" method of playing. He devised a system in which a single directing mind brought scenery, costume, stage lighting, and actor into artistic unity. Berlin received these players with wholehearted enthusiasm, as did the audiences in other European cities where they played. Antoine and his Théâtre Libre in Paris felt their influence. Stanislavsky, when he founded his Moscow Art Theater, borrowed directly from the Saxe-Meiningen group and also welcomed into his theater Craig and his revolutionary ideas. Other leaders appeared. Adolphe Appia set down in printed analysis the principles of the new method in staging plays, and Max Reinhardt was soon to begin his bold experiments in staging.

Although many of Craig's actual practices were necessarily discarded and others were extreme and impractical, and although he himself was unable to apply his own ideas to practical usage, his concept became the basis for others in this country to develop and utilize. Simply expressed, this concept regarded the creation of scenery as a unit factor having the principles of art. It was an interpretation of the play in style and mood, the design of which was to create not a reproduction of the actual in painted perspective but a work having the qualities of selectivity, proportion, rearrangement, intensity, and emphasis—all of which would convey the inherent qualities of the play. Not only the scenery but the lighting and costumes as well were designed with the same principles, so that each, besides being an artistic unit in itself, bore an artistic relation‐ ship to the other.

Productions continued to attain a high artistic standard, but the actors were still arranged in formalized positions, a carry‐ over of the technique of the past. They were not expressing the qualities of the play no matter how ably they acted their roles. The visual aspect of the actor conveyed none of the qual‐ ities of the play; sometimes the formalized and artificial arrangement and movement actually contradicted or fought against the qualities of the drama that they were meant to interpret.

The need for direction of the actors to contribute to the total art expression of the production is apparent. The actors themselves without the help of scenery, lighting, or costumes should on a bare stage convey the very style and mood quali‐ ties that the other factors of production contribute. The direc‐ tor then becomes as much an artist as the scene designer. His materials are actors in place of paint and canvas. He must shape and form his group using principles of art and with reason has to coordinate conception and form.

B. DIRECTING THE ACTOR AND THE ACTOR GROUP

For a further understanding of the director's principles let us use the dance as an example. A solo performance of a spring dance is an individual expression of the feeling of spring. A good dancer is able with movement and posture to convey to an audience the connotation of spring. If, however, we work out the dance pattern for eight dancers, training them mi‐ nutely, and then place these eight on a stage in a double row of four; and if now we let each dancer give individual feeling to the routine, the inherent qualities of spring will not come across the footlights. The eight dancers will convey the feeling of spring less ably than the solo. The mood and emotions of the eight placed in arbitrary form, even though each dancer is expressing "spring" to the utmost, have little tonal connota‐ tion to the audience. because we are dealing no longer with the problem of the individual but with that of the group.

No group in which each individual member is expressing an emotion or idea can convey that emotion or idea to an audience. For such individual expression is what the old-fashioned stage manager or stage director worked for; what the actors did, or where they went so long as they did not cover one another and so long as they took a position subordinate to that of the star, did not concern him. To such a director each individual actor was a soloist who expressed his own part. A cast of eight, grouped arbitrarily on the stage, with each expressing his own characterization perfectly was a directed play. This manner of directing fails to give any tonal connotation as far as an audience is concerned. Today only when the relationships and visualization, movement and rhythm, of the group convey the emotional qualities of a play do we consider the play completely directed.

Our modern dances of "revolution," "famine," and "reaping," to mention a few, are not dances of individual expression but of group relationship and movement. In *Les Sylphides* and *Union Pacific* as done by the Ballet Russe de Monte Carlo one sees the difference between the old form of dancing and the new. One sees also the difference between the old-fashioned play directing and the new. The first is a disassociated series of solos, *pas de deux,* trios, and choruses; the latter is a semi-pantomime of violent and contrasting activity coordinated by rhythm and connotative business—all controlled by the principles of composition.

The foregoing paragraphs show clearly the essential difference between coaching and directing. In coaching we are concerned with the individual; in directing we are concerned with the group.

The well-staged ballet contains in the group entity not only the art expression of the choreographer but also perfection of conception and technique, of feeling and thought in the individual. The choreographer has spent his imagination, knowledge, and energies on each individual as much as he has on the effects of the group. And so does the play director.

This relationship of the director to the individual besides his relationship to the group must be emphasized strongly.

The play director must also train, coach, and labor on the speech, voice, expression, and body movement of each actor. Nothing discussed hereafter under the Five Fundamental Elements of Directing is to be understood as meaning a neglect of the individual actor or of the consideration of the auditory coaching of a play which is an inherent part of the dramatic performance—both are requisites of a good director. This book is called not *Play Directing* but the *Fundamental Elements of Play Directing*. This does not mean, however, that because the five elements deal solely with the visual aspect of a production we must look upon the auditory considerations in play production as unimportant. The play director, moreover, who hopes to succeed professionally must also know dramatic construction and playwriting as well as the coaching of speech and acting and the methods of group expression. But again, though dramatic technique is touched upon but lightly in this volume, it does not follow that it is unimportant. Nor does it follow that speech, body expression, and the study of the role which are treated briefly in this volume are any the less important.

By play directing, therefore, we mean the presentation of a play on the stage for an audience interpreted in terms of dramatic action and dramatic sound and in terms of the emotional and intellectual concepts of an author's script.

C. The Five Fundamental Elements of Directing

In the following chapter we deal briefly with the sound, or auditory, portion of the interpretation and proceed then to concentrate in detail on the action or visual aspects. Furthermore, we do not deal with the intellectual and emotional concepts but merely with those elements which furnish the means of conveying these qualities. These means we shall refer to as the five fundamental elements of directing. They are composition, movement, picturization, rhythm, and pantomimic dramatization. These constitute a five-note scale of play directing. These in different combinations and degrees of emphasis are the means by which a director may express the emotional and intellectual qualities of a play.

The director must use parts of each element in every play that he produces. Although every play according to its nature and the characteristics to be emphasized uses a varying degree and combination of the fundamental elements, every directed play must contain some use of all the elements.

The five fundamental elements together with their principles are drawn from the different elements of painting, dancing, and music. Play directing is a combination of the elements of these arts and not an entirely separate and new art. Frequently the principles taken from one of these arts are slightly modified to meet the demands of the new medium. Especially is this true with the elements of painting, since, in directing, the third dimension becomes an additional factor to be considered.

Part II

THE ACTOR

III

Necessity for Technique

AT FIRST consideration it might seem that there would be little demand for a section on the various phases of acting. Already there are a number of excellent texts for the development and training of actors. However, not included in these specialized books are many things that a director expects a beginning actor to know, even though the actor is thoroughly drilled in voice and body expression. The following pages are devoted to material on elementary stage technique for the actor and on acting as it concerns the individual actor, material that the director as coach must know and that should serve as common terminology between director and actor. The beginning actor will find this material of extreme importance. However, our intention is not to develop an actor by thorough instruction in this sort of knowledge but merely to assist a promising actor in obtaining and holding a position in an acting company.

The acting profession today is crowded—perhaps too crowded. Competition in obtaining a part, even a small one, is keen. A professional director is impatient with raw material because he has more important things to do than teach a beginner, no matter how gifted he is, the fundamental elements of stage technique. He gives directions and expects them to be followed. He is occupied with the playing of a scene as a whole; and when directions in movement and coordination are bungled by the player of a small part because he cannot understand them, the director is justified in his impatience. The existence of a large group of more experienced actors does away with the necessity of putting up with the inexperienced.

The stock company which was originally the training school for many distinguished actors is rapidly disappearing. Schools of the theater and of acting are now an important source from which the professional theater may draw young actors. Besides

these there are the so-called "summer companies" to which
the amateur from school or college is now rushing for professional experience. These summer groups, for the most part,
are taking the place of the old stock companies. We find in the
New York theater-program notes that so-and-so began his
professional theater work with this or that summer company.

Directors of summer theaters are so overrun with requests
from beginners that they do not have to bother with the
would-be actor who has not had sufficient experience. The
applicant must have learned from his own study or from his
previous work in amateur companies—college or community
—or in dramatic schools all that is expected of him—stage
deportment, which includes promptness at rehearsals, coming
with a pencil for notes, readiness for all entrance cues, ability
to take "direction" by understanding the director's vocabulary
and approach, how to study and approach his part and his
characterization, how to adjust himself to the company and
to the manner of playing.

Summer theaters usually devote one week to producing a
play. This is altogether too short a period for the director to
stop the rehearsals to teach while he is directing. Fundamentals
must be mastered before joining a company so that the director
may work on characterization, on the timing of the play, and
on the hundred other matters that absorb his mind and energy.

According to existing conditions then, the beginner today
must be more than a beginner; he must have had some experience even to begin. This experience is in essence derived from
exhaustive reading and studying with teachers.

Knowledge of any art is gained through a process of deduc
tion from what has already been created successfully: it is that
constantly repeated form and manner known as technique.
Time has shown that there is a "best way" of executing an
idea; major exceptions and variations of the original accepted
manner of doing exist, but these are variations of what is
ordinarily done. Technique in any art is teachable, and it is
universally agreed that a beginner will do best to learn those
elements which have been long accepted before he experiments
with a new technique and manner of expressing his idea,
whether it is an idea in a play or in a characterization.

Mere instruction in an art cannot make an artist out of a person who has no inherent quality or natural tendency or feeling for the art. Instruction, however, in any art and particularly in the art of the theater is experience condensed in ordered form. Without question, practical experience is the best teacher, but that oft repeated saying does not mean that each actor must spend ten years of his life in the trial-and-error approach to acting—that he must by a long-drawn-out experience teach himself. Teachers of acting and books on the art have gathered and arranged the experience of many years so that a beginner can benefit by this experience in two years instead of ten. Good instruction, whether in personal contact or within the covers of a book, is condensed actual experience. This section on acting is not a theoretical or idealized treatment of what acting is; nor does it cover in detailed analysis the development of body and voice for expressive response. But in it is contained not only the terminology that the director has in common with the actor but also the fundamentals that a director expects an actor to have mastered.

Since, therefore, we make no pretense of developing a person into an actor, there is no need to discuss the moot question of whether acting can or cannot be taught. We take for granted that the beginner has unusual and excellent natural talent for acting. Without this talent and this experience it will be extremely difficult for anyone, no matter how gifted, to succeed in obtaining even a chance to show his ability. Although the author sincerely believes that this information is of extreme importance to the actor of talent, he is the first to admit that, unfortunate as it may be, an actor could know and be able to execute all that follows hereafter and still be a very bad actor. That is the mystery and often the tragedy of any art.

IV

Elementary Stage Technique for the Actor

THE DIRECTOR must have an absolute knowledge of the elementary stage technique for the beginning actor. He will find that in directing amateurs much of his rehearsal time will be spent in teaching them these technical principles.

The beginner, interested in acting and endowed with emotional feeling for a character, often rushes into acting without consideration for the articulate playing of the part. He relies on the inspiration of the moment and, not having technical control, defeats his purpose by disregarding important fundamental technicalities. These technical considerations involve (1) the relation of the actor to the parts of the stage, (2) his relation to the audience, (3) his relation to other actors, and (4) the visible and smoothly executed way of handling himself in relation to certain properties and business. These points in themselves may seem of negligible importance. They are, however, of infinite value in conveying a precise and clear creation to an audience. They are the coordinating positions and "timed" movements which will arise in practically every play and in the playing of all characters.

Without the knowledge and execution of these "do's" and "don't's" the actor will fail to consider the audience, will upset the other actors, and will confuse the group ensemble. His playing will be rough and untimed, and a jerkiness will enter into his work and spoil the flow of his scenes. If he is at all sensitive, he will feel immediately the crudeness and awkwardness of his execution of the simple ordinary actions. He must, accordingly, master this coldly calculated technique which is comparable to the five-finger piano exercises that enable the pianist to play without technical consideration when he is performing a long run in a concerto. This technique is the foundation through which talent is expressed and without which talent is impotent. Each point should be learned so thoroughly that it becomes a part of the actor's physical coordination and motor responses. He should have little or no consciousness of them but should execute them as a natural body expression. They should be practiced with all seriousness and so mastered that they may subconsciously underlie all further effort.

The moment that a point is violated, the resulting awkwardness and the breaking of the timing should be felt by the actor. He should immediately sense this; but should he fail to do so, the director can quickly by technical explanation correct his manner of execution. The terminology should, therefore, be known so that he may understand the director's instruction.

A. Stage Positions

1. Right and Left Stage

All stage directions of right and left are given from the stage's right and left as the actor faces the auditorium. This means that the director working from the auditorium must reverse his idea of left and right. The full direction should be "cross to stage right," but this is usually shortened to "cross to the right." "Go to the right" means "stage right" though not necessarily the actor's right, for he may be turned with his back toward the audience. In such a position of back to the audience, stage right is then the actor's left; and in any directions given to him, look or go to the right must be taken as meaning stage right.

2. Downstage

This is a term used for that part of the stage nearest to the footlights and the audience.

3. Upstage

Upstage is near the back of the set away from the footlights. This terminology is the result of the historical convention of the stage's having a floor that sloped from the rear down to the footlights. For this reason the audience could easily see those people in the rear, and the star, who usually kept upstage of the other actors, would have a higher position and be more easily seen by the audience than the supporting cast.

4. ABOVE

This term is used virtually as a synonym for "upstage of," as when an actor crosses upstage or behind (from the point of view of an audience) another actor or a piece of furniture, property, etc.

5. BELOW

This is used when an actor crosses on the downstage or in front of another actor or a piece of furniture.

6. STAGE AREAS

Since the actor must know how to distinguish by name one part of the stage from another, it has been found expedient to divide the stage into the six so-called *areas:* down left and up left; down center and up center; down right and up right. Note that there are in addition stage positions that may be designated center, right center, and left center. These positions are

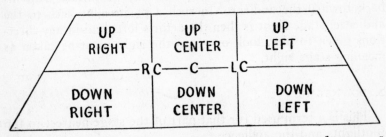

Chart showing division of stage into "areas" and designated "positions."

between the areas. These areas are named from the actor's point of view: right, left, and center.

Exercise in stage positions

An actor on the stage with a table RC and a chair LC may be given the following directions: Begin DL, cross above chair to UC, L, C, UR,

R, below table to C, DR, RC, above table, C, UR, above table and below chair to L, above chair to UC, below table to R, DC, upstage of the table, DR, UL, downstage of table, UC, downstage of chair, above table to R, and DC.

B. Body Positions

For many years actors faced the audience on important lines or speeches. Comedy was also "pointed" in this manner. The old technique was to direct the speeches to the first rows of the balcony. Today drama is more realistic, and plays are being acted and directed accordingly. It is not necessary to act directly to an audience; although the face may be of great benefit in conveying the intellectual and emotional expression of a part of the play, the body is able to express just as much as the face if it is handled correctly. So, too, can the voice. A well-projected speech can be conveyed to the audience even if the actor has his back to the footlights. Today the actor's position on the stage must bear relationship to the characters on the stage as well as to the audience. In realistic playing a good actor never looks directly at the audience. He keeps within his picture-frame stage. Sometimes, when an actor is giving voice to lofty thoughts and ideas, he naturally looks away from the person to whom he is talking. Under these rare conditions, the actor may look at the side wall of the auditorium with his head slightly lifted. It is needless to say that no actor should ever look closely at the people in the front rows of the theater to recognize friends.

We shall first consider the body positions of the actor in relation to the audience. These are important not only for receiving directions but for adjusting an actor to the style of the production. Without going into style at this time, we shall merely state that some plays require and some directors insist that the actors play with varying body positions. Some companies play with the body full front to the audience; others, with the body slightly turned away; and still others, turned so much that even the backs are frequently toward the footlights. It must be constantly remembered that the turn of the body and not the turn of the head is what determines the style or manner of tone of a performance. When the director says "turn in and blend more," it does not mean keeping the body full front and turning the head in but rather just what the words mean literally: "Turn the body from full front away from the audience and toward the other actors on the stage."

Since there is little agreement among directors as to this technique, one of the first things that a new member of a company must notice is the body positions of the leading actors or the majority of the cast and adjust his own body position to harmonize with them.

1. THE BODY IN RELATION TO THE AUDIENCE

a. A "full-front" position is with the body and head directly facing the audience.

b. A "quarter position" is approximately forty-five degrees away from the audience, or the turn from full front toward the audience halfway to profile.

c. A "profile" position is a ninety-degree turn so that the side of the body is to the audience.

d. A "three-quarter" position is at a point halfway from profile to full back.

e. A "full-back" position is with the back directly to the audience.

Whether these positions are to the right or the left does not enter into our present consideration.

2. TERMINOLOGY OF BODY POSITIONS

In order to obtain the blended, or pictorial, effect he desires, a director often wishes a change in the body position of his actor. The following terminology will be used by him to relate an actor's position to other actors and to the picture, or composition:

a. To "open up" is to turn more of the body around toward the audience or, for example, to change from a profile to a quarter or full-front position.

b. To "turn in," or "close in," is to turn away from the audience and toward the center of the stage, resulting in giving more profile or back to the audience.

c. To "turn out" is to turn more of the body to the audience and more away from center, so that more of the face and body are toward the side of the stage. On "turning out," an actor "opens up."

d. To move "two feet downstage" is to move perpendicularly toward the footlights a distance of two steps, being careful to maintain the body position.

e. To move "two feet up" is to move perpendicularly away from the footlights a distance of two steps, again being careful to maintain the body position.

f. To move "forward three feet" is to walk in the direction in which one is facing a distance of three steps.

g. To move "one foot back" is to step back from the exact position in which one is standing a distance of one step.

h. "Blend in" is a general direction entailing minor changes of body position so as to obtain better relationship to other actors.

Exercise in body positions

Bare stage except for table RC and chair LC: Actor C, full front, taking the following positions: Turn profile, two feet upstage, one step forward, turn three-quarter to R, full back, three-quarter to L, two feet downstage, full front, blend into R, profile, turn out, turn in, two feet downstage, two feet forward, three-quarter position to L, profile to L, upstage three feet, full back, one-quarter to R, turn in.

Exercise in body positions and stage positions

Bare stage except for table RC and chair LC: Actor start C, then full front, turn in to L; cross to L, three-quarter position to L; cross above chair to C, one-quarter position, two feet upstage; cross below table to R, DC, blend in, two steps forward, two steps down; cross up to L to L of chair, full back, two steps to R, two steps down, two steps to L, one-quarter to R; cross below table to R; cross above table to C, below chair to L, profile position to R, full front, turn in; cross to RC, turn in, turn out; cross to DR, three-quarter position, two feet upstage, three feet forward, one step back.

3. POSITIONS IN RELATION TO OTHER ACTORS

The standing position of two people who are playing a scene may be such that they "share a scene" or are in profile or that one may "give the scene" to the other.

a. When a scene is shared, each person is presenting three-fourths of his face and body to the audience or is in a one-quarter body position.

b. In a scene played profile, the actors face each other directly, and the audience sees the face and body of each in profile.

c. When one actor gives the scene to the other, the latter is upstage of the former, who must turn to a three-quarter body position to face him.

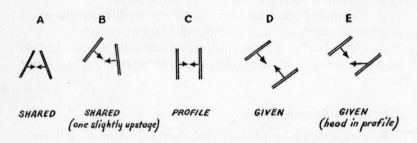

A	B	C	D	E
SHARED	SHARED (one slightly upstage)	PROFILE	GIVEN	GIVEN (head in profile)

The most frequent position is to share a scene (*A* on chart). An actor should take this position immediately when the scene is between two characters, unless the nature of the scene is one that requires a profile or a given position. Great care should be taken to see that both actors are directly opposite each other and that neither is slightly upstage of the other. There is nothing more common with the beginner than to take a position slightly above the other actor. This is a breach of elementary stage etiquette, and it shows either bad manners or ignorance. "Getting upstage" on another actor, unless definitely indicated, will cause immediate complaint from one who knows his technique. To go directly and literally opposite the other actor should be a movement that requires no thought.

When there is a *slight* backing off or "giving" in a scene, this movement should be made back on the very same parallel line and *not* slightly upstage. Moving slightly upstage is known as "working upstage." A first-class actor simply does not work upstage on another, except where the director orders it for a particular effect of interpretation.

When the speeches of both people are very important and

the reactions of each are equally so, another treatment of the shared position can be used. The positions of both actors are more easily "opened up" to the audience for a big scene by having both face one-quarter turn in the same direction and having one actor slightly upstage of the other (*B* on chart). The content of the scene must allow this position to be the picturization of the two people. This relationship is apt to connote secrecy, introspection, confessions, denunciation, and many other violently emotional states.

The "direct-profile" position is similar to the shared except that it is more intense and is used in scenes of an intense, exciting, and climactic nature (*C* on chart). Often it will be the culmination of a scene that starts shared. Cross-questioning, accusing, or denouncing scenes use the direct-profile position.

The given position (*D* on chart) is used on occasions when the main interest of a scene obviously rests in one person and when his speeches are long and narrative and the "giver" merely has an occasional remark or question. The dialogue of a scene very easily determines from its import and meaning whether it should be a shared or a given scene. The only exception to these positions is in the case of old-fashioned stars who insist that virtually everybody give them the scene. Their excuse is that it is important for the audience to see their reactions; but in most cases they will "take the scene" whether their reaction is important or not. This sort of star technique is rapidly disappearing, and today an actor of a smaller role, if his part of the scene is important, can share the position with even the leading actors. But, again, a beginner on joining a company should watch carefully the general relationship of technique of the cast toward the leading actors. If a beginner finds himself unable to share his scene with a leading player, he can hold himself in a given position and on his important lines keep his body in given position and turn his head profile (see *E* on chart). This same treatment is used when for certain reasons the placement of one actor *A* is necessarily upstage of the second, *B*. *B*'s lines for a short time become very important to the play, and they are necessarily given to *A* upstage. This treatment is frequently and easily used when there is a wide distance on the stage between them. With *A* on stage up right and *B* on down left, the head of *B* can very easily be kept profile and merely the eyes directed upstage toward *A*.

This is a definite steal, but it is successfully used because the audience cannot detect the angle between the horizontal line along which *B*'s head is directed and the line that his head would make were it turned directly upstage to *A* (see Figure F). *B* accordingly will seem to the audience to be speaking directly to *A* upstage, and yet his voice will be more clearly audible and his expression in profile more readily seen.

F

d. When three or more people are on the stage, the scene may be given first to one and then to another by means of the body positions of each. The actor to whom the scene is given takes the scene by turning more nearly full front to the audience, and those giving it to him turn toward him and slightly more away from the audience. By shifting this focus, first one and then another will take the scene.

e. The instruction "focus" directs the actor to turn both body and face directly toward another actor or object, usually upstage.

f. "Dress stage"—when one actor, *A*, crosses in front of the other, *B,* it is necessary for *B* to cross to approximately the point that the moving actor *A* has left. When there is a group of three in a triangle form *A*, *B*, *C*, and *C* crosses right, in front of, or below, the group, the actor *B* at the apex of the triangle crosses down from the apex to approximately the point that the moving actor *C* has left. This is called "dressing stage" and involves the principle of balance in the stage picture. Furthermore, by "coming down," *B* gets into a position to share the remainder of the scene with *A*. The experienced actor does this without being told.

g. The term "steal" is used with various meanings. Stealing is very frequently a derogatory accusation and refers to an actor's taking the attention or focus of the audience when, considering the value of the scene, he should not have it. If *A* is having an important speech and *B* waves a handkerchief or a fan or moves conspicuously for any purpose whatsoever, this is stealing. It was done frequently by the old stars who likewise always kept the forward position on the stage. Today, disturbing movement such as this, when the focus of attention is elsewhere, is again bad etiquette and is not done by the best actors. Beginners sometimes do know, but more often do not know, when they are stealing. Sometimes pure ignorance of what distracting business and movement do to a scene and an over-enthusiasm and desire "to act" will lead them to keep up a perpetual commotion, thereby upsetting the focus on the actor to whom the scene belongs. Actors who are not speaking the emphatic lines of the scene should, of course, act and react, but they should express their emotions in an inconspicuous manner. Never under any circumstances should they do any distracting piece of business—like fixing dresses—or make any noise such as jangling bracelets. A beginner should never steal deliberately. He should constantly watch his "feeling" for a characterization and see that it is not conspicuous when the immediate part of the scene belongs to somebody else.

To steal, however, is often used legitimately as a stage direction. It has already been referred to above under *c* in relation to body and head position. It is often used by the director when arranging the position and pictures of a group—when, for instance, he wants an actor to get into a certain position in an inconspicuous manner, such as by taking small steps, so as not to divert attention from the actor with the important lines.

If *A* is upstage left in a group and the focused attention of the audience is on the right stage, and the director then wants to have *A* downstage for a later speech, *A* can steal down right in an unobtrusive manner and be there at the right time without the audience's being conscious of his movement. "To work" is a synonym for steal in this sense. For instance, you work downstage during the scene. Other words for this kind of movement are "ease down" or "up" and "drop down."

To steal is also used legitimately when an actor varies from
the actual, or lifelike, position so that he may become more
articulate and clear to the audience. For instance, a person on
a throne in real life is always approached directly in front.
When on the stage a throne is placed upstage with A on it, and
B is required to approach it, the realistic position for B is
directly in front of it with his back to the audience. But a very
important scene between A and B follows. B cannot play it
with his back to the audience. His first approach, therefore,
will be to kneel, not directly in front of A but slightly to one
side; and then, as he rises, he will definitely swing upstage so
that he opens up and can play opposite in profile or with his
body slightly downstage but with his head in profile. This stealing will necessarily arise in many instances besides those in
which a throne position is involved.

To steal, or "to fake," is also used to mean to pretend. If a
prolonged bit of realistic business which is not necessarily
important is taking too much time, an actor fakes it, cutting
short its duration by eliminating some of the detail or taking
less time than it would actually. Eating and drinking in general
are faked on the stage. Frequently unlocking a window or
door, tying or binding a person, using handcuffs, and packing
or unpacking bags is not carried out in minute detail.

   h. "To cover" is to get downstage of another actor or
important object and thereby block him or it from the audience's view. Usually it is bad to cover, and the responsibility
for not covering is with the downstage, not the upstage, actor.
However, the upstage actor is expected to be quick to aid in
uncovering; and if he can move his position slightly, thereby
saving the downstage actor from an awkward move, he should
do so. It is surprising how quickly professional actors will
hesitate to carry out directions that necessitate covering another actor. Few beginners have any consciousness about it and
so should quickly learn to sense such a situation.

There are times, however, when covering must be done if
certain business or properties are being faked. An actor faking
the playing of a piano can well have another actor cover the
keyboard. Turning the body slightly upstage aids in covering
the use of a dagger or a gun. In lighting a lamp when there is a

necessary coordination between the action of lighting it by the actor and the action at the switchboard, the actor should cover the lamp and definitely block off the audience's view from seeing the actual business. This is also true of switching on or off lights from a side switch. An actor, furthermore, besides covering the switch, must always keep his hand on the switch until the lights on stage have changed; he should do the same when turning off the radio—keep his hand on the knob until the radio is silent. When turning on a radio the actor should allow time for it to warm up. Of course the sound man must also take into consideration the time of warming up.

Exercise in stage position of one actor in relation to another

Cast: *A* and *B*.

Set: Double door upstage C, table RC, chair LC, lamp on table, light switch to left of center door.

At start *A* is DR; *B* is L. *A* talks to *B*; *A* crosses to C, share scene; *B* gives scene to *A*; *A* crosses to below table; *A* turns one-half to R; *B* shares scene with *A*; both facing one-quarter R; *A* crosses to LC, *B* dresses stage; *B* crosses to R; *A* and *B* focus on center door; *A* crosses DC; *B* crosses DC; *A* and *B* share scene; *A* and *B* in profile scene; *A* speaks of life's ambition; *B* goes to UR; *B* crosses to UL; *B* turns off light switch L of door C; *A* crosses to center of table LC and turns off lamp; *B* crosses DL; *A* and *B* have a scene; *A* crosses below chair LC; *B* draws dagger and stabs himself.

4. THE STANDING POSITION

Actors should stand still on the stage except when their movement is definite and set. Too many inexperienced actors are apt to shift from one foot to the other constantly and to make nervous and jerky bodily movements. Poise is extremely important. Beginners should watch this most carefully and train themselves to stand in repose even when expressing the more violent emotions. Furthermore, they should stand with their weight on the balls of their feet. This enables them, whether they are talking or listening in a scene, to seem alert and attentive. When the weight comes on the heels, the body is apt to slouch, and the character seems inattentive and inactive.

5. SITTING POSITIONS

The attention of the audience must not be broken by an actor's turning to look for his seat. In most cases he should approach the seat beforehand and feel for it with the back of the leg. If he tries to take a step toward the chair, his action of sitting will be poorly timed. Of course this looking for the seat when it is the natural expression of a character is not only legitimate but should be slightly exaggerated and pointed.

a. When a woman is sitting, one foot should be extended slightly in front of the other—one foot partly under the seat or both in front. With a man, both feet should be planted on the floor in the same plane. Girls should not cross their knees on the stage unless it is particularly or definitely in character; and men should not conspicuously, if at all, pull up their trousers before they sit down.

b. In rising and sitting it is very easy to slip into one's own personal manner, and especial care should be taken by the actor to keep in character. Oftentimes ingenious character business can be thought up and inserted.

c. Many chairs on the stage face profile or upstage. It is always advisable when sitting in such a chair to open up by sitting in a profile or three-quarter position. One should not sit far back in an overstuffed chair when it is down right or down left.

d. This opening up is particularly necessary when a character must sit downstage and talk to a person upstage, as is already shown in Figure F. In such cases it is inadvisable on important speeches to turn constantly to the upstage person. The head may be turned occasionally toward the general direction of the upstage character, or the body shifted slightly downstage while he is talking. This opening up, together with tilting the head up, prevents the head from being tipped in such a manner that the top of the head is toward the audience, thereby covering much of the actor's face.

e. When two people are sitting on a sofa and the sofa is on a slant, the actor sitting at the upstage end of the sofa should sit on the front edge, and the actor sitting downstage should sit far back in the seat. The actor having the most lines in the scene should sit upstage.

6. RISING

In getting up from a chair an actor should have one foot in front of the other; he should lean forward and put his weight on the front foot; he should push up with the back foot, lift himself up, and put forward the rear foot for the first step. Here, again, characterization will change this procedure, as old people will often get up with strained difficulty.

C. TURNS, GESTURES, AND KNEELING

1. Turns are ordinarily made so that the actor faces the audience in the turn. Exceptions to this rule are when the turn toward the audience is obviously awkward and unnatural, because the body is already turned more than halfway around the complete turn. In this case the body turns toward the new position in the shortest distance. For example, if an actor is turned a three-quarter position upstage and he is turning for an exit behind him, he does not turn to profile and complete the semicircle turn but rather turns upstage directly. Then the back has picturizing value from delivering a line over his shoulder. This movement is called "turning in."

2. In gesturing and holding or passing objects on the stage, care should be taken that the actor does not cover himself in the process. He should gesture or hand something to another actor with the upstage hand whenever it is possible—as it almost always is. Especially should care be taken if an arm is raised, as the downstage arm will cover the head. Often the natural movement would be to use the right arm; yet if it is the downstage arm, the left arm should be used.

3. It is also better to kneel on the downstage knee, because that opens the actor up to the audience. Incorrect handling of these problems may mean the loss of important lines or facial expressions.

Exercises in turns, gestures, and sitting

Cast: *A* and *B*.

Set: Table with lamp RC. Sofa at LC. Double door up C with light switch to L. Window DL. Chair DR. Chair DL. Door RL.

A and *B* at C; share scene; profile; *A* crosses to window DL; turns and speaks. *B* crosses to sofa LC; *A* speaks to *B; B* crosses to *A; B* hands *A* a letter; *A* crosses DR; *B* crosses to DR and kneels; *A* crosses to window, stands on chair, and addresses mob outside during which he gestures profusely. *B* crosses up C; takes three-quarter position to R; turns to *A; B* turns on electric lights at L of C door; *A* crosses to *B* up L. *A* crosses to sofa and sits upper end; *B* crosses below sofa and sits lower end; *A* rises, crosses DR; *A* speaks to *B; A* sits chair DR; *B* rises; *A* speaks to *B; B* sits on sofa; *A* rises; *B* crosses to window DL. *A* and *B* focus on lamp; *B* crosses above sofa to table and puts out lamp. *A* turns three-quarter right; *B* goes to window DL and addresses mob with many gestures; turns, crosses to DC. *A* turns; *A* sits DR chair; hands *B* a letter. *B* turns and exits up C door.

D. Approaches

Two general types of approaches must be recognized: the straight line and the curved.

1. DIRECT

When an actor approaches another in the same line parallel to the footlights, he makes the simple direct approach—defined as a straight-line advance to a person or thing.

2. CURVED

In the exercises so far, the approaches have probably been direct. This has invariably left the crossing actor in an awk-

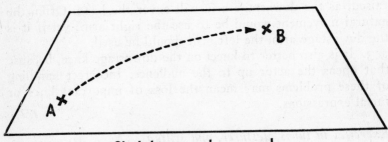

Slightly curved approach

ward position, and in order to share a scene he has had to take a jerky up- or downstage step to arrive directly opposite the other actor. This movement is bad and can be avoided by a slightly curved approach. When an actor must approach another character who is in an up- or downstage area, he is forced to make the curved approach. The curved approach digresses from the straight line and reaches the object after an unnoticeable curve in order to get opposite the other actor instead of above or below him and into the same line with him. If the actor to be approached is downstage, the curve is a downstage curve; if he is upstage, the curve is an upstage one.

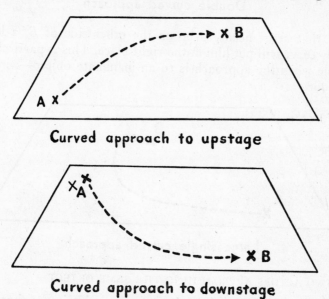

Curved approach to upstage

Curved approach to downstage

Obviously the curved approach is invaluable in many cases for keeping the actor open to the audience, for sharing the scene with the other actor, for softening a cross, and for getting the greatest effect from a costume.

3. DOUBLE CURVED

When an actor has to approach another actor or property, like a door or window, that is almost directly above him, it is advisable to make a double curve so as to arrive directly opposite him or it.

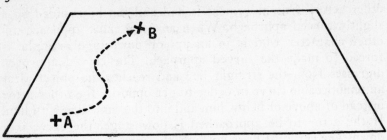

Double curved approach

If that actor needs to be on the other side of *B*, a large single curve will put him in the right place. This is particularly usable when the approach is to an inanimate object—window or door.

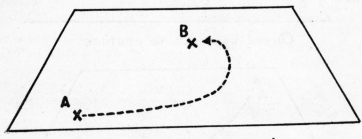

Large single curved approach

4. TWO ACTORS APPROACHING THE SAME OBJECT

Approaches and crosses become more intricate when two people are involved. Such problems arise when two or more people approach an upstage window from down right and down left. If the object to be viewed outside the window is to the right, the actor on the right must make the curve, and vice versa. The approaches must be timed so that the person who is to stand next to the window arrives first.

In any approach the actor should always take position directly opposite the other person (shared position) until told to take up- or downstage by the director.

It is generally agreed that objects outside a window will be placed as follows: If the window is on either of the side walls,

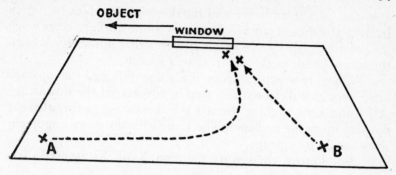

Two actors approaching same object

the accident or the person offstage is usually downstage; if the window is on the rear wall to right or left, the object outside is toward the center. If the window is center, the director must settle which way the focus is to be. All these positions are settled in this way so that, in looking out, the actor will be opened up. The actors accentuate their positions by opening up more than they would open up in reality. Most windows are higher than the street, and consequently the gaze is directed down, except when the actor looks at objects of nature such as trees and mountains.

5. CROSSING

a. An actor must take the shortest and most direct line in crossing to a person, an object, or an exit. He cannot circle about furniture or other people if that circling takes him out of the natural direct line of crossing. If it is desirable for an actor to cross above furniture and the direct line would ordinarily take him below it, he must work upstage with a motivation or a steal before it becomes time for him to cross, thus making the direct line of crossing above the furniture. This does not retract what has been said about the curved approach which is a technical movement and will not be noticed by the audience.

b. Excepting servants and characters who are to be stealthy in their manner, actors pass in front of each other, because when an actor passes behind another he loses his hold on the attention of the audience and it takes time for him to regain it. An actor should cross in front of (below) other actors when the cross is made on one of his speeches that allows it or when there is a break in the other actor's speech.

c. When two actors cross the stage talking, the upstage actor should walk about one step in advance of the downstage actor and turn slightly toward the downstage actor, thereby opening up to the audience. The actor with the more important lines should be upstage.

d. For "cross" in scripts the sign X or Xs is used; frequently, the word "go" or "come."

Exercises in approaches

1. Repeat the exercises on pages 51 and 53, putting in straight and curved approaches where they should be used.

2. Set: Armchair DR. Window DR. Table and lamp RC. Window RC. Double arch up C. Sofa LC. Door DL. Armchair DL.

Cast: *A* and *B*.

At start *A* and *B* are DC; *A* Xs to chair DR; *B* goes to table RC; *A* sits DR; *A* and *B* look at accident out of window DR; *A* and *B* rush up to window UR; *B* Xs to sofa LC; *A* comes to R; *B* sits upper end sofa; *A* Xs to *B*; *A* and *B* go to C door and look L. *A* and *B* walk to door DL; *A* and *B* walk to window DR. (*A* is doing most of the talking.) *B* Xs to left of table RC; *A* Xs to R of table LC; *A* hands *B* a letter.

E. Position of Doors and Windows

Doors and windows are designated as follows: Those on the right stage wall are down right and up right; those on the left stage are down and up left; those on the rear wall are up right center, up center, and left center. Care should be taken to recognize at once the difference between up left and up left center, as up left is in the side wall and up left center is in the back or rear wall.

In old scripts you will find these doors referred to as R-1, R-2, R-3 and L-1, L-2, L-3. On both sides the 1 is the opening in the flat nearest the downstage, or proscenium; and 3 is the opening farthest upstage. Even in modern scripts these designations are frequently used to indicate entrances in exterior sets—they are the openings between the wings.

F. Opening and Closing Doors

Except in designated instances, an actor should close the door after entering. Practically all stage doors swing offstage, with the exception of outside doors which should swing onstage. Doors in the side walls are hinged on the upstage side. In entering by a side-wall door, take hold of the knob with the upstage hand, and open the door; enter; take hold of the knob with the downstage hand, and close the door. This technique keeps the actor opened up to the audience during his entrance. In entering at a door in the rear wall, if the hinges are on the right, the opening should be done with the right hand; and, after entering, the closing should be done with the same hand. If the hinges are on the left, both opening and closing should be done with the left hand.

G. Entering and Exiting

1. CUES FOR ENTERING AND SPEAKING

The cue for speaking cannot be taken as the cue for entering. The entrance cue must precede the speech cue by the amount of time necessary for the actor to come on stage and hear his speech cue. This statement is, however, modified according to the place where the speech is to be delivered. If it is supposed to be heard from offstage, one cue may be taken; if delivered at the door, the entrance cue precedes the speech by a very short space of time. Ordinarily, a character on entering the stage should speak by the door and not wait to walk to center stage.

2. CHARACTER ENTERING

It is always essential to start getting into character before an entrance. "Step into the character's shoes" five or six steps before the entrance, being certain to open and close the door in character.

The relation of the character to the room is often woefully

disregarded, to the detriment of all reality in the stage picture. An actor should not think that he is entering a stage but that he is a definite character entering a certain place; and his relation to the place should be immediately shown. By his action or reaction to the set upon entrance, the owner of a room should establish himself as such. A butler should enter the drawing room in a manner that clearly distinguishes him from a salesman. A friend of the family, the son of the house, a formal guest, a prospective buyer, a salesman, a burglar, and so on indefinitely, although each may enter by the same door during the course of the play, has each his distinctive way of entering. The enrichment by pantomime is what makes the play live and breathe and establishes the characters.

3. BUTLER ENTERING

A definite procedure has been laid down for the entrance of butlers, maids, and footmen. If this entrance is up left center, the servant takes a position full front to the center side of the door. If the door is up right center, his position is to the left. If the door is directly center, he stands at the side that has the hinges. If it is a double door or arch, either side is correct. If he is announcing an arrival, he leaves the door open. If he has been rung for, he probably closes the door. When he has announced the character, and the arrival has entered, he exits and closes the door.

If the door is in either side wall, his position is always upstage of the door, so that the entering person is below him. In taking his position he usually faces profile; that is, his body position is parallel to the side wall. Some directors, however, prefer to have the announcer of an important character, when the entrance is on the side, face directly front with his body at right angles to the side wall. An actor accordingly should be prepared to change quickly from the first procedure to the second if the director so wishes it.

Butlers should not announce until they are in place. A butler's cues are therefore extremely difficult. For entering, the cue should be early enough to allow him to enter and get in place before speaking on his line cue. If he has been rung for and his line is the equivalent of "You rang, sir," he should say this in the doorway itself, assuming a formal body position, and not take time to get into his announcing position.

If, on entering, a butler has a scene with an important character, he should take his position either as if he were making an announcement or in the door. If it is a short instruction, he remains there. If there are enough ensuing speeches to make it even a short scene, he should work down during the first two lines and play directly opposite the other actor, being very careful not to steal with a slightly upstage position.

If the butler brings in mail, paper, a visiting card, or something of a similar nature, he goes directly opposite the character, again being careful not to play upstage. Very seldom will a servant come into a room and approach a character before he speaks. When the content of the scene demands it, the actor must time his entrance so that he not only enters but walks to the person to whom he is to speak and is there for the speaking cue. This is difficult, because he cannot hurry, and also he cannot get there and wait for his cue.

Butlers' parts are usually short. If the actor can handle them by himself, he is a great pleasure to the director. If he cannot, he will waste a great deal of both the director's and the cast's time. He should himself see that the timing of his entrance is perfect and smooth. He should be mannered, formal, and correct in his speech and action but not stiff and forced. His movement must not be slow enough to drag but must be slower than that of other characters. He should be very polite and, until he has finished speaking, never turn away from the person whom he is addressing.

4. SEVERAL CHARACTERS ENTERING

When a number of people enter together from a side entrance, the speaker, with few exceptions, should enter first. He then can pick up the cue more quickly; and furthermore, in addressing the actor following, he can "open up" to the audience. When the entrance is in the rear, the speaker often comes second and addresses the first to enter. There are times, however, when he comes first, such as when the remarks are either general or definitely to someone on the stage.

5. THE EXIT

The technique of leaving the stage differs little from that of entering. Character must be maintained. The character, if important, should keep open by making a curved approach to the exit. The actor should open a door on the side wall with the upstage hand, exit, and close it with the downstage hand. Doors in the rear wall are opened under conditions established by the approach; as always, the upstage hand should open it unless the exit requires the back to the audience.

6. TWO CHARACTERS EXITING

When two people exit, the talking character leaves last, either addressing the person in front of him or delivering his words back to the character on the stage.

It is often effective to deliver a final speech before exiting just as the door is reached; or a speech may be broken, the first part delivered in the room and the rest at the door as the actor turns. This depends upon the situation, but it is generally bad to have a long cross and exit hold up the following dialogue. It is permissible, however, when the exit is very much a part of the dramatic action of the play or the emotional mood of the character.

An example of a difficult exit for two people is the following: A and B are down right talking. A is right of B. They are to exit together. A is to have the last line of the scene. B reads his last line and turns to exit. He crosses and opens door. A delivers his last line while he crosses. A exits through the open door, and B follows.

This may also be handled so as to emphasize or point the last line to greater advantage. The same situation exists; only this time B, after his next-to-the-last speech, crosses and opens the door. A follows and gives his next-to-the-last speech. As A reaches B, B gives his last speech; A crosses B, stands in the door, turns to face B, and delivers his last speech.

If the door is in the side wall, the exit is simple. When the exit is in the rear, it is more difficult: If the actors are down-stage right or down left, the main speaker on the exit should start upstage first. If the speaker is nearer the center, it is simpler as he keeps ahead, talking over his shoulder to those behind, thereby opening up. If the speaker on the exit should happen to be near the side wall, he must of necessity cross in front of *B*, turn back to talk to *B*, and keep ahead of him on the way upstage. The curved approach is necessary in either case.

If *A* and *B* are sharing the scene, center, and an exit is made upstage, they both turn in and walk upstage. If the lines are decided, they keep abreast of one another but turn their heads as far in profile as possible. If *A* has more to say or is more important than *B* in exiting, *A* keeps slightly ahead of *B* and turns to look at him.

7. ENTERING AND EXITING THROUGH CURTAINS

When a person enters through curtains and is compelled not to disclose backstage, such as going out through the act curtains to make an announcement or exiting through curtains that if opened will disclose another set, he must keep the two halves of the curtains so that they overlap and one is down-stage and the other upstage of him as he passes through on a nearly horizontal line. As the actor steps through, with the downstage hand he pulls slightly the downstage half in the direction in which he is going and with the upstage hand pulls the rear behind him.

When he turns to exit through these curtains, he strikes the upstage curtain with his upstage hand before he is ready to leave; when he turns, he will be able to see the break in the curtains by the streak of light showing between them where he has struck them apart. He then slips his upstage hand ahead of him to hold the upstage half of the curtain ahead of him as he passes through again on the horizontal line. With his downstage hand he pulls the downstage half behind him, keeping the lap as great as possible during his exit just as during his entrance.

When the backstage may be shown, the actor takes the two

halves of the curtains with his two hands, parts them, and steps through in a vertical line. His exit may be accomplished in a similar manner.

(NOTE: It is when walking upstage in any of the preceding ways that the stage directions of left and right must be carefully watched. Directions are stage left and stage right and in most cases the actor's, but here it is directly the reverse: any direction of right will mean the actor's left.)

8. ENTERING FROM RIGHT OR LEFT

Whenever a character enters or exits through an open door or arch upstage, care should be taken to find out whether he comes in from the right or the left stage. As the space between the rear wall of the set and the backing is supposed to be a hall or room, the direction from which they come in or go is important. And, again, if he is exiting, he will have his back to the audience so that "off left" will mean to turn to his right.

9. POSITION AFTER CALLING THROUGH A DOOR

When an actor has to go to a door to call another character offstage, he usually, after calling, steps back three or four steps and waits for the person to enter. This leaves sufficient space to keep the actors from being too close to one another during the ensuing scene. It is, however, technically obvious and arbitrary. If possible, it is better to find a motivation for this opening up. The actor who has called can cross away from the door to some position in the room. If this is undesirable, the caller can approach the side door from above and, after calling, step up slightly and allow the person entering to pass well on to the stage before turning and seeing the caller who comes down and shares the scene with him.

10. ENTERING AND EXITING AT REHEARSALS

At rehearsals when there are no doors with which to practice, the actor should roughly time his cue for entering. When he has entered, he should stamp his foot fairly loud so as to let the other actors know that he has entered. This is a convention of rehearsals and is a definite aid to the actors and director. Frequently an actor will give the same loud stamp on his exit through the imaginary door to acquaint the actors remaining with the fact that he has departed from the set.

Exercises in entering and exiting

1. Set: Window DR. UC arch with drawn curtains. Door DL. Chair DR. Table RC. Sofa LC. Chair DL.

a. Each student enter and exit, opening and closing door DL.

b. Each student enter and exit through curtains UC, being careful not to disclose backing to arch.

c. *A* sitting DR. *B* standing by *A*. They exit off DL—*A* does most of talking.

d. *A* and *B* on sofa (*A* upstage of *B*). They exit UC to R. *B* does most of talking.

e. *A* and *B* on sofa (*A* upstage of *B*). They exit DL. *A* does most of talking.

f. *A* sitting DR. *B* standing by *A*. They exit DL. *B* does talking.

g. *A* sitting DR. *B* standing by *A*. They exit DL. *A* does talking.

h. *A* looks out window DR; *B* enters to center from R, Xs to window DR, and looks out. *B* Xs to sofa; *A* and *B* hold scene; *B* sits in sofa; *A* Xs to R of table; *A* and *B* look off C to R; speaking, *A* and *B* exit C to L; *A* and *B* enter C from L, *A* speaking; *A* and *B* X to DL and exit DL; *A* and *B* enter from DL, *B* talking; X to C; *A* and *B* hold scene at C; *A* and *B* exit UC to R, sharing scene.

2. Character enters.

Set: Any room. A real door UC.

Cast:
A	The lady of the house.
B	The butler.
C	A woman newspaper reporter.
D	Woman friend.
E	Man newspaper reporter.
F	*A*'s old father.
G	Burglar.
H	*A*'s child.
I	Friend of a friend with a letter of introduction.
J	The husband who owns the house.
K	The daughter's friend.
L	Salesman.
M	The blackmailer.
N	The maid.

Problems: *a.* Each in character enter separately, close door, react
to room, and sit.

b. Each student do each character.

Exercise on butler's entrance and positions

Set: Window DR. Door (practical) LC. Chairs DR and DL. Desk
RC with chair right of it. Sofa LC.

Cast: Sir Andrew.
Mr. Baxter.
Carleton, the butler.
Lady Dora.
Mr. Easton.
Lady Faywood.
Sir George George.

*Sir Andrew is at his desk RC; Lady Dora is on the sofa LC; Baxter
is standing C.*

SIR ANDREW: Now really, Mr. Baxter, I'm afraid it's impossible.

BAXTER: But I must find out what you ate for breakfast.

SIR ANDREW: I must say good-by.

BAXTER: Just one moment more, sir. Do you eat oatmeal or just toast
and tea? If you don't mind, sir. [*Enter Carleton.*]

CARLETON: You rang, sir?

SIR ANDREW: Will you please show this man to the door.

CARLETON: This way, sir. [*Baxter and Carleton exit.*]

SIR ANDREW: His nerve is unbelievable.

DORA: There is no peace from the minute your name appears in
the newspapers.

SIR ANDREW: I don't even dare go out in my car.

DORA: Yesterday they photographed me as I left the house. [*Enter
Carleton.*]

CARLETON [*giving letters, papers, etc., to Sir Andrew*]: The evening
post, sir.

SIR ANDREW: A queer thing, this publicity, Carleton. Don't ever let
in those newspaper reporters again.

CARLETON: No, Sir Andrew.

SIR ANDREW: Never again, not for one minute.

CARLETON: I'll see to that.

SIR ANDREW: Give the paper to Lady Dora.

CARLETON: Yes sir. [*Turns to Lady Dora.*] The evening post, m'lady.

DORA: Thank you, Carleton. [*He turns to exit.*] Oh, and Carleton.

CARLETON: Yes, your ladyship.

DORA: Be certain to see the windows by the front door are locked.

CARLETON: Yes, your ladyship. [*Exits.*]

DORA: Andrew, did you tell Carleton you wanted the car tonight?

SIR ANDREW: Won't a taxi do as well?

DORA: I prefer our own.

SIR ANDREW: But the newspapermen will follow us more readily. [*Enter Carleton.*]

CARLETON: There's a gentleman called to see Sir Andrew.

DORA: Has he an appointment?

CARLETON: No, m'lady.

DORA: You said he was out?

CARLETON: He is very anxious to see him.

DORA: Sir Andrew won't see anybody else today.

SIR ANDREW: What's his name?

CARLETON: He would not give his name.

DORA: Don't you know, Carleton, that Sir Andrew will receive nobody who is unwilling to give his name?

CARLETON: He said it was very important, m'lady.

SIR ANDREW: I can see nobody without a name.

CARLETON: Yes sir. [*He exits.*]

DORA: It's preposterous.

SIR ANDREW: I've told him many many times.

DORA: Well, you must tell him again. [*Enter Carleton.*]

CARLETON: Mr. Easton. [*Enter Easton. Carleton exits.*]

EASTON: Good evening, Lady Dora. Andrew, how do you do?

SIR ANDREW: The press have been driving us mad.

DORA: A certain Mr. Baxter has been a nuisance. [*Enter Carleton.*]

CARLETON: Lady Faywood. [*Enter Lady Faywood. Exit Carleton.*]

DORA: How do you do, my dear?

FAYWOOD: And you, Dora. Andrew, many happy returns of the day. Oh, Mr. Easton, I didn't expect to find you here. How are you all?

DORA: Not so well. We are so constantly bothered by the press. [*Enter Carleton.*]

CARLETON: Sir George George. [*Enter Sir George. Exit Carleton.*]

ANDREW: My dear George, how do you do?

GEORGE: Very well, and you?

DORA: Not so well. We are so constantly bothered by the press.

SIR ANDREW: A certain Mr. Baxter is determined to know what I eat for breakfast. [*Enter Carleton.*]

CARLETON [*aside to Sir Andrew*]: The very important gentleman has a name this time, sir.

SIR ANDREW: Show him up.

CARLETON: Yes sir.

GEORGE: By Jove, that's funny. I never thought of thinking what you ate. What do you?

SIR ANDREW: Toast and coffee and marmalade, and you . . . [*Enter Carleton.*]

CARLETON: Mr. Baxter.

H. LISTENING

Too much cannot be said about the value of listening and the development of the art of listening on the stage. It is much more difficult to act without words than with them, but the two kinds of acting are equally important. If a character drops out of the scene the moment he stops speaking, the illusion of reality is immediately broken. This is bound to happen unless, firmly grasping the role, the actor reacts characteristically to every person and line in the play, as a character following the thoughts of the others. Reactions should be made when the actor is one of a group, but, as already noted, they should be made softer than when he is the focused or emphatic figure.

When the actor is in the midst of a scene and the other person is speaking, the silent actor should

1. Listen. Then, even before the speaking actor has finished his speech, he should

2. React to the idea of the speaking actor, then

3. Think of his idea in reply,

4. Take his breath, and

5. Speak on cue.

I. ASIDES AND SOLILOQUIES

The aside is a short speech delivered at a time when other characters are on the stage. It usually expresses audibly what the character is thinking or what he knows that the other characters do not know and what the playwright wants the audience, but not the other characters, to hear.

Modern plays do not contain these obsolete conventions of the drama. If they do and are supposed to be plays of modern times, they are poor plays. If the other parts of the play are as poor as the asides would indicate, it is probably not worth producing. If, however, asides are in a modern play and it seems best for certain reasons to produce it, or if the play is of an earlier vintage, as Oscar Wilde dramas are, and is receiving a modern production, great care should be taken to see if the asides cannot be cut out entirely and the substance of them given in pantomime.

If it is impossible to cut the asides, the actor should read them, not directly to the audience yet turned from the other actors on the stage with detailed business and pantomime on the lines and with a reading in a lower than speaking tone. The emphasis should not be on the lines but on the pantomime and expression that accompany them. The other actors should be concerned with minor and inconspicuous business or movement.

In the classic dramas the asides are an integral and legitimate part of the play. Furthermore, they are most important in establishing the style and manner of the historical production. They should be spoken directly to the audience. While the aside is being delivered, the characters on the stage who are not speaking may hold their positions, or "freeze." In a serious production of an early play it is inadvisable for an actor to glance at the front row of the audience and cup his hands at his mouth to prevent the other characters on the stage from hearing what he has to say. If the production is a burlesque one, such procedure may prove effective.

The soliloquy is a long speech delivered when the actor is alone on the stage. The contents may be direct exposition, planning, plotting, explanation of situation, or, in the highest form, thoughts and mental predicament. Like the aside it frequently may be cut, and pantomime substituted. If in a modern production it cannot be cut, a great deal of business and pantomime should be introduced and blended into the dialogue. A soliloquy is also spoken with softer volume and not directed to the audience.

In the classical dramas it may be spoken directly to the audience with the actor coming down to the footlights to deliver it, or it may be more blended. This will depend upon what the director has chosen to use for the style or manner of production.

In the modern-dress version of *Hamlet* Basil Sydney in delivering the famous "To be or not to be" never once directed it to the audience but lighted a cigarette, stood upstage looking off through a French window, came slowly downstage with pacing and thoughtful movement to a backless bench near the footlights, and then lay down flat on his back and continued to smoke.

J. Opening Up and Covering Positions and Business

If the preceding technique of movement and positions has been analyzed carefully, one will discover that it is planned primarily and basically so that the audience will see the actor. All the actor's technique is arrived at in order to keep the character in correct relationship to the other actors and, at the same time, to include the audience so that it may see what is taking place as well as the facial and body expression which conveys the mental and emotional state of the character.

We have already practiced covering, or masking, such things as the switching of lights. This action is covered deliberately so as to conceal a mechanical process which might not be coordinated. The majority of the business in a play, however, should not be covered but deliberately opened up for the audience.

"Business," or "bus.," in acting is movement connected with the handling of property or a definite pantomimic action. It may be executed while the actor is speaking or while there is a distinct pause in the flow of dialogue. Some business is faked and covered. Frequently it is accomplished with no marked attention to it, but more often it is done with great emphasis so that the audience is distinctly aware of it.

At rehearsals all business is worked out carefully along with all movement and positions. In stock and even in New York production rehearsals the actor at the first meetings reads aloud, but in a lower tone than his lines, the written business in his script. In stock he is apt to read all directions, and he learns his business just as he does his lines. The actor should always do the business in pantomime at all rehearsals, taking care to imagine each individual step of the procedure in the use of the property. He should allow as nearly as possible for the time that it will take to execute action when it is actually being done with the property at dress rehearsals and performances. This careful "timing" of the use of a property at rehearsal will save the actors and director hours of time at the dress or property rehearsal. With due consideration and imagination it may be gauged correctly. Along with the timing problem the execution of the business in relation to the audience should be planned. Is it to be covered or open, held down or emphasized?

When business is involved and includes movement over a part or all of the stage, an actor will do well to get to a rehearsal early several times in order to plan and time action to the actual space. Any long and involved business requires this special rehearsing.

We shall now consider examples dealing with classifications and techniques mentioned above.

1. CASES OF DELIBERATE COVERING

a. Eating and drinking on the stage

In most of the cases of covered business so far, the covering has been done deliberately because it involved either mechanical consideration or inconvenience from eating a considerable amount of real food while keeping the lines of the play going. The faking of eating food needs further exposition.

Actors do not like to eat "property" food or to drink quantities of cold tea or other faked substitutes. Not only is it unpleasant to consume quantities of such stuff night after night, but, owing to the convention of not speaking when the mouth is full of food, talking becomes extremely difficult.

All phases of this business are faked. When there is eating to be done, the actor spends a great deal of time cutting or breaking the food. The food is usually soft and easy to swallow. Eggs in one form or another are used for all sorts of other food. Actually, very tiny pieces of the food are put into the mouth. The actor with a tiny morsel eats it with jaw movements suitable to a larger mouthful. This is pure pantomime, but it must be convincing if it is to convey the effect of a regular mouthful. Very little is served, so with a few small mouthfuls and a great deal of cutting up, the actor leaves on the plate most of what has been served. If he is sitting with his back to the audience on the downstage side of the table, he of course eats nothing but fakes the whole process of putting food into his mouth, cutting it up, and reaching for articles.

Whenever possible, receptacles are used that are not transparent. Often the liquid is faked so that only water is used or else nothing at all. Whether there is something or nothing in it, the actor tips the cup or mug as if he were drinking but allows none or very little of the substance to enter his mouth. He then must be sure to swallow or to pantomime swallowing so that the cords of the throat may be seen to move while the cup is raised to the lips.

If the liquid is in a transparent glass and can be seen by the audience, the process is a combination of the two preceding elements of eating and drinking technique. The glass should seldom, if ever, be full. If it ever happens that a beginner is to pour out a liquid and give it to a more experienced actor to drink, he should be told never to fill the glass. Three-quarters or a bit over half full is sufficient. Then the actor drinks just a little, pretends to drink more, and finally ends up by leaving the glass nearly as full as it was when it was given to him. There are, of course, exceptions where the lines point to the fact that the liquid is all gone or the actor has to drain it, but in these cases very little is in the glass to begin with.

The actor usually manages to keep his hand around the glass so as to cover just how little actual liquid there is in it. If the liquid is being faked and the actor is supposed to drink a long draught, care should be taken to allow him sufficient time. Only too often does an actor drain a mug too quickly and accordingly disclose the faking.

If the drink is supposed to be a strong one (liquor should always be faked), the actor must be certain to pantomime according to the character's natural reaction. This consists in making faces of varying intensity and sometimes even coughing. Even a habitual drinker has a definite facial reaction. It is important for an actor to eat and drink convincingly on the stage.

b. *The actor's handling of shooting, stabbing, and suicide*

It is easy to imagine that in any of these situations a great deal of masking and covering is employed. In killing a character by shooting, the killer must keep at a distance from the one killed. This will lessen the danger of fire or injuries from the wads in the blank cartridge. The killer should, except in extreme cases, be below the one to be shot, so that there is no shooting at or toward the audience. The actor shooting should aim the pistol slightly downstage of the to-be victim; the audience will not be aware of this steal. If the actor to be shot at is downstage of the shooter and on one side of the stage so that he is near the side wall, the shooter can aim slightly upstage of him. The aim should never be toward the audience. If it must be and the killer must be upstage, he must then be covered by another actor or be directly above and covered by the one to be killed. Then the killer can shoot down on to the stage floor just above the downstage actor, and the steal will not be seen by the audience.

If the killing is to be done with a dagger, as in many of the Shakespearean plays, again the actual killing must be covered. The director may want the scene to be done in one of many ways, but in any case the actors should be able to realize the problem and help him. If the director has the killer upstage of the other actor, the stabbing may be done in the back of the other, thereby covering. If the thrust is to be in the front of the victim, then the killed may turn and cover the blow himself.

If the killer is downstage, he himself must cover the thrust by covering the victim.

The stabbing must be started with great force and a violent motion and lessened in speed as the knife approaches the body. As soon as the dagger is covered, the thrust is directed away from the person. A dagger goes into a body more easily than it is withdrawn—consequently, much forceful effort must be used in pretending to withdraw the weapon. Nothing will disclose this faking more obviously than quickly and easily withdrawing the knife.

When the weapon is not a knife or dagger but a sword, as in a duel, the same treatment of covering is employed, and the actor passes the sword between the upstage arm and the body. Often the sword's point should show behind the body. The apparent force when it is withdrawn must again be panto-mimed.

The weapon used in any of these last cases must be disposed of immediately in order to keep the audience from seeing the lack of blood on the instrument. It may be thrown on the floor toward a far corner of the stage. It may be wiped off at once on something that can be disposed of and kept out of sight, or it may be returned immediately to the scabbard. But it must be kept out of sight.

The actor stabbed should *not* fall immediately. He staggers a moment. He will help the illusion by grasping the part of the body shot or stabbed and by showing a definite reaction of agony as he sways and partially sinks. After this reaction it is good business and more convincing if the actor breaks his fall by first falling against a piece of furniture and supports him-self by it as he sinks to the floor. Only the last part of the action is a complete fall. In falling the knees are the difficult part to protect. Once the knees are down, the fall on the hip and down is easy.

If the fall is from the full standing position, the actor must be sure that the feet stay down on the floor and do not bounce up.

He should plan to have his head more downstage than his feet, as these are ugly and apt to give a humorous aspect to a corpse.

If an actor has to help carry a body offstage, he should see that the head of the victim is higher than the feet. In most cases he should be on the downstage side of the body, as the prone figure is apt to be ludicrous, and covering it is a valuable aid in maintaining the mood of the scene. In carrying a body offstage the head should go out first.

In suicide the actor must himself cover the method from the audience. Usually he uses a knife, because it is the more easily masked. He begins partly open to the audience; as he thrusts the knife toward himself with great feigned strength and effort, he turns upstage. He must not let the knife fall, but he must keep it in his hand as he falls. His falling is the same as before, staggering until he gets one knee down and then falling on his hips.

In turning a gun on oneself the action should also be feigned. The shot should be directed, parallel to the body, at the floor. There have been instances when the gun has been kept in the pocket, which again means that the shot is made directly in front and parallel to the body or that the shot has been fired behind. It is also possible to turn the back to the audience and shoot directly at the floor.

A gun that goes off during a scuffle is fired in the following manner: The actors get into a clinch with their bodies and downstage arms, leaving an open space on the upstage side. When in the firm grip of the other, one shoots at the floor. The actor who does not shoot is the one who struggles violently while the shooter cocks the gun and fires.

Guns are nearly always fired on stage and not off, as many people think. A property man offstage has a cartridge ready; and if the on stage gun fails to go off the first time, the offstage gun will be fired. An actor should have this arrangement with the stage manager or property man. It should be settled how many attempts the actor should make; usually only one is made before the prop gun is fired.

2. EMBRACING AND KISSING

If the embrace is performed while both actors are standing, the correct position is arrived at by first taking practically a natural dancing position. The right hand of the boy is placed under the left arm of the girl and around her back toward her right shoulder. Instead of taking the girl's right hand, the left hand of the boy either goes around the girl's waist or high on her upper arm or on her right shoulder blade. The girl then puts her right hand on the boy's left shoulder, on the lapel of his coat, or around his neck, or she may smooth his hair. Her left arm is around his right shoulder. The boy should place his downstage foot below the girl's downstage foot and very close to it. He then puts his weight on it so that his general body position is leaning slightly forward. This covering will result in the audience's seeing the two in close contact, but as a matter of fact only the downstage sides of the actors are in close contact, and there will be considerable space between them on the upstage side.

In kissing, the girl, whether standing or sitting, should tilt her head upstage, and the boy his head downstage. This is to be done whether the kiss is actual or covered and faked.

The treatment of the kissing varies very much with the director, the company, and the professional standing in the company of the two people kissing. That is, if a beginner is to kiss the leading lady, he should at least start by covering. If it is not satisfactory in the auditorium, the director will correct it. Because of varying circumstances it is impossible to state the technique with much certainty. The covered treatment of the kiss, however, is one that the beginner should practice during his early experience with the amateur companies and should invariably use when he first rehearses with professionals. How the kiss is handled is one of the practices that he should watch carefully when he joins a company.

The covered kiss is executed by the boy's turning the girl's head slightly upstage and bringing his own directly below hers. His head will cover and mask the process, as his face will be directly upstage and his shoulders and the back of his head toward the audience. From the waist down he will be in profile.

When the head is in this position he can either not kiss at all or can put his lips on her cheek or chin, or he can put his face to the side and back of her neck.

If the couple is sitting on a sofa and the man is downstage, the covering is as simple. If he is upstage, the procedure is similar except that the girl will do the covering.

At the earliest rehearsals an actor seldom ever practices the embrace but merely stops for a literal second and says "kiss over." At later rehearsals when the lines have been learned and the script is out of hand, he will mechanically execute the technique of slightly turning and covering. He holds his head and lips in correct position but does not complete the kiss. This will be done for the first time at dress rehearsal.

The technique of the kiss can be practiced in pure pantomime and does not need a second person.

3. CHARACTER AND UNEMPHATIC PROPERTIES AND BUSINESS

Character properties and business are used mostly to convey characterization to an audience rather than to clarify the story or idea of the play. Much will be said later about their choice, their variety in use, and their relation to line and timing of the play. For the present we are concerned solely with their relation to the audience.

Character properties consist of fans, shawls, sewing, flowers, books, canes, brief cases, cigarettes, pipes, glasses, papers, and the like. They have been selected by the actor for an enrichment of his characterization. Their use as a general rule is unemphatic as far as the audience is concerned. Occasionally they may be used for a "laugh point," and they are sometimes tied up with the plot; but these are exceptions, and when they occur, the properties would be included as emphasized plot props or business.

Whether covered or open, the use of such properties should not be overdone. They are the objects with which an actor must be careful not to steal. Distraction and confusion of interest can result from their playing an important part on the stage. Waving a fan will cause great visible damage; rustling a newspaper will disturb auditory focus. Lighting a pipe or a cigarette or slowly pouring wine will hold up the delivery of lines when the scene should be progressing rapidly. A beginner should watch these interruptions of focus and timing. He should be certain that they are kept down to their proportion of value to the scene as a whole. They are to be definitely blended. If the entire audience does not see or is not impressed with them, there is no injury to the play.

It is best for an actor to use character properties on his own lines and speeches.

4. EMPHATIC PROPERTIES AND BUSINESS

Just as character properties and business are unimportant except for the enrichment of characterization, story, or plot, properties and business in themselves are often vitally important to the progress of the play's action. Great care must be taken to plant and open up such properties and business to the audience.

The actor should handle the telephone with due consideration for the audience. He should be above or to the side of the object on which the telephone is placed. The mouthpiece is held slightly below the mouth of the actor. The actor begins with his body either definitely profile or in a three-quarter position. If the conversation is short and only fairly important, he does not change his position; if it is long and important, by slow degrees the actor turns full front.

Now that we have touched on the telephone in connection with opening up, we shall take up a second important consideration of telephone scenes, one that is much abused.

In telephone conversations the replies should be very carefully planned, and the pause held during the time when the actor should listen and react to what is supposedly being said. For the reply, it should be held a slightly shorter time than is necessary. An actor must always in his own mind fill in what is being said.

Exercise in telephone conversation

   1. Plan place and time of holding.

   2. Write out the speeches of the person on the other end of the tele-phone.

"Operator, I want Wellington O three four O . . . . I did not say Wellington O three O four. No, that's wrong. . . . Wellington . . . yes. Hello. Let me speak to Smith. What? No such person? Is this Wellington O three four O? Well, I want to speak to Jack Smith. Isn't this O three four O? And nobody named Smith there? Hello, operator, I want Wellington three O four. Thank you. Hello, is Jack Smith there? Hello, Jack. This is Henry . . . Henry Jones. Well you ought to be glad it's five-thirty. Yes, Mac held up the arrest purposely till after the papers came out. Yes. I'm on the job. Sure. O.K. First send over the papers. The insurance papers. Then send over George. What about the laundress? I want her now. Yes, now. Why he's somewhere in the building. Sure. He's been here. He's on the job. All right . . . Sure. Oh, quit fussing about him. And listen. . . . Will you keep off this wire? He's the best reporter there is. He did? Well, what did the captain say? Oh, same thing, eh? Well, thanks for trying, anyway. And good-by. Wait a minute . . . Has Mac started over yet? That's bad. Well, kiss him good night for me. Good. Why sure, come over yourself. Sure. Good night."

5. SOBBING

When an actor sobs on his arm, on another actor's shoulder, in the embrace of another actor, or into a pillow, care should be taken to see that the mouth is not covered—that there is space open in front of it. The forehead and not the face should be laid on the arm, and this will allow the mouth to be protected and the words audible. When an actor cries in the lap of another actor, the upstage side of the face must be in the lap with the front facing out toward the audience.

6. PLANTING AN OBJECT

We have seen how the use of the dagger or gun must be covered, but in their "planting" they need not only be shown to the audience but shown in such a way that the attention of everybody in the audience will be held by them. Usually early in the scene the author will call attention to them in the lines of the play, and by this pointing the suspense values will be increased. The actor must, however, do his share of pointing. The lines tell us of an unusual Indian knife which is now used as a paper cutter. The actor must pick this sharp and threatening object up and examine it in such a way that the audience will see just how full of potential danger it is. The property must be opened up so that it registers with all.

Here is a story of a jewel robbery. The pearls or the necklace or the rubies are to play an important part in what is to follow. Not burlesquing the action, the actor planting them should hold up the property, run his hand over it, and even admire it. It must be opened up and focused. The object becomes more important for the moment than does the actor. An inanimate object takes possession of the stage focus. Innumerable examples might be cited, but the same principle of pointing emphatic objects becomes an emphatic business or pantomime.

An actor may be called to light a lamp, turn on a switch for the side lights, close a window, pull down the shade, put another log on the fire, close a door, get a book and sit. Nothing emphatic is necessarily in this. It is just business; but if this is followed by his taking a paper from his pocket and putting it in the fire, this last bit becomes emphatic. He will open up and point the paper from his pocket before he throws it into the fire. As a matter of fact he will probably take the paper out of his pocket and point it for the audience before he does any of the business. In this way he will establish a suspense that is held. But he returns it to his pocket, then does all the business, and then points it again but not so strongly before he puts it in the fire.

Whenever an actor has a definite business pantomime and he has been alone on the stage, he must make a slight noise with the last business so that it may serve as a cue for a speech offstage or for an entrance. This may be an accidental rattling of fire tongs or putting down a glass heavily, a slight cough, hitting a chair, or sitting down heavily.

Following is an exercise in which every move and each use of a property is of vital importance to the audience. Each action must be opened up yet be blended into a natural relationship of the actor to the stage room.

Exercise in emphatic pantomime business

The stage directions are taken from *Interference,* by Roland Pertwee and Harold Dearden. Copyright, 1929, by Samuel French, Ltd. All Rights Reserved. Reprinted by permission of Samuel French.

The scene concerns the attempt of Sir John Marley to cover up the murder of Deborah Kane by poison. Sir John believes that his wife, Faith, committed the crime and desires to protect her and make the case appear to be suicide.

The set is the living room of Deborah Kane's flat.

On the DR wall is a fireplace. Across angle of back and R wall is a curtained window recess with a French window and little balcony. There is a glass-paneled door in C of back wall. This door leads out to the elevator and main hall. To the L of this a passage which leads into kitchen.

(The stage is still dark. The body still lies on the bed. Footsteps. A shadow passes the glass panel of the front door. The shadow pauses. There is a ring at the bell. Pause. Another ring. Sound of a key in the lock. Sir John Marley enters very quietly [swell of gramophone until

door shuts] and closes door. He is just visible, lit by the glow of the passage lights.)

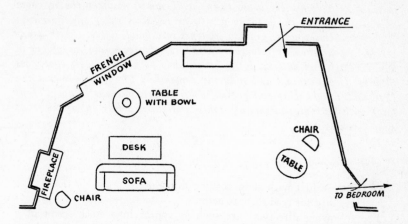

SIR JOHN (*gently*): Anyone here? Miss Kane! [*Goes to writing table R, puts latchkey on it, then lights match. Finds the switch, and lights go up. He stands looking around the room. Sees Deborah.*] Miss Kane! [*Moves to her side and kneels, take her hand, and turns her over on her back.*] God! [*He goes down to bedroom L. Returns to table, picks up tumbler, smells it. Is just about to telephone when he sees Faith's bag lying on the floor R. At the sight, for a moment his mind becomes blank with horror. He picks up the open bag, examines its contents, takes the cheque he wrote for her, and puts it in his coat pocket. Glances at his wrist watch. His eye settles on the poison bottle which he recognizes as one of his own. He covers his eyes with his hand and sits thinking. Suddenly he straightens up with a new and intense expression. From this point onward his actions are extraordinary. He takes gloves and a black silk handkerchief out of his pocket, puts on the gloves, takes off his coat, places it on chair at back of table, picks up poison bottle from table, tries to remove its label with a knife from the tray. He then empties the poison tumbler into the bowl of flowers on the writing table; places poison bottle in a glass of water which he takes from jug at back. Takes brandy bottle, thoroughly cleans it with handkerchief. This done, he replaces brandy bottle on table center. He then removes poison bottle from glass and scrapes off the red label, which he puts on the table C and places poison bottle in Deborah's right hand. At this moment the voices of two men are heard approaching; their shadows appear on the glass window; they stop; one rings the bell; they are evidently calling on Deborah to try to get a drink; the other per-*

suades his friend that it is too late; and they go away talking. At the sound of voices and the appearance of the shadows, Sir John is arrested in what he is doing. He backs to the wall, moves down to the bedroom door L, hesitates; the men go away; he registers relief and hurriedly carries on. Rinses glass, pouring contents into bowl, wipes it with hand-kerchief; pours brandy into the glass; wipes knife; wraps his gloves in handkerchief, and puts the lot in his trousers pocket. He takes coat, goes to door. Looks around and suddenly remembers the label; comes down C to table; picks it up and puts it in his pocket. Returns to door, opens latch with his coat, switches off lights, and passes gently out of the front door, latching it.]

General exercises in stage movements and positions

1. Do these first with actor reading direction.
2. Have director read them to actor.

The following directions are such as appear in a stock script of a Broadway farce. Each section constitutes those for one character. After each direction hold the position as if a scene were to follow which you are to share in every case with somebody. Other person may be standing on whichever side of you is convenient. All properties are to be used in pantomime.

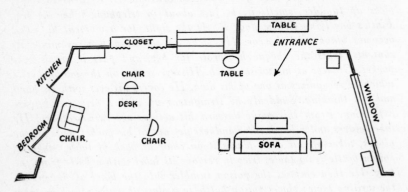

Exercise *a*.

1. You enter LC quickly, carrying traveling bag to C, coat to sofa LC, grip by door of up C. Hat on table by door LC alcove.
2. C.
3. Follow to RC.
4. X to C.
5. Take (Xs) to LC.

6. Stroll up to C.
7. X to chair L of desk, sit.
8. Rise, go to C.
9. Bring grip to sofa, and begin to open it. Your back is toward RC.
10. As you bend over grip:
11. Turn embarrassed.
12. To LC below sofa.
13. Put grip up by closet C.
14. To C, embrace her (she on right).
15. Cross to DL.
16. X to C, embrace her.
17. Take position at door up LC for exit.
18. Exit LC.

Exercise *b*.
1. Enter R-1 crossing in front of desk to RC; then up to door LC; when you reach a position near end of sofa, the doorbell rings. It stops ringing, and telephone on desk rings. You turn sharply and go toward telephone. When you are nearly to desk RC, telephone ceases, doorbell rings. The business is repeated three times. You grow more and more confused. You finally take coin from pocket and flip it. Indicate that doorbell wins, go to desk, lift receiver off telephone. You open door, take paper, cross with paper to desk, answer telephone. "Hello, what is it? No, sir, this is the home of Mr. Johnson. This is his house. When he's home. But he's not home. Yes, Mr. Jones lives here when Mr. Johnson's not home. We expect him any minute. You didn't bother me. All right. Yes, good-by."
2. X to chair L of desk RC.
3. Sit chair L of desk RC.
4. X front of desk to R.
5. Drop down a little.
6. Beckon to back of you with thumb.
7. X to RC front of chair L of desk.
8. Go up to CL of stairs, and then come down to above chair L of desk.
9. Cross to C.
10. Start to R-1, stop at DRC.
11. X to C.
12. X above sofa to window L.
13. Look at object offstage.
14. X to door LC.
15. Come down a little.
16. Circle above desk to R-1.

17. Let Amy pass in front of you. Keep above door to give Amy a clean exit. Feed the scene with ad-lib business.

18. Exit R-1.

Exercise *c*.

1. Enter LC.
2. Work down toward sofa.
3. X to foot of stairs up RC.
4. Sit at desk.
5. Pick up telephone, "Hello," decide not to telephone.
6. Sit L end of bench RC.
7. Rise. Start toward door LC.
8. Snatch your coat from sofa LC, and start to R-1 below desk. Change your mind, and X to L of desk.
9. S to R, get grip from settee RC.
10. Put grip on table C of door LC.
11. Talk as you go to actor at C.
12. Sit on upstage arm of sofa LC.
13. X to R-1. Open door, and call "Amy," who enters. Take your position.
14. X to L end of desk RC. Sit on desk.
15. X to R end of settee RC.
16. Sit.
17. Rise, and steal UR.
18. Business. Begin to attract attention of actor *A* at L, but you fail. Business repeat. When actor *B* turns and sees you, you pretend to be trying to catch a fly.
19. Exit up RC, giving speech before you exit.

Exercise *d*.

1. Your head appears at top of stairs URC. You sneak down, come to R of desk, pause, listen, cross to sofa LC, look in grip, and sink on sofa.
2. Rise, circle back of desk, cross to door LC, pause, hesitate, come back to L of desk front of chair.
3. You hide behind upstage end of sofa, LC.
4. You appear below sofa, creep out, take box out of grip, open box, take out necklace, put box back in grip, put necklace in your stocking.
5. Rush back and forth between R of desk and downstage end of sofa. Business three times. Go to R of desk, grab glass, take up pitcher, pour water into glass, and start to exit RC. Change mind and X to DR.
6. Begin drinking from glass, wandering aimlessly about RC, put

glass on desk, take it up again, ad-lib until water is all gone. Then put glass on upstage end of desk.

7. Begin dusting in a senseless way various articles, finally knocking telephone over; you pick it up and begin dusting it by wiping it on your dress. Put receiver to your ear. In telephone, "Yes, yes, yes, yes, no." X to R of desk. Pick up glass, drain it, put it down as a cue for some-body to enter.

8. X to door C. Speak, and exit.

9. Enter C, X to R-1, turn on electric switch on upstage side of door.

10. X to up C.

11. X to DL in front of sofa.

12. X to window L, and look out.

13. X to door C, open it, start L of it, hold door open. Close door, and work DRC.

14. X to R-1. Give speech and start to exit, then dash to desk R side, searching madly on it for something. Circle above desk to L side, search on desk, look under cushion on chair L of desk; then dash to sofa, tumble pillows about, lift up seat cushion of sofa, finally discover paper under cushion. Having found paper, your excitement subsides instantly.

15. Sit on sofa, and talk to somebody upstage.

16. X to DR, call "Amy," who enters.

17. X to exit RC.

V

The Body, the Voice, and the Role

WITH THIS understanding of the actor's technique of handling himself in relation to the audience and to the other actors, we now begin a wholly new attack: the actor in relation to himself—his body, his voice, his role—free from any stage technique.

Under body and voice only the salient and most used principles will be touched upon. Those chosen are the ones most likely to arise during rehearsals. As we mentioned earlier, the following exercises are not given to train and develop an actor but rather for the beginner to keep practicing as the singer would practice musical scales between public appearances. These exercises will also furnish a step-by-step outline on which the teacher can elaborate with his own lectures and demonstrations. These sections have been handled at such great lengths by whole volumes that to proceed with more detail would be to repeat what has been already ably accomplished.

A. SUBJECTIVE AND OBJECTIVE ACTING

1. METHODS OF OBJECTIVE CREATION OF CHARACTER

The purpose of acting has always been to re-create a character from life upon the stage. Formerly and until fairly recent times, this re-creation was achieved by having the actor visualize the physical characteristics in detail. Then before a mirror he would watch himself imitate the manners, the gestures, and the movements of a character. Spending hours in this critical and analytical study, he would acquire the mirrored way to hold palsied hands, to turn his head or stoop his shoulders, to lift his eyebrows, or to twist his nose.

There was a time, and not long ago, when the way to express the different emotions was catalogued. The face and voice took on stereotyped expressions and tones which were learned by imitating a teacher or coach. Actors handed them on to actors, and teachers handed them on through books for generations. Again the neophyte studied these emotional expressions before a mirror. The actor studied the character from the outside and saw and heard himself playing the role.

This approach to the reproduction of a character is known as the objective method. In its use the actor is on the outside of himself, looking at himself as an object of speculation and analysis. With this consciousness of his manner of body and quality of voice, it was almost impossible to get within the real character and to convey to the audience that sense of reality, of depth, and even of sensitivity which we demand today—not only in our acting but also in our plays.

In the days when the theater was theoretically and practically an artificial and resplendent world this method produced great actors. They very likely pierced the depth of human nature even though encumbered by all this manufactured outer surface. Today nothing is considered more detrimental than the practice of acting before a mirror, because it results in self-consciousness and stilted movement which lacks spontaneity, conviction, and reality.

2. IMITATIVE METHOD IN MODERN DIRECTING

We have, however, a very definite "carry-over" of a phase of this objective method in our theater of the present day. Too many of our directors and, unfortunately, our teachers received their early training when this approach was common. Although for the most part the mirror has disappeared, the teaching of imitation is frequent. It is the easiest and shortest way to make an actor read a line or do a bit of action correctly; the director does it himself and has the actor copy him. This is doubtless because many of our directors were formerly actors, many of them disappointed actors who know only one way to coach—that of doing a thing themselves and having the actors imitate them. A good actor does not necessarily make a good director, and, conversely, a good director does not make a good actor. Frequently the general aspersion cast upon directors is that "he was such a bad actor that he had to take to directing." Without attempting to settle that dispute, we should point out the well-known fact that the best singing teachers and operatic coaches have not been singers themselves. Rather they have known the best ways to shape the technique of the singers and to draw out from a gifted voice the emotional expression. Coaching the singer or the actor is seldom successfully accomplished by the method of imitation.

Some of these "successful" directors who still treat their actors like so many puppets or trained dogs—by reading each line and each speech, by furnishing every external characteristic, and by demonstrating every moment of action for the actor—are in many cases the directors who believe that directing a play is merely a question of reading; whereas such things as the positions on the stage, the movement and business of the characters, the interrelation of character to character, the locale, and the many other elements of directing that we shall discuss later under the Five Fundamental Elements of Directing they consider immaterial and inconsequential. Such ignorance is the result of a lack of knowledge of what a director does or should do in staging the play in our present-day theater. To these directors, devoid of such knowledge, all action is at right center, left center, or center. Their furniture arrangement in every setting will be a table with two or three chairs or their equivalent on one side of the stage and a sofa on the other. Their direction consists of having actors sitting or standing by these pieces with their body positions quite open to the audience as they give elocutionary dramatic readings. Other directors of this same category employ a more costly and imaginative scene designer who provides a richer furniture arrangement. Then, after spending two weeks with the cast sitting in a circle and reading their lines by themselves day after day, these directors eventually transport their actors to the stage, seat them in a broken circle of chairs, and again have them read lines hour after hour for the last week before the opening.

The first type of director is rapidly disappearing as the result of old age; the second, the result of a fad of a few years ago, is also passing. The great danger of the former method is the development of inhibitions and complexes in the actor;

the breaking up of these is treated elsewhere. The purpose of this material on the actor is to furnish the director with the tools by which he may bring out the proper results from the actor, not through imitation or coercion but through explanation and imaginative suggestions.

3. THE ACTOR AND THE IMITATIVE METHOD

The actor, too, must prepare himself against the stultifying effects of direction through imitation and be ready to supplant stiltedness with spontaneity. Especially is this important today in the motion-picture studios where directing is conducted along these lines and where the sequence of takes requires the actor to jump coldly into an emotional scene whose motivation and stimulation for the emotional states lie in an earlier scene.

A recent example of this was related to me by an actor just returned from Hollywood. He was playing the part of a boy who hated and did not believe in war. This boy had never fared well with his father. One morning at breakfast, however, while the war is on, he receives news that three of his closest friends have been killed in action. The boy decides to go and fight; the father approves of his decision and, for the first time in the boy's life, is kind to him. This kindness breaks down the antagonism of the boy toward his father. A long dramatic scene follows during which the father and son compare confidences, yet each not wanting to show the great love that has developed between them. This episode was told in three scenes. The order of the shooting, however, of these three scenes was completely reversed. The final scene which required the playing of mixed and complicated emotional states was taken first. One month later they played the "making-up" scene and three weeks later the boy played the "breakfast" scene which contained the motivation for his going to war.

Under such conditions the drilling in the reading and playing of mixed emotional states as a distinct and individual technical problem is a great advantage. The pure reading approach is a valuable and practical experience. However, time is showing that the best actors for the system encountered in motion pictures are those who have played a long time in the methods of the theater. These actors have gained much experience in a procedure where emotional states have been arrived at through a natural order of receiving stimuli. When, then, in the motion-picture technique, they are required to jump coldly into an emotional state, they are able to recall such states from memory and can do away with immediate stimuli.

All this is more easily said than done, but the young actor who is required to submit to objective coaching should learn early to receive such instruction in an objective state of mind. He should first watch or listen from a perfectly mechanical point of view, whether it is a movement, a look, a voice tone, or an expression of emphasis. Then he should grasp the meaning or idea behind the instruction by noting quickly what idea has come out of or is conveyed by the new treatment. After this it is the simple process of combining the objective or technical execution with the subjective feeling and meaning.

4. THE ACTOR AND THE FUNDAMENTAL ELEMENTS OF DIRECT-
ING

For those actors who must work with the director who leaves it to them to feel the movement and business, it is necessary to learn certain principles of directing and to apply these to themselves. In this respect the material in this book, though written from a director's point of view, becomes invaluable information for the actor. Many an actor has admitted that this is the very thing he does—supply his own movement and business—when he is left alone by the director. Such an actor viewing the scene from a director's attitude has added treatment upon treatment so that the actual director out front has believed that the part was being played solely as the natural expression of the actor grasping the characterization. The fact is that the experienced actor does know a great deal about directing, especially the purely technical side. He is unable to grasp more, solely because it is a mental impossibility to be a contributive part of the whole and to grasp the whole in itself at the same time. That is why contributive directing from the actors without a guiding hand does not make for unity of impression.

Nevertheless, whether the actor is working under a director who believes that directing a play consists solely in letting each actor act to his heart's content and accordingly has to direct himself or under one who believes in contributing to the play and its expression by his ability to dramatize the inherent characteristics, mood, and meaning—in either case the actor who understands the simple fundamental principles and theories of directing will achieve an infinitely better coordination between himself and the director. If after the director asks him to make an arbitrary movement without the technical, business, or character motivations being explained the actor anticipates the reason for such a movement, unquestionably this actor is bound to be in closer accord and understanding with the director. Many a time, after a piece of direction, a good actor will grasp the reason for the direction even before the director has a chance to give the first few words of explanation. These are the actors with whom a director most enjoys working. Every beginning actor should try to grasp direction quickly, and the way to achieve that faculty is to understand some of the simple elements of directing.

5. BASIS OF SUBJECTIVE CREATION OF CHARACTER

The subjective method of re-creating a character from life consists first in getting the body and voice in a thoroughly relaxed condition. Neither body nor voice must feel restricted or be inhibited, awkward, tense, or stiff. The actor should not be mentally conscious of either. When these external obstacles have been eliminated and the full freedom of the body and voice from muscular strain has been achieved, the mind is then in a condition to create an image. This image, however, is not to be of a physical event but instead must be a stirring up of former emotional states that the actor has experienced. This internal feeling will slowly grow and will eventually express itself through the body, taking form in body mimicry, expression, and gesture. The voice, too, as the mouth shapes the words, will bring out the inner emotional feeling in a concrete expression. With this external manifestation of an inner feeling we have the basis for the subjective creation of characteri-

zation and emotional states. The energy from the inner feeling
will work on the deeply ingrained lines of a past, and out of
this a natural spontaneous reading will pour out through the
actor's vocal equipment. This attack, remember, is only the
beginning; there is much more to be done to carry the inner
feeling and imagery to full expression.

B. SUBJECTIVE CREATION AND STAGE TECHNIQUE

Before proceeding further with the subjective method of
creation, let us pause to consider and understand the relation
of this pure creative imagery to the abundance of technical
considerations that we have minutely detailed in the preceding
chapter. For the moment let us disregard the voice and concentrate solely on the movement of the body.

Let us suppose that the emotional energy seeking expression
through the body gives the body an impulse to move, to run
hastily toward a door and rush out of the room. It is easy for
us to understand how such an outward expression could occur
in violent action. Performed in the actor's own sitting room,
this outward expression would present no particular problem;
it would be the natural emotional outlet. But now let us
transfer the sitting room on to the stage. Let us suppose that
the actor is to run the width of the room and exit out of a
door down right or, better still, to run across the room and
exit out of a door upstage center that has to be opened and
closed. When to this movement must be added very important
lines for the full outward expression of an emotional state,
the problem becomes much more complicated. The actor must
make a curved approach so as to arrive upstage in an open
position; he must open and close the door, and so on. Clearly,
the problem becomes one of letting the inner re-creation of an
emotional state give expression to an outward movement that,
controlled under stage conditions, must be made with technical
consideration, restriction, or modification. It is largely for
this reason that the need for mastering stage technique becomes paramount. These technicalities must become so much
a part of the unconscious motor reactions that, when the impulse from the emotion comes, the body will naturally and

without thought or consciousness fall into technical form.

Let us consider another simple adjustment of inner impulse to technical control. We have already mentioned that when an actor sobs on his arm he must leave the space in front of the mouth open so that the audience can hear what is said. The natural physical movement of this action is to throw the arm on the table with the head face down on it.

Demonstrations

1. Have the actor do the natural physical movement of sobbing on his arm several times. His arm will probably come across his eyes, covering his nose and most of his mouth. The table will be in front of whatever part of the mouth is not covered by the arm.

This movement will be completely without technical control and unsuited to any consideration of a group of people interested in what he is saying. Now have the actor perform this movement with technical control so that the space in front of the mouth remains open.

2. Have the actor mechanically and arbitrarily and with no emotional feeling put his arm on the edge of the table. Have him throw his head down so that the forehead and not the nose rests on the arm. Have him do this several times until he performs the action without any thought of his motor physical reaction.

The movement is now under technical control and takes into consideration the group of listeners. Moreover, this second way of performing the movement is neither false nor insincere. If possible, the actor, having mastered the technical form, may now awaken his emotional impulse and without thought of technique, stage, or audience express his inner emotional state. This simple demonstration tells the complete story of the relationship of emotional expression to technical control. This is why the actor must study and master technique first so as to get it ingrained into his system as a part of his natural body reaction. Following this technical mastery he may work freely on the development of inner emotional states and their outward expression.

So far we have dealt only with the body and have not touched upon the voice in relation to this theory. We shall come to it later. For the time being we shall consider the necessary basic physical conditions of getting the body ready for the outward expression of the emotional creation.

C. BODILY RESPONSIVENESS

Before the body or voice is able to express subjectively the concepts of the character and its emotional state, it must be freed from muscular strain and tightness which restrict, inhibit, and fetter the person not only on the stage but in everyday life. Mental consciousness can often be broken down by physical exertion. The more the actor is mentally tied up the greater is the physical action required in order to achieve flexibility and mobility of action.

The exercises that follow are only a few of many that a director will find invaluable for actors as practice work in relaxing the body. Those given here are sufficient for the usual requirements that a director expects of an actor, since they cover not only the separate parts of the body but the whole of the body itself. If an actor spends a great deal of time on these and constantly reviews them, later when he is working on other subjects and even after he has appeared in public he will keep his body relaxed, responsive, and naturally graceful. The conscious actor should never cease to practice these exercises for the continued maintenance of a relaxed and responsive condition of body and voice.

Exercises in relaxation

Relaxing the entire body:

1. Hold the body erect, the arms over the head, reaching as high as you can. Slowly bring the arms down, then drop the head, then the shoulders, then bend at the waist, then relax the knees until the body is hanging as much like a rag or bent-over scarecrow as you can make it. Then slowly straighten the knees and pull up the body as though a string were tied to a point between the shoulders, first straightening at the waist, then the shoulders, then slowly the head, leaving the arms hanging loosely at the sides. This exercise should be used not only during a practice period but at any time during the day when the body becomes tense.

2. Folding and unfolding. Hold the body erect, alert, the arms and

hands reaching as high as possible above the head. Slowly relax the arms, dropping them to the sides on the count of five. As they pass the head, let it relax and drop slowly to the neck. Then let the shoulders go, then relax at the waist, the arms always leading the body as it folds down. Then soften the knees, drop on to one knee, on to both. Then fold the entire body up into as small a ball as possible on the floor. If this process has been properly followed, the body should be completely relaxed, and the position one of utter comfort. Hold this position for five counts, and then slowly unfold, reversing the process, the mid-point of the back below the shoulders leading up. First up with one knee, then with both, then straighten at the waist, pull up the shoulders; let the head come up last. No tension whatever should be allowed to come in the unfolding process, but the relaxation attained in folding should be kept throughout. Repeat, folding on the count of ten, holding five counts, unfolding on the count of ten. This exercise relaxes the body and then brings it into position in complete poise.

Relaxing the different parts of the body:

For the head:

3. This exercise will be successful only if it is practiced with complete relaxation of the head, neck, and shoulders. The arms are permitted to hang normally at the sides. Drop the head on to the chest, then roll it around in a complete circle four times to the right and four times to the left. Then enlarge the movement to include the shoulders. Enlarge it still more so that the waistline becomes the pivot point. Then return to the second movement and finally to the head movement, bringing the head back into position.

For the torso:

4. Stand with the feet set firmly but slightly apart. The knees should be kept flexible throughout this exercise, ready to give with the flow of the movement. Now make an entire circle with a center point at the waist as pivot starting to the left, going as low as you can, then coming up to the right; reach as high as you can (the arms are free at the sides), and then make the same circle starting to the right. When the body is making the movement with ease and a strong flowing motion, let the arms follow through, but be careful that the body continues to lead, the arms merely carrying through the movement.

4a. Take the same circle on the diagonal, first with the body slightly turned to the left and the right foot forward and then with the left forward and the body turned to the right.

For the arms and legs:

5. Whirl first the right and then the left arm in a circle, letting the movement come from the torso and be carried through the arm. Then let both arms follow through their circles at the same time. They should be

completely relaxed, and all the impulse of the movement should come from the shoulder.

6. Let the arms hang loose at the sides. Start the left arm swinging slightly. Increase the movement until the swing goes through as large an arc as you can easily make with the arm relaxed. Gradually decrease the arc until the arm hangs easily at the side again. Repeat with the right arm. All this movement should come from the shoulder.

7. Stand with the weight on the right foot; start the left leg swinging like a pendulum, at first slightly and then increased. Be careful that no strain slips into this movement and that it is kept a free and easy swing from the hip. Increase the movement as much as you can easily, and continue until the leg seems to swing of itself. Then slow down the movement, and stop it easily. Repeat with the right foot and leg.

8. Stand with the weight on the right foot, the left leg hanging freely but not raised so that there is any strain on it. Shake the leg, then just from the knee, then just the foot itself, then the entire leg again. Drop it easily to the ground, change the weight, and repeat with the right leg, knee, foot, and leg. During this exercise the rest of the body should be relaxed, and no tension should come into the shoulders, neck, or any other part of the torso. It is best to keep the head poised and not look down at the leg.

For the hands:

9. Shake the hands one at a time, letting the movement come through the arm from the shoulder so that the hands themselves are completely relaxed. Then shake them together. Then move the fingers as rapidly as you can, one after the other, as though you were touching the strings of a harp. Be sure that you bend each finger at every joint with each movement. Keep the hands relaxed throughout, then go back to the shaking movement; shake them as hard as you can, and then drop them easily at the side.

10. Imagine that a heavy, but very soft, velours curtain is hanging before you. Reach as high as you can, and bring the hands down the curtain, keeping the feel of the velours as you come down.

Relaxation for the breaking up of a fixed inhibition during rehearsal or a performance:

11. Raise the hands high up over the head, then lower them to the sides. While you are doing this, start walking in place. Increase the speed of raising the arms as you change the walking to a running in place.

11a. The same, only instead of walking and running in place, walk and run around the room.

11b. The same, only now add to the action the speaking aloud of the speech, over and over again. This will be difficult. Stop and say the speech.

D. Vocal Responsiveness

In the study of the elementary stage technique for the actor we have seen that there is a technique that must be learned so thoroughly that the movements of the actor on the stage may be accomplished with little or no thought. Then we have seen how the body must be made to relax so that it is in a free and unrestricted condition to express the creative concept of character and emotion. Now we come to a study of the voice for its use on the stage.

In real life ordinary speech is for the most part monotonous, unemotional, and weak. The words are usually poorly enunciated and often irrelevant. Little regard is had for color, variety, emphasis, or unity of vocal melody. Few people with the exception of speech connoisseurs notice such deficient speech equipment in everyday life. But put that naturally distorted yet passable voice on stage, and many of the defects immediately become apparent to the layman. The magnifying qualities of the stage on voice are the same as on movement; getting up out of a chair in real life is generally done in an awkward, clumsy way, but on the stage this bit of business must be done with ease and grace and inconspicuously.

Hence, the voice must be handled so that it will be pleasing, flexible, colorful, strong, varied, and impressive. The words and sentences must be spoken in a clear, articulate, and harmonious manner. The phrasing with use of emphasis must be liquid and expressive. Developing the voice is a matter of technique; the vocal organ, like the body, must be trained so that its qualities will not only arrest the attention of an audience but convey with ease the thoughts, the imagery, and the inner emotions that call for expression.

As with the body, the voice must be trained so that its correct use will come to an actor without consciousness. The actor who is consciously aware of his voice restricts it from being the free organ and faithful conveyor that it must be to express the inner emotions and ideas. So there is not only work to do to prepare the voice for technical proficiency but exercises to make the voice relaxed, receptive, and flexible. Only when this is done will the director have actors with voices prepared to respond to and convey the subtleties of inner feeling.

With the many excellent texts written on the voice and voice training, it is not our intention to enter into a detailed treatise on the subject. The director, however, will find that such study fully covers the requisites for a well-trained voice which he should expect to find or to develop in his actors.

1. BREATHING

Most of the faults of the speaking voice are due to poor and incorrect breathing. People who breathe incorrectly are not able to get enough air into the lungs. They have little control or the wrong control in letting this air out as they speak. They spend too much breath on the first part of a sentence and have only a little or a forced breath left to complete the important part of the sentence. If they do attempt to hold sufficient breath, they tighten the vocal cords and become tense in the throat so that they hinder rather than help the speech. When once a person has achieved correct breathing, many of the other voice difficulties will take care of themselves. Accordingly, we shall discuss first what constitutes correct breathing and, second, what exercises will help develop it.

Proper breathing demands the correct use of the diaphragm, lungs, and intercostal muscles. Most people breathe with only the upper part of the lungs instead of using the diaphragm and the full lung capacity. The diaphragm is a muscle that forms the floor of the chest cavity. Upon its control through the correct use of the abdominal muscles depends the control of the voice. In inhalation the diaphragm straightens out, allowing the lungs to expand and fill with air. In exhalation the reverse takes place. We exhale as we speak. To control the breath in speaking is therefore a matter of controlling the contraction of the diaphragm so that breath is forced out of the chest cavity in a smooth, steady stream. We need to consider the exercises that will strengthen the diaphragm and train the actor to use it properly in speaking.

Exercises for the development of breath control

These exercises will help the actor to speak a sentence correctly so that he will have sufficient breath to give the increased emphasis that is necessary for the final words. It will also make it possible for him to give long speeches with the desired climactic effect and to phrase correctly long sentences.

In practicing the following exercises, be certain to keep the voice steady without jerks, breaks, or wavering. Under no conditions should the exercises be continued after the breath is gone by straining or forcing the air by means of tightening the throat muscles or collapsing the chest. The chest should be kept firm and expanded at all times; the throat must be opened and relaxed throughout.

1. Take a deep breath, and see how far you can count. This exercise should be practiced until you can easily count sixty on the exhalation of one breath. Be careful never to force the count. The moment the breath is forced by rasping or the throat grows tense, stop and begin again until you can count sixty without effort.

2. Take a deep breath and exhale slowly, issuing a constant flow of the sound *s,* while someone counts aloud. This should be practiced until the count of forty can be reached on one exhalation.

3. Inhale deeply, and exhale with a continuous *ho-o-o-o* sound as you walk. Keep the sound steady. This should be practiced until you can walk twenty-five steps on one breath.

4. Take the gymnastic position for arm circling—the two feet apart, chest high, head back, the arms extended at right angles at the sides. Make small circles with the arms, and count with each circle made. This should be practiced until you can count thirty-five, keeping the voice steady and firm.

5. Take other gymnastic exercises; and by constant practice in correlating them with breathing, develop the breath control so that you can increase the number of counts possible on one exhalation.

6. See how many times you can repeat the following sentence with one breath: "Now is the time for all good men to come to the aid of their country." With each repetition be sure that the greater emphasis is on "aid of their country."

7. Repeat the foregoing exercise, and with each repetition of the sentence increase the intensity and volume with which it is spoken. Build the whole so that the final repetition is the strongest and greatest in volume.

8. Take the sentence "Now is the time for all good men to come to the aid of their country while the little gray fox jumps lazily over the broad white fence," and repeat it three times on one exhalation. Again be careful to emphasize the ends of the two clauses.

9. Draw a diagram representing the inflection of the sound from a sea wave breaking on the shore. Repeat "Now is the time for all good men to come to the aid of their country" so that its sound will have the same inflection as the diagram.

10. Take the vowel sounds *ee* and/or *eh, ah, aw, oh, oo,* and repeat them with the sea-wave diagram in mind, building with each repetition to a final climax. Be sure that your vowel sounds are full, open throat, and clear.

11. Exercise: *Cataract of Lodore,* by Robert Southey.

2. VOICE QUALITY

The correction of a second common fault of the inexperienced actor lies in the development of a good voice quality. Too many beginning actors have harsh, high-pitched, nasal, and generally unpleasant voices. A student who is taking his acting work seriously will try to develop a pleasing and appealing voice. There is no better way of gaining the immediate attention of the audience than through the beautiful sound of a musical voice. This has become particularly apparent in watching and listening to the sound motion pictures; here everyone appreciates constantly the greater appeal of one actor over another, not only through personal appearance as in the silent movies but through the beauty of the voice. Furthermore, because of the sound motion pictures, more people are becoming conscious of voice quality and are carrying a stricter critical sense of these qualities when they attend the theater.

Before working directly on voice quality, it is necessary to perform certain exercises to get the throat in a thoroughly relaxed condition. This is as fundamental for the voice as it is for the body.

Exercises for relaxing the throat

1. Yawn, and then speak, first the syllable *moh,* then the word *more,* and the sentence "The more unconsciously that can be done the better."

2. Take the sentence "More can be done about speech than can be said," and say it:

a. Yawning before each word.

b. Yawning before each of the three phrases.

c. Yawning once and then speaking the entire sentence.

3. The test for an open and relaxed throat is as follows: Without voicing them, speak the syllables and the words *ho, ha, hey, home, whey, what, where, whoa.* If no rasping sound results, the throat is open and relaxed. Now speak the syllables and words aloud, but before speaking each one make the test as above. This test of not voicing a word first will help prevent the actor from hurting his throat in a scream; it eliminates the tension and tightening of a throat that usually comes when he must scream and should be applied immediately before the scream.

3. RESONANCE

After the throat is thoroughly relaxed and open, we should begin to work for the first element of voice quality—resonance. By resonance is meant the element in voice quality that gives the overtone, vibrancy, and brilliance to the tone. Resonance brings out the most appealing quality of the voice; it is the element most responsible for stimulating emotional contact with the audience. Accordingly, we should work to develop this quality of resonance in the speaking voice. Experiments have shown that the chest, the back and upper part of the roof of the mouth, the nose, and that part of forehead just above the nose will act very much as a sounding board in a piano. If you strike a note on a keyboard and listen to it acutely, you will hear the aftertone or overtone of the note resounding. This is the beauty of the tone. Our problem is to utilize these "sounding boards" by learning to throw our words up to strike one or more of these resonating chambers.

Without entering into the actual physiological structure that accounts for quality, we shall explain one practical and psychological way to obtain resonant tone.

Say the word "one" as you probably would naturally, with the sound coming through the mouth without striking the sounding board. Then with a conscious effort throw the sound against the back part of the roof of the mouth, being particular to hold the *n* sound. You will notice its resounding quality.

Alternate the two ways of saying "one"—first without this resonance and then with—until you are perfectly certain that you understand what the quality of resonance is and how it is gained. Notice how as you increase the intensity of the *n* sound the passages of the nose tend to quiver. The emphasis on *m* or *n* sounds is excellent for improved nasal resonance.

Exercises for resonance

In order to help improve resonance and develop an appealing voice quality, work on the following exercises. Be sure to practice them slowly at first, so that you consciously make and hear the overtone of each word that you speak. Then increase the speed until you are speaking at a natural rate; that is, let your consciousness be thinking of the sentence itself, leaving the resonance to come of itself. Note the words that are most conducive to obtaining resonance.

Be sure that the breath stream is not only well supported but directed forward, through the mouth for oral sounds and through the nose for nasal sounds. We omit here exercises for chest and head resonance.

1. *Nasal resonance:* Be sure that the soft palate is free from rigidity and sluggishness:

a. Chant *nga, ng, nga, ah.* Feel the vibration of the nostrils on *ng* and the freedom from vibration on *ah.*

b. Consciously throw the sound against the roof of the mouth, and say "One, up, nine, up, one, up, nine, up," etc.

c. "He said a pun in fun, and she ran with her fan in her hand."

d. "He 'phoned in a low tone to ask for a loan, and I rendered a penned note sending him funds."

e. "Running round the town like flying sand, singing simple sounds, I ended all my ranting noise and soon regained my long-lost poise."

2. *Oral resonance:* Be sure that the throat and back of the mouth are open and free from strain and that the lips and tip of the tongue and soft palate are flexible, light, and sure in their action. The breath should be sustained without effort and directed well forward through the mouth. Concentrate on eliminating nasality entirely. Practice on the following sentences which contain few nasal consonants:

a. "And now abideth faith, hope, charity, these three; but the greatest of these is charity."

b. "After life's fitful fever he sleeps well."
c. "Variety is the very spice of life."
d. "Be there a will, then wisdom finds a way."

4. PITCH

The second element in voice quality is pitch. We all know that in the several musical scales there are a great number of notes. The human voice encompasses many more speaking tones in its range than can be charted musically, since it is able to sound the many gradations between the notes of the musical scales. The actor's pitch is his tone place on the musical scale; his range is the distance between and number of different pitches on the musical scale that he is capable of using. This variation in pitch is generally known as intonation, or inflection, of the voice.

We must consequently develop a flexible range of pitch and learn which notes we should use in the various demands of acting. It is generally agreed that the tones of the middle register are the most pleasing for the natural voice on the stage, leaving higher and lower tones, or pitches, for expressing the different emotional states. The higher pitches are for exasperation, terror, fear, hysteria, nervousness, and other phases of nervous emotion. The lower pitches are for the deeper states of emotion, such as love, religion, grief, or deep sincerity. Accordingly, it is very necessary for the actor who must be able to express a great variety of emotional states to have a wide range of pitch.

Exercises for the development of range in pitch

1. Say the syllable *ho-o-o-o* in your normal speaking tone. Then say it on each note of the speaking scale, going down by half notes to the lowest pitch that you can reach and returning to a half note below normal. Continue, starting with the half note below the normal and returning to a half note below that. This will develop the lower register. Repeat the exercise, going up the scale to the highest pitch that you can reach without strain and returning to a half note above the starting point. This is for the development of the upper register. At first you can use a piano for this exercise.

2. Use the following sentence in the same manner as the *ho* of the first

exercise, speaking the entire sentence on a single tone each time: "I love his avowal." Be sure to prolong the vowels to their full value.

3. Repeat the following sentence in a low, deep register, and analyze its meaning from the contents and the reading. Repeat in a high register, and see how the speaker's meaning changes just from mere change of pitch: "Father, I am paying your compliments to the lady; madam, I can conceive of nothing equal to the happiness of pleasing you, and the pleasure of being your husband is a glory which I would prefer to anything else on earth."

4. Pronounce the following sentence with as many different emotions as possible, and note the use of different pitches for the different emotions: "I shall never go away."

5. ENUNCIATION

The next main common fault of the inexperienced actor is poor enunciation and pronunciation. In everyday life poor diction is a frequent and generally accepted fault, but on the stage it becomes a serious failing. The audience cannot understand the actor with poor enunciation. The magnifying power of the stage makes the natural faults of both pronunciation and enunciation stand out clearly and obviously.

Good diction depends upon the clear and correct sounding of the vowels and diphthongs (pronunciation) and the distinct articulation of the consonants (enunciation), especially those at the beginning and end of a word.

Since the voice depends a great deal on vowels for it beauty, expression, and carrying power, particular attention should be given to the pitch, emphasis, and duration of vowels. Too long a hold on vowels will make the voice monotonous and drawling. If the vowels are slurred, the speech will not be clear. Vowels, therefore, should be pronounced smoothly and easily.

In everyday speech, the final consonants are apt to be neglected and slurred; and whereas one may not be caught slighting them in ordinary speech, when an actor is on the stage his neglect of these final letters is apparent even to an undiscriminating audience. The final *ed, t, th, ing, d, f,* and *v* are the letters most likely to be slurred. *Wh* at the beginning of a word is apt to have the *h* eliminated in careless speech. *D, k,* and *g* are

difficult almost anywhere in a speech and need special attention; and the letter *r* presents a problem all its own. Standard
stage diction requires that this consonant remain unpronounced
and unsounded except when preceding or between vowel
sounds.

Great care has to be taken not to make the words of a speech
sound like the words in a column of a spelling book. They must
not have equal emphasis or stress. The meaning of the lines
must never suffer because of overdistinctness. Lines may be
spoken with the greatest clarity and still have the inflection,
variety, and proper stress to carry the full meaning of the line.
The chief reason that overcarefully enunciated sentences become so artificial is not because of enunciation but because of
the emphasis, or stress, on each word; the lack of phrasing in
the sentence; and the lack of properly proportioned stress to
bring out the important word, usually the final ones in a dramatic sentence.

Faulty enunciation results from incorrect or careless lip
movement and tongue movement and from a tight jaw, mostly
due to laziness in the use of lips and jaw. Faulty enunciation
also results from tension.

Exercises in enunciation

1. To work on the loosening of the jaw, roll the head around, with the
neck as a pivot, keeping the jaw loose. Then roll it saying the alphabet.
This also relaxes the throat.

2. Practice opening and closing the jaw with the motion of biting,
taking one large bite after another rapidly without touching teeth.

3. Speak the following syllables in succession, opening the jaw wide on
the *ah* sound and closing it between syllables: *pah, fah, tah, lah, kah, dah.*

4. For the lips:

Speak the following exercises first without voicing the sound and without any whispering sound but with complete formation by the lips. Then,
when the lips have become accustomed to making the shapes for the
words, speak the sentences aloud, being careful to enunciate clearly and
distinctly.

a. "Now is the time for all good men to come to the aid of their
country."

b. "The little gray fox jumped lazily over the broad white fence."

c. "Father, I am paying your compliments to the lady; madam, I can conceive of nothing equal to the happiness of pleasing you, and the pleasure of being your husband is a glory which I would prefer to anything else on earth."

d. After practicing these three sentences many times, say them silently in a different order, and be sure that everyone in the class can tell which one of the three you are saying at the time.

e. "Around the rugged rock the ragged rascal ran."

f. "She sells seashells by the seashore."

g. "Peter Piper picked a peck of pickled peppers; where is the peck of pickled peppers Peter Piper picked?"

h. Do the following exercise for the full value and clarity of the vowel sounds. Do it as written, then substitute an *l,* and afterward an *r,* for the *m.* Repeat all three also adding the same consonant to the end of the syllable. *May, mah, mă, moh, maw; mē, mĕ, mī, mĭ, miu, moy, mow, moh, muh.*

i. "Teddy took great care to drop his music roll."

j. "Singing songs, making mongs, taking tongs, baking bongs, ringing gongs, selling wrongs."

k. Read aloud, without chorus repetition, the patter song of the Major-General from Gilbert's *Pirates of Penzance.* Pay particular attention to the enunciation of each word. At first the reading will be slow. Repeat again and again until you can read the song in two minutes.

Song—Major-General*

I am the very model of a modern Major-Gineral,
I've information vegetable, animal, and mineral,
I know the kings of England, and I quote the fights historical,
From Marathon to Waterloo, in order categorical;
I'm very well acquainted too with matters mathematical,
I understand equations, both the simple and quadratical;
About binomial theorem I'm teeming with a lot of news—
With many cheerful facts about the square of the hypotenuse.
I'm very good at integral and differential calculus,
I know the scientific names of beings animalculous;
In short, in matters vegetable, animal, and mineral
I am the very model of a modern Major-Gineral!

*From *The Pirates of Penzance,* by William S. Gilbert.

I know our mythic history, King Arthur's and Sir Caradoc's,
I answer hard acrostics, I've a pretty taste for paradox
I quote in elegiacs all the crimes of Heliogabalus,
In conics I can floor peculiarities parabolous.
I can tell undoubted Raphaels from Gerard Dows and Zoffanies,
I know the croaking chorus from the *Frogs* of Aristophanes,
Then I can hum a fugue of which I've heard the music's din afore,
And whistle all the airs from that infernal nonsense *Pinafore*.
Then I can write a washing bill in Babylonic cuneiform,
And tell you every detail of Caractacus's uniform;
In short, in matters vegetable, animal, and mineral
I am the very model of a modern Major-Gineral!

In fact, when I know what is meant by "mamelon" and "ravelin,"
When I can tell at sight a chassepot rifle from a javelin,
When such affairs as sorties and surprises I'm more wary at,
And when I know precisely what is meant by "commissariat,"
When I have learnt what progress has been made in modern gunnery,
When I know more of tactics than a novice in a nunnery,
In short, when I've a smattering of elemental strategy,
You'll say a better Major-General has never *sat* a gee—
For my military knowledge, though I'm plucky and adventury,
Has only been brought down to the beginning of the century;
But still, in matters vegetable, animal, and mineral
I am the very model of a modern Major-Gineral!

6. PROJECTION

Projection, or carrying power, is the ability to convey the spoken words a distance. As children, when we make ourselves heard by a playmate farther up the hill, we yell. Now, yelling is opening the mouth wide, retracting the tongue, tightening the throat muscles, and forcing the tones. It results in what is called a diffuse, or undirected, nonfocused tone. This is nearly always accompanied by a high and shrill pitch. Obviously, when we are acting before an audience, we cannot yell. Not only is it unpleasant, but also it is unintelligible.

In order to be heard when playing in a large auditorium, an actor is presented with a problem. He cannot yell. He cannot take a high pitch with the ordinary voice. (Unfortunately, he often does both.) What he should do is to *project*.

Projection involves support of tone both by diaphragm and by voice placement. For good tone support the actor must have excellent breath control, for only with the ability to take deep breaths correctly and to let the breath out with great conservation can he project successfully. Practice humming and other resonance exercises. The actor whose tone is well placed and well supported is sure of reaching his audience. A third factor in the process is careful enunciation. The actor's lips and tongue must be trained to execute his ideas with freedom, flexibility, and force.

We shall see shortly the need for the actor to express with the voice the different emotional states; but first we must stress the point that only through projection is he able to convey emotions to the audience. He cannot express emotional states by shouting or yelling.

When projection has been developed so that it becomes a natural part of both stage and ordinary speech, the audience will be able to hear and understand what is said, whether the actor faces the audience or the rear of the stage. Projection cannot have too much practice.

Exercises in projection

1. Use again the Gilbert patter song from the previous exercises. Speak directly into the auditorium from the stage.

    a. Begin low, and think solely of projection, focusing and directing the tone at one point.

    b. Increase volume gradually through several repetitions.

    c. Give the first part of a lyric as a projection exercise, standing profile on stage; then with back to the audience. Use large volume in each case.

2. From the stage, practice yelling a sentence to the rest of the class sitting in the farthermost part of the auditorium. Then, in a well-modulated voice, give the same sentence over again using projection.

7. EMOTIONAL RESPONSIVENESS

Sincerity, depth, and conviction of feeling as expressed through the voice are conveyed to an audience only when that feeling comes from an internal energy in the body. Otherwise the emotional expression of the voice sounds hollow, false, and forced. This type of dramatic reading is frequently heard and easily detected over the radio. The romantic, heroic tones in many a broadcast of the romantic operetta, as well as the portrayal of character parts and emotional states in "dramatic sketches," are empty, insincere, and unconvincing—often they are embarrassing. This is because the readers are acting from the neck up. There is no body feeling, no inner creation. Certain conventionalized tones and mannerisms of voice are arbitrarily used. It is voice for voice's sake, tone for tone's sake. There is an objectivity in voice use that warrants comparison with the study of body expression before a mirror. The voice stands without support, and the emotional expression exists disassociated from body.

Many people have a capacity for strong emotional feeling but are unable to express this with the body because of physical inhibition or with the voice because of vocal inhibition. We have seen that when an actor feels emotions but is unable to express or project them, the best correction for the situation is exercises for body relaxation. The same holds true for the voice; exercises for voice relaxation will develop the ability to express emotions through the voice. The throat and vocal cords need to be in such a physical condition that the voice will express the entire gamut of emotions. For visual and auditory expression, both body and voice must have freedom, elasticity, and a sense of natural rhythm.

This ability to express emotion through the body and voice is called responsiveness. It consists of getting the body into a relaxed condition and then feeling the emotion and allowing it to pass through the relaxed and passively receptive vocal cords. It is absolutely essential for the expression of real emotion in the voice that the inner body receive the emotion first, then the external body, and finally the voice. This procedure for preparing the voice to express the emotions of the internal created image is closely similar to that of preparing the body.

In executing the following exercises it should be constantly borne in mind that the body must first be in a relaxed condition. It is probably wisest to review many of the body relaxation exercises before doing each of the exercises in responsiveness, although the student may find that as he becomes more able and experienced he can get the body into the proper receptive condition by mere conscious relaxation without actual body exercises.

Exercises in emotional responsiveness in the body

1. Lie down flat on the floor; take plenty of time to relax the body and mind.

a. Hear a noise.

b. Feel a snake crawling along by your side.

c. See somebody about to walk on you.

d. Your mouth is open, and a fly has flown in.

e. Smell smoke.

2. Sit in a chair. Relax. Feel and express:

a. Horror.

b. Joy.

c. Pity for yourself.

d. A tremendous religious experience.

e. Regality and stateliness.

f. Humility.

g. Yourself as the center of attention of a crowd.

h. Yourself very much out of the group. (You know nothing about the subject of conversation.)

i. Yourself explaining something to a group of children.

3. The following differ from the previous exercises in so far as the process of feeling the emotion will be slower in arriving and will build to a greater expression.

Sit in a chair relaxed. Drop your head down; close your eyes; drop your hands in your lap. Feel as if you were about to go to sleep. Then feel anger; keep feeling it more intensely until you cannot keep your eyes closed and then until you cannot sit still any longer.

Do the same with the following emotions: joy, hatred, love, religious ecstasy, grief.

4. Responsiveness followed by pantomimic action.

Lie on the floor and relax; sit in a chair and relax; stand relaxed. Then feel and express:

a. The moment before an experience in your own life when you were terrified and then the moment of reacting to the fear

i. When you are afraid of a mouse.

ii. When you have to go down cellar at night in the dark.

iii. When you come back from the cellar.

iv. When you are lost on a mountain.

v. When your house is on fire.

vi. When you walk by a cemetery alone at night.

vii. When you are sure that there is nobody in the house and then you hear footsteps upstairs.

b. An experience of joy at

i. Receiving a Christmas present.

ii. Receiving a string of pearls.

iii. Receiving the most important social invitation of the winter.

iv. Reaching a mountaintop.

v. Winning an athletic contest.

c. An expression of anger

i. When you cannot find your schoolbooks and it is late.

ii. When your younger brother or sister tells your parents that you are in love.

iii. When you are falsely accused of a minor crime.

Exercises in emotional responsiveness in the voice

1. Sit in a chair and relax; drop your head down; close your eyes; drop your hands in your lap. Then think of the following phrases expressing the emotion. Keep thinking of them and feeling the emotion until the phrase is given vocally. Be sure that after each phrase you begin the following one in a highly relaxed condition. Be sure also that no consciousness or thought, except the one sentence, creeps into consideration; that is, do not think how you have seen it done or how a person would do it or even how it should be done. Do not be surprised or discouraged at how long it will take you to utter the phrase or that if you wait too long you will become conscious and think you cannot do it—this is a typical and natural state to show when consciousness or an inhibition sets in.

a. "I can't stand it!"

b. "Oh, it's marvelous!"

c. "I hate you!"

d. "My darling!"

e. "Oh, heaven help me!"

f. "Oh, why did I do it!" and then with
   "Why did she have to die!"

Note the difference in the emotional feeling and expression in these two different phrases, the first being more introspective.

2. Sitting in a chair and leaning on a table, relaxing each time:

a. See your father drop dead, and give a vocal response.

b. Hear footsteps above you; hear them descend the stairs and come to the doorway. When the door opens, give a vocal response.

c. Be eating spinach, and get a mouthful of sand.

d. Be tied in that chair, and be tortured. Supply your own words without thinking of what you are going to say.

e. Be tied in that chair, and smell smoke which tells you that the house is on fire.

Exercises in the feeling of an emotion

(First internally, then through body expression, finally giving it vocal and physical reactions.)

Use a full stage for the expressive movement in the following. In each case supply your own sentences. They are to continue as long as your physical reaction does.

a. You are having a nightmare. A tiger is pursuing you. You are running on sand and can make no headway. The tiger nearly gets you, and you wake up.

b. You are lost on a mountaintop and are calling for help. You eventually collapse.

c. You are on the seventh floor of a house. The house is on fire. Discover that the door to your room is locked.

d. Enter a room, to find something on which your brother's life depends. You hunt for it all over the room, think you find it when you have not; and finally, when you are in despair, find it and run out of the room.

e. You are about to be hanged. Make your confession.

Exercises for two people, employing body, voice, and action

For speeches, first whisper the alphabet; then repeat, using full vocal utterance. Repeat by whispering improvised lines—with or without sense —then repeat exercise, giving the improvised lines full vocal tones and expression. These exercises are most valuable if there is no consciousness of the sentences' correctness.

1. Simon Legree beating Uncle Tom.

2. *A* is a professional actor or director. *B* is an amateur actor. *B* has not been doing his scene satisfactorily for *A*. *A* nags *B* more and more. *B* loses his temper. *B* is tired, nervous, and overwrought. *A* and *B* quarrel with each other. *B* becomes hysterical. *A* gives up in despair.

3. Stage the return of the prodigal son. *A,* the son, first makes his plea to *B,* the father, who is adamant. *B* finally relents, agrees to forgive *A,* and accepts his return.

8. VARIETY IN SPEECH

If the preceding exercises have been ably done and the student stops to recall his voice sounds, he will notice that he has utilized a large and contrasting range in his vocal expression. This brings us to the element of variety in stage speech.

Variety is one of the greatest factors to consider in the theater. Just as it is important in all phases of production and directing, so is it in the use of the voice by each member in the cast.

One of the greatest faults in the speech of real life and with the voice of the inexperienced actor is monotony. Words are spoken in one continuous straight line of pitch and emphasis, the same degree of loudness or softness, the same pattern of melody. Imagine a violinist just playing one note on the middle register.

Monotony is due primarily to the lack of emotional feeling on the actor's part. Perhaps the greatest aid in gaining variety is the approach through responsiveness. Later we have an analysis of the technical considerations, but far more important than these are the contrasts that are arrived at through the minute shadings of the emotional states inherent in dramatic speeches. When each sentence in a speech is given the correct expression, variety is bound to result. This is variety of emphasis. Another element, which we have already touched on, may at first seem a different point, but basically it ties up with responsiveness in its contribution to variety. That is pitch. For instance, we have already noted that the different pitches of the voice denote different emotional states. You will remember that the lower pitches denote sincerity, deep feeling, and fervor and that the higher pitches convey hysteria, excitement, and joy. When the student actor has succeeded in training his emotional feelings and when he has learned to express them through a relaxed body and voice, he will of his own accord arrive at different pitches for the different emotional states.

In addition to variety of emphasis and pitch, we have:

1. Variety of tempo of speech in delivering lines.
2. Volume or intensity of projection.
3. Tone: quality of voice including resonance and placement

E. Bodily and Vocal Responsiveness in Subjective Acting

Now that we have worked to get the voice in a neutral, relaxed, and responsive condition, let us work on an exercise in subjective acting whereby we may achieve true emotional expression in body and voice. The exercise should not be studied or thought out. The actors should not have an opportunity to read it until they are on the stage. The approach is to have two actors read the exercise through on stage. They must be in the relaxed and responsive state for which we have been working. By repeatedly reading and acting it out on the stage, without a single instruction from the director-teacher as to positions, gestures, reactions of body, variety, build, or emotional expression with the voice or body movement, they should see how highly developed they can become in these respects, merely through the repetition of the scene.

In doing this scene, as in all scenes on stage, the actor should make full use of his imagination; he should concentrate on the actor playing opposite him so that, unmindful of the audience around, his mind will focus on the scene rather than expend its energy elsewhere. There should be a strong sense of communication between the two actors in order that the action of one will find reaction in the other. This last comes not only from listening to what the other actor has to say but from observing his manner of saying it as well.

Host *A* is approached by guest *B*

A. How do you do?

B. How—What are you looking at?

A. How do you do?

B. Are you looking that way at me?

A. I'm really very glad to see you.

B. I know you are looking at my nose.

A. Won't you sit down over here?

B. Don't look at my nose.

A. This seat is very comfortable.

B. I hate you when you look at my nose.

A. Come.

B. I hate all the world. They look at my nose. It drives me mad.

A. You are my husband's sister. I am very fond of you.

B. No, you're not. You are laughing at my nose. You're not **fond** ⟨...⟩ me, and I hate you. Good-by.

F. The Study of the Role

1. ASSIMILATION AND VISUALIZATION

You have seen by the preceding exercise how, if your body and voice are in a relaxed and responsive condition, by reading a part over and over again a definite feeling for the character seeps into your whole nature. You have seen how, in responsiveness, you have let an emotional feeling work into your system and have found for it a natural expression in body and voice.

Assimilation of a part is very similar to this except that, instead of having merely one emotional reaction to consume, we now have, for the first time, a whole series of traits and emotions that constitute the character. Assimilation is the response to a character as you read the lines in the play over and over. You accomplish this much as you did in your exercises in responsiveness. If you feel and think the lines, then your assimilation will give vent to expression in the body and voice. One needs to read and reread his part. Furthermore, he needs to give vent to this character in body and in vocal expression. In learning his part, the actor needs to yield himself to it in business and movement and in the character's natural expression in language, even though they may be irrelevant to the immediate action of the play. That will help the actor to assimilate the feeling of the part.

As soon as you have assimilated a part that you are to play, you should work with imagination to visualize that person— what his face looks like, what sort of hair he has, how he holds his shoulders, how he walks, how he sits. You can go even further and think what sort of things he has to eat for breakfast, for dinner; you should know what he considers a good time, how he spends his spare time, how he makes his living, what kind of people he knows and comes in contact with, what he thinks about them and about life in general. Does he know what is going on in the world or just in his town or merely in his own neighborhood? Often it is possible to think of somebody within your own experience who is like the character. Often you will see him on the street, in streetcars, or in stores. The main point is either to draw the complete figure vividly from your recollections or to search about you for people that look, think, and act like that man. Along with this process of visualization you should consider the reasons for all the characteristics that you find in this character. Why does he walk as he does? What is there in his experience that makes him think, look, and act as he does? How did he choose his means of livelihood? Did he choose it, or was he forced into it? To these and many similar questions the actor must find the answer before he can understand his character thoroughly.

Demonstrations

a. Demonstrations in assimilation (subjective approach):

1. A blind man walking along the street with no help.
2. A movie star getting off a train.
3. A lame man running to catch a boat.
4. An old man putting a log on a fire.
5. A child in the zoo or at a circus.
6. Little Red Riding Hood discovering that her grandmother is a wolf.
7. A Hindoo at the hour of prayer.

b. Demonstrations in visualization:

1. Select a character from a play with which you are familiar. Do not imitate or pantomime him, but describe him fully, and tell much about him that is not told in the play according to the enumeration given under Visualization.

c. Demonstrations in assimilation and visualization:

1. Show the reactions of a character at the following ages to the dropping and breaking of a glass of water: seven, fourteen, seventeen, twenty-one, thirty, forty, seventy.

2. Have the girls in the class act out the nursery rhyme of Little Miss Muffet, when Miss Muffet is four years old, seven, fourteen, seventeen, thirty, sixty, seventy.

3. Have the boys in the class be introduced to a girl, and show their reactions at the ages of fourteen, seventeen, thirty, sixty, eighty.

4. The expression and reactions of a character, which you should first describe fully, in a trial when he has been (*a*) convicted, (*b*) freed.

5. Take a character from a play, and act out his reactions to a situation in the play. Then take the same character, and confront him with a situation that is not in the play.

6. Take the exercises under responsiveness, and do them at the ages of seven, fourteen, eighteen, twenty-one, thirty-five, forty-five, sixty, eighty.

2. OBSERVATION

Let us now consider a problem in characterization in which a certain part of the expression is necessarily from observation rather than from visualization; then let us see how we make a study of physical traits a part of the subjective characterization. Certain traits are characteristic of extreme old age and of middle age, and others are out of the norm in regard to physical carriage and voice. Certain ones are also characteristic of nationalities such as the Italian, Scotch, Irish, French, Indian, and Negro. All these have physical and vocal mannerisms that are outside the possible visualization (or normal response) of anybody who has not been closely associated with these types or observed them closely. The actor who is to play such a character part must find a similar person in real life and carefully watch his physical and vocal actions. After observation, he must imitate from an external point of view the body and vocal mannerisms.

In order to adjust this observation to the subjective method, it is absolutely necessary for the body and vocal observations to be practiced until they become an absolute part of the unconscious physical expression and coordination of the character. When, and only when, the body posture and the vocal idiosyncrasies have been mastered so that the actor need have no conscious consideration of them, it will then be possible to approach such a part from the subjective point of view. Only then is the actor ready to forget the observational study and revert to his subjective expression of the visualization of the character. He is ready to throw himself into the emotional and mood states of the character and continue with his vivid expression of them. He has adjusted himself so that his bodily and vocal response to a subjective interpretation will include the idiosyncrasies and mannerisms of the character.

Pantomimes from observation

1. An old lady in a hotel lobby.
2. A soapbox orator.

3. A Polish woman with two little children at a bargain counter.

4. The entrance, ordering, eating, paying, leaving, etc., of a person you have seen at a lunch counter.

3. THE TECHNICAL STUDY OF A PART

a. Suggestions for memorizing

A good way to memorize a part is to take it scene by scene, a scene constituting the period from a time at which the character enters until the time he leaves. The actor should analyze accurately the definite points of thought development and know what facts he is bringing out to the audience and to what point he arrives in the development of the play.

Secondly, he should read the complete scene aloud three or four times, other people's speeches as well as his own, being certain that he knows the continuity of the scene. Next, he should read his own speeches over many times. Then he should take the cue of each of his speeches and say over the cue and the speech as one continuous unit. He should continue this last process until his lines are learned. The way to have someone hear his lines is to have that person read him the cues before his speeches and check him on his lines. An equally good way is to write the cues in succession on cards and then read the cues to himself, saying the speeches that follow. Be careful not to add a "well," a "but," an "oh," or an "uh," to the beginning of each of your speeches.

b. Emphasis in the sentence

The important words of a dramatic sentence, it should be recalled, come at the end, and the important parts of a speech are the last sentences in it. Accordingly, this is the time for an actor to practice his breath control and apply it to his speeches. He will then have sufficient breath to last during the entire sentence so that he can lift the final words of the sentence with greater clarity and volume.

He should, furthermore, determine what words earlier in each sentence need to be stressed in order that the entire sentence may be clear. Usually the important words are one or two at the beginning, the verb, and the final words. Let us take for example:

1. "You mean you want to discuss it without me here?" The underlined words are sufficient to convey the idea to the audience.

2. "I should even go further and say that any man who is loved by her is an extremely lucky fellow."

c. Interrupted sentence

Whenever a line in a play is incomplete in its statement of thought, it is known as an interrupted sentence. The actor needs to handle this with great care in two respects. First, he must always continue in his own mind the thought of the interrupted sentence and supply one or two of his own words, so that there is a moment when both characters are speaking—the person interrupted and the person interrupting. The second point which is extremely important is that the interrupted sentence must be built up, in pitch, tone, volume, or some other way that will make it stronger at the end than at the beginning. The usual tendency is to reverse this process.

d. Thinking out loud

In thinking out loud, as when enumerating a list of things, the working of the character's mind must be made apparent during the thought pause; illustrative movement used; and the situation made as real, vital, and interesting as possible.

e. Seeing or hearing something for the first time

On seeing or hearing something for the first time, the character must take care to express the quality of unexpectedness and surprise. He must not anticipate the unexpected sound or sight but must "build" the movement or speech preceding the break and stop suddenly. At that moment the actor sees or hears the thing but must not be too quick in locating it. Then comes the bodily reaction to it, and after that the speech. In seeing something unexpectedly, like a letter on a table or a jewel on the floor, the actor in passing usually crosses slightly beyond the object and then steps back or turns to pick it up. This is true to real life. The mind and body are usually so intent on an objective that there is momentum enough to continue after the sight of an interrupting object registers in the mind. The body is stopped only after it has passed the interrupting object. When a noise is heard, the movement of the head accompanies the hearing; the eye then moves in the direction of the sound; the head and body turn toward it; and finally the character may walk in that direction to investigate.

f. Laughing, crying, or other emotional outbursts

When laughing, crying, or other emotional outbursts are accompanied by lines, the technical principle to keep in mind is that of separating the laughing or crying from the lines so that the line values are preserved. The outbursts should be executed between the lines and on lines that are obviously not important. The order should be line, line, sob, line, sob, line, sob, sob.

g. Calling a person not on stage

In calling a person not on stage an actor (as he enters) must not be seen to sweep the stage with his eyes and then call a person obviously not there, but his call must be the culmination of a preceding speech or movement. Often he can call before he gets on stage and stop abruptly in repeating the call as soon as he gets on stage and sees that the person is not there.

h. Character props

The actor must choose his character props with deliberation and plan minutely his use of them. Too often is the consideration of hand props neglected, and seldom are any used that are not specifically called for by the script. They are often helpful in establishing character and in playing certain scenes. A cane, an umbrella, a brief case, glasses, or gloves a man may use to good advantage in enriching his characterization. A woman may use handkerchiefs, beads, a parasol, a fan, a lorgnette, sewing, a scarf, as well as many other articles. The choice of these is determined by the characterization, but the use has to be determined by the actor. First, he must have variety in handling them. He must not use them all the time. He had best not use any one for more than one act. Each one of these has many uses. Take the cane, for instance: The actor may lean on it to one side or behind him; he may merely hold it in his hand; he may point with it, slam it, or hold it behind him; he may hold an end in each of his hands, in front of him or behind him; or he may go through the process of laying it down on a table with his hat and picking it up. There are still other uses. A prop should be used for effect and should never become a hindrance. Such props can frequently be used for pointing comedy or for emphasis on plot or idea lines.

4. VARIETY

We have seen that if the actor has his body and vocal responsiveness well developed, a great deal of variety will naturally result. He needs, however, to study his speeches further to see whether or not his natural responsiveness has taken care of all the necessary variety. Whether the speech is short or long, this technical consideration has to be made. Even if the speech is so short that it contains only two words such as "Stop, stop!" we have to get variety in the reading of those two words. They cannot be said in exactly the same way. (Incidentally, this applies to any repetition, especially when it is in succession.) If one enlarges this "Stop, stop!" to "Where am I to go? Oh, where am I to go?" we have again to consider the problem of variety. In both these cases the first one may be louder and stronger than the second, or the second may be louder and stronger than the first.

When a speech is a long one, we can begin the first sentence low and the second one a little bit higher, and so on until we come to the last sentence in our highest pitch, fullest tone, and greatest volume. Or we may begin a speech with the first sentence pitched high and then drop the second and begin a build. If the speech will allow for it in its content, we can begin high, drop it, build, drop it, and then go even higher. In any speech of emotion there must be this element of variety in the delivery of the different lines.

The method of attaining variety selected for a speech must correspond to the inherent build of the speech itself. This contrast is easier in emotional passages. In narrational ones it is much more difficult but none the less imperative. Often the actor in narration and description will have to superimpose an artificial variety upon the different sentences in order to make them contrasting and varied. Whenever there is a series of words, phrases, or clauses, they should invariably have a built variety; that is, each one should be greater in tone, volume, or intensity.

5. INTELLECTUAL UNDERSTANDING

Now that the actor has mastered the ability to visualize his character and to express that visualization with technical control, he must next give his attention to the intellectual understanding of the play and of his part:

a. He should first gain a perfect understanding of the idea of the play.

b. He should know thoroughly the story and its different complications.

c. He should determine the purpose and contribution of the main characters to the play.

d. He should determine the purpose of his character to the story and idea.

e. He should discover any descriptions of himself in his own speeches, including any physical characteristics mentioned.

f. Then he should determine the purpose that his part plays in every scene in which he appears and the purpose of every action that he performs. If he does not have a great deal to do in a scene, he should be perfectly conscious of what is going on in that scene and what his character's reaction is to it so that he may listen the better. He should recall his visualization of his character in physical terms, determining his make-up, his costume, his body standing position, his walk, his sitting position, his manners, and what properties he should have in playing the part.

g. He should adjust this visualization to the demands of the different scenes.

h. He should decide on the lines that need to be emphasized for the understanding of the story by the audience.

i. He should determine his comedy lines.

j. He should determine his breathing places in each long sentence.

k. He should determine the purpose and thought of each of his lines. Also he should read over carefully the lines of the other characters in each scene during which he is on the stage and determine his character's reaction throughout. This is to help him in his reaction.

l. He should plan any business or pantomime that is expressive of his character and determine where it could be put into the play.

m. Through full use of his imagination he should think out what his character is doing when he is not on the scene of action, that is, on stage.

n. He should think why the character enters each time he does and what is in his mind when he enters.

o. He should understand thoroughly why he leaves the stage.

p. He should notice the intensity of the other players in the first rehearsal after they have learned the business and their lines and see that his own is similar to the others.

q. He should see that when he is making an important speech he is in an important position in the stage picture.

6. CONSERVATION AND BUILD

In studying a part, the actor should consider the question of conservation and build. By conservation we mean holding back, in this case certain characteristics, until later in the play. A great failing of the less experienced actor is his attempt in the first scene to disclose too many phases of the character, whereas a more experienced one will disclose one or two new characteristics with each scene in the play.

By building, we mean the increased enrichment of the characterization as the play progresses, so that in the last scenes we have still to discover new traits. One of the best ways to approach this is by planning in the early study of the play what traits of the character will be disclosed in each scene of the play. An excellent way to do this is to make a list of the qualities of the character after you have read the entire play twice, and then divide them among the different scenes, choosing the most likely ones for each scene.

An actor should also look out for the conservation and building of the emotional intensity of a role during the play as a whole. Even if the part demands great emotional expression at the beginning, it should be held down; or, if it cannot be, the first scenes should be played with great intensity. After the drop the actor can begin a gradual build. In this case care should be taken that the first scenes do not exceed the emotional intensity of the later scenes of the play.

Not only are conservation and build of the emotional qualities necessary for the play as a whole, but they should be closely watched for each individual scene so that there is an increase within each scene. Such a consideration of the emotional conservation and build is necessary for the general emotional effect on the audience; and also it furnishes variety and constantly renewed interest, avoids monotony, and allows the actor to reach the audience first by a natural emotional contact and then to lead it into the same emotional states that he himself reaches. If he begins in a high emotional strain, the audience will not be in a condition to receive that emotion, and the actor will fail to attain emotional contact with it. As a result it will never be moved to the heights to which he is moved. If, on the other hand, the actor begins in an emotional state approaching that of the audience, the emotional contact will be made, and his audience will live his emotions with him.

So far we have seen how acting consists of a relaxed and responsive body and voice expressing the visualization of a character and have observed the restriction or control through technical considerations that is necessary when this visualization is put on the stage.

7. SUSTAINING A ROLE

In our exercises we have worked for visualization in character, in several different movements, in several different ages, and in several different actions and reactions to situations. Thus we have grasped the character, his age, and a large number of his reactions. Now we need to see how these various parts are to be related and tied together into a whole. This tying together is called "sustaining a role." It is the filling in, between the high moments of action and reaction and detailed business, with an equal amount of emotional intensity and with continuous body and vocal expression, so that a complete continuity results through the entire course of the play from the actor's presentation; it is the development of a complete character in a unit of action.

Demonstrations in sustaining a role

1. A cafeteria. Have different characters, one at a time, select a luncheon. From the pantomime show the audience what food it is they are selecting and picking up. See that the characterization is sustained between the choices.

2. First obtain your visualization of a seven-year-old child. Think out his movements and natural manner, then the way in which he would act and react in the following pantomime. Do it again as a fourteen-year-old and at seventeen, twenty-one, thirty, sixty, and seventy. The scene is in a dining room. The character is alone in the house. Notice how the whole pantomime changes as the character and age change.

a. He enters the room and wonders where everybody is.

b. He is at first surprised and then does not mind it.

c. He hears that it is raining, goes to the window, raises the shade, and *sees* that it is raining. Whether or not he pulls down the shade is left to the actor to determine. He then busies himself with setting the table. Be sure that this is done according to the character of the person.

d. After the table is set, he goes to sit down; where and how are left to the characterization to determine.

e. He does something to amuse himself. What?

f. He hears a terrific noise offstage. Reaction?

g. The character finds for himself a solution of the noise and turns to a new kind of activity. What?

h. The noise is repeated. Reaction? He ends with going to the door and locking it. The storm outside definitely increases.

i. He turns a third time to a different activity. What?

j. Almost immediately the noise is repeated again. Reaction?

k. There is a pounding on the door of the room. Reaction?

l. A voice tells the character that it is the return of a member of the family. Reaction?

Pantomimes for sustaining a role

A play does not consist of the sustained continuity of a single person but rather of several people each carrying out his own continuity. With great regard and consideration for the problems that evolve when more than one person is on the stage, work out in pantomime the following exercises; be sure to include many of the principles of the actor's stage technique as well as of directing, especially the establishment of time and place, emphasis, picturization—all done with a proper degree of variety.

1. The scene: A wharf with gangplank leading to a boat offstage. The boat is about to depart.

The action: There are two people taking tickets at the end of the gangplank. Have as many people as you wish go aboard the boat and as many friends as you wish seeing them off. Each passenger and each friend should be a definite characterization with typical business and manner of departure, etc.

2. The scene: A barker before a side-show tent at a circus.

The action: Have six people enter, listen to him, and react according to their characters. The characters should be contrasting and furnish many different reactions.

3. The scene: An art gallery.

The action: An artist is copying a masterpiece. Many different contrasting people come in and view the pictures.

4. Form a group along the stage from left to right, and imagine it to be a line waiting to get into a movie.

(Again let each character take on a marked contrast to the others, and think up considerable business of what would happen in the line.)

5. A Sunday-school picnic.

6. A barbershop.

7. A melodrama.

The cast: *a*. A mother, about sixty years old. She has had a hard life with a great deal of physical labor, many disappointments. She is cheery and pleasant through it all.

b. A boy about twenty, very vigorous, alert, and strong, has had little education and a hard life and has been going with a gang of crooks, although because of his mother's careful bringing up he still has a fine, tender side to his nature.

c. A young sister, about seventeen. She has had little schooling and has had to work hard to help support her home.

d. Three plain-clothes policemen, alert and quick to grasp a situation.

The scene: A living room in a tenement: after midnight. The stage is empty.

The action: *a*. The boy enters in a manner that shows the following:

He does not want to meet anyone in that room. He is not certain whether his mother and sister are up or have gone to bed. After entering, he looks for a place to hide a bundle of clothes. Where he is to hide the bundle is left to the actor's imagination. He is still stealthy. For one thing, he looks out of the window to see if anybody has followed him and then pulls down the shade and lights a lamp. He then takes a bag from a closet and packs it for going away. He takes material from the dresser and from the closet. In doing this, he should choose very carefully what articles he would pack and show clearly what they are.

b. While he is in the midst of this packing, his mother enters. She has just wakened and heard him. He pretends to be doing nothing. They talk about casual matters. Finally she sees his bag half packed. He tells her that he is going away on a business trip that night. He wishes to be left alone. He asks her to go. They embrace, he knowing that it is probably good-by forever, and she thinking it a good-by for a short time. She leaves.

c. He continues to pack, more hurriedly this time.

d. The door opens, and his sister enters. He finishes his packing, answering her questions. He then sits down and starts to write. She asks him further questions. He is distracted between the letter writing and the questions. He asks her to go. She does not want to. Finally she goes.

e. He finishes his letter which is a farewell one to his mother, puts out the light, goes to the window, looks out, crosses the room to the door, opens it—and three plain-clothes policemen enter. His reaction. Their reaction. One covers him with a gun; two others search him and the room. They find the bundle that he had brought in at the beginning. He tries to escape; a chair is upset; they seize him. The mother's voice is heard calling offstage. Their reaction. The son motions the men that if they will not tell, he will go with them.

f. The sister bursts in. The mother follows. Reaction. The policemen act as the son's friends, and the boy introduces them as such. They shake hands, not as policemen but as friends, with the mother and sister. They start to go. The boy crosses and takes his bag, returns to the door. His mother runs to him, embraces him once more; his sister does the same.

g. The policemen and the boy exit. In the exit be sure to visualize it so that, although the policemen are acting as friends, they show in their positions and relationship to the boy that they are arresting him.

8. Take any play, and tell it in story form. Act out the story in pantomime so that it is entirely understandable to a person who has not read the play.

Part III

THE FIVE FUNDAMENTAL
ELEMENTS OF PLAY DIRECTING

VI

The Media of the Director

THE MATERIALS with which the director works to express
the play are two: the actor and the stage. As with the other
arts, there are certain important facts that the director must
know about the characteristics of his materials.

A. THE ACTOR

1. BODY POSITIONS

The actor on the stage has a changing tonal quality, as in
any one spot his body changes its relation to an audience.
By relation to an audience we mean the numerous positions
that the actor may take, from facing the audience directly to
turning his full back on it.

The tonal quality we shall designate in various degrees of
strength and weakness. These words, strength and weakness,
we use not only in describing the position of the body to the
audience but also in regard to the various positions on the
stage and later in relation to various movements. A clear
understanding is necessary at the outset. Strength and weakness
are not synonyms for goodness and badness. There is no ap-
proval or disapproval, commendation or aspersion in the
application of the terms. Strong positions may be bad, and
weak positions good. This terminology is merely descriptive of
the relation of body positions to the audience.

In considering the strength and weakness of the body on the
stage, it must be constantly borne in mind that we are concerned with the tonal value of the body position alone in its
relationship to the audience. All the other factors, such as place
on the stage, level or height of person, color of costume, or
lighting, must be eliminated from consideration in the demonstration of these points on body positions. These are all

modifying factors, and, as we shall see later, they will build up a weak body position or soften a strong one.

There are five designations in the relation of body position to audience:

a. Full-front position to the audience is very strong.

b. One-quarter turned-away position is still strong but less so than the full front.

c. The profile, or one-half turned, position is less strong.

d. The three-quarter turned-away position is weak—the only really weak position.

e. The full-back position is as strong as profile but, other things being equal, not so strong as a one-quarter turn.

The reason for the proportionate strength and weakness of these body positions is that the greatest emotional contact with the audience comes from the full-front body and face, and this emotional contact diminishes as the position of the body gradually breaks its close contact with the audience.

Demonstration

1. One person will show the relative strength of the standing figure in its several body positions in relation to the audience.

2. Test the comparative strength and weakness when the figure turns to stage right or stage left.

3. Test the comparative strength and weakness of one figure in relation to a second figure on stage by change of body position.

B. The Stage

I. AREAS

The stage is divided into three definite parts by two equidistant imaginary lines running from downstage to upstage and perpendicular to the footlights. These parts are designated as right, or R, center, or C; and left, or L. R and L are from the actor's R and L and not from the audience's or director's. The director must learn to use these terms glibly when speaking to the actors.

Considering the strength of these three parts of the stage, we find that C is the strongest, that R is strong, and that L borders on the weak.

If halfway between upstage and downstage we draw a line parallel to the footlights across these three parts, we shall divide the stage into six major areas, each having a designated name.

UP RIGHT	UP CENTER	UP LEFT
DOWN RIGHT	DOWN CENTER	DOWN LEFT

Demonstration

With a figure full front, note the relative strength of each area by having him stand in each area of the stage successively.

All other factors being equal, the results of the strength of each area should be in this order: DC (strongest), UC, DR, DL, UR, UL. Both UR and UL are too weak to be used for important scenes unless they have other factors of composition to strengthen them.

For the moment let us consider the peculiar phenomenon that we have noticed from the demonstration—the fact that right stage is stronger than left stage. Why this should be so is an unsettled fact in the psychology of aesthetics. Years of tests in the classroom have shown it to be a fact but have given no satisfactory reason. The obvious reason is that we are naturally inclined to look from left to right in reading and that we carry this inclination into all phases of observation. In looking at a painting the first glance is in the left direction; and in the theater, as the curtain rises at the beginning of an act, the audience can be seen to look to their left first in taking in the immediate impression of the stage setting.

The Chinese theater roughly substantiates this theory. Orientals read from right to left. In the technique of their stage, the important position is on the right as you look at the stage or, in other words, on stage left. Here are placed the chairs not only for the important actors and the more important members of a family but also for the higher social positions of court life. If a scene is between the hero and the villain, their highly technicalized stage convention demands that the hero sit on the right side of a table as you view it and the villain on the left. We have no such set conventions, but the fact remains that with us the left side of the stage, as we see it, is more dominating.

A seeming contradiction rises from the fact that in newspaper make-up the right-hand column is considered more important than the left; it is the place for the most important news. But this may be eliminated as a contradiction, since the right hand pulls the paper more readily toward the reader and also because the front page is not considered a single unit but a series of many different units. Many other arguments than our natural tendency to read from left to right may be found for the theory that stage right (or the left side of the stage as we look at it) is stronger than the opposite side, but the real psychological basis remains unsolved. That stage right is a strong area has long been known in the theater. Not that the area has ever been used until recently as a valuable and strong area, but it has been recognized that in a scene between two or three people the actor standing on the spectator's left has an advantage. Aware of such an advantage, the stars always took this position second to center. This technique was early carried over to the cinema. The motion-picture star always sees to it that he or she is on this side, especially in close-ups of two or three people.

2. PLANES

The stage is divided into an indefinite series of imaginary lines parallel to the footlights. These imaginary lines, or planes, are as long as the scenery opening and as wide as the actor standing in the plane. All other factors being equal— that is, the position of the body and the level and distance from left to right being the same—the figure downstage, or near the footlights, is stronger than the figure upstage, or near the rear wall. The degree of strength of the actor lessens proporrionately as the figure withdraws upstage.

Demonstrations

1. Have a person take a certain spot downstage in a full-front body position and retreat slowly backward, or upstage, on the many lines perpendicular to the footlights.

This would seem a contradiction to the often told stories of the star who likes to stand upstage and the minor character who strives to get upstage of the other minor characters when the star is not present. This apparent inconsistency is due to the fact that when two people are on stage, and figure A is on an upstage plane to figure B, the downstage figure must turn and face the upstage figure A. In this case the strength that A derives by forcing B to face or turn up to him allows A the stronger and more opened-up body position, while in turn it forces B into a weaker and more closed-in body position (we discuss this factor under Emphasis and Focus). This difference in body positions is what makes up for the weakness of an upstage plane.

2. Place A and B on stage C. Have B downstage of A but facing upstage to A who is on an upstage plane. Now change the facing positions so that A faces stage left one-quarter position, while B faces stage right one-quarter position. If they are in the same C area, with all things being equal, B should become much stronger.

The actor must consider planes in his approaches to other actors in a different plane. These are the cases where the curved approach is used—the approach that brings him in the same plane with the person to whom he has moved. In any kind of approach a figure must come to the other and remain in the same plane, unless the director specifies otherwise. The actor, furthermore, should be conscious of the technique that he is required to use when speaking to an actor in a plane upstage of him. In such a case the downstage actor turns only his head slightly upstage and talks in a profile position with occasional glances upstage.

3. LEVELS

By levels is meant the height of an actor above the stage floor. A few of the different levels in their relative proportion of strength, beginning with the weakest, are lying on the floor; sitting on the floor; sitting in a chair; sitting on the chair's arm; standing; standing on one step, two steps, three, etc., until he reaches the height of a stairway or high platform. Ordinarily, the higher the level of the figure the stronger his position.

The exceptions to this are those cases in which the level of the actor in relation to the stage floor is in sharp contrast to that of the other actors on the stage. This is so because the attention of the observer is attracted by that which is out of the norm of regular vision. An example of this is an actor prone on the ground or sitting when the remainder of the group is standing.

Demonstrations

1. Show the relative strength of different levels.
2. Seven people on the stage in the same plane. They all stand, then all sit, and then all take different positions of sitting and standing.
3. One figure on the floor, six sitting.
4. One figure sitting, six standing.

Exercises

To test the relative strength and weakness of body positions, areas, and levels to one another.

1. Two actors in the same plane will test the relation of strength between the different body positions of one standing and the different body positions of the other, using the different levels. For example, is the person standing profile of equal strength to a person sitting full front?
2. Do the same between the different body positions and areas. For example, does a three-quarter position DC have the same strength as a full-front position UR?

With this understanding of the inherent quality in the positions of the actor and the areas, planes, and levels of the stage, we are ready to consider composition.

VII

Composition

COMPOSITION IS the structure, form, or design of the group. It is not, however, the meaning of the picture. Composition is capable of expressing the feeling, quality, and mood of the subject through color, line, mass, and form. It does not tell the story. It is the technique; it is not the conception.

A. DEFINITION

Composition is the rational arrangement of the people in a stage group through the use of emphasis, stability, sequence, and balance, to achieve an instinctively satisfying clarity and beauty.

B. EMPHASIS

The first factor of composition for us to take up is emphasis. As every art product must have its emphatic element, so every stage group must have its emphatic figure or figures. The director's first problem resolves itself into that of selecting the figure upon whom the eyes of the audience should rest immediately. This is determined by the importance of the character in the scene being played and by the importance and length of the lines being spoken. Naturally, in any written scene, the important speakers should readily be seen as well as heard. The composition should emphasize this figure so that audibility of voice is reinforced by visibility.

An amusing example of the lack of this factor in staging is illustrated by the remark of an estimable person who was asked about the quality of production of a newly established summer-theater company. "Oh," she said, "they did excellent work, and we enjoyed them ever so much. But there was one very peculiar thing about them—you never knew who was speaking. You could hear them, but your eyes were always trying to find out who it was that was speaking. And no sooner had you found out than somebody else would begin to speak."

The director must always make this question of who is speaking clearly answered in his stage group no matter how realistic or naturalistic he wishes his style to be. There is no excuse for not having an emphasis—an emphasis that must necessarily change from figure to figure as the scene progresses in the play. He may even have to emphasize several figures at the same time. He must also use a wide variety of methods in emphasizing his characters and not resort continuously to the same method, as this creates monotony and is technically unimaginative. The director, accordingly, must utilize every means of composition at his command to obtain emphasis on that person and the relative emphasis on other people in the group in proportion to their relative importance to the emphasized person.

Then, again, the director may have on the stage a large number of people, even a crowd. How is he to save the important characters from being swallowed up by those around? In a scene in which a character has been unimportant up to a certain moment, how does the director make this character become important, or "take stage"? All these demands require a knowledge of how to obtain emphasis.

C. Methods of Obtaining Emphasis

The simplest methods are the uses of the strong body positions, areas, planes, and levels. We have discussed these four factors above under the Media of the Director, and we have seen how each one in itself contains a definite value described as varying degrees of strength which contribute to this first factor of composition-emphasis. Emphasis may also be obtained through contrast. If actual demonstrations are made, what is meant by each type of emphasis mentioned below will be apparent.

1. THROUGH BODY POSITION (See Plate I: *She Stoops to Compromise.*)

The strong body position is one of the simplest methods of obtaining emphasis. In a group of people on stage standing in various body positions the one with full-front body position will receive the emphasis. In realistic productions, however, the strong body position is seldom practical to use alone, because the positions of the actors need to bear relation to one another.

2. THROUGH AREA (See Plate I: *She Stoops to Compromise.*)

The strong area position is used often in emphasis. If a group of people is spread over the stage without much form, the actor in the center area will take on emphasis, other things, such as body positions, being equal. However, if other factors giving emphasis enter into the stage picture, then the emphasis from strong area position is only relatively true.

3. THROUGH PLANE (See Plate VII: *Decade.*)

With other factors, such as body positions, equal, the downstage plane is the strongest. A figure in this position will receive emphasis. In the use of planes for emphasis, however, many other factors such as focus enter into consideration, as we shall learn later on. For this reason the strong plane can seldom be used alone.

4. THROUGH LEVEL (See Plate II: *The God Innis.*)

Levels present a much used method. The attention of the observer is attracted by what is higher than the regular line of vision. If a group on the stage is sitting, and the important person stands or sits on an arm of a chair or even sits in a chair with a higher seat, he will be emphasized.

A scene in which a person is allowed by the content to stand on a chair is one where level is used for emphasis. An example of this is in *Trelawney of the Wells* when Trelawney says farewell to her actor friends. They toast her, but before doing so she is invariably lifted up on to a chair. The star of the past decades liked the advantage of height for her first appearance and often maneuvered to make a sweep down a flight of stairs, only to remain standing a step or two from the bottom.

5. THROUGH CONTRAST (See Plate III: *Russet Mantle.*)

We find that a new factor now comes up for evaluation. An actor in a position that is in sharp contrast in relation to the positions of the other actors will receive emphasis, even though this position is considered weak in itself. This method of obtaining emphasis is known as emphasis through contrast, or counteremphasis.

It occurs frequently and in many different forms. Below is given one example of each of the four factors that we have studied so far.

a. Body position: If all the members of a group take the strong one-quarter body position and one takes the weaker three-quarter, or full-back, position, by sharp contrast alone the weaker position becomes emphatic.

b. Area: If all the members of a group take full-front body positions in the DC area, and one takes the full-front body position in the UL area, by sharp contrast the weak area position becomes emphatic.

c. Plane: The example under *b* also serves as an example of emphasis through contrast for plane. Down center area is a downstage plane; up-left area is an upstage plane.

d. Level: The actor prone on the ground or sitting when the remainder of the group is standing will receive emphasis by sharp contrast.

Demonstrations in emphasis

1. Have a group of six on stage stand facing front in a straight row. No one will receive emphasis.

2. Have each of the six take a different body position so as to see the different values of the body and to see which takes the emphasis.

3. Have each of the six take a full-front position in a different area. Emphasis from area strength.

4. Have each of the six take different levels. Body position must be the same.

5. Have the six figures all stand, all sit, all take different positions of standing, sitting, and kneeling. Analyze the relative degree of emphasis for each of the six figures.

6. Have five figures take a one-quarter position and one take a full back (contrast of body position).

7. Have five stand full front and one sit; then have the one figure kneel (contrast of level).

D. VARIETY IN EMPHASIS

Since composition adds beauty to the stage picture, it is important at this point, before taking up the other factors of emphasis, to consider one of the most important contributors to this quality of composition—variety.

Although variety is applicable for use in all the elements of composition—emphasis, stability, sequence, and balance—it is especially to be used in the factors of emphasis: body position, areas, planes, levels, space, repetition, and focus. Monotony is a quality to be avoided in most phases of life and is absolutely taboo in art except when uniform usage is to gain a special effect and purpose or accomplish a specific style. Except for the unusual play, variety is demanded, and in direction variety is deeply engrained in the details of composition.

Considering variety in these first four factors of emphasis—body position, areas, planes, and levels—we find that there are endless opportunities for its application.

1. VARIETY IN BODY POSITIONS (See Plate I: *She Stoops to Compromise;* Plate III: *Russet Mantle.*)

With the eight different body positions possible, one can easily imagine the monotony of having most figures on the stage hold only one, for instance, full front, during the course of the entire play. Variety in body position is obtained (*a*) by having one figure use many or all of the possible body positions during the course of the play, (*b*) by having as many different body positions as possible used in any one scene by the different figures.

2. VARIETY IN STAGE AREAS

The most elemental way of obtaining variety is to use different areas for successive scenes and to vary the use of one area with two or all areas in successive scenes. This is known as "between-area playing," or "breaking up." In using this form of variety one should always consider the number of scenes already played in a given area, as well as whether a scene is to be played within one area or between several areas. The term "scene," as used in this connection, designates the action between new entrances and new exits.

Exercises in variety in areas

a. Variety between areas

1. Play the following scenes in order to get the greatest variety in the placement of scenes in an act.

Scene 1: Two people playing DR, using one area.

Scene 2: Three people playing DR and UC, using two areas.

Scene 3: Four people playing DL, using one area.

Scene 4: Seven people playing DR, DL, UC, UR, using four areas.

Scene 5: Two people playing DC, using one area.

Scene 6: Nine people playing DR, and four UL, using two areas.

Scene 7: Nine people playing two DR, two UR, three UC, one UL, one DL, using five areas.

Scene 8: Nine people playing one DLC, one DRC, three UC, two UL, two UR, using five areas.

Scene 9: Three people, playing DC, using one area.

2. Have seven pieces of furniture on the stage grouped according to playing areas. Place seven people on the stage, and work out the largest number of positions that they can take, considering the problem of variety between areas.

3. The maximum number of positions between areas.

a. Set: Nothing. Cast: Two people.

b. Same as *a* with five people.

c. Set: Three benches. Cast: Three people. Use only the three playing areas.

d. Set: Six areas of furniture. Cast: Two people.

e. Same as *d* with five people.

Besides variety in the use of areas, one should have variety within the area. An area may be one-sixth of the stage, or it may be one-tenth. Actually in production an area is not so much a proportionate part of the stage as it is a unit of furniture or furniture grouping. For example: a large armchair, although it might be near another piece of furniture, is often considered an acting or playing area. This is especially true if the armchair stands beside a fireplace or has a footstool in front of it. Instead of having a figure just sit in such a chair, twelve to sixteen different positions may be found in relation to it. They contribute the factor of variety within that area. This is known as "breaking up within the area."

b. Variety within the area

1. One person about one chair.
2. One person in one chair.
3. One person on the floor.
4. One person on floor before, another in, chair.
5. One person on a flight of stairs.
6. Two people in one area. No furniture.
7. Set: One armchair. Cast: Two people. Problem: One in chair and one around chair.
8. Set: A sofa. Cast: Two people.
9. Set: A table and two chairs. Cast: Two people.
10. Set: A fireplace and one chair. Cast: Two people.

There have been several plays in which one character for physical reasons has not been able to move out of a chair or off a sofa. This becomes a difficult problem for the handling of variety. In directing such scenes, the amount of variety in body positions, areas, planes, and levels that the other figure or figures may use can be appreciated: different standing positions around the sitter, different positions of leaning, sitting, etc. The stationary figure may use a large variety of sitting and reclining positions. The full scene consists of one figure breaking up within the area, while the other figure will make use of the principle of breaking up between areas.

c. Variety between areas and within the area

1. Set: One armchair. Cast: Two people. Problem: Maximum number of positions, first within the area and then between areas.
2. Set: One bench with back. Cast: Two people. Problem: Between areas and within the area. Maximum number of positions with both moving at different times.
3. Set: Three benches with backs, in three front areas. Cast: Three people. Problem: Maximum number of positions.

Up to now we have dealt only with the positive, or active, aspects of variety. There is another aspect, however, that comes from the arrangement of furniture and the conservation

of areas. In a play of one setting, two considerations are
necessary as regards variety. The first of these is the arrangement whereby as many units of furniture as possible are obtained. (For possible arrangements of furniture to obtain
playing areas see Plate VII: *Decade;* and Plate XX: *Passée.*)
Each of these units really constitutes an acting area. Occasions
arise when as many as eleven different acting units may be
obtained. The second consideration comes in the conservation
of areas when the same arrangement of furniture must be
used during the course of the three acts. In such cases there is
need to refrain from using all the acting areas in the first act
and even in the third act. Conservation for the third act comes
from saving for the important scenes in this act only some of
the acting areas that have not been used for important scenes in
the previous acts but have been used merely for the minor
people.

3. VARIETY IN PLANES (Plate VIII: *One Shall Be;* and Plate
   XIX: *The King's Coat.*)

Since the stage has three dimensions, it is important that stage
groupings take this third dimension of depth into consideration
and make use of more than one plane in composing the stage
picture. Objects, views, and groups in life are three dimen-
sional; a stage grouping that has this quality will become more
lifelike than a group of people who have practically only one
plane in their arrangement. One seldom sees a minstrel-show
line-up of people in life. Such a line-up on stage, even though
it may curve slightly, is practically in one plane. Even though
this form is suitable and satisfactory for minstrel-show patter
and jokes, the use of one plane causes the figures to fall into
a straight line, and the stage picture consequently is monotonous, flat, hard, and unnatural. In more advanced problems of
directing when style is considered, flat compositions will be
found usable for formalized, conventionalized, and arbitrary
plays. For the present we are discussing the realistic style of
directing, and in shaping the positions of our actors in terms
of composition we should realize the contributing values of
many planes.

The straight line, then, whether it is parallel or diagonal to the footlights, gives an objectional and obtrusive quality to a composition. Lines, therefore, should be carefully avoided by the director in the realistic styles. For some reason actors readily form straight lines, and the director is forever having to take such a form out of his composition. There are two ways to eliminate it: (*a*) by forming irregular groups out of the figures in a line; (*b*) by using a variety of planes so as to have some figures in a lower plane, or downstage, and others in an upper plane, or upstage. Aside from the sheer breaking up of the line, the whole composition becomes more interesting when many planes are utilized. (For variety in body positions and planes see Plate I: *She Stoops to Compromise.*)

This variety in body positions and planes produces a greatly enriched treatment of the line; moreover, the three-dimensional quality obtainable in the stage composition adds a depth, a richness, and a lifelike quality to the form. Especially is this treatment essential in ensemble scenes and in scenes between two people. Just as we have seen the need for varying the placement of scenes in the different areas, we now should value the effectiveness and need for varying planes.

Demonstrations

1. Place eight figures in row in a downstage plane, all facing front.
a. Have ✕2 back up halfway to rear wall.
b. ✕3 halfway to ✕2.
c. ✕4 halfway to ✕3.
d. ✕5 clear to rear wall.
e. ✕6 back one step.
f. ✕7 and ✕8 halfway to rear wall.
2. Have each take different body positions.
3. Have each take different levels.

4. VARIETY IN LEVELS (See Plate IV: *Taken from Life;* Plate VIII: *One Shall Be.*)

The vast importance of levels lies in their unlimited possibilities of varying the stage composition. When the large number of possible levels in an ordinary living-room set—stools, chairs, sitting positions on arms of sofas and chairs, sitting positions on a table, standing positions, stairways and steps leading into the room—are considered, one can easily picture the extent of variety obtainable. When variety in level is considered in relation to and combined with variety in body positions, areas, and planes, the possibilities are almost endless.

These four factors alone would prevent the director from repeating the same composition in a one-set three-act play. Yet each one of the factors of composition to be discussed here contributes further variations to the total composition.

E. OTHER METHODS OF OBTAINING EMPHASIS

I. THROUGH SPACE (See Plate V: *Done Got Over.*)

To the emphasis from the strength of body position, area, plane, and level and the contrasts, we now add another powerful factor of emphasis—space. Space around a figure gives it emphasis. Emphasis may be obtained by greater space around a figure compared with that around the other figures or by separating a figure from a group by means of space.

Space is frequently and wisely used. It is the easiest method and, accordingly, can be much overdone. Many a star uses it constantly and monotonously. In my experiences I have seen absurd treatments of intimate scenes merely because the star would not allow the subordinate characters to come near her. The most flagrant case was in a death scene where neither mother, father, husband, nor nurse was allowed to come near the star in her death agony but had to keep a respectful distance, that is, respectful to the star. In this scene the emphasis should rightly have gone to the star, not because she was the star but because her action was the emphatic action of the scene. The family could have been close, even touching the star, and other means of emphasis could have been used, had the actress and director known their business.

Demonstrations

1. Have seven people on stage take full-front positions in a straight row. All take even spacing, except one.
2. Try the breaking of the even spacing with each one consecutively.

2. THROUGH REPETITION (See Plate XVII: *Venice Preserved;* notice the doge.)

Whenever a figure is repeated by another figure at a short space behind it, the front figure is emphasized. As the number of the rear figures is increased, the emphasis is increased. Thus an actor is more emphatic when supported by two attendants than by one; a king with a court in attendance is more emphatic than a rebel leader with two followers. In the cases where the attendants or followers increase to any large number, space becomes a contributing factor of emphasis.

Not only do other actors serve as a repeat-motif in emphasis, but furniture will also act in this capacity. An actor standing by or sitting in a high-backed chair is emphasized by the mere repetition of the perpendicular line from the chair. A door frame also serves the same purpose, and far too often do certain stars loiter by one on an entrance. (See Plate VI: *Crabapple.*)

Besides the repetitive line we have the contrasting factor of the horizontal line to obtain emphasis. The horizontal line of a table, a sofa back, or even a couch emphasizes a figure not by repetition of line but by contrast of line. With a person playing a scene lying on a couch, space, as we have seen, is not the method of emphasis. Three or four figures standing above and kneeling below the couch, so long as they keep a predominantly perpendicular line of themselves, will emphasize the horizontal figure.

Demonstrations

1. Have seven people on stage take full-front positions in a straight row. Place a high-back chair beside and partly behind one. Place a table in front of one. Again emphasize a figure other than the center figure so that it is a clear example of the emphasis from the furniture and not from the area.

2. Place a figure RC and another LC, one-quarter body position on the same plane. Place a third figure to the L of the LC figure and slightly behind it. The LC figure should be emphasized.

3. Same as before but this time with a table in front of the RC figure. These two groups should now be equally emphasized. Have the RC

figure sit in a regular chair to R of the table. The RC figure should lose in emphasis and become slightly weaker. Try the RC figure sitting in a high-back chair. The two groups should be of equal value in emphasis.

Exercise in emphasis without the use of focus

Experiment with a group of seven figures in practicing emphasis using body position, area, level, space, and repetition, with the added possibilities from the contrasting factors. In this case the same plane must be constantly used; otherwise the element of focus will enter into the composition.

3. THROUGH FOCUS: DIRECT, COUNTER-, AND INDIRECT (See Plate XVII: *Venice Preserved;* Plate X: *The God Innis.*)

In the demonstrations and exercises so far used, a warning has constantly been given to keep all figures in the same plane. Consequently the emphatic value of the different areas has necessarily been neglected. This avoidance of the use of different planes has been done consciously; for if one figure were placed downstage or upstage of another figure (always remembering not to cover), a direct line would be formed between the two figures. This line has an emphasizing quality. It illustrates the use of *direct focus*.

FIGURE I

FIGURE II

To give a figure *direct focus* is to emphasize it by use of *actual line*—either by one line created by a figure downstage of the one to be emphasized or by two lines created when a third figure is also downstage of the emphatic figure. In the first instance we find that when two, three, or more figures are in a diagonal line on the stage the figure on the upstage end, whether it be up left or up right, is the focused and therefore the emphatic figure (see Figs. I and II). This use of focus is an example of an exception to our earlier statement that the downstage plane is more emphatic than the upstage one. In the second instance both lines converge to form the apex of a triangle in which the apex is the emphatic placement. Basically both instances are the result of the *actual line* focusing or terminating at the desired place or person. Actual line does not mean a solid line but the placement in the line of a series of figures in such a manner that the sweep of the line of vision of the spectator is from one person to another until the eye comes to the focused person.

a. Demonstrations

1. Form a diagonal line with five figures facing full front with equal spacing between them.
2. Form a regular triangle with five figures facing full front with

equal spacing between them. The actual line is further reinforced by the direction and feeling of movement from the body as it is turned toward the focused figure.

3. The same as before, but this time with the bodies turned toward the apex figure. The actual line is frequently reinforced by the tops of the heads of the actors in a gradual sweep either up or down toward the focused object; or it may be reinforced by figures on a planned series of levels.

4. The actual line may also be strengthened by the use of arms or legs pointing in the direction of the focus.

5. In realistic drama actual line through use of parts of the body is too extreme a method. But even in realism an occasional pointed hand or crossed knee will serve the same purpose.

In addition to actual line for obtaining *direct focus* we have the *visual line*. A person standing on the street looking constantly at an object will attract others to do likewise. The same principle holds true on stage. Up to now we have constantly referred to the body position, and that has meant a literal position of the body and not just a turn of the head. Now, regardless of body position, we find that a group of actors looking at one point will cause the audience to follow their lines of vision to the same point. This is one of the simplest methods of gaining focus and must be done with great conservation. When done, it should be used with a great amount of counterfocus; this we shall discuss later. The use of actual line and visual line gains a very strong focus, and except in rare instances it should be avoided in realistic directing, as it becomes hard, formal, and monotonous. (See Plate IX: *The King's Coat*.)

b. Demonstration

If two lines of figures lead in direct focus to an emphatic person, and their bodies and faces are directly focused on the apex, we have a case of actual and visual line focus. If the figures turn their backs to the focused figure and look in the opposite direction, the apex figure is emphasized merely by actual and not by visual line. If seven figures are scattered around the stage so as to avoid any obvious triangle, and the bodies all take different positions but with the heads all facing the emphatic figure, we have a clear example of the part that visual line plays in emphasizing a figure.

Visual line is especially effective when the focused object is offstage or when it is a very small object on stage or when it is deliberately covered as in the case of a physical fight, a mutilated body, a killing, or a corpse.

c. Demonstrations

1. Place five figures scattered at random but not covering one another from the sight of the audience. All face DR; then all look UL and offstage.

2. Place two figures *A* and *B* downstage C on their knees with backs to the audience; they focus down on floor of stage. Place a third figure *C* upright with body turned toward offstage but focusing on spot above *A* and *B*. Place a figure *D* down left focusing on same spot. Place a figure *E* C focusing down and a figure *F* UL in a full-back position.

The basic treatment of two figures focusing on a third, the apex, is often considered as the only form of emphasis; this we have found to be untrue, as we have already discussed several methods of obtaining emphasis. To these already mentioned we have, in addition to the diagonal line and the triangle, the semicircular formation. Theoretically it can be argued that the semicircle has a far different connotation; except to an acute observer it appears as a different and varying form of the triangle. The focused figure can stand either in front and in the middle of the semicircular form or in the form itself with a very slight added assistance from a small space, a slightly higher level, or a more advantageous body position. Even with the reinforcement from one of these methods, it is actually the circular form that does the emphasizing; the actual line itself will achieve the focusing, but visual line will add to its strength.

d. Demonstration

1. Place seven figures in a large semicircle, each facing front.

2. Have the center figures take one step forward. Have one on the side step forward.

The triangle, resulting from the converging of two lines, actual or visual, has the emphatic person focused at the apex. It is easy to form in directing. Its use is bound to be frequent,

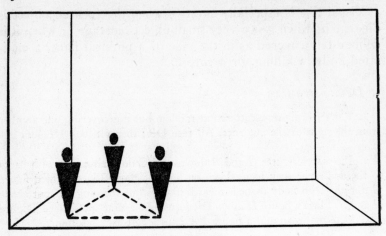

FIGURE III

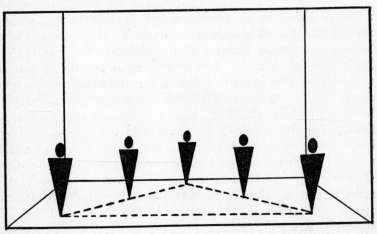

FIGURE IV

even though the obvious triangular form is extremely monotonous, hard, and formal in the realistic play.

Overemphasis is as great a fault as underemphasis or no
emphasis at all. For every play directed in which the audience
is unable to discover who is speaking, there are hundreds that
use a hard overfocused form, not only once or twice but constantly in the course of the play. This allows for no beauty, no

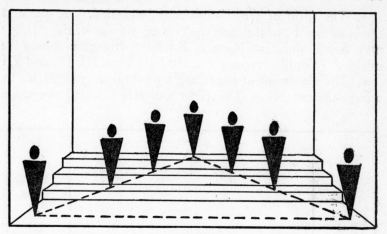

FIGURE V

subtlety, no realism, no tone or mood. In order to see what to avoid hereafter, it is advisable to give a demonstration in which every imaginable factor of emphasis will be piled on to one person.

e. Demonstration

1. Place a figure UC, standing on a stool in a full-front body position. Place three figures leading downstage on stage R and three figures doing the same on stage L. Have a distance of four feet between the apex figure and the first figure on each side. Have distances of two feet between each two figures on the sides. Have each side figure take a three-quarter body position and face the apex figure. Place two figures behind the apex figure, one on each side but standing on the stage floor.

2. Analyze each factor of emphasis in this composition.

To avoid overuse of the obvious triangular form, means must be studied whereby the triangular focus may still do its service of emphasis but do it without being obvious and formal to an audience. We have several ways of disguising its hard form and of obtaining variation in its use. Each of the following variations are to be demonstrated.

a. The size of the triangle may be varied, not only in the different successive scenes but in the same scene.

b. The form of the triangle may be varied. The angle at the apex may be of different degrees or the legs of the triangle may be of different lengths. Isosceles triangles should be avoided. (For illustrations of *a* and *b* see Figs. III, IV, and V.)

c. The placement of the triangle on stage may be varied by using different areas. The right and left sides of the stage

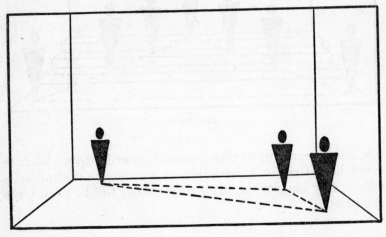

FIGURE VI

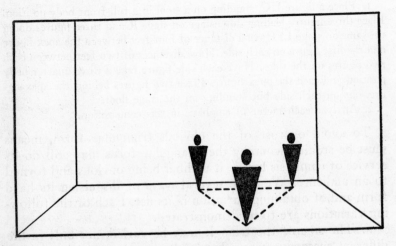

FIGURE VII

being softer in tonal values than the center, the placement of the triangle in these areas gives an entirely different quality.

d. Its placement may be varied by changing the relation of its base to the footlights. Furthermore, the apex may vary its position in relation to the legs; it may be up- or downstage. Usually the apex is upstage and the legs downstage, but often the context of the scene allows the apex to be down and the legs up or the apex to be to one side of the stage (see Figs. VI and VII).

e. The lines of the legs of the triangle when more than three figures are used may be made irregular; the several figures making up the legs may break up slightly the straight-line formation leading to the apex.

f. The space between the figures forming the legs may vary; the figures in the leg of the triangle may be closer to the apex figure than to the figure at the base of the triangle, or vice versa.

g. The levels of the tops of the heads of the figures may be of different heights. This is done by having some figures sit, while others kneel, stand on steps, etc. Even though the actual triangular form may be quite regular, different levels resulting from different positions will disguise the basic form.

h. Figures added to the basic form, thereby creating a double triangle, are of tremendous aid in keeping the triangle from becoming obvious, especially when the added figures are unimportant so that they may be placed upstage of the emphatic, or apex, figure. From this upstage position the added figures form an actual line down to the apex; and even though they may not be seen from all parts of the house, they contribute a richness and depth to the composition.

Direct focus, besides the use of the actual and visual line and the triangular form, may be strengthened by the use of *counterfocus.*

This works on the same principles of contrasting factors that we have seen demonstrated by the contrasting level and by the contrasting horizontal line in repetition. Not only does counterfocus serve as a strengthening element, but it also adds variety to the triangle.

f. Demonstrations

1. Place a figure on stage; have a second figure stand below and to the R, focusing on the first figure. We have direct visual focus. Now have the DR figure turn to the R in a three-quarter body position. The focal emphasis of the first figure is now just as strong as if not stronger than before.

2. To this arrangement add a third figure, and have it stand (*a*) above and L with back toward the first figure; (*b*) DL with profile toward L; (*c*) DR below the first figure with profile toward R; (*d*) one step to the R, above the first figure, in profile.

If two lines of several figures lead in direct focus to an emphatic person with the faces and bodies facing this person, we have, as we have seen, a case of an overemphatic actual and visual focus. This composition may still retain sufficient focus if a small proportion of the group—two or three—face and look in a direction other than that of the emphatic figure. (See Plate XIII: *Rogue in Bed;* Plate XI: *This Fallow Ground.*)

g. Demonstration

First label each figure with a letter beginning with the DR figure as *A*, the middle figure as *B*, and the upstage figure as *C;* on stage L begin with the upstage figure as *D*, the middle figure as *E*, and the DL figure as *F*. All six begin with actual and visual focus on *X* at UC. *A* faces directly offstage R in a profile position; *B* focuses on *A; C* focuses on *X*. On the left, *D* turns and focuses on *B; E* focuses on *X*. *F* focuses on *E*. Each figure takes a different spacing from the other and steps forward or backward from the straight line of the triangle so as to give it an irregular form.

The focused strength of *X* is not injured because the contrasting, or counter, body position of *A* and *B* and *D* and *F* strengthen not only *X* but *C* and *E* as well, who in turn strengthen *X*.

Counterfocus is the contrast of the actual line of the body positions. It can also be created by the contrast from visual line. This is sometimes called indirect focus, but it is always difficult to separate the emphasis that comes from actual line from that which comes from visual line, as they both appear in most cases of counterfocus.

h. Demonstration

Using the form and labels of our previous demonstration: *A* focuses on *B; B,* on *C; C,* on *D;* and *D,* on *X.* If these figures are spread out over the entire stage with their bodies in several contrasting positions but with their heads doing the focusing, we find that *X* is finally greatly emphasized by the eye which wanders from one to the other before reaching the emphatic *X.*

We have learned the purpose and methods of emphasizing the important figure in our stage composition. We may obtain emphasis by the proper use of (1) body positions, (2) areas, (3) planes, (4) levels, (5) space, (6) repetition, and (7) focus. We may vary our use of focus in the common triangular form by change of size, form, position of apex, or placement of the triangle or by a variation in the spacing, in the straight-line formation, or in the levels of the figures making up the triangle or finally by the addition of figures to the basic form or by the use of counterfocus. Furthermore, we have learned that counterfocus, besides the contrasting factors in body positions and levels, strengthens emphasis.

The following exercises are given as a summary of emphasis up to this point.

Exercises in emphasis in the use of focus

1. Work out the different ways of varying the triangle, and devise forms additional to those described. Use seven figures.

2. Spread seven figures over the stage in any way that has no form or emphasis. Rearrange them so that there will be an emphatic one.

3. Place a figure DR, using six other figures to emphasize it. Do this for each area of the stage. Be sure to use a great variety in your method of emphasis.

F. KINDS OF EMPHASIS

So far we have discussed the emphasis of one person. More often in a play, however, we need to emphasize more than one. In some scenes or climaxes of a scene it is sufficient to emphasize one person, but on the other hand most scenes require the emphasis of two people. Occasionally we have scenes that require two, three, four, five, six, or even seven people to be emphasized.

We have four kinds of emphasis:

1. Direct.
2. Duo-emphasis.
3. Diversified.
4. Secondary.

1. DIRECT

This is the arrangement of figures on the stage so that the attention goes directly, easily, and quickly to the one emphatic figure. It is accomplished by one or more of the means of gaining emphasis already discussed.

2. DUO-EMPHASIS

This is the arrangement of figures so that the attention goes to two of equal importance in a scene. It is used when the essence of a scene in the script is carried by both people, or, as we call it, in an "equally divided scene."

Demonstrations

The simplest form of an equally divided scene is when two people, each taking a one-quarter or profile position at center stage, face each other.

To enrich this, place (*a*) a table between them; (*b*) a high-back chair on stage L of table, and have one sit (here the chair and table strengthen the weaker level so that the two figures are of equal importance); (*c*) two figures adding repetition to the stage right figure, and three figures in a semicircular formation around the stage left figure (once again we have emphasized the two figures so as to make them of equal importance). (See Plate XIV: *Venice Preserved;* Plate XVI: *The God Innis;* Plate XXIV: *Merry-Go-Round.*)

In (*b*) and (*c*) we have shown the great problem in duo-emphasis— the finding of different methods of emphasis. Analyze the factors of emphasis that are used for each.

Whenever two figures of equal importance are in a scene of a realistic play, the methods of emphasis should be different for each figure. The same method of emphasis leads to symmetry; it is usable in plays of a particular style quality. In realistic plays such scenes are frequently those of extreme opposition where figure *A* is antagonistic to figure *B*. The additional figures used to emphasize *A* are usually his supporters in the scene; that is, they are on his side and of the same mind and opinion. This is likewise true of those emphasizing *B*.

Frequently there are likely to be one or more people on the stage who are not tied up with either of the two emphatic groups, who are neutral in their opinion. In the case mentioned above of opposition between *A* and *B* the placement of these neutral figures, especially if there are several, is usually center upstage of *A* or *B* and midway between them. They are in "no man's land," as it were. They can serve as a shifting focus, sometimes looking toward *A* and sometimes toward *B*. Care must be taken that they do not change their focus in unison. If, however, there are only a few people in this scene and *A* and *B* have only one or two supporters, then neutral *C* may be placed down right or down left, provided there is room for sufficient space between *A* and *B*. The problem of the placement of the neutral figure belongs not so much to composition as to picturization which we come to later. Composition, however, involves the placement of figures in their technical tie-up, and it is on this ground that we discuss the problem here.

Besides the neutral figure, we often have a figure who has been neglected by the author. A character who has been important in the play up to a particular scene when the author completely neglects him, except possibly for a line or two, is called a "suspended figure." Such a character is a sign of poor writing technique, but it occurs frequently, even in good plays. The suspended figure, neglected by the author, must not be ignored by the director. The natural impulse is to leave such figures at one side of the stage or out of the picture; this is definitely wrong. An important character who is on stage but who has, for the major part of the scene, little or nothing to say must be placed in the picture, usually in the center between the two emphatic figures who are carrying the scene. But certainly even if the center is not the correct placement for this figure as far as the picturization of the emotional relationships is concerned, he must have an emphatic placement in the compositional arrangement. Suspended figures may have a defi-

nite placement in the scene from the point of view of emotional
relationship or picturization; but if they do not and are neutral
emotionally, then the up-center position is always a possibility.

3. DIVERSIFIED (See Plate VI: *Crabapple;* Plate XVIII:
   Chantecler.)

This is the most difficult form of composition, but one that
is frequently called for in an ensemble scene in many plays.
Every play has many "twosome" scenes, but it is usually poor
technique in playwriting to have most of the play carried
by scenes between two or three people. It is likely to become
obvious, mechanical, monotonous, and unclimactic. The playwright, accordingly, uses scenes of general ensemble which
include five, six, or seven of the principles. Ensemble scenes
may be of the sort that has been described above under Duo-
emphasis; although any number may be present, the greatest
amount of the dialogue and thought of the scene is carried
by two characters.

On the other hand an ensemble scene may be the discussion
by a family in which all seven of the characters are important,
if not every minute, at least at repeated and frequent intervals.
These seven figures must then be placed in a composition
whereby the attention of the audience may go from one character to another—to a third, to the first, to the fourth, to the
fifth, to the second, the sixth, etc. All seven are alternately important, and all may immediately, with a slight change of body
position and without movement from one part of the stage to
another, take the focus of the composition. A great many plays
have a scene of this nature: the first act of *Icebound,* the second
act of *Outward Bound,* the second act of *The Truth about
Blayds*—the list is too long to enumerate.

Demonstration

The first consideration in creating a composition of diversified emphasis
is to spread the seven figures roughly over the stage on the different pieces
of furniture. Break the monotony of even spacing by having two sit on
one sofa, another on the end of a desk, etc. Be sure to avoid straight lines
but use many planes and areas. Have each actor take a different body

position. In a composition such as this no one person is emphasized. Great care must be taken that focusing from line does not stop at any one figure but carries on from one to the other and that even the seventh figure carries the focus back to an earlier figure. The group should be so arranged that the eye, left to roam without the aid of sound, should go from one figure to another. Here, again, we have an opportunity to use many different methods of emphasis—one might say every method. Those serving as counterfactors may even move to the extent of taking a direct focus while reciting their lines and then after finishing return to their original positions.

Give a number to each person. Then as that person's number is called he should turn his body or head to open up and recite four or five letters of the alphabet. The next number should continue with the next letters of the alphabet. Call them in various orders:

a. 2, 3, 7, 5, 1, 4, 6.
b. 1, 5, 3, 7, 6, 2, 4.
c. 1, 6, 1, 3, 1, 4, 1, 2, 1, 5, 1, 7.

After using all three of these tests, choose one, and rehearse it so that the members of the group know from whom they take their cue. Now repeat it without calling the numbers.

In (*c*) you will notice that 1 is definitely more important than the other numbers. Readjust the composition so that, although all are equally important, 1 is definitely more emphasized than the others.

4. SECONDARY (See Plate XIX: *The King's Coat*, figure DR with arms folded.)

At first a secondary emphatic object may seem very similar to duo-emphasis. There is no desire to split hairs over terminology, but the placement and emphasis of a secondary figure are definitely different; more often than not it is neglected. A secondary emphatic figure may be in a group that has only one major emphasis, or it may occur where there are two, three, or even four other emphatic figures.

The clearest way of explaining fully the secondary focal point is by means of the well-known story of Solomon. Two women appear before him claiming motherhood of a babe. He listens to both and then commands that the infant be cut in half and that one-half be given to each woman. The impostor agrees, but the real mother cries out to give the whole infant alive to the other woman.

In staging this scene we have three emphatic figures: the king-judge, the mother, and the other woman. The infant is of course important even though it has no lines; it is a clear illustration of secondary emphasis. The king and the women must have distinct and evenly contrived emphasis, the king perhaps slightly more than the women. The infant, however, must be placed in a position where the actual lines from the placement of the three emphatic figures will convene, where all three may focus by look as well as by line from the hand when referring to it. The infant never takes the emphasis of itself.

Frequently, but not always, the secondary emphasis goes to the character about whom the scene is played. The person may or may not have occasional lines. Often, too, a character who is saying little or nothing but whose reactions to the situation are of great importance receives secondary emphasis. It may also go to a character who is surveying a scene, not having at the time much to say, but who will later become a major part of it. This frequently happens to a principal who momentarily does not have much to contribute but who later in the scene takes full leadership or control. The figure then goes from a secondary to a duo- or even a single emphatic position. This change from a secondary to a primary emphatic position, brought about by a character's walking into the new composition at the psychological moment, is much stronger for gaining emphasis than in the case of one who remains in an emphatic position when he is at the time not emphatic.

Inanimate objects such as a ring, a mortgage, a piece of furniture, or even a body or corpse frequently come into this category.

G. Offstage Emphasis

We have seen minor instances of offstage emphasis in the emphasis given to an entrance of a particular character when somebody looks through a window or door and says that so-and-so is coming. This is a simple but clear case of bringing the focus to what is offstage. Greater and more important instances occur frequently in plays. A description of any action offstage, such as an accident, a gathering of a mob, an army marching off to war, all these are part of the emphasis in stage composition.

A specific case is the death of the poet's wife in the well-known fantasy *Will o' the Wisp,* by Doris Halman. Actually the narrator or narrators describing the event to someone on stage for the benefit of the audience would seem to be the emphatic point; but in these cases the window, or rather what is outside the window, becomes the focal point; the audience must be able to visualize clearly the action outside. The window or door, accordingly, through which the action is seen should be the main apex of the form that the stage group shapes for this scene.

The best placement of the door or window for such a scene is on the side wall either right or left. This allows the figure or figures describing what they see to remain opened up. Occasionally, as in *Will o' the Wisp,* it is necessary for certain reasons that the window be placed in the rear upstage wall of the set. The problem here of including the audience in the description becomes more difficult. In both these placements it is necessary to motivate one or more characters to remain on the side of the stage opposite the opening so that the narrator may have a motivation to open up completely, as he must when talking to these characters; in this way he includes the audience. This becomes extremely important when the opening is in the rear wall. In this instance the narrator must see offstage action either to the right or to the left so as to remain on the diagonal. The character listening must be motivated to remain on the opposite side of the stage from which the action occurs.

Whether the opening is in the center or rear, the listening figure on the opposite side forms a line that contributes to the focusing of the offstage action. Usually with only two figures on stage this line is a straight diagonal form which, as you will remember, brings the emphasis to the upstage end—in this case offstage.

In addition to offstage action, we have a large group of dramas where the environment plays such an important part in the events of the characters' lives and actions that it practically becomes a character in the drama—a character, however, that never appears. The destructive sea, the oppressive mountains, the deadening plains, the sun-scorched wheat fields, the turbulent slums, the deserted and lonely prairie, the bigoted neighbors, the little grove of trees where the only child lies buried—these all have played an important role in one drama or another. These cannot be physically brought on stage; nearly always they are fully described by the characters early in the play. A crude method of emphasizing this offstage character is to have a large window in the rear wall through which the audience may see it in painted canvas. This is far from being effective. Actually it is far better to have the opening in the side wall where the audience may not see the unconvincing paint and canvas and to have an actor build the description so vividly that the audience imagines the terror and oppression of the natural elements by the power of the words. Given a design where the actor describing and the offstage thing described are the emphatic parts, the atmospheric environment may be so vividly impressed on an audience that for the duration of the play they feel the values toward nature that the author desires them to hold. Such a scene must be emphasized among the scenes of a play, and this can be achieved through the form of the composition which is one of the greatest aids to the visualization of this offstage character.

Since this problem of the scenery and the scenic description has arisen, let us digress for a moment and comment upon it. The power of the descriptive word is far greater than any stage reproduction of nature in impressing the mind and stimulating the imagination of the audience. For instance, Shakespeare's description of Cleopatra's barge creates a far more magnificent object than any stage designer, builder, and painter could produce. But this, as you will immediately reply, is a classical play. That is true, and, what is more, it was written at a time when a theatrical production had little or no scenery, when the playwright had to design his own and light his production by the use of words. As soon as painted settings and electric lights did this work for the playwright, he promptly left these values to be conveyed by the producer, omitting so-called description from his script. When today we give full productions to plays that were written either during a period when the playwright put these values into his work or by contemporary playwrights who choose to make use of the word, two unfortunate results follow: (1) The verbal description belittles the attempt of the designer and technician, and the audience realizes the shortcomings of the attempt to reproduce nature; (2) the descriptive speeches cause the play to drag. Since the eye is quicker than the ear to catch the idea, the audience catches the idea from the scenery no matter how poor or good it may be; the words seem and are superfluous. The scene drags because the audience has absorbed the idea immediately upon seeing, and yet the dialogue continues on and on. Furthermore, when the eye has been filled, it is impossible for an audience to concentrate on its own imagination.

This understanding allows us to determine from the play whether or not the reproduction is to be in the setting or is to be left to the imagination. If the author has not put the environment into the script, then the producer must; but if he has, it is best to omit as much of that which is mentioned as possible. This holds true whether the play is classic or modern.

H. Emphasis on the Important Entering Character

This is planting the important character (not the actor) by "building an entrance." It is very important but should not be overdone during any one production. The methods given below strongly build an entrance; but even if none of them need be used for an entrance, great care should be taken that a character does not enter without the audience's seeing him, unless, of course, it is expressly explained in the script that he is not seen. This is not to be confused with an entrance that the other people on stage should not notice. In this case the entrance must be very carefully emphasized for the audience. Not only do the following methods employ visual emphasis, but some command the attention by sound and a pause before entrance:

1. One person comes down a flight of stairs and then pauses for a line at foot of stairs. This entrance employs both level and space.

2. A group comes down a flight of stairs with the emphatic figure using space between him and the group.

3. A minor character enters through a door, stops, focuses on door, and principal enters.

4. A minor character (servant) opens double doors, takes position, and principal enters.

5. A group of people are not focusing on an entrance; a figure enters, stops short, and the group focuses.

6. An important character entering as one of the group enters last. The others should enter one right after the other at regular short intervals, take their positions, pause while the last gets to his position, and the principal enters. The pause before the emphatic entrance should be twice as long as the regular and rhythmic entrances of the minor characters.

7. A knock on the door, a pause, and entrance.

8. The character speaks offstage and enters.

9. The use of noise offstage: blowing of automobile horn, others speaking, loud orders, mumblings of mob, formal announcements as for a queen, etc.

10. The character offstage is seen passing by a rear window; pause; entrance by a door on the side.

11. A character on stage hears someone coming, speaks to a third character, and focuses.

12. A character on stage hears something, stops short, goes to look out of door, returns, goes to a mirror to primp, and focuses on entrance.

13. Loud talking on stage builds up to a height and suddenly stops short as emphatic figure enters; pause before the next speech. In this case focusing need be done by one or two figures only.

14. A pause (term—holding for an entrance) either in movement or in dialogue.

15. Topping in voice and amount of movement by entering figure.

Exercises

1. Each group demonstrate two of the foregoing methods.

2. Prepare an emphatic entrance, not on the list, when other people on stage do not see the entrance.

Of course any unusual entrance is of itself emphatic. The simplest is that of an entrance through a window. Others include sliding down a banister, falling immediately after entrance, entering through a "trap door" or a hidden panel, entering backward and then turning. This last is frequently used, especially if the person has lines to speak to someone offstage. In "dream plays" a very effective entrance is made when a character appears apparently out of nowhere by coming through an unseen slit between the flats on the side wall. Similarly, when a character who has been hiding behind curtains or furniture since the beginning of the act suddenly appears either on an empty stage or in a full scene his presence has the unexpected, or surprise, element that emphasizes.

The methods of building or emphasizing an entrance or exit are endless, but all utilize in some manner the principles of composition. Often two or three methods are used to emphasize a single entrance, but this is usually too obvious and artificial. Several years ago in New York, two stars of great importance were required by the play to enter together. For stars of such magnitude to enter together was out of the question, so their build-up was of even greater magnitude. The script reads

BUTLER: Mrs. B! Mr. A! [*Mrs. B comes in followed by Mr. A, and the butler exits.*]

In the performance the entrance was executed in this manner:

1. *A* and *B* were heard quarreling offstage. (The voices were easily recognizable.)

2. *C* on stage rushed to the window and looked in their direction, announcing to *D* who was coming. He then returned to a position that did not obstruct the view of two large windows to the audience.

3. *B* passed by window talking back to *A* and then turned forward. *A* strolled slowly along. Both passed out of sight.

4. A pause while they were out of sight.

5. *B* made her entrance through a door on the upstage right side wall (much applause). She then took her position on stage left.

6. *A* entered just as *B*'s applause was beginning to die down (greater applause).

There was hardly another device that could have been squeezed into this. The execution may seem endlessly long; actually it was beautifully timed. *A* was the star of slightly greater prestige and so took the choice of entering second. As we have seen, the last entrance is stronger. Moreover, *B* warmed up the audience and by starting the applause prepared it to go one better on *A*'s entrance.

The same principle is apparent in the arrangement of curtain calls where the minor characters come out first and warm the audience for the appearance of the stars.

Such build-up entrances are seldom seen today, as their obviousness is apparent even to the rare theatergoer. A director, however, should plant the important character just as the playwright does. Furthermore, after the important character has entered, he should "take stage"; that is, he should hold the focus of attention for a reasonable time so that he may be clearly introduced as a character both visually and orally.

I. SPECIAL PROBLEMS IN EMPHASIS

While on the topic of emphasis it is best to discuss particular kinds of scenes that require special handling in emphasis. These are various types of table scenes, crowd scenes, and scenes where the emphatic figure or figures are definitely related to parts of the setting, as in a throne-room scene or a courtroom scene.

1. IN A TABLE SCENE (See Plate XVI: *The God Innis,* illustrating placement of characters at tables.)

Of all scenes that involve great maneuvering of the figures so as to protect the important characters, none is more difficult than a dinner scene. These do not occur frequently but frequently enough to require careful study. In the former days of staging the handling of these scenes was easy, because theatrical convention allowed us the privilege of seating everybody on the upstage side of a table, thereby keeping all characters open to the audience. Today, however, realism has crept into the theater so that this can no longer be done, except in scenes of formal banquets or dinners of royalty which we shall discuss later.

Today, if more than three people sit at a table, some must sit downstage of the table with their backs to the audience. This is unfortunate, as the figure downstage is not only in a difficult position but covers the figure on the upstage side of the table as well. How to avoid this becomes our immediate problem.

The best shape for a table is round. This allows a small steal in the placement of the people. Instead of seating the people perpendicular and parallel to the audience, they may sit near to each other; instead of sitting north, south, east, and west, which would be the perpendicular and parallel result, they should sit northeast, southeast, southwest, and northwest (see Fig. VIII). In this latter arrangement more of the faces are seen. NW and NE may steal slightly nearer to each other, and SW and SE may also not only work slightly upstage but take profile positions.

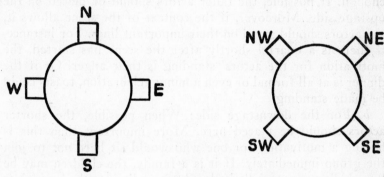

FIGURE VIII

If there are to be more than four at the table and a long rectangular one is necessary to allow these open positions, this can easily be achieved by placing the table on a slant. This necessitates the set's being triangular in form, for the long side of a table in the center of the room should be parallel to the side walls of the room. Furniture should be placed in relation to the set. With the diagonal line given by a rectangular table, the positions are opened up. We find the emphatic position to be the upstage end with third emphatic place on the upstage side nearest this; the second and fourth in order of emphasis are on the downstage end; and the fifth and sixth, on the downstage side. The reason for this ordering is that those on the upstage side are somewhat injured in emphasis by the people on the downstage side. Those on the lower end can easily open up and even move slightly away from the table, stealing to a profile position. If it is impossible to slant the table, and its position is parallel to the footlights, these same positions still hold good in their emphatic rank. If people are sitting on the downstage side, the ends are still the most important positions; but if there is nobody downstage, then the upstage side becomes the most emphatic.

When it is necessary for six or more to sit at the table, there are certain ways to counteract the many disadvantages.

a. For the upstage side: It is possible to use higher seats or to place pillows in the chairs. This steal on level will not be noticed and is particularly good for actors who are not tall enough. If possible, the taller actors should be placed on the upstage side. Moreover, if the context of the scene allows it, the actors should stand on their important lines. For instance, if there is a quarrel shortly after the scene has started, the motivation for the actors' standing is their anger. Or if the dinner is at all formal or even a minor celebration, toasts could be made standing.

b. For the downstage side: When possible, the shorter actors should be placed here. More important than this is finding a motivation for one who would sit here not to join the group immediately. If it is a family, the children may be late to dinner, especially if they have no lines at the beginning. Or those downstage may finish earlier and rise. If they can do neither of these, the characters may be such as would lean over when eating; youngsters particularly may do this. If those downstage have a conversation, it is easy to motivate their sitting sideways and open up in profile when speaking. Or possibly the people downstage could get up and pass the food.

c. For the end positions: The people at the ends may very easily open up in their chairs. Or they may easily find motivation, particularly if they have finished the meal, to move their chairs slightly backward, arriving at a more informal position.

Of these various possibilities, one would seldom, if ever, use all in any one play. One or two devices are possible, however, in almost every situation.

Unless the class of society depicted dictates otherwise, regular table etiquette should be carefully observed at any dinner scene: the food should be served on the left side of the characters; the finished plates should be picked up on their right side;

the hostess should be served first, to name a few of the many points of etiquette. Great care has to be taken at rehearsals to time the serving so that a waiter will avoid passing in front of a character at the table who is speaking. At banquets and royal meals, furthermore, there should be many waiters. One for every two people is none too many to effect a change of plates quickly and in unison.

The seating of royalty as in Molnar's *The Swan* or the seating of people and speakers at a banquet is very simple. In these cases the table should be parallel to the audience, for no one is supposed to be on the downstage side, although the ends are used. The most emphatic position is in the center place on the upstage side, but this does not always go to the emphatic person, since here the problem of rank enters into consideration. The king or toastmaster occupying center place may be only a minor character in the scene. The lower side, however, being clear of obstruction, allows the emphatic figures to sit on different sides of center so as to make these positions the emphatic ones. The two or three characters who are most important should not be placed next to each other but should have space between them to allow opened-up positions for them during speeches. Except for this consideration, the placement of the people, beginning at center and running to the ends, should be in diminishing rank and importance.

A buffet meal is much easier to stage than an ordinary dinner scene. It is wise, therefore, to make use of it in a play whenever possible in preference to the other. A few of the people may draw up to a table, but most of them should be scattered over the room. As each must serve himself, usually at the side or rear of the set, care must be taken to avoid crosses in front of a character speaking.

2. IN A CROWD SCENE

Although it is impossible to discuss here the many problems of large-scale or mob productions, frequently in a simple play the director is confronted with scenes in which a figure must address a group several of whose members have important lines that must be emphasized. I have witnessed scenes in which such a problem has beaten the director. He has had the emphatic figure face the audience while the figures whom he was supposed to be addressing stood at his side or behind him. I have seen such an arrangement even when the emphatic figure was supposed to be stirring the group to bloody revolution. I have seen the emphatic figure swamped by the surrounding mob so that only a few members of the audience were able to see him and then only intermittently. I have seen groupings in which all members of the mob who had speeches were so completely covered that you neither saw the mob leaders nor heard what they were saying.

As a matter of fact, the problem of emphasizing the important speakers in a crowd is quite simple. The easiest method, of course, is to use a level. The principal speaker should be placed on a higher level upstage center, and a motivation should be found for so doing. This higher level may be his standing position as he talks to his followers who are sitting on the ground or on various objects about the scene. Or it may be the step of a flight of stairs or a building; it may be a chair, a soapbox, a curbstone, a tree stump, a chair, a table, or whatever other possible positions the setting may motivate. But level he must have. With the level to give him advantage, no matter how far upstage, he may dominate and control the scene. (See Plate II: *The God Innis.*)

With the speaker on a higher level, the majority of the crowd should be to the left and right of him, with a thinner grouping in front. When possible the groups in front should be made up of children, shorter people, or figures who through exhaustion or some other motivation would sit on the ground. But even if none of these is possible and full-grown figures must be in front, at least the higher level will make him head and shoulders above the rest and thus give him an advantage that is often sufficient. The placement of groups to the left and right of the speaker allows him an excuse to cover the full extent of the stage in addressing first one side and then the other.

There are almost always in such a scene several people in the crowd who need to be emphasized. Their placement needs even more careful consideration. The best places for these are down right and down left—positions that are quite strong. These positions allow the figures to open up at least to a three-quarter position when addressing a person upstage and even allow them to steal to a profile position quite frequently. Furthermore, when addressing a figure next to them, they can open up fully to the audience.

Members of the group whose important contribution is comments among themselves should be placed downstage center nearest the footlights. As they talk together, often they can motivate turning away from the speaker and opening up to the audience. If, however, they must address the main speaker often, the best positions are on the two sides of the stage. As the worst positions are those up center nearest the speaker, only those members should be placed there who have occasional speaking or shouting of short lines.

Where the architectural background allows levels lower than the main emphatic position, these are excellent for secondary emphasis. When no levels are possible, the emphatic figure should be placed stage left or stage right facing the group who stand opposite him on a slight diagonal going downstage. The member of the crowd to be emphasized should be opposite the speaker and a little in front of the crowd; the second is downstage; and the third is halfway between the first and the second. The third is also often at center near the footlights.

Now that we are dealing with crowds, two other considerations, not necessarily concerned with emphasis in crowds, should be taken up. First, when a larger crowd than can be handled or put on stage expediently is required, the crowd should straggle offstage but within vision of part of the audience. This conveys the impression that the crowd continues to an indefinite distance offstage. Secondly, a crowd should not be grouped too closely together but far enough apart to allow complete freedom of bodily movement. This spacing of the crowd also serves to give the impression of a larger crowd than is actually on stage.

These general principles of emphasis in a crowd scene apply not only to actual crowds of large numbers but also to smaller groups, such as a delegation, a small revival meeting, a choir rehearsal, or a schoolroom.

3. WHEN THE EMPHATIC FIGURES ARE DEFINITELY RELATED
   TO PARTS OF THE SETTING

a. In a throne-room scene (See Plate XVII: *Venice Preserved.*)

Although this problem does not occur so frequently as to make its staging a major consideration, it does arise occasionally, and it needs to be understood. It occurs not only in throneroom scenes but also in any meeting or gathering of people with a chairman or speaker of importance. In many ways the problem is very similar to that of emphasis in a "crowd scene."

The place for a throne in most directors' minds and in all scene designers' is along the upstage wall. The opportunities for setting off to full view of the audience the regal splendor of a throne are most tempting. Very often this position is correct; the king should have all the emphatic elements to build him up—center area, level, space, and repetition, as well as a spotlight and a brilliant costume. This position, however, is so emphatic that it is impossible to build anybody else in the scene sufficiently to approach him in strength. All characters that address him are forced to speak with their backs to the audience. At most, a three-quarter body position is possible from the side. For this reason this placement should be used only when the content of the scene definitely warrants such an emphatic position.

In many plays, however, the characters subordinate in rank are far more important and emphatic as far as the scene in the play is concerned. The king and the scene designer in these cases have to be sacrificed, and the throne should be placed along the right or left wall. There can. be a slight steal on bringing the throne out a foot from the wall, and the level itself can be lowered—this brings the actual position of the throne right or left center. At such a position both the king and the other important figures may receive equal emphasis. A figure may also easily steal upstage of the king to deliver an important speech. Approaches, moreover, are simpler to handle, and the king remains sufficiently emphatic for his rank and for his character in the play.

The throne can also be placed on a diagonal so that its

position is actually up right or up left. In this case the whole ground plan of the throne room has to be designed on the diagonal. Such a setting allows the king to be in a one-quarter position and allows the important figures approaching him to be upstage of the king, taking either a one-quarter or a full-front position.

As we mentioned earlier, these placements come into consideration at any meeting or gathering of people with a chairman or speaker of importance. The speakers, for instance, in the meeting scene of *The Enemy of the People* are the sole emphatic figures, and their placement should be upstage center with their listeners sitting or standing with their backs to the theater audience. More frequently, however, some speaker from the floor has a great deal to say in answer to the chairman. In such a situation the meeting should be staged profile to the theater audience or at least on the diagonal.

b. In a courtroom scene

In staging a scene in a courtroom we have in many ways the same problem as in a throne room. In these scenes, however, we have a greater restriction in so far as the arrangement of the various portions of the setting are determined for us by the actual layout of a real courtroom.

The layout of a real courtroom takes in the following factors:

1. Judge's bench on a high level along center of wall opposite the spectators.
2. Witness stand on lower platform with chair and railing around it, close by at left of judge's bench as you look at it.
3. Door leading to judge's and lawyers' rooms at right of judge's bench.
4. Jury box with two rows of seats along the left wall.
5. Door leading to jury rooms on left wall above jury box.
6. Clerk's table directly below the judge's bench.
7. Tables for lawyers and principal witnesses in front and slightly to the right and left of judge's bench.
8. Window along the right wall.

A railing usually separates the spectators' benches from the actual courtroom area. Either of the two doors may lead to the detention rooms.

In reproducing the real courtroom on stage, we must make certain modifications of the aforementioned arrangement so as to arrive at the correct position for the emphatic factor of the play. The emphatic factor may be witness, the jury, the spectators, etc.

The best procedure in arriving at this modification is to draw a ground plan of the real courtroom and then decide the emphatic element in the play. Consider the emphatic element as placed along the rear, or upstage, wall; draw a line across the plan (taking out the fourth wall) on either the straight or the diagonal. This then becomes the floor plan for your setting. It must be constantly remembered that, as in the throne room, the right and left walls are excellent places for emphatic positions.

The regular layout of the courtroom on stage is one in which the judge's bench remains up center against the rear wall. In this case the necessary changes demand that the spectators' benches along with the tables of the lawyers' and the principal witnesses' be placed on stage right in the same relation to each other. This clears the space in front of the bench and places the lawyers in an emphatic position at right. We also steal on the witness stand by bringing its position slightly forward so as to be on a downstage plane to that of the judge. This allows space on each side of the witness stand so that the lawyers may approach the witness in profile position. In the regular layout the witnesses are constantly the important people and are emphatic above every other factor in the act.

There are plays in which the jury is the emphatic factor. They should take the emphatic position along the upstage wall. This would mean that the judge would be downstage right with the witness stand up right and the lawyers' tables left. The wall opposite the judge would be vacant, and the spectators eliminated. There have been plays where the spectators were important and the jury eliminated. In fact there is a courtroom play for every kind of emphasis.

Owing to the fact that the actors' positions are bound to be tied up with the set, this method of determining a ground plan is an excellent approach in many other types of settings besides the courtroom.

J. STABILITY

(See Plate XII: *Murder in the Cathedral;* Plate XXIV:
The King's Coat.)

Stability is the factor of composition that pulls or ties down the picture to the stage. It confines and defines the space. It is the factor that satisfies the innate sense in the human being for coordination of ourselves and all that we see with the force of gravity. Pictures without stability seem to fly off into space and for this reason are displeasing. This is easily demonstrated by placing a group of seven people all upstage; no matter how much this group is broken up, there will remain a peculiar dissatisfying feeling as one looks at it (see Fig. IX).

FIGURE IX

After the important figure or figures are emphasized, the next step in composition is to add stability. In scenes with two or three figures in which only one or two areas are used (no more than two), stability will always enter into the arrangement without any conscious consideration from the director. This is because such area playing becomes a focal unit, and the audience eliminates the rest of the stage from consideration. But the moment all or nearly all the areas are used and the visual aspect includes practically the full stage, then the factor of stability becomes an important conscious consideration.

Stability is arrived at by having a weight of a figure or figures at the down right or down left areas or both. Sometimes a group standing or sitting, or in a mob scene, squatting or lying on the ground at down center, can be used as the stabilizing factor to tie down a group largely up center (see Fig. X).

FIGURE X

When the number in the entire scene is large, as in a mob scene, we find that the stabilizing weight must become greater than in a scene with six or seven people where usually one person on one side of the stage is sufficient or, at the most, two people either one on each side or both on one side. The stabilizing element necessary to tie down the stage picture varies in proportion to the number in the entire picture. The more weight there is upstage the more weight is needed for stability. If a large crowd is used upstage and on a high level, several figures are needed in both downstage areas.

A diagonally straight or broken line of figures placed anywhere on the stage has an inherent value of stability. The line can begin center and run up left or up right; in either case stability is included. The diagonal line also includes emphasis: Whatever figure is on the upstage end, that figure becomes emphasized, since the eye has a tendency to run to the end of a line before it stops. The diagonal line, therefore, is an instance of both stability and emphasis.

This is also true of a triangular form in which the apex is on stage, left or right, and the legs of the triangle are one short and one long—with the long leg beginning anywhere but basically being a straight or broken diagonal line. We have seen an example of this under offstage emphasis.

K. Sequence

(See Plate VIII: *One Shall Be;* Plate IX: *The King's Coat;* Plate XXI: *Chantecler.*)

In focus, line has been used to tie the different figures together into a whole stage unit. Line has made each figure a part of the stage composition. Frequently, however, we have instances in which the exigencies of placement do not permit three or more figures or groups of figures to be tied together by line. So much space is necessary between the figures or groups of figures that they seem to bear no relation to one another but instead appear like several unrelated figures or groups. Large family scenes; tea, dance, or cocktail scenes; or many exterior scenes in which the people as far as meaning is concerned have no relationship present this problem. Considered purely from the point of view of meaning, these figures or groups are quite independent units, but from a compositional point of view they must be brought together into a single one. These disintegrated parts which cannot be united by line may be tied together by space.

Sequence is the tying together of units on a stage by space. This established space must have a regular recurrence or a recurrence of a proportion of that space. Sequence, speaking more broadly, therefore, is space relationship. In effect it is a regularly recurring accent. It is rhythm in composition, rhythm of distances between figures or groups of figures on the stage.

a. Demonstrations

1. Take the space between two figures *A* and *B* as a unit; the space from *B* to *C* should be multiples or divisions of that unit. Place *C* at a distance equal to half the space between *A* and *B*. Place *C* at a distance equal to twice the space between *A* and *B*. In this last example,

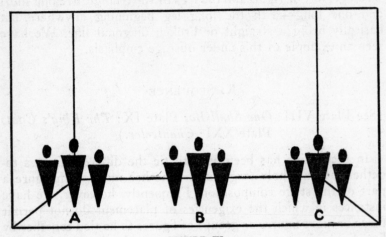

FIGURE XI

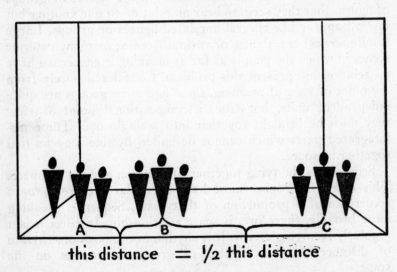

this distance = ½ this distance

FIGURE XII

the figure C, since it has the greatest space between him and the others, is isolated and, therefore, becomes emphasized.

2. Place three figures equidistant from one another; A on stage R, B C, and C on stage L. Add two figures to each basic figure. Have the groups bear no relationship to one another; that is, figures of one group must not focus on other groups but must keep the focus of attention within their own groups. These three groups of figures will appear as three separate units which are in no way tied up into a whole unit composition. This is the sort of composition that a director does not want, as it distracts the audience. To correct this, divide the distance between A and C into thirds; place group B one-third of the distance between A and C, so that the space sequence becomes the unit between A and B and twice the space unit from B to C. A is now on stage R; B on stage RC; and C on stage L (see Figs. XI and XII).

By this use of sequence, group C, although it is off by itself L, will be tied up into the compositional unit.

3. Try space relationship with three figures tied up to one. Establish a good distance between A and B; repeat this distance between B and C; but double the distance between C and D. Repeat this with halving the distance between D and C. Discuss your findings.

Rhythmic spacing is not confined in its use to straight lines. It may be used (1) in a triangular formation, (2) in a semi-circular formation, (3) in a diagonal line, (4) or in an irregular formation by the placement of each figure in a different plane.

b. Demonstration

Place four figures in each one of the aforementioned formations. Cover the entire stage, and use rhythmic spacing or sequence in each case.

Figures in sequence may be on different levels as long as the spaces between them are in space relationship. It makes little difference if A and B are sitting and C is standing. Of course here the contrast in levels will increase C's emphasis, as well as space, if C is standing at a point twice the distance between A and B.

In crowd scenes, figure A, raised high above the massed group with a space that jumps from the crowd to him, will not be tied in to the picture so well as if two or more additional

figures were spaced so as to show sequence from the crowd
to him. Both these instances should be worked out (see Figs.
XIII and XIV).

To give a scattered effect or an illusion of a mass of people,
space should be used in arithmetical progression.

FIGURE XIII

these figures added to supply sequence

FIGURE XIV

c. *Demonstrations*

1. Place *B* a certain distance from *A*; place *C* twice that amount from *B*; *D* three times that amount from *C*; *E* four times that amount from *D*; and *F* five times that amount from *E*. Place each figure in a different plane. The figures should not focus on one another, but each should busy himself with a different activity. Place each figure in a different level and body position.

2. Instead of using only single figures, to *A*, *D*, and *F* add one more figure. We now have both groups and single figures. Add another figure to every unit except *D*. Now we have units of one, two, and three figures. Each figure in each group should bear no relationship to any other group but his own. Give each group a focus with use of variety so that each group differs from the other.

Sequence is most important as a means of tying the composition together when it is broad, spread out, and covering the entire stage. Diversified focus nearly always requires the use of sequence. Even in scenes that require a figure to be away from others of a group, there is a limitation of distance at which the figure may be away from the group; beyond this point the figure will be ignored by the audience.

L. BALANCE

There is a human tendency when looking at unevenly balanced scales to push up the overloaded side. The longer one watches it the more irritated one becomes at the unevenness. This is true in painting or photography as well; if one side of a picture is overloaded, the observer immediately senses it and in time starts lifting his shoulder in an unconscious reflex action as a compensating gesture. More often than not, viewing an unbalanced scene is distinctly unpleasant.

When one part of the stage composition is equalized in weight with the other, the composition is said to have balance. This is an important factor in giving a pleasurable and satisfying effect—the constant purpose of composition.

1. WHEN QUESTION OF BALANCE ARISES

Balance is utilized in full stage or at least in four-area composition and in all compositions of two or more figures that

employ both halves of the stage. In speaking of full-stage or
four-area composition we mean those compositions in which
the figures are in two groups made up of one or more figures
with an area or more between them. We need not consider
balance in small unit compositions in which the group of figures
is placed in one or two adjoining areas. Here, as with stability,
balance comes of itself, since the spectator dismisses the remaining areas from consideration. Theoretically, in this instance the factor of balance should undoubtedly be taken into
account, but in actual practice the director need not consider
it, for he arrives at balance, as at stability, from the consideration of other factors such as emphasis. As in small unit compositions, we need not consider balance in compositions that
employ one-half the stage only.

2. SETTING, FURNITURE, AND COSTUME RELATED TO BALANCE

Before going further into the problem of balance we must
first consider the relation of the setting, furniture, and costume
to balance. The setting and furniture should be balanced in
themselves so that the balance of the actors will not be affected.
The entire background of the actor should neutralize itself in
balance. This is important; for if the setting should have a
strongly focalized point, it would continually counteract the
focal point in the director's composition, or else the director
must be forever taking the set focus into consideration in
balancing his own composition. The same holds true for costumes. Since the different hues, brilliancies, and saturations of
color have varying weights, the costumes must have their own
relationships in weights for the principal and minor characters.
As this relationship in the well-produced play will correspond
to the director's evaluation of the emphatic and unemphatic
characters, the question of costume balance need not enter into
the consideration of balance in the director's stage composition.

3. PHYSICAL BALANCE

Balance is weight against weight, so the stage must be
thought of as a large balance scale with the fulcrum at any

point on an imaginary line dividing it into two equal parts, right and left, and running perpendicular to the footlights. This imaginary center line, running from downstage to upstage, is as long as the depth of the setting. Furthermore, the arms of this scale with fulcrum as axis can pivot to assume any right angle to footlights, that is, from second to first position. Physical balance, then, is definitely the theory of this scale and is needed to obtain equilibrium between the two halves of the stage.

a. The simplest way to obtain balance is by having an exactly equal grouping on both sides of and equidistant from the imaginary center line. This is known as *symmetrical balance.* (See Plate XVII: *Venice Preserved;* Plate I: *She Stoops to Compromise.*)

a. Demonstrations in symmetrical balance

NOTE: In doing all demonstrations under symmetrical and asymmetrical balance great care should be taken to have all figures relatively of the same weight—that the strength from body positions, areas, planes, and levels is the same for all figures; that focus does not enter into consideration. As an attempt to eliminate strength from the factors of emphasis, it is best to do all exercises with the body of the figures standing and facing full front. Even with such precaution it is difficult to eliminate strength gained from area and focus.

1. Place one figure three feet to the right of the center line of the stage; place a second figure three feet to the left on the same plane.

2. Place three figures in a close grouping at the same positions on each side (see Fig. XV; see Fig. XVI for use of same figures in asymmetrical balance).

3. Now imagine the fulcrum as turning on its axis so that the line of the arms of the scale is a diagonal. On this diagonal place one figure four feet to one side of the axis; place a second figure on the other side at the same distance.

4. Do the third demonstration, using five figures for each side.

5. Turn the line of the arms of the scale at any angle, and place two groups of two figures each in symmetrical positions. Then add a third group at the axis; move this up- and downstage on this center line.

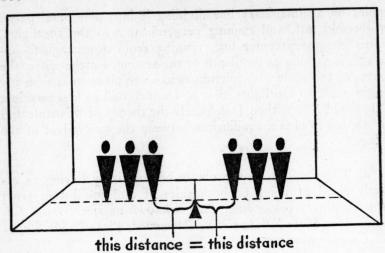

this distance = this distance

FIGURE XV

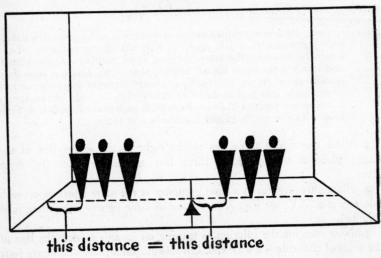

this distance = this distance

FIGURE XVI

NOTE: The group on the axis will not change the weight of either side. In the balance of a stage composition those figures on the center line do not add any weight to either side; therefore they can be disregarded in considering the balance.

6. Experiment with symmetrical balance using different numbers of figures at different distances from the axis, at different turnings of the

arm of the scale at the axis, and with the fulcrum moving up and down center line.

Although symmetrical balance with its many variations allows for a large variety of positions, it leads to a certain monotonous and obviously mechanical grouping on stage. Its form being set and geometric, it is not conducive to a realistic treatment of the stage composition. It is, however, extremely effective for conventionalized and formalized styles. Alternated with asymmetrical balance it is suitable for modern farces and arbitrary comedies. There was a period in directing when physical balance was practically the only method used. The classic, the Shakespearean, the Restoration, and the Nineteenth Century Romantic drama, besides our modern opera, utilize physical balance almost entirely.

b. The second form of physical balance is *asymmetrical balance*. If a figure is placed a certain distance from the side wall on one side of the stage, it will balance another figure placed on the opposite side of the center line at the same distance from the fulcrum.

In this form of asymmetrical balance, the eye of the audience unconsciously but quickly divides the stage into two halves with the figures in the same relation to each half. These halves balance as two separate units. (See Plate IV: *Taken from Life;* Plate X: *The God Innis;* Plate XXI: *Chantecler.*)

b. Demonstrations in asymmetrical balance

1. Place a figure DR two feet from the right wall; place a second figure two feet to L of the center line on the same plane.
2. Increase the number of figures.
3. Pivot on its axis the line made by the arms of the scale to any angle.
4. Vary the distances from the wall and fulcrum.

A form of asymmetrical balance used more frequently than any other form of physical balance is that of unequal numbers of figures. It is best explained by an example:

When figure *A* must balance figures *B* and *C, A* will balance if he takes one ordinary step away from the position where *A* would be if he

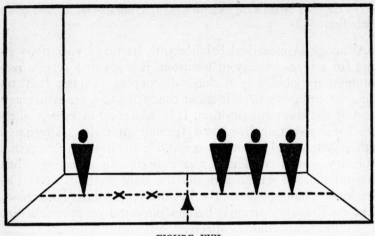

FIGURE XVII

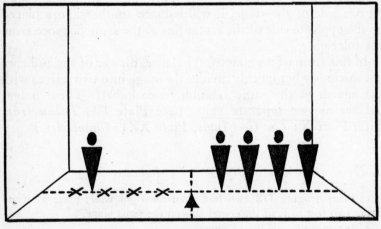

FIGURE XVIII

were balancing *B alone*. When *A* must balance *B*, *C*, and *D*, he must take another step away; but in balancing *B*, *C*, *D*, and *E* he need take only a half step more away (see Figs. XVII and XVIII).

In other words the weight of four or five figures in a group does not change materially with the addition of more figures. Because of this a point can be found at which *A* does not need to retreat farther away in order to balance any additions to the group. When levels are included in the increase of weight, the problem remains practically the same. One step up on a level adds as much to the balance as a step away from the fulcrum. If the group opposing *A* continues to increase after *A* has stepped away twice or three times, *A* need mount only a step at a time for every two or three additions to the crowd until, as in the example above, he does not need to mount higher. (See Plate IV: *Taken from Life;* Plate VI: *Crabapple;* Plate XXII: *Spring of the Year.*)

4. AESTHETIC BALANCE

When realism, or verisimilitude, in stage grouping and mood from compositional form came into the staging of play, physical balance alone could not solve the problems of balance. It was necessary to turn to the art of painting and apply to the stage the painter's principles known as aesthetic, or occult, balance.

At first aesthetic balance will seem difficult and involved, but after a while it will be easily applied, as it is the most common and frequently used kind of balance. (See Plate V: *Done Got Over;* Plate VII: *Decade.*)

In doing the demonstrations of physical balance we have noticed how difficult it has been to elminate the weight on certain figures derived from the principles of emphasis; frequently it has come by angling the line of the arms of the scale on a diagonal whereby those figures downstage have focused on those upstage. In this single example we have one of the main points of aesthetic balance. Downstage is a stronger area than upstage, yet the nearly full-front body position of the upstage figure is stronger than the three-quarter body position of the figure downstage. Not only is the strength of the body position counteracting the weakness of the upstage area, but the line focus as well from the downstage figure to the upstage figure adds a far greater strength to the upstage figure. These two contributing values of full-front body position and focus, therefore, make the upstage figure far stronger and heavier than the downstage figure.

Since in obtaining aesthetic balance the director deals with the comparative weight, or strength, of the emphatic figures, we should review here the values of the factors of body position, area, plane, level, space, repetition, and focus, so that we may obtain a balance between the various figures by various means. We shall find that aesthetic balance is virtually a balancing of equal emphases.

a. Demonstrations

1. Balance the weights of two figures, using merely body position, area, and plane. Try to eliminate focus from entering into the placements.
   a. Place one figure UR and one DL. Find the body position of each that will equalize the strength of each figure.
   b. Does a one-quarter position DC balance a full-front position UR?
   c. Use a profile body position for one figure and a three-quarter position for the second. Find out in what areas these body positions will balance each other.
2. Balance the weights of two figures using body position, area, plane, and level.
   a. One figure sitting and one standing. Use only one area. Does the figure standing profile balance the figure sitting full front?
   b. The same using area.
   c. One figure on a throne balancing one figure before the throne.
   d. One figure DR on the floor. Find the area in body position to balance the weight of this.
   e. One figure on a throne UC. Even though it cannot be done, try to find any area or body position to balance this.

So far these demonstrations have balanced figures merely by the strengths or weights gained from body position, area, plane, and level. The emphases from space, repetition, and focus, which offer far more complicated problems, require much more experimentation.

b. Demonstrations

Using as many figures as are necessary, balance:
1. A figure emphasized by a circle of figures with one at the apex of a triangle.
2. A figure on a level with one using repetition.
3. The important figure in a sequence of four with a single figure with space.

4. A figure sitting, built up by any furniture, with one built up by repetition.

5. A figure built up with focus with another built up with a different focus. Try at least three different methods of this.

6. One figure lying on the floor, surrounded by a semicircle of five focusing on it, with a group of your own composition.

7. One man completely surrounded with girls, kneeling in a circle on the floor, with your own focused figure.

8. One figure on a throne UC with another in any position and with any emphasis that you desire.

It is evident from these demonstrations that all figures who are contributing to the strength of an emphatic figure are not considered in the balance so long as the emphatic figures are equally balanced.

So far we have used one focal point balancing another. Now we must consider one focal point balancing two. We shall begin with single figures.

c. Demonstrations

1. Place two figures in profile; opposite these find the body position and plane of one that will balance the two figures.

2. Have seven figures in a group balance one figure. Here you will notice that

a. The one figure will be upstage of the group. This gives him a stronger body position while the figures in the group are forced into weaker body positions.

b. The group acts as a focus.

c. The one figure is reinforced by space.

d. The weight of the mass of figures is not the total weight of the individual figures in the group. The aggregate weight of a mass of figures increases only slightly with additional figures.

To test this add seven more figures to the group; the one balancing figure will require only a little more weight.

3. Have two figures balance five. Use all forms of emphasis.

4. Have seven figures all equally balanced. Do not forget to use variety.

5. Place a figure at a piano with three figures about him. Arrange them so that they balance eight figures sitting.

In this case the figure at the piano is strengthened by the piano, and the three figures will have to be weakened as much as the eight sitting figures will have to be strengthened. This process is often used, that is, the weakening of an overemphatic figure when it has to balance a figure or a group of figures that are necessarily limited in their power to be strengthened.

6. Have four figures sit roughly around a table at center stage; place a single figure of great importance away from them in such a manner that he will balance the four figures at the table.

7. Place seven groups of two, three, and four figures each scattered over the stage. Three of the groups are emphatic; balance two of these against the one. (This will result actually in one's being emphatic and two relatively secondary, whereas the remaining four groups become weakened so as to have no weight value.)

8. On each side of a table on stage R two figures are having a scene. Both are equally emphatic. Place five figures in five different places on the stage so that none of them is in the scene and none is included in the balance of the composition.

The weight of the mass is our first introduction to mass as a factor in composition. Mass is a very important determinant in composition. For the time being, however, we shall consider it as a part of balance.

Mass, as defined in the dictionary, is an assemblage of things that collectively make one quantity. In directing, the "things" are figures. A mass, therefore, becomes a quantity of figures considered as a unit.

Mass may have a focal point of its own; usually it has few or no characteristics. But whether it has detail (composition within itself) or no detail, mass does have a definite weight which must be considered in balance. We have dealt with undetailed mass in one or two demonstrations above. We have seen how the weight of the mass does not amount to the total of its parts; in other words, seven people in a mass do not have an aesthetic weight of seven times the individual. In both physical and aesthetic balance, after a mass of three figures is reached, the added weight lessens with each added figure until, when a mass of about seven figures is reached, the weight does not increase materially.

With detail in the mass, however, its weight increases. By detail we mean a small composition within itself: as a small space around one figure who has a few lines and who must be protected from being swallowed up by the group; or a great deal of whispering among the figures of the group; or the action of an unimportant figure who has been killed or has fallen to a low level from exhaustion; or the variety of positions in the group scattered on several levels. The value to the director of knowing these varying weights is to aid him immediately in increasing the weight of the opposite unit that is to balance the mass.

Balancing mass against mass is simple, but balancing mass against individuals requires great dexterity and experience.

As we have seen, there is weight to space; furthermore, there is weight to an expansive distance. For instance, if a figure stands on the part of the terrace that has the sea or the mountains beyond as background, that figure has greater emphasis and weight than a figure on the other side of the stage backed by the house. The latter figure would need a build-up strength if he were to balance the one surrounded by an expansive distance. In a case such as this great care has to be taken with the lighting in the distance and behind the figure. Bright lights behind a figure make it impossible to see the person.

The theory of strength added by an expansive distance is also true for a figure standing in front of a large window or door. Not only is distance here helpful in strengthening a figure so that greater strength is needed to balance it, but the frame of a window or door acts as a repeating or contrasting line to the figure, thereby adding more weight or strength.

In summary, aesthetic balance is the achievement of equilibrium in the stage composition of the strength or weight of the emphatic unit or units. All unemphatic units bear relation and contribute to the weight of the emphatic unit or units.

The weight of the emphatic unit is the degree of strength created by any of the factors of emphasis—body position, area, plane, level, space, repetition, and focus.

Any unit may be balanced in any part of the stage, provided its emphasis is equalized in strength in its relation to another emphatic element or provided the single emphatic element is equalized in value with the unemphatic elements related and contributing to it. (See Plate VII: *Decade;* Plate IV: *Taken from Life;* Plate V: *Done Got Over;* Plate XXI: *Chantecler* [Chantecler faces Peacock].)

M. Effect of Composition on the Emotions of the
Audience: Mood

(See Plate I: *She Stoops to Compromise;* Plate XII: *Murder
in the Cathedral;* Plate XIV: *Venice Preserved.*)

It is a well-known fact that the human being is moved emotionally by shapes. In nature we experience emotion when
looking intently at a mountain or when looking at a broad, flat
plain. A tall tree may stimulate in us as powerful an emotional
state as the huge flat expanse of the sea extending to the limit-
less horizon line. Living in a small house at the bottom of a
valley or at the foot of a mountain gives the occupant a feeling
of being shut in. The close surrounding mountains stir us to
different emotions: Some may feel cozy and warm; others may
feel oppressed, shut in, and stifled. But no matter whether the
reaction to the closed-in surroundings is pleasant or unpleasant, it acts as a stimulus to the emotions.

So strong is this effect on the human being that, whether he
is conscious or unconscious of it, when viewing a piece of art
he feels a kindred association with what he feels when watching
excessive shapes in nature. The great perpendicular slabs that
form the skyscrapers of Radio City or the single shaft of the
Nebraska State Capitol or the Washington Monument all
arouse in man an emotional reaction. Huge masses like the
pyramids in Egypt or the Coliseum in Rome affect us differently
from the lofty tree or the inspiring tower. The perpendicular
line sends us heavenward; the horizontal makes us want to
relax. The weight of a large mass may impress us even to terror. The large open courts of the colleges at Oxford affect
us very differently from the cramped catacombs in Sicily.

Shapes, then, are made up of line, mass, and form. The emotional feeling aroused in the spectator from the arrangement
of line, mass, and form is known as *mood.* We are not considering, at this time, all the aspects of mood in a dramatic production but merely mood resulting from composition.

Though every element in nature or in architecture includes
these three factors of shape, usually only one of them has
greater emphasis and, therefore, a resulting domination. From

the domination of the kind of line, the kind of mass, or the kind of form we receive our emotional feeling, or mood. This is true for all spatial art; painting, particularly, adds the factor of color.

Color plays a vitally important part in the study of composition in painting, yet in this study of play direction it is omitted completely. In painting, color affects the principles of emphasis, stability, and mood. Its omission here is due to the fact that in actual stage production it is furnished by the costumes and scenery and not by the director as such in his directing. The director may design his costumes; but if so, he does it not as the director but as the designer of costumes. If he does not design them, he is cognizant of what they will be and has approved them. In either case there is a system of color determination and arrangement that distinguishes the important figures and that expresses the mood of the play. The color blends and emphasizes. The costume designer's scheme will not conflict with the director's scheme for handling his figures; rather, the two schemes will coordinate and support each other.

Even when an unimportant character, dressed in a neutral or unemphatic color, does become important for a short scene, the director by any of the means for obtaining compositional emphasis will make that character emphatic, emphatic beyond the power of color in the other figures to detract. No matter how vibrant or brilliant the hues of a costume are, it may be subordinated to a less emphatic color by its placement in the composition. If there still is a slight consciousness on the part of the audience of the important character during a scene that at the moment belongs to an unimportant figure, that is not necessarily bad, for it keeps the former in the total picture; after all, the important character should seldom be forgotten entirely.

Just as the art of painting has taught us much about what to do with our actors when on stage, it now has much to teach us about the effect that line, mass, and form of our composed picture have upon the audience as they watch it. Most people in looking at a painting merely observe the subject; few appreciate the beauty of the composition; and only a very few go deeper to appreciate the treatment of line, mass, and form and its success in conveying a mood to the spectator—a mood, as we shall later see under Picturization, that is identical with the subject matter.

The best way to discover this mood from line, mass, and form is to subtract the parts of each realistic object that make it a recognizable thing and to reduce these to their basic line, mass, and form. For instance, place a thin piece of paper over the pictures in the Appendix, and draw straight lines for the dominant lines, masses, and forms of the figures. Be certain to trace the outer frame of the entire picture itself, so that the abstract shapes will be in relation to a definite space. On viewing this abstract arrangement of shapes the spectator can now detect the factors of line, mass, and form and from them feel an emotional quality which immediately creates a flow of imagery in the spectators' mind, an imagery that rises out of or is qualified by the emotional quality. The emotional quality may be one of joy, of pity, of great terrorizing impressiveness, of sorrow and oppression, of loneliness, of peace or turmoil, of quaintness, or of universality, and the imagery expressed will be in terms of such qualities or mood. This process of stimulus, mood, and imagery is a rapid one; the spectator gets it either immediately or not at all. Almost all physical places and scenes in life, and even the qualities of writing, have a dominant feeling; this mood may be expressed to the spectator by the abstract shapes arrived at from the amount, kind, and dominance of line, mass, and form.

So far we have analyzed and deduced the emotional quality or feeling that comes from a picture. Now let us analyze further the feeling or mood that comes from the different kinds of predominating lines, masses, and forms.

Dominant quality is stressed because, though every picture will contain some line, mass, and form, only one of these factors will be utilized by the composer more than the other two. Each factor, moreover, will have a variety of treatment; in a composition in which line is dominant there will be some horizontal and some vertical lines, but one or the other of these will be predominant. A composition in which mass is the dominant factor will have some concentrated mass and some scattered mass, but one will be used more frequently than the other.

I. LINE

Dominant lines in a stage composition are arrived at from the position of the bodies of the figures. Reclining positions, many sitting positions, a general evenness in the heights of the tops of the heads—these are some of the ways in which a director may obtain the predominant horizontal line. A great number of standing figures, use of levels, very tall people or headgears—all these stress the perpendicular line.

Lines in a composition may be classified as horizontal, perpendicular, and diagonal. These may be treated in a straight, curved, or broken manner to obtain additional effects.

A dominance of *horizontal lines* creates a restful, an oppressive, a calm, a distant, a languid, or a reposeful feeling in the spectator. Horizontal lines express stability, heaviness, monotony, restfulness, and other like qualities.

Perpendicular lines express height, grandeur, dignity, regal or forceful impressiveness, frigidity, spiritual or ethereal qualities, or soaring and aspiring qualities.

Diagonal lines are seldom used, but on the rare occasions when they are they express a sense of movement or an unreal, an artificial, a vital, an arresting, a bizarre, or a quaint quality.

Straight lines express strength, sternness, formality, severity, simplicity, nearness, regularity.

Curved lines express naturalness, intimacy, quiescence, freedom, gracefulness, flexibility, coziness.

Broken lines express informality, disorderliness, humbleness, smallness, quaintness, independence.

Obviously these types are not all distinct and separate. Perpendicular lines may be straight or curved; horizontal lines may be straight or broken; but when the director achieves these combinations, he obtains different and mixed values. Broken perpendicular lines give a feeling of violence; broken horizontal lines, a casual feeling.

Or consider the contrast of feeling created by the use of broken horizontal lines and straight horizontal lines in the same composition. The former give the feeling of oppressiveness, languidity, and coziness, whereas straight horizontal lines give the feeling of sternness and strength. Such a composition could be a scene at the beginning of *The Lower Depths* or the final scene of *Beyond the Horizon* where the characters have disintegrated under the destroying forces of the environment.

Let us reverse this process so that we begin with an actual situation in a play and from there decide the feelings or mood and from those the dominating lines that will express those qualities. It is the living room of a New England farmhouse after supper. The family consists of a grandmother, a father, a mother, an older son who has worked all day, a son in school, and a younger daughter. Such a scene calls up in us the qualities of rest, repose, coziness, intimacy, informality, casualness, independence, and quaintness. The lines that will express these qualities are horizontal, curved, and broken.

For the purpose of showing the sort of mixed feelings that arise in situations in a play, let us suppose that a neighbor enters into this farmhouse scene and suddenly begins a vigorous fight with the elder son. In the midst of the qualities that we had in the beginning we now need conflict, or a vigorous and arresting contrasting value. The perpendicular lines of the two figures, strengthened by the diagonal body attack of one and the raised arm (level) of the other, will supply the contrasting value. At this time we must not consider the handling of this situation in terms of picturization. We are merely interested in the treatment of lines in composition to express the desired mood effect.

2. MASS

Mass is a group of figures as opposed to the individual. Its weight is an important consideration under balance; the impression of mass on an audience is an important consideration under mood effect.

Is the effect of a scene on the director light, dainty, delicate, charming, and gentle; or is it heavy, ponderous, severe, austere, and massive? Does the scene show power and strength? Is it full and rich? All in all, mass consideration is the impression of a degree of lightness or heaviness.

If large numbers of people inherently produce an effect of heaviness and small numbers produce an effect of lightness, it is apparent that the use of weight by a director as a mood effect is limited by the author's inclusion in the script of the number of people in a scene. This, however, is not wholly true, because the director may handle a group of seven or eight figures so as to give a mass effect; in working on a new script he may persuade the author to include more people in a certain scene; and in crowd scenes the director himself determines the number of figures in the crowd, the number of attendants to a regal or military personage, and the number of listeners and figures for atmosphere. For a light effect the director naturally employs fewer figures.

Let us study a specific example: A man is going to perform public prayers in a public place to invoke rain which the community needs badly. The number of townspeople that turn up to join in the prayer is at the director's discretion. The stage can be crammed to capacity, or it can be sparsely filled. The application of this approach would guide the director to examine the feeling of the scene and to determine from that the number of figures required. If it were a seriously religious scene in a tragic play, the stage would be filled to overflowing. If it were a light, fantastic comedy, the number of figures would be much less with greater space between each one.

If the scene does not call for a crowd of people but only for seven to eleven figures, the decision of the director rests upon whether these few are to be divided into masses of two, three, and four figures or he is to treat them individually. Can you imagine the difference between three masses of figures and nine figures treated individually? Can you react emotionally to the mood effect of the two treatments? If so, then you have mastered the ability to decide on the treatment of mass in a stage composition.

The mere statement of the scene and the nature of the play should immediately stimulate an impression to the practical director of the use that he is to make of mass in the composition. Each scene has an inherent weight to be conveyed by mass which gives a specific value or mood effect to the audience.

3. FORM

Form is significant in expressing through compositional arrangement the mood effect of the subject. To be sure it seldom needs consideration in twosome or even threesome scenes, but the moment the scene becomes ensemble in effect, then form is one of the first qualities to determine.

Form may be (*a*) symmetrical or (*b*) irregular, (*c*) shallow or (*d*) deep, (*e*) compact or (*f*) diffused.

Each one of these arrangements of form has a totally different mood effect; the director should give special attention to the expression of a scene in terms of form. Variety in staging a play is obtained by a great variety in form during the course of the action. So expressive is form that, as the subject of the play progresses in its various manifestations, so will the form.

As with line, let us analyze the mood effects of the different arrangements of form:

a. Symmetrical, regular, or repeated form expresses formality, artificiality, coldness, hardness, quaintness.

b. Irregular form expresses a casual, an impersonal, a realistic, an informal, or a free quality.

c. Deep (multiplane) form expresses warmth, richness, mellowness, sincerity, realism.

d. Shallow (single-plane) form expresses quaintness, artificiality, shallowness, excitement, effectual and alert quality.

e. Compact form expresses warmth, force, horror, power.

f. Diffused form expresses indifference, coldness, turmoil, defiance, individualism.

The possible combinations of form, as well as the combinations of line with form, will give mixed emotional effects. An irregular compact form is entirely different in effect from an irregular scattered form. What is the effect? What is the effect derived from a symmetrical deep form in contrast to that derived from an irregular shallow form? What is the effect from a scattered form with perpendicular lines in contrast to that from a scattered form with predominant horizontal lines?

Although the sensing of the emotional effect obtained from form or line-and-form arrangements may be difficult at the start, the director will eventually visualize scene after scene in a play that he is reading in such terms, rather than in terms of technical composition or in terms of minute picturization of the subject matter. He will learn first to feel certain qualities in his scene and then will strive to convey this feeling to an audience in a general manner of composition; the arrangements of details will follow afterward.

This treatment of the composition from the emotional effect of shapes on an audience is one of the most marked ways in which a director demonstrates his real artistry—his real interpretive power. It amounts to developing an ability to visualize the qualities of a scene in a play and to reproduce these qualities on the stage. The way to accomplish this is through the determination of the correct lines, masses, and forms. It is extraordinary how the untrained mind of the beginning director will be prolific in this creation. In a short while he will conjure up the desired mood effect of the scene that he has read. In this he should be as free as possible from the confining stage directions and details of the text. He should be relaxed, carefree, and away from all disturbances so that he may create without interference of any sort.

Demonstrations

Often it is possible to imagine the mood effects by the mere mention of a scene from a play. To test our powers in this respect, let us first describe the mood effect that we receive from the following scenes and then explain how we are to convey this feeling to an audience by means of line, mass, and form. Great care must be taken not to picturize or to visualize these scenes photographically but merely to describe the feeling and execution.

1. A large cocktail party in the tastefully decorated New York studio of an elocutionist.
2. The family at home in their apartment on Park Avenue, New York.
3. The annual dinner of a large corporation in one of the leading New York hotels.
4. The family at home in their sun parlor on a Sunday morning.
5. Explorers on a West Indian island.
6. The emperor receiving an envoy in his throne room.

7. Tourists visiting Chinatown at midnight.

8. The inhabitants of a large slum house in the courtyard on a Sunday afternoon.

9. The arrival of a new little girl in the receiving room of Miss Munchin's School for Young Ladies.

10. Mrs. Jordan is about to die and is not allowed to see her family of children and grandchildren. They are waiting in the living room of her house at Veazie, Maine.

11. A conspiracy of five men in a cellar.

12. A cabaret on the roof garden of a high building in New York.

13. A group of visitors in Westminster Abbey.

14. The Land of Nod.

Exercises in composition

NOTE: Try to keep interpretation from creeping into the composition.

1. One composition with one emphatic figure from each person in the group.

2. One composition with duo-emphasis from each group.

3. One composition with diversified emphasis from each group.

4. One composition with offstage or secondary emphasis for each group.

5. One composition with a mood of grief.

6. One composition with a mood of joy.

7. One composition with a mood of loneliness.

8. One composition with a mood of turmoil.

9. One composition with a mood of oppression.

10. One composition with a mood of peace.

VIII

Picturization

AFTER WE have mastered the technique of procuring articulate and pleasing arrangements and the manner of obtaining a mood value from our compositions, we are ready to place meaning into the stage picture. Already in doing the exercises under composition, we have found it difficult to prevent meaning, or a storytelling quality, from entering. Now we are ready to concentrate on this very factor which is called picturization—the second fundamental element of directing.

A. DEFINITION

Picturization is the visual interpretation of each moment in the play. It is the placing of characters so as to suggest their mental and emotional attitudes toward one another so that the dramatic nature of the situation will be conveyed to an audience without the use of dialogue or movement. (This visual interpretation of the play should be developed as fully as the auditory.)

B. RELATIONSHIP BETWEEN COMPOSITION AND PICTURIZATION

Composition contributes the rational ordering and rearrangement of technique and the mood of the subject, and picturization contributes the meaning, or thought, or subject, in a stage group. One might say that picturization is the concept, and composition the technique. Concept is the author's creation —his thought, meaning, or subject. It is his imaginative contribution without technique. It is his own personal expression or invention of the mind.

Concept and technique in any art should be related, with composition expressing the feeling or mood of the concept. For instance, if a good picture is stripped of its picturization or

storytelling elements of the emotional relationship of character to character, leaving only its arbitrary line, mass, and form
(the composition), an emotional quality or mood of the subject matter will come across to the audience.

In the teaching of painting, the instructor frequently turns
a picture upside down when analyzing its composition. He does
this in order to remove all meaning from the painting so that
the class will consider only the composition and its mood and
not confuse both with the subject. In the teaching of play directing this process is impossible, but the way to obtain an analysis
of the composition in a stage picture is to have each person on
the stage eliminate all body expression and relationship to
another person—in other words to become a mere automaton
or inanimate figure.

C. Body Expression and Relationship to Other Characters

(See Plate IV: *Taken from Life;* Plate II: *The God Innis;*
Plate XXIV: *The King's Coat;* and study body expressions and
relationships.)

In life the relationship of one person to another and the
body expression of the person himself have a definite storytelling value. Instinct keeps us away from those whom we dis-
like, suspect, oppose; near to those whom we trust, endorse,
agree with, love. This picturization of the emotional state tells
the director where to place each character in a scene in relation to the other characters. You will notice that under the
section on Composition we have always talked of "figures,"
never of person or character. Now for the first time we begin
to talk about characters, since we are considering the character
in emotional relationship to another character.

We shall begin first with storytelling positions by means of
which two persons through their body reactions and body relationship will recall to us certain experiences in our life that will
tell us what they are acting. We shall then bring character into
the exercises in order to establish an emotional relationship.

In the following exercises notice how certain scenes pictured
around one piece of furniture will vary considerably in their

power to convey their meaning to the audience when played around another piece of furniture. Be certain, therefore, to choose the right piece of furniture for each scene.

Exercises in use of one or two areas

1. Storytelling pictures.
Set: One table, two chairs, and a sofa.
Cast: Two people.
Picturize
a. One scolding the other.
b. Telling a story.
c. Whispering.
d. Equally divided quarrel.
e. Confession.
f. Formal conversation.
g. Two women telling stories.
h. Two men telling stories.
i. Two children telling stories.
j. Waiting for a decision.
k. Two women, one calling on the other.
l. Two women gossiping.
m. Two men gossiping.
n. One woman selling something to a second when the second does not want to buy.
o. One man selling something to another man who does not want to buy.

2. Storytelling arrangements.
Set: A fireplace and one armchair.
Cast: Two people.
Picturize
a. Old people.
b. Children.
c. Lovers.
d. A quarrel.
e. A long narrative told by a man.
f. A long narrative told by a woman.
g. A confession.

3. Character and storytelling pictures.
Set: A door.
Cast: Three people.
Picturize farewell:

   a. Husband and wife saying good-by to
     i. Friend.
     ii. Son who is going to school.
     iii. Son who is going to college.
     iv. Son who is going to war.
     v. Son who is going to prison.
     vi. An unwelcome guest.
   b. Father ordering son out of house.
   c. Farewell of two lovers.
  4. Character and storytelling pictures.
Set: 1, 2, 3.
Cast: Two characters.
   a. Two mothers whose children have quarreled.
   b. Two fathers whose children have quarreled.
   c. Two sisters greeting each other after a long interval of separation.
   d. Two brothers greeting each other after a long interval of separation.
   e. Two sisters saying good-by to each other.
   f. Two brothers saying good-by to each other
     i. When the separation is to be short.
     ii. When the separation is to be long.

Frequently we have a more difficult emotional relationship to picturize, as, for example, one of a mixed emotional state: love and anger, as when two lovers quarrel; or hatred superimposed upon two who originally loved. This latter occurs in a play in which two business partners of twenty-five years' standing have come to a fundamental difference of opinion and belief. Their business is put up for auction; we find them both bidding for it.

To gain a clear understanding of picturizing a mixed emotional state, let us work out the picturization of the two lovers who have quarreled. This becomes a problem of mixed emotional body positions and expressions.

The way to approach the problem is to make a picturization of the one basic emotion which in this case is love. Let us place each character in the center of a sofa. The connotation of such a background setting is helpful in itself. Now move each as far apart as possible; this separation helps to put the element of quarrel into the picture. Next have them turn their backs to one another. This last move has emphasized the element of quarrel too strenuously, so an added touch must be given the picture by having one or both run the downstage hand back toward the other and rest it on the edge of the seat.

D. Title of the Scene (Concept)

So much for exercises in simple picturization. We now turn to the process of applying the principle to the play. We spoke of picturization as embodying the author's concept at each moment of the play. In order to express the concept we should understand what each moment of the play has to say. This brings us to a discussion of the scenes of a play.

1. SCENE DIVISIONS AND TITLES

A play is composed of many scenes (in the French sense). Each scene represents an idea incidental or pertinent to the main story or idea. The scene is often marked by the entrance of a new character who changes the subject matter as a part of the progressive thought in the unity of the play. It is possible, of course, that two subjects or thoughts may be carried on in a scene by the same group of characters. A scene of this kind must be necessarily treated as two scenes, but the division is an arbitrary one made by the director according to each individual idea or purpose put there by the author. The director must divine the author's purpose, because without a knowledge of the purpose of a scene, picturization cannot be created with meaning. The purpose or subject of each scene, therefore, can be definitely titled, in the same manner in which many of the previous exercises have been titled.

The director cannot be urged too strenuously to analyze the basic purpose or idea underlying each scene in a play, because now, under picturization, he must express graphically the dramatized situation by placing his characters on the stage in storytelling positions and emotional relationships.

Before we continue to the manner of executing picturization, we should first practice the division of a play into scenes.

A clear illustration of dividing a play into scenes will be found in the following synopsis of a certain play:

a. *A* sees *B* at a tavern and forces a conversation.

b. *A* tells *B* a personal but horrible story.

c. *C* and *D* (*A*'s sisters) at home receive a call from *E*. (*A* had formerly been engaged to *E* until *C* and *D* broke the engagement.)

d. *A* returns home and has a love scene with *E* who first (i) refuses and then (ii) kisses *A*.

e. *C, D,* and *E* have tea (*A* refusing to sit at the table).

f. *C* and *D* have a fight before *A* and *E*.

g. 1. *F* (to whom *E* is now engaged) arrives.

2. Is greeted characteristically.

3. Has tea.

h. While at tea *C* and *D* insist upon showing to *F* paintings by *A* to which *A* objects and at which *E* is embarrassed.

i. *E* and *F* depart.

j. *C* and *D* carry away the paraphernalia.

k. *A* decides to murder *C* and *D*.

l. A persuades *C* to buy poison to kill their old dog (insinuation).

m. *A* starts a row between *C* and *D,* telling *D* to break a dish dear to *C*.

o. *C* and *D* struggle to get dish.

p. *D* breaks dish with *C* and *A* looking on.

q. *D* goes to her room in anger.

r. *A* gets *C* to take cocoa to *D* to reconcile *D*.

s. *A* pours poison in cup of cocoa while *C* is out of room.

t. *C* leaves, taking poisoned cup of cocoa to *D* while *A* looks on.

u. *C* finds empty bottle of poison.

v. *G* (maid) discovers *C* with empty poison bottle.

w. *C* is arrested by two policemen; *G* accuses *C; A* is pretending grief while actually he is glad.

Although this synopsis does not have a title for each scene, it is necessary to supply one.

a. A meeting.

b. A confession.

c. A formal call.

d. A formal love scene.

e. A tea scene.

f. A fight between two characters with two looking on.

g. Four greet one.

h. Two show paintings to third while fourth objects.

i. A departure.

j. Clearing a tea table.

k. Decision to murder.

Exercise

1. Title the remainder of the scenes in the synopsis.

E. Classification of Scenes (Technique)

The author not only has a purpose for each scene in his play but has decided by what technical manner he is going to convey that purpose. Here, again, we have a minor instance of concept and technique. Any scene in a play may fall categorically into any one of the four kinds of technical arrangements.

I. SCENES OF INCIDENTAL ACTION

These are scenes not pertaining to the main action but, nevertheless, scenes of activity through which exposition, atmosphere, or presentation of characters are woven. They are scenes of a tea party, a sewing circle, a game of bridge, one character calling on another, a reporter obtaining news, etc., in all of which the action, although fully developed, is of itself not so important as the dialogue that runs through it, leaving aside the "how-do-you-do's," "two lumps," "your deal," etc. Once in a while they may contain main action dealing directly with the main story, but more often they are scenes of irrelevant action to which exposition of great importance is superimposed.

In the old days scenes of incidental action were pure declamation, for the audience's benefit, of a long expositional dialogue between an important character and her maid companion or confidante. In the later drama they became scenes between two servants (one new and one old) dusting furniture while they laid the foundation of the story or elaborated on the characteristics of the principals. In time the exposition became more cleverly handled, and we had scenes between a secretary and a newspaper reporter or scenes in a waiting room. There has been a definite improvement in the treatment of the exposition until now, in the present-day drama, it is usually incorporated into real action and often carried by the principal characters.

2. SCENES OF BACKGROUND

In these the locale, setting of place, or time is established, and the dialogue and emphatic incidents carry the main thread of the story.
Examples:

1. A scene on a bridge where there is continual movement of people passing by, traffic noise, etc.
2. The waiting room in a doctor's office or in a hospital with internes, nurses, and visitors passing through.
3. A restaurant where the diners and waiters come and go.
4. On the deck of a ship just before sailing.

Background scenes are established by the playing of the minor characters during and after the principals play the main scene. Sometimes the background action continues through the principals' scene, although it is always diminished in its amount.

3. SCENES OF MAIN ACTION

These contain the main situations of the story in which the plot is in graphic or dramatized form. In such scenes the background, if present, thins out while the attention focuses on the graphic unfolding of the story.
Examples:

1. Arrest of a principal character.
2. A confession.
3. A father putting his son out of the house.

4. SCENES OF DRAMATIZED EMOTIONAL RELATIONSHIP

In these the play of character upon character, the picturization of the mental and emotional attitudes of characters upon each other, forms a graphic picture. They are scenes of mental and psychological states and attitudes.
Examples:

1. Six people at a houseparty suspect each other of a theft.
2. Five crooks mentally torment a rich old lady.
3. A husband persuades his wife to borrow money for him from her father, and she does not want to.

4. A manicurist tries to inveigle a rich man into a compromising situation, in order to trap him before a hidden witness, and he refuses.

F. Inherent Mood Values on the Stage

After we have determined the subject and title of a scene and analyzed it for its technical classification, we would seem to be ready to place our characters on the stage, but before we do this we need to know more facts about the stage than we have learned so far.

1. IN AREAS (See Plate IV: *Taken from Life;* use of DR area for a warm, informal scene.)

Upon a more acute examination of the areas of the stage we find that each area not only has its own value of strength and weakness but also a definite feeling or mood value. We do not know the psychological reason for this, but after many years of experimentation we find that a mood value does exist for areas. These mood values of areas, like color, line, mass, and form, have a tonal quality that can be verbally described. The best way to understand this is to arrive at your own conclusions through demonstration.

Going a step further we find that the subject of each scene in a play has an inherent mood which can also be expressed in tonal qualities. We know, furthermore, that each scene will convey this mood more convincingly if it is played in the area with the corresponding mood value. Although the mood of the subject of the scene should harmonize with the mood of the area, the following classification of the mood values of areas, expressed in terms of tonal qualities and scenes that the mood

UR	UC	UL
DR	DC	DL

value suggests, *should not* be taken to imply a rigid, unbreakable rule by which a scene must or must not be played; it is given more as a guide.

In deciding where a scene should be played many factors governed by the script on hand must enter into consideration.

Mood values of areas in terms of tonal qualities and suggestive scenes.

Tonal Qualities in Each Area	*Scenes Suggested*
a. Down center: hard, intense, harsh, strong, climactic, great formality	Quarrels, fights, crises, climaxes
b. Up center: regal, aloof, noble, superiority, stability	Formal and romanticized love scenes, scenes of domination and judiciary nature, royalty
c. Down right: warm, informal, close intimacy	Intimate love scenes, informal calls, confessions, gossip, one character observing a scene of others, long narratives
d. Down left: not so warm as down right; distant intimacy, formality, introspection	Conspiracies, casual l o v e scenes, soliloquies, formal calls, business matters
e. Up right: soft, distant, unreality	Romance
f. Up left: soft but seldom used by itself; must have o t h e r f a c t o r s t o strengthen it. Infinity, ghostliness	Supernatural scenes, background scenes

Exercises in coordinating the mood value of area and the subject or title of scenes

1. Two people compose a picture suggested in the chart for each area of the stage successively and show the suggested mood of each area.

2. Repeat each picture in an area different from that which is suggested in order to sense the conflict in mood values of title and area.

In many plays the same idea expressed by a particular character or the dominance of a particular character keeps recurring. In such cases the character can wisely be placed in the same area, usually on the same piece of furniture, for each recurrence of idea or dominance. The audience will gradually associate this area with the particular character or idea. Such use of area, however, should not be handled too blatantly but should be disguised in order to avoid obviousness. One way to do this is to have another character or other characters use the same piece of furniture for a short time in the course of the play. This also contributes a definite value of variety.

It often happens that an identical situation occurs at the beginning and at the end of a play, showing a complete cycle of a day or of a character. The same principle as expressed above follows: The use of the areas, the positions of the characters, the dialogue, and the movements are approximately duplicated to accentuate or make clearer the idea of the play.

2. IN PLANES (See Plate XIV: *Venice Preserved;* use of up-stage planes for a scene of violent action.)

Planes are so tied in with the mood values of areas that a word should be said about them. The stronger the emotion in a scene and the more important the scene the farther front it should be played, using the downstage planes. The upstage planes, aside from scenes that suggest softened areas, are good for background scenes or for unimportant characters in a scene of main action. Scenes of extreme physical violence, such as shootings and stabbings, are usually placed upstage, since for aesthetic reasons the violence must be softened.

Frequently a director has a scene in which there are many people who for atmospheric purpose carry on dialogue that should not be heard by the audience, but who necessarily are near to the important characters. In these cases the director should confer with the designer to arrange an alcove or a small room into which the audience may look. This area beyond the normal stage planes may be a reception room, a cocktail bar, etc. Its position may be center or, better still, up left. This establishes these added upstage planes as a place for the withdrawal of characters, left without lines, to *ad-lib* in silence. Their business has to be carefully worked out when added upstage planes are used in this manner. The convention we establish that people in these planes cannot be heard is quickly accepted by the audience. To safeguard this illusion, we must take great care to see that no one in the "nonhearing" planes speaks aloud or speaks to somebody downstage of these planes. If the character must speak, he should come forward and step out of the nonhearing planes.

There are cases when so much necessary dialogue has to take place away from the minor, or background, characters that the directing of such a scene has been solved only by having the main set become the withdrawing room, with a large opening in the center showing the reception room in which the background action takes place. The main set, then, becomes a withdrawing room into which the principals and a few others may stray to carry the story of the play. In cases of this kind the full business of continual background action has to be directed minutely.

The upstage planes in the form of alcoves or other similar recesses are excellent places to set dreams, return of the dead, ghosts, and other supernatural scenes. In all these instances the beginning of the scene should start in these upstage planes even though, as the scene progresses, it is better to bring the characters forward by degrees in order to utilize the center planes.

3. IN LEVELS

Levels, as can be readily seen, also have a definite feeling, or mood value. An actor's level can often correspond to the emotional tone of the character—a humble character can be in a low level, and a regal one on a high level. Often the changing use of levels can represent the building or diminishing of an emotional state of a character. (See Plate II: *The God Innis;* the level of the emphatic character corresponds to the character's emotional tone.)

In a certain production of *Oedipus Rex* the changing use of level corresponded with and brought out the progressive steps of the king's downfall. The production was staged on an immense flight of steps. At the opening of the play we saw the king on the highest level—grand, prosperous, master of himself. As each tragic implication bore down upon him we saw his gradual descent from step to step, although at times he ascended again as the obstacles diminished. Not until the end, when the tragic downfall had reached its depths, did we see the king on the lowest level nearly prostrate on the stage floor.

Exercises in placing scenes in their proper mood area, plane, and level

1. Place in its proper area each of the picturization exercises on pages 205 and 206.
2. A mother talks to her dead son.
3. A captain, disgraced by defeat, reports to his superior.
4. The king enters and denounces the superior for treason which brought about the captain's defeat at battle.

G. Creating the Full-Stage Picturization

With a complete understanding of the many considerations of the title or subject of a scene and its technical classification, of the mood values of composition, of the stage itself, and of the emotional qualities of body expression and relationship, as well as the imagination to dramatize, the director is ready to practice the full-stage picturization.

The thought process of combining the director's imaginative concept with the several technical considerations is one that will vary considerably. From experience it is found that the beginner had best separate the many steps and do each in turn. As he acquires more experience, the steps in the thought process become blended until a fully experienced director will think of the expression of the situation directly in terms of mood values and technique. It will seem to be only one creative process.

With the strong belief that a director should begin with a separation of concept and technique, the following procedure is offered for the blending of picturization and composition, both of which should be obtained for each scene of a play.

I. SEVEN STEPS IN ITS CREATION

a. Analyze the scene so that it may be definitely titled: whether it is a scene of struggle, of love, of forgiveness, of oppression, of suspicion, etc.

b. Determine the mood qualities that are inherent in the title: if it is a title of suspicion for a situation in which six people are each suspecting the others, we should have awareness, unrest, nervousness.

c. Express the nature of the mood in terms of mood value of composition such as line, mass, and form. Then express this in technical terms of composition: whether the composition is compact or diffused, large or small, regular or irregular, flat or deep, etc., with all the different combinations of these. In the situation of six people suspecting each other, we have isolation in space, diffused mass, and irregular line and form; and we see these in terms of closed-in focus, indirect line, uneven sequence, and a great deal of counterfocus together with irregular body position.

d. Visualize the background of the situation, characters, and setting: the forces that brought about the situation, the social standing of the characters, the environment where the situation takes place, and frequently the time of day and season. In the six people suspecting each other the situation has been brought about by a robbery. The characters might be people of high social standing, and the environment might be the drawing room of one of these people; or the characters might be gangsters, and the environment a hide-out. In this second instance the picturization would assume totally different qualities from those in the first.

With a clear knowledge of what the situation is, of the mood qualities inherent in the situation, of the mood values of composition that will express the nature of the mood; and with a clear conception of the entire background (situation, characters, and setting), we may now transfer our mental picturization on to the actual stage.

e. Roughly place your characters in the proper parts of the stage and in a manner that will express their emotional attitude or relationship of their primitive emotions in terms of their cultural and environmental background.

f. Apply the factors of composition that will, in particular, stress the emphatic characters or objects.

Having roughly related our characters, we now work for articulation and a clear-cut quality. We make definite use of our technical knowledge of composition, applying the proper emphasis and the necessary stability, sequence, and balance, with a careful eye to avoiding monotony.

g. The last step in the complete creation of our picturization on stage is the attitude of the individual actor.

Have your actors individually give their emotional body expression and reaction. Most of the individual picturization is probably instinctive with the actor, as a result of the emotion that he is striving to portray, or it may often be the result of his technical skill resulting from his observation. If he is defiant, he will stand with his feet firmly planted and lean forward with the body erect; if he is frightened, he will cringe; if he is humble, he will relax and slightly bow his head. This physical accompaniment of emotion in the human being is a universal language that he speaks and, just as the picturizing arrangement of the group, arouses an immediate conception of emotion and emotional relationship in the audience.

In arriving at our final picturization we have worked from the general to the specific. We first made known to ourselves the title for which we would work, and then through a series of steps starting with a rough sketch we have arrived at a detailed visualization of it.

After the picturization is completed, check on each individual factor, and make sure that the picture tells the title, the story, and the background.

2. PRECAUTIONS

Make certain that

a. Your composition is not obvious but is subtle and varied. The placement of your emphatic characters should correspond to the mood of the area, and the center area should not be used in every picture for the emphatic figure. Occult balance should be used more frequently than symmetrical.

b. The treatment of the picturization is not trite and too conventional but shows an imagination, an individuality, and a richness in detail which come from acute observation of life.

c. The actors react in character and in terms of the content of the scene.

d. Disorder is avoided in the picturization of great emotional stress. Disorder comes from violation of the principles of composition, with no regard for emphasis. No matter how disorderly a mood may inherently be, you cannot be disorderly in your composition. Whenever it is desired to portray confusion on the stage, it must be orderly, or composed, confusion.

3. SUMMARY

Analyze

a. What the title of your situation is.

b. The mood inherent in the situation.

c. The mood expression in terms of composition.

d. The background.

Then

e. Place the actors on stage to express the emotional relationship between them.

f. Apply the elements of composition for emphasis and articulation and for pleasing and varied effects.

g. Have the characters express their individual attitudes.

4. APPLICATION

Now let us work out together the steps in this thought process from title to complete visualization, using a definite title.

Example: Two women before Solomon, each claiming to be the mother of the child.

1. The title of the situation is two people seeking justice of a third: Solomon is justice; the two women are the seekers of justice; the child is the claim.

2. The mood values inherent in the title are impartiality, firmness, appeal, anger, and hatred.

3. The mood values of composition are those of strength, stability, balance, and loftiness of justice, as well as those of vigor and intensity of excitement. One feels a seemingly conflicting note from a diagonal line crossing a broad and strong perpendicular line.

4. The background of the situation is a mother's struggle for the possession of her child whom another woman has claimed as her own. The two women are of low birth, and the scene takes place in Solomon's court.

5. The placement of the figures in the proper parts of the stage and the expression of their emotional relationships are as follows:

Solomon should be placed dead center, high on a level (throne), and should be strongly emphasized by repetition of line coming from guards standing behind him. The mothers should stand before Solomon as far as possible from each other, with their body positions in antagonistic attitudes to each other yet leaning forward toward Solomon (their appeal). One of the women should have an arm raised to give the prolonged diagonal line. The women should be equidistant from Solomon to bring out his impartiality toward them and his inability to decide which the mother is. The child should lie horizontal to Solomon on the floor of his throne; in this position the child is equidistant from the two women and in possession of Solomon; since the child is the motivation of the scene, it should receive secondary emphasis.

6. Application of the factors of composition for emphasis and articulation:

Solomon should have preeminent focus. The mothers should have strong equal emphasis yet in varied methods. In addressing Solomon they will have to steal on their body positions so as to open up. In the entire scene there can be additional details of councilors, etc. Any raised arm must avoid covering the face. In most picturizations there is the need for slightly added changes to vary the triangle and obtain balance, but in this one the basic form is necessarily symmetrical.

7. The individual attitudes of the characters: This picturization presents more common problems than is ordinarily supposed. The mothers have two basic emotions to portray at one time—the hatred toward one another and their appeal to Solomon. These two conflicting emotions are expressed by having the body leaning and focused toward one object, while the arms point toward another. The head may turn toward either object. As we have already mentioned, the arm of one woman *A* may be raised toward Solomon, while her head may be turned toward the other woman *B*. As the raised arm gives great emphasis, with the bodies of

both *A* and *B* leaning toward Solomon, *B* may have her head toward
the king, but her arm may be pointing toward *A*. In this way we get
variety between *A* and *B* without duplicating exact positions, and yet
each is of equal strength and importance.

With these steps we have completed our picture of the emotional
relationships and have expressed visually the meaning of the scene; we
have used composition for its technical unification and its form for its
mood contribution. We have used that moment in this story when each
woman is putting forward her case at the same time, just before Solomon
makes his decision. Continue the story in two or three pictures to the
point where Solomon makes his decision by holding up the baby in a
feigned attempt to cut it in half. Notice the slight but telling changes
in the dominancy of the women and Solomon. Continue with the picturization of the whole story. Analyze in each case what you have done.

In this approach to directing a play we have a picture for
every scene; but as soon as we put movement (our next fundamental element) with picturization we have a picture that is
ever changing. In the finished product, therefore, the picture
does not remain static during the entire length of a scene but
changes slightly as the action or the emotional reaction of the
principal characters changes. The motion picture is a series of
static pictures which pass so quickly, one after the other, that
the eye does not notice any break between. So it is with the
stage picture within a particular scene. There is a definite and
constant kaleidoscopic but small movement reflecting the general progressive values in the scene. Nothing is more peculiar
in watching a play, in which the director has arrived at a picture
and held it continuously until it was time to change, than to
see all the people rise or move of a sudden and form a new
picture, only to hold this until it is time to move again. The
small changes in a picture often alter the meaning of a scene
entirely.

Referring once again to the Solomon story, we can tell the
whole tale with very little movement between a series of individual pictures and tell who the mother is and who is not. The
picture remains practically the same, yet by small changes of
strength and weakness, by change of emphasis, by climactic
movements we may hear the story from *A* and from *B;* make
it seem as if *A* were the mother, as if *B* were the mother, as if

both might be the mother; show the varying doubts and certainties of Solomon; show his decision; show the women's reactions to the decision; show Solomon pronounce his decision by starting to cut the baby in half; show the real mother's reaction, the false mother's reaction; show him bestowing the child on the natural mother; show him reprove the false mother. There may be possible still further minor changes which would show more minute changes in the story. Each one of these is a picture. Running one slowly after the other, we have the complete dramatization of the story which would be understandable to a deaf person, even if he did not recognize the Biblical tale.

An excellent picturization does all this: It tells the story in visual terms so that someone deaf or a foreigner could understand the story and characters of the play.

Demonstrations

1. A judge, a defendant, a lawyer, a jury.
2. A family of three with a young son, and a friend who has come asking the boy to go on a camping trip with him, when the family has already planned to take the son an automobile trip with them. They leave it to the boy to decide.
3. The members of a houseparty of nine all suspect one girl of having committed a theft. (She is innocent.)
4. A boys' club at an election, when they are waiting for the returns from the voting for a new president. The ballots are being counted in the next room.
5. A New England family at home in the evening; the eldest son returns from the Far East and introduces his new wife to them. Although neither the son nor his wife know it, the family sees that she is covered with scales.

Exercises in picturization

1. Set: Six pieces of furniture.
   Cast: Six children.
   Picturize: Fourteen positions.
2. Set: Six pieces of furniture.
   Cast: Six people.

Picturize:

a. A scolding.
b. Telling a story.
c. Whispering.
d. Equally divided quarrel.
e. A confession.
f. A formal conversation.
g. A quarrel.
h. Expression of grief.
i. Surprise.
j. A gossiping scene.
k. Conspiracy.
l. Good news.
m. A dinner party.
n. A death scene.
o. Shakespearean death scene.
p. A tea party.
q. Cross-questioning scene.
r. Pleading scene.
s. One suppressing five.
t. One boring five.
u. Six hunting for something.
v. Six suspecting one another.
w. One addressing a jury.
x. Theater lobby during an intermission.
3. One original picturization from each member of the group.
4. Title the photographs in the appendix.

IX

Movement

A. Contribution of Movement

MOVEMENT, THE third fundamental element of directing, is the stage picture in action. It comprises the moments of picturization in their ever changing aspects. Although movement exists in those passages from picture to picture, it must of itself have a definite picturizing value. In discussing the situation of Solomon and the two mothers we have already included the use of the smallest amount of movement during the changes from one picture to another. This increases by degrees until we arrive at a great deal of movement, movement that becomes an important factor and that must be considered as an active contributive quality of a play in performance. Just as we learn the principles of composition and picturization from painting, so we learn the contributions of movement to the stage play from the principles of movement in the dance.

Like composition, movement has a technical value and a mood value. Movement, such as exits and entrances or the hiding of an object, is supplied by the author for the necessary action in the progression of the story and also by the director for emphasis, variety, and mood expression.

B. Values of Different Movements

As with body positions, areas, planes, and levels, stage movements have certain definite values. These must be learned and so absorbed by the beginning director that any wrong movement will be immediately sensed by him.

All movement may be generally valued as strong and weak, but again we must point out that these terms do not mean good and bad. They are merely the evaluation of movement; there is a right time to use strong and weak movement, as well as a wrong time, depending upon the character and his line of dialogue and the situation.

1. BODY MOVEMENTS

A strong movement of the figure is stepping forward, straightening up, placing the weight on the forward foot, rising from a chair (lower to higher level), raising arm, or walking forward.

A weak movement is stepping backward, slouching, placing the weight on the rear foot, sitting down, lowering the arm, walking backward, or turning around and walking away from a figure or object.

In the general flow of movement, the value of the final movement before a pause, as for the delivery of a speech, becomes the dominant impression of the full movement. For example, if we desire a figure to be strong, while the script requires it to sit and yet at the same time be strong, the figure sits (weak movement) and then suddenly becomes strong by sitting very erect or by executing a large gesture. The reverse of this is also true: If a child is sitting on the floor and her mother enters to admonish her, the child rises (strong movement) ; but since under the admonishment she should be weak, she may hang her head and put her weight on her rear foot.

In this movement from strong to weak or weak to strong is evident the first influence of the dance. The increase in the amount and size of these strong and weak movements is of itself a dance.

2. STAGE MOVEMENTS

Not only does the movement of the figure have its strong and weak values, but the lines of movement of the figure on stage have their own values as well.

a. Relative strength of movement

The following charts give the value of the lines of movement of the moving figure not only in the strong and weak stage movements but also in their relative degree of strength and weakness.

Here, again, we notice that a strong stage movement followed by a weak body movement is made weak. For example,

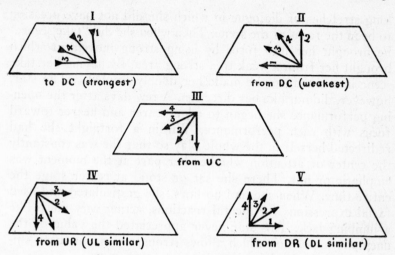

Charts showing relative strength of movement

if a figure walks from upstage to down center and sits, the general value is weak unless he makes a strong body movement after sitting. Likewise, a weak movement followed by a strong body movement will be made strong, for example, walking from downstage to upstage and turning full front for the final lines. This is the only possible way of making a final exit definite, strong, and emphatic.

Movement from a weaker to a stronger area is very strong. This is an excellent way to strengthen important dialogue and business or to make a figure emphatic. As a matter of fact a figure kept unemphatic until the crucial moment will become stronger if you give him a strong movement going from a weak area into a strong area than if you keep the figure in a strong area continuously. This principle is basically true in many phases of directing. For instance, there is a limit to the time that a director can keep the focus of emphasis on an actor who has few or no lines of dialogue, no matter how important he may be as a star or as a character or how much he may be acting during his period of silence.

Stars do not believe this fact and want to take the attention during all moments that they are on stage. A few years ago a very fine director kept a star in unemphatic positions during long stretches of dialogue in which she did not have occasion to be in the focus of the scene. Then when she did "take scene," he brought her into focus by using strong movement which brought her from a weak to a strong area. By having her take scene in this manner he made her doubly emphatic. The star, however, did not like her direction. A few days after the opening performance she began to edge nearer and nearer toward focus with each performance. Within a fortnight she had redirected herself in the whole play so that she was constantly the center of attention whether her part at the moment was emphatic or not. There she sat or stood at center stage the entire time. When she had no lines, she gesticulated and used facial expressions for mental reactions, acting very much like a jumping jack. This star never appreciated the value of the unemphatic position which allows strong movement to an emphatic position in the composition.

Occasionally there are plays in which the central character is on stage the entire time or nearly the entire time. In such cases the director simply has to find moments in which the actor will be unemphasized during long stretches of time. The resulting build from weak to strong can then be handled excellently for dramatic purposes.

b. Movement related to level

Movement from a lower to a higher level is strong. This is apparent not only in the simple cases of the body slouching and then straightening out but in movement up flights of stairs as well. An interesting phase of movement with level is one in which a weak movement becomes neutralized by a strong one; the weak movement in walking directly upstage to a raised exit is balanced by the strong movement of going up the steps. The figure will not gain dominant strength unless it turns before exiting.

c. Length of movement

A long distance to walk ordinarily weakens a movement, especially an exit. For this reason it is wise for the director to move his figure fairly near the exit before the actual exit movement. The weakening value of the long walk may be neutralized by a more rapid than normal one, or a long walk for entrance or exit may be built up for royalty by a formalized procession of guards and courtiers.

There are other ways also by which a weak exit movement may be strengthened. All of us have seen the leading lady take a gentleman's arm to support her exit. Both figures "turn in"; but although she has his arm, she keeps as far as possible away from him, usually a little ahead, talking violently to him as they make an exit from down to up center. Such an exit strengthens an inherently weak movement.

d. Movement related to ground plan

The values of these stage movements must be considered in the placement of entrances and exits in the director's ground plan for the designer. In general, important entrances should be made through upstage openings—up center being the strongest position for entrances, since it allows the entering figure full-front body position, possibility of strong movement coming downstage, and focus of emphasis from the other figures downstage. Important exits should be made through down-right openings, because the moving figure's profile is stronger than his back and the line of movement from center to right is stronger than that from center to upstage.

Final exits of figures are usually more important than entrances, as they frequently stress the keynote of the character in the play. In considering the ground plan this importance must be decided, especially if there is only one door in the set, as is often the case, or if the exit of the figure must be necessarily made by the same opening through which he entered. Exit openings, therefore, should have preference over entrance openings. Accordingly, if we have one door only and the exit of the heroine going out to commit suicide is the climax of the play, the exit becomes more important than the entrance. In studying the chart of relative strength and weakness of movements (page 225) to decide the placement of this exit, we find that I-1 is excellent for an entrance but bad for an exit as in II-2, whereas II-1 is better for an exit than for an entrance as in I-3. The opening, therefore, should be placed down right.

Exercises in the general evaluation of movement

Set: Doors DR, UR; fireplace on R wall between the two doors. Door UC with two steps leading into room. Window at center of L wall; door DL. Stool in front of fireplace; sofa facing front at right angles to fireplace; chair at C, L of sofa, facing fireplace. Desk in front of window with chairs at L and R of desk. Bookcase UL.

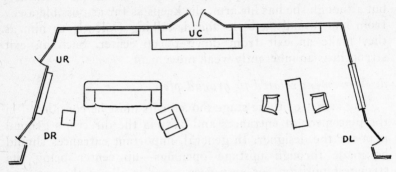

Problem: Have one member of the class do each exercise, and have class decide whether the movement is strong or weak.

The exercises should be performed by someone who has memorized each movement so as to show the direct relation of stage movement to the dance. The speed of execution in this demonstration should vary.

1. Figure *A* enters DR, Xs to chair C, sits.
2. Rises, Xs to door DR, closes door as he turns toward C.
3. Xs up to door UR, opens door.
4. Xs to UC, stops, turns toward UL.
5. Turns toward DR.
6. Xs to chair C.
7. Turns toward UC door.
8. Xs to UC door, going up both steps; turns on top step toward DL.
9. Sits down on top step and then straightens up.
10. Rises, Xs to window L, and looks out.
11. Turns around toward desk.
12. Sits in chair L of desk.
13. Buries his head in his arms on desk.
14. Rises, Xs to bookcase UL, and takes out book.
15. Xs to sofa.
16. Sits on sofa.
17. Stretches out on sofa.
18. Sits up.

19. Rises, Xs to stool.
20. Sits on stool.
21. Rises.
22. Turns toward fireplace.
23. Turns toward C.
24. Xs to C, then turns toward UR.
25. Turns front, then sits on arm of chair C.
26. Rises, Xs to door DL, and looks out.
27. Runs and Xs to chair R of desk, looking toward door UC.
28. Xs to above sofa and turns front.
29. Xs to right of desk, then sits on desk with feet of chair right of desk.
30. Xs to L above desk, stands on chair left of desk, and looks out window.
31. Jumps off chair and turns toward UC.
32. Turns and then Xs to below chair C.
33. Xs to stool, then sits with back toward audience.
34. Turns front, then buries face on knees.
35. Rises and Xs above sofa to door UC.
36. Xs to C and then turns toward UR.
37. Xs to door UR, turns toward DL, and exits by door UR.
38. Enters door UR.
39. Xs to door DL.
40. Xs to door DR and exits.

3. VALUES OF MOVEMENT FROM LEFT STAGE TO RIGHT; RIGHT STAGE TO LEFT

Repeated experimentation has shown that a figure or group passing from left stage to right stage gives the effect of stronger movement, as well as a greater amount and force of movement of the figure, than movement from right stage to left. Of the many possible reasons why this is so, one is convincingly understandable: The normal movement of our eyes is from left to right, probably on account of our training in reading. In looking at a panorama, whether it is actual or photographic, we begin at our left and follow through to our right.

We do the same thing when looking at the stage. When a figure or group walks along the normal direction of our vision, there is a certain ease or harmony between the eye and the moving figure. The figure goes along with us until he is offstage. With our eye going from left to right, it means that the figure is passing from right stage to left stage.

When, on the other hand, the figure goes from left stage to right stage there is a certain clash with the follow-through of our eye which, as we have seen, naturally travels from right stage to left. This clash, or resistance, in vision makes us feel that the figure is stronger than when it travels along and in harmony with our vision.

The sense of harmony, or ease, with one movement and sense of resistance to the other create definite values of weakness and strength respectively which, in turn, express definite mood qualities.

If the figure or group, therefore, is to enter with a sense of strength, it should enter from left stage and go to the right. Processions, groups, or lines of figures imply with this strength that they are going to something definite or important with an anticipation of success. Also, if a group comes from victory or success, it enters from the left stage.

In contrast to this: If the figure or group goes from right stage to left, it is weaker and, therefore, is retreating or going to defeat or to something indefinite and uncertain. If the group returns from defeat, it comes from the right stage toward the left.

Armies usually go to war marching from left stage to right. If they return victorious, the movement is also from left stage to right; if defeated, from right stage to left.

Peculiar as this phenomenon may be, it becomes clear and evident from demonstration. In a short time the beginning director will readily sense the degrees of strength and weakness in the two movements and will apply the proper movement when called for in a scene.

Demonstration

Scene: An army storming a castle.
Problem: Is the castle on stage right or stage left?
1. Decide its position from the principles described above.
2. Try the castle on stage L.
3. Try the castle on stage R.

For the mob storming the castle use about nine members of the class; space them at intervals with the majority on stage L when the castle is at R and vice versa. Have each take a different position of hurling a rock, shooting an arrow, using a battering ram, shaking fist, etc. Each should be in a different body position. Place one figure on a level behind and at the top of the castle which may be two flats.

This demonstration will show clearly that when the castle is on stage right the fighting is much fiercer.

Exercises in left and right movement

Picturize the following lines of people, and see that the line of movement faces the right way:

1. Going to a dining car on the train.
2. Going to war.
3. Waiting for free bread and soup.
4. Climbing a difficult mountain.
5. Going to a grave.
6. Dancing a war dance.
7. Leaving a house forever, sadly.
8. Arriving at a summer hotel, tired out after a day's trip in an automobile.

Closely allied with left and right movement and its implication is movement of an entering figure crossing to a stationary figure either standing or sitting. We have here the basic conflict of which is stronger—the movement or the stationary figure. The placement of the chair or desk around which the rest of the ground plan is often designed depends upon which figure is to be victorious. The figure moving from left stage to right is stronger than a figure placed right center. In such an instance the entering figure is more important and emphatic than the figure at right center whom he is approaching. In contrast to this when the stationary figure is more important, he should be placed left center, as that position is stronger than that of the entering figure coming from right stage to left. In both these examples the movement has greater value than the area. The strong movement is stronger than the strong area; and vice versa, the weak movement is weaker than the weak area.

Demonstration of movement related to stationary figure

Place a figure on a chair LC facing R; have six figures offstage R enter one at a time, cross stage to LC, bow, speak part of the alphabet, and depart off R.

Reverse chair and figure to RC; have the six figures enter one at a time from the L and repeat the same movement and exit.

Which of these movements emphasizes the sitting figure, and which emphasizes the entering people?

Exercises

Picturize the following groups of figures, and see which is the better line of movement:

1. One figure approaches a king.
2. One figure appears before a judge; another waits to go before him.
3. Two children who have misbehaved come to their mother to confess.

4. DIAGONAL MOVEMENT

Diagonal movements from down right to up left or from up left to down right or from down left to up right or from up right to down left have four different values and implications.

As a general rule they are less strong than lines of movement parallel or perpendicular to the footlights, but the diagonal line is longer and seems much more so than these others. It seems to traverse a great distance and even seems to extend offstage. Whenever an exit or an entrance is so vitally important that it practically becomes the subject or title of a scene, the diagonal line is properly and wisely used.

Demonstrations

1. Test out for the class each one of the four diagonal movements, and decide their relative strengths and weaknesses.

2. Decide the exit of *A, B,* and *C* under the following conditions:

A room in *A*'s house. *D* has come to visit and stays on and on, fighting with the servants and asserting herself until *A* can hardly call her home her own. After many minor situations which are unbearable for *A*, her daughter *B* and her son-in-law *C* come to help *A* pack and to take her from her own home, leaving *D* alone. They think that by this stratagem

D will leave shortly; but instead *D* is delighted, as she has some relatives whom she wishes to have visit her in *A*'s house. *D* is victorious; and *A, B,* and *C* are defeated.

So important was this scene that the doors were purposely designed into the set in order to dramatize the departure of the defeated.

Find the diagonal exit for *A, B,* and *C* and the position for *D* who cheerfully says good-by as each of the three departs with a short pause between each exit.

3. The same situation, except that this time *D* does not want her relatives to visit her. She is left alone, sad. In this situation *A, B,* and *C* are strong and victorious; *D* is weak and defeated.

5. SUMMARY

These four divisions of movement are all concerned with the values of sheer movement: first with body movement, then with general stage movement, next with right and left movement, and finally with diagonal movement. Just as in areas, we have seen what the values are and then what action or sort of scene these values suggest.

C. MOVEMENT AND DIALOGUE

As in picturization, the use of movement depends upon the script. Later on under Mood of Movement we shall see the manner of choosing the amount and kind of movement.

With an understanding of the values of sheer movement our next problem is to find the relationship of these values to the lines of dialogue. In contradiction to the often heard lament of beginning directors that they can find no legitimate reasons for interpreting movement out of dialogue, the motivation for much of the movement in bringing a play to life arises from the meaning or mood of the line of dialogue. More than this, all movement should be related directly to the line, except in those instances where movement has a connotative value of its own.

1. VALUES OF LINES

Just as in the case of body positions, areas, planes, levels, etc., so too we find that lines may be classified as strong or weak. The point to remember, however, is that weak speeches or lines may be as important and as emphatic as strong ones. In so far as they are strong or weak they have a definite relation to movement; every sentence of a play has an inherent movement. In this respect a play, speech by speech, may be likened to a dance. The inherent movement may be strong or weak, or it may be a static movement that is as much a part of movement as movement itself. Static movement, as in dance, is the timed pause; it corresponds to a rest in music.

The line, moreover, may be made strong or weak according to the movement given it, or we may change the meaning of a line by the movement given it. What, then, determines our evaluation of a line and the interpretation that we give it? The interpretation of any one element in a play—the character, the scene, the dialogue, etc.—depends upon what dramatic value can contribute most to the main purpose of the play. Therefore, in determining the evaluation of any line it is considered not in itself but in relation to this greatest dramatic value which is associated with the whole.

It is necessary to learn to sense the values of lines. To a large extent, this is an intuitive faculty, but we suggest below the possible kinds of lines with their appropriate movement:

a. The absolutely positive and strong line of dialogue should be used with strong movement only. These are lines of command, determination, defiance, optimism, threat, etc., the characteristics of which are positive. "Look here: I'm not going to stand this!" "Do as I say or you go out!" "There's no question about it, he'll win." These are positive lines demanding strong movement.

b. The negative and weak line of dialogue should be used with weak movement only. Lines of doubt, defeat, introspection, fright, hopelessness, frustration connote a negative quality. "What a mess I've made of it!" "I swear to you I feel the whole weight of the denunciation." "I am disgraced, impeded, and baffled here . . . and I have no way out." These are negative lines demanding weak movement.

c. The line that is part strong and part weak, either beginning weak and ending strong or beginning strong and ending weak, demands movement to correlate with the strong and weak parts of the line.

"If I stay, we'll go on making ourselves miserable . . . we must call it quits now!" The first part of the line takes a weak movement; the second, a strong movement.

"Sir, you must believe me. . . . Ah, yes, I can tell, it's all quite useless." The first part of the line takes a strong movement; the second part, a weak movement.

An exception to the use of a strong movement on a positive line or a weak movement on a negative line is found in comedy where for incongruity we may make use of a strong movement on a weak line or vice versa. It is a common stock in trade of the comedian's technique to make a weak movement like backing away as he calls out: "I'll punch you on the jaw!"

Demonstration

Demonstrate on stage the examples given above. First do the line with the correct use of movement as illustrated; then do it with the opposite value of movement. You will find that the correct use of the movement reinforces the sentiment of the line.

d. Many times in order to emphasize the correct interpretation of a line it becomes necessary to evaluate that line by the movement given it. The line can be made positive or negative according to the movement related to it. For illustration let us take: "I'm the one that's being made a fool!" By giving a strong movement to the line a positive statement is made by which the character asserts his indignation: "I'm the one that's being made a fool! (And I won't allow it!)"

But by giving a weak movement to the line the character assumes an ineffectual and self-pitying attitude of mind: "I'm the one that's being made a fool! (And there's nothing I can do about it.)"

e. Related to the foregoing are those lines whose meaning depend on the movement given them. "Yes, it's wonderful!" Give a strong movement to this line, and the character means what he says. Now give a weak movement to the line, and the opposite effect is achieved: The character does not believe that it is wonderful. The movement has changed the meaning of the line. It becomes evident that before we can decide the movement required by a line we must first make clear to ourselves

the right interpretation of the line in reference to the character
and the situation.

f. Sarcasm is a positive line with a negative meaning and
will take either a strong or a weak movement according to
the meaning.

Demonstration

Work out the movement for the lines of sarcasm spoken by Henry
in the following dialogues:

1. SHE: He longs to be free . . . he said so himself.

    HENRY: Yes, so as to be able to see you again . . . having been
touched by your pity.

2. HE: He'll talk her out of her fright.

    HENRY: She's not afraid, doctor. Don't you believe it. The thing
bores her rather.

3. SHE: History says — I don't know whether you know it or not —
that . . .

    HENRY: Yes, I know. You are most faithful to history, my dear.

Do each line of sarcasm first with a strong and then with a weak
movement. In each instance decide which is the more effective.

2. MOVEMENT ON, BEFORE, AND AFTER LINES

When possible the movement should come *on* the line. As
a rule lines are never held for movement unless, of course, the
pause is used for a definite dramatic effect. Lines that need no
particular pointing up should have movement come on the line
when movement is called for. A movement that is illustrative
of the line should come *on* the line. Sometimes when movement
is boldly illustrative of the line, a movement separated from
the line will soften the general effect.

The movement *before* a line is made when it becomes
essential to attract attention and emphasize the line as the
important thing. This is an instance of "pointing" the line. The
actor first attracts attention to himself by making a strong
movement and then stops or holds the movement just before
speaking, thereby giving the line definite emphasis. Such a
movement may be standing or making a strong stage movement
or gesture with the hand. Important lines and words that

contribute directly to the story or idea or both demand this kind of pointing. Movement is only one of many ways of pointing a line. Often for greater emphasis or variety it may be used with one or more methods of line pointing, such as

1. A pause in movement, business, or voice before the line or the important words.

2. The actor taking an important position, as coming down into a stronger area.

3. A contrast in the quality of tone when speaking the important line or words, as going from a full tone to a whisper.

4. Raising or lowering the pitch of the voice.

5. Speaking the important words with staccato.

6. Retarding the tempo of the line.

When pointing a line with proper movement and business it is important to have precision, especially in the playing of comedy. Apropos of this, all movement should be definite and simple in execution, for movement, more than anything else on stage, attracts the greatest attention.

Usually the movement before the line must be strong if the line is to be emphasized; but if the movement itself is to be emphasized rather than the line, then the movement before the line must be weak. A character who turns upstage (a weak movement) and then delivers his line is emphasizing the movement.

The movement *after* the line will likewise emphasize the movement. The delivery of the line attracts attention and gives emphasis to the movement immediately following. Here again, as a rule, the movement after the line must be strong if it is to receive emphasis; otherwise if it is weak, the line receives emphasis. Lines that follow movement are those which have finality.

Exercises in relating movement to dialogue

1. Take any play and find
a. Five positive lines requiring movement.
b. Five negative lines requiring movement.
c. Five lines part strong and part weak.
d. Five lines that are positive or negative according to the movement.
e. Five lines that change meaning by the movement given them.

f. Five lines of sarcasm.

g. Five lines that you can move on.

h. Five lines that you can move before.

i. Five lines that you can move after.

j. Five lines that you cannot possibly move on.

2. Execute these lines on stage with their respective movements.

3. Show ten different ways of pointing a line or the important words.

Important as movement is to a play, it is a dangerous and difficult factor. Like the old saying about fire, it is a fine slave but a bad master. If as a director you can conquer it, your play benefits; but if you are at a loss as to how to handle it, it will destroy your play.

3. MOVEMENT RELATED TO EMPHASIS

a. Movement and dialogue

Movement commands a great deal of attention. It will make the audience look at it rather than listen to a speech. No matter how much a director builds up the emphasis of the speaker, a small movement from an unimportant figure will distract the audience's attention. What little of directing we have covered so far boils down to the audience's looking at what we want them to see and hearing what is necessary for them to hear to understand the play. Let one of the minor female characters appear with a fan and unconsciously use it when she feels that it is in character, and your work of hours crumbles like a house of cards. For this reason, the fan, even in costume plays, is seldom or never used on the stage. A star will often use one, but a star will immediately spot it if a member of the supporting cast is seen with one. The amateur or beginning professional is delightfully naïve about bringing a fan on to the stage.

Like the fan, small doodads on dresses, handkerchiefs, jewelry also are distracting. They are small, but they are expressive of the whole danger arising from unwise movement. In plays with mobs, it is extraordinarily hard for the director to obtain the necessary reaction and movement and still protect the important lines.

b. Dialogue and background movement

The technique required by a player of Cyrano in the fencing scene, where the actor has one of the most beautiful passages in poetic drama and must fence throughout, presents a problem in control of movement. In fact all *Cyrano de Bergerac* is so difficult as far as the action of background crowds is concerned that one has to abandon all attempt at realism and direct it under the pretense of pure romanticism, having the crowds freeze on passages of important verse.

c. Actor's individual dialogue and movement

Because of the power of movement in attracting attention, it has become the custom in the theater for an actor to make his movements on his own lines rather than on those of someone else unless the lines being spoken are very unimportant. This is wise because (1) an actor can judge the best of several lines to move on and (2) he can decide the relation of the line to the movement.

The easiest line on which to make a movement, such as a cross or exit, is one in which the line describes, explains, or is expressive of the movement.

Examples: Excuse me, but I've got to go.
Come on, I'm in an awful hurry.
We'll go ahead slowly, and you can catch up.
Good-by, everybody, good-by!

The figure can cross to an exit on all these. In spite of the distracting movement, enough of the words will be heard, and the movement itself is explanatory of the line.

d. Entrances and dialogue

This is equally true of an entrance. Unless there is a very definite reason for not doing so, an entering figure should begin to speak immediately. Many actors feel that they should walk to their position after entering and then begin to speak. When this is done, there is a break in the flow of the scene.

When an act has several entrances in it, such as a first act, the general effect resulting from pauses for unimportant speeches is one of hesitation and jerkiness. Actually an entrance speech is seldom so important that it needs a holding of the figure. When it does, it is better to hold the actor by the door for the full pointed effect and then have him move on his second speech. But lines like the following can be spoken while the character moves:

> I just stepped in with some wine jelly for poor Mrs. Jones.
> Hello, Anna. How do they like your garden?
> How do, Mr. Neil? Mrs. Neil? Ellen?

An entering figure nearly always has a speech. It is much easier for an actor to have the first speech on entering. Only occasionally does a person on the stage have a speech to a person entering. When this is so, the entering figure should keep moving to a position on stage all the while the actor on stage is addressing him. This prevents the entering character from being "suspended" any longer than possible before he gives his first line.

e. Crosses and dialogue

Crosses and movements are usually made in front of the other figure with whom the character is conversing. That is another reason why the speaker should move on his own line. When a cross is made behind another actor, the moving figure passes out of focus and breaks his power of holding attention. By moving on his line and crossing in front, he can still hold this attention until he has finished and at the same time allow the other figure to pick up his cue and continue the attention and interest in the scene. Minor characters, like servants, do make crosses upstage of the principals.

f. Exits and dialogue

When a figure leaves the stage, it is nearly always best for him to be near the exit for his last speech. A usual method is for an actor to give part of his speech, make his cross, and then give the rest at the door. Even if a figure does not proceed with his exit in this manner but must deliver his last speech, let us say, near center stage and then exit, the director should see to it that the figure is fairly near the exit door so that the cross to the exit is not too long and does not hold up the lines and flow of the scene.

If an exit is very important or if it has value as comedy in line or business, the people remaining on stage should hold their lines for the exit. Also, they should hold their lines if the character exiting is not supposed to hear what is said after he leaves. The smooth flow of a scene is so important that unless there is a definite and important reason for an emphatic exit, dialogue should not be held for actors leaving the stage.

4. RELATION OF MOVEMENT TO DIALOGUE IN A PACING SCENE

In a pacing scene the relationship of movement to the dialogue must be carefully considered, and the movement planned so as to preserve the lines. A pacing scene may develop out of the character, the mood, or the style of the play. Its control, manner, and variation depend on the nature of the situation.

In the execution of a pacing scene the movement must be organized into a definite pattern. This is most important so as not to confuse the audience. A disorganized pacing scene would have your audience wondering where the actor is going next, thus distracting from the lines. The pattern established for the scene may be a repetition of definite planned movements in the form of a triangle or straight lines or any regular form that best expresses the nature of the situation. By unobtrusively establishing this pattern, we draw the attention of the audience to what the actor is saying and not to what he is doing.

The pacing may be done by the person speaking, in which case he points his own lines either by stopping before he speaks or by speaking on strong movements only. The others, if they have lines, speak while he is taking weak movements.

Or the pacing may be done by the nonspeaking person, in which case the pacer points the speaker's lines by his movement.

To cover the general procedure in handling pacing scenes, we shall consider the technique involved in cases where the pacing becomes violent.

a. Placement of actors

The nonmoving actor is placed in a strong downstage area as far as possible from the mover. The mover is placed in weakened areas; his movement may be roughly from up center to down left.

b. Lines of the nonmoving actor

His lines are spoken loudly and while the mover is making a weak movement or while the mover is in a weak body position. To bring enough emphasis to himself, the nonmoving actor should make a slight movement before or after his lines, as the case may be. In the instances where the lines of the nonmoving actor are particularly important, the mover should stop pacing, often occupying himself with business.

c. Lines of the mover

He emphasizes his lines by stopping and holding the movement for the line and then picks up his pacing in a faster tempo. Or he emphasizes them by speaking on strong movements, like coming downstage or going from left to center. Or he may speak as he opens up or just before a turn if he is going into a weak movement. He should get variety in the pointing of his lines by using all the methods mentioned.

d. Planning of the movement

In the pattern of the movement he will use a regular form like a triangle. The movement may go from up center to down left to up left and back to up center. It must be subordinated to the lines. Once the pattern of movement is established, he should use a movement out of the basic form for variation. This, however, should not be carried too far; otherwise the pacing becomes disorganized and confusing. For variety again the actor may use different body positions and different positions within the pattern for the delivery of the speeches. As the scene progresses the speed of the movement should be increased or decreased, depending on whether the scene calls for a build or for a diminished ending.

Demonstration

1. Let each group work out the technique outlined above, using letters of the alphabet for lines.

   a. Do one scene where the speed of the movement increases as the scene progresses.

   b. Do one where the speed of the movement decreases as the scene progresses.

NOTE: Each group present a different pattern of movement.

Exercises in pacing scenes

1. Let each group work out a pacing scene where the pacing is done by the nonspeaking person. Use letters of the alphabet for lines.

2. A pacing scene from *Her Husband's Wife,* by A. E. Thomas, Act II, page 67 (Samuel French ed.)—see excerpt at end of this chapter.

   Problem: Irene is angry and expresses this in pacing. The window through which she looks is ——— ? Uncle John is amused at her fury and teases her. The problem is to

   a. Determine the placement of the window and actors.

   b. Determine the lines on which she can move to preserve her own lines and the lines of the uncle.

   c. Establish a pattern that will subordinate movement to the lines.

   d. Get a continual flow in her movements.

   e. Get a build in her movements.

   f. Obtain variety in her form of movement.

   g. Get Uncle John's laugh lines over.

3. A pacing scene from *Othello,* Act III, Scene 3—see excerpt at end of this chapter.

   Problem: The pointing of one person's lines by the movements of the second person.

D. MOVEMENT AND PICTURIZATION

In the demonstrations of Solomon and the true and false mothers, as we proceeded with the various pictures that told the meaning of the whole story, we found that movement crept into the process of going from one picture to another. In this case the movement was of secondary importance, and the resulting picture the dominant part of the exercise. It is true that in many plays the movement between the scenes is of secondary importance, but usually the movement itself between pictures is just as important as the pictures themselves. Not only does it relate itself to the over-all mood inherent in the pictures, but it is as telling as the pictures themselves.

1. STORYTELLING QUALITY OF MOVEMENT

Under Areas we have seen the storytelling quality that is conveyed by figures at a distance from each other or in close relationship. Now, the actual strong movement that brings *A* from stage right to *B* on stage left has a storytelling quality. The distance between two figures cuts down the emotional intensity between them. There is not a close or strong emotional relationship. As they draw nearer to each other in any emotional condition, their positions grow stronger, more intense, and therefore more climactic; the love grows more fervent; the anger, more vehement; the situation, more intense. The change in this emotional relationship is known as "low to climactic position."

Under Breaking Up we saw the opportunities for a variety of positions. This also holds true in picturization; as the figures draw nearer to each other during a scene, the emotional intensity of the movement increases and contributes to the climax of the scene and at the same time makes clearer the meaning of the scene.

2. PLANNING PATTERN OF MOVEMENT TO OBTAIN STORYTELL- ING QUALITY

We have already seen how placing our characters to picturize the emotional relationship helps us with the static placement of the people for a scene. We shall now see how the changing of the emotional relationship of character to character gives us the movement for an entire scene.

1. The scene

Let us imagine a scene between a superintendent of a reform school and one of the boys. The superintendent has caught the boy in a position that leads him to think he was attempting to escape. The boy is at first belligerent, and the superintendent is firm and severe. The latter, not being able to get the boy to confess by this means, next tries to persuade him to tell, offering him his confidence and doing him a friendly act by putting a blanket around him, as it is night and he is cold.

The boy does not respond but turns on the superintendent and tells him what he thinks of him, the reform school, and life in general. He is thoroughly denunciatory. He is bold and frank because he knows that he will receive the severest punishment in any case.

The superintendent then tries to win the boy's confidence by telling him of certain events in his own life. The boy becomes interested. The superintendent's disclosure shows him that this superintendent was once in the same situation. The boy softens, relents, and confesses. The superintendent professes his affection and future personal interest in the boy. The latter agrees to do the right thing and be the superintendent's friend and supporter.

b. The analysis

1. Upon close analysis we find that there are five distinct changes of emotional relationship in this scene. Accordingly, there are five distinct picturizations of the scene, and the transitions from one to the other will give us the movement.

2. First we have the two opposing characters who are obviously placed opposite each other on the far sides of the stage.

3. The next change of emotional state is when the superintendent pleads with the boy. He will come over to the boy. Meeting with no success, he will return to his own side.

4. The boy's next state is one of attack upon the superintendent. Accordingly, as this part of the scene progresses, he approaches from his place by degrees, going over to the superintendent; and since, at the end, he is still antagonistic, he will return to his former position.

5. The next state is when the superintendent tells the boy the story of his life. He comes part way toward the boy but turns away from him because the narration is so difficult for him that he cannot give it to the boy directly. He comes part way because he is more sympathetic than he has been heretofore. As the superintendent tells the story, the boy, at first indifferent, gradually becomes absorbed and is drawn closer to the superintendent. Accordingly, he begins by being in an aloof picturization and slowly turns and walks over toward the superintendent.

6. Then in the final lines in which they are in mutual understanding, they are together in the same area at the center of the stage, possibly shaking hands.

From this example we see that the change of the emotional relations between two or more people on the stage leads to a definite pattern, a definite combination of static emotional picturization and movement. We shall discuss this point under the consideration of motivated movement through character pattern.

If an actor is put physically into a picture with the correct relations to the other people in the scene, in the correct body position for the mood in which the speech is to be given, and given the correct movement for the transitions and changes in emotional relationship, he will instinctively read the speeches of that scene with greater intelligence and emotional depth than if he is in the wrong picture or no picture at all.

E. TECHNICAL DETAILS IN REGARD TO MOVEMENT

1. BUILDING A SCENE SOLELY BY MOVEMENT

a. Methods

In building a scene to a climax, voice and tempo as well as movement are important. Our problem at the moment, however, is to practice building a scene by the use of movement only. Movement will build a scene if we increase the amount and size; change the value, placement, and tension; and use contrast.

Following is one arrangement in the use of these methods:

1. Increase length of movement from short at the beginning to longer.
2. Increase number of people moving.
3. Use contrasting movement.
4. Use shorter movement.
5. Go from weak body positions and levels to strong.
6. Increase tension of the movement.
7. Use stronger areas.
8. Increase the number of people crossing one another.
9. Increase the amount of small movement.
10. Go from individual to group movement.

Demonstration

Work out the arrangement outlined above in building a scene solely by movement. First use five persons; then use ten.

b. Conservation of movement

At the beginning of a scene that demands a build you will find that the inherent interest of the situation usually holds in itself so that the amount of breaking up required is small in contrast to the amount and acceleration of breaking up necessary in the latter part of the scene. The control of the methods of building and the proportion of breaking up are also dependent on the characters who may or may not be able to hold scenes in themselves. In building a scene, therefore, we must be careful not to unload all our means at one time but to work out a progression that will give a smooth build in relation to the situation and the characters. This is necessary for conservation and variety.

2. PARALLEL AND COUNTERMOVEMENT

As a rule, parallel movement and countermovement, that is, two persons moving in identical or directly opposite directions at the same time, are to be avoided. These movements, however, are sometimes effective in comedy or farce. A slight retarding of one person's movement will break up parallel and countermovement. This, as in the case of all other such rules, has specific exceptions.

3. CONTRASTING MOVEMENT

This movement can often be used to great advantage. Compare a mob going off to the right in victory with a lone figure going off to the left in defeat. The contrast of the movements heightens the value of each.

4. HANDLING OF VIOLENT SCENES

Unless we are intentionally doing a scene of this kind for its horror element, all violent scenes should be softened and blended into the whole of the play.

In a murder the scene preceding the actual killing should be "built up," very often by movement, and the killing should follow rapidly. Generally, the actual execution of the death should be muffled by using a weak area. The body should fall behind furniture or somewhere so that it will be partially covered unless it is important to have it visible to the audience in the following scene. The same holds true for suicide by shooting, which in most cases should also be carefully muffled by having the actor's back toward the audience and by placing the scene in a weak area. Refer to what was said in Chapter IV, Elementary Stage Technique for the Actor, regarding the actor's handling of shooting, stabbing, and suicide.

5. HANDLING OF LOVE SCENES

a. General principles

With amateurs we need to take advantage of the connotative value of the softened upstage areas for our love scenes. The actors will blend into the picture, add more of a romantic flavor to the scene, and feel less self-conscious than if they were downstage in close contact with the audience.

The director should keep constantly in mind the fact that the sense of the emotion of love should be stimulated in the audience rather than in the actors. This can be done by means of romantic picturization. We need to picturize most graphically, as that will hold the interest of the audience in the sheer beauty of the picturization and will tend to make the actors less self-conscious by keeping their minds on the business. In romantic positions they will also read their lines with more feeling.

The third principle to consider in a love scene is the postponement of the actual embrace which the actors reach at the end of the scene. Far too often directors place the actors downstage, either standing center stage or sitting on a sofa, for an entire scene; whereas the scene of love-making can begin with the actors somewhat apart. The movement, then, that accompanies the scene can be such as to draw them slowly and by degrees closer and closer together from the farther sides of the area used for the scene. In this way they are in actual close proximity for only a short time at the end of the scene.

If romantic picturization is consistently worked out, the love interest will be constantly conveyed to the audience.

b. *Example in procedure*

As an example of these principles, let us block out the picturization and movement for a love scene.

Let us play the scene around a sofa placed upstage center and slightly to the right. (If the scene has to be played standing, it is possible to play it behind a chair or table but in any case in a softened area.) The girl can sit on the center of the sofa early in the scene, and the boy can stand on the right side of the stage when the scene first begins to take on a love interest. He can cross from where he is standing to the right end of the sofa. He can hold his position there for several speeches. Then he can move along behind the sofa until he is leaning over from behind the girl. From this position he can come around the left end of the sofa and stand there. He can then sit on the arm of the sofa and then on the left end of the sofa itself. The girl can easily find lines that will allow her to move over to the right end of the sofa. The boy can then move toward the center, then closer to the girl until he is on the right end with her. He can then place his arm upon the back of the sofa, then take her left hand in his left. He can bring his arm from the back of the sofa down to her shoulder, and finally he can kiss the girl.

This manner of handling a love scene is possible in many cases, whether the scene is played around a sofa or not. Love scenes are often played about a piano, a mantelpiece, an armchair, a table, a window, the lower steps of a flight of stairs, or a mantelpiece and sofa together, etc. But in all cases, the actual embracing should be postponed by the building up of romantic positions that bring the lovers increasingly closer together.

For amateurs a good principle to follow is to have the love scene played about a piece of furniture rather than standing center stage. Furthermore, it is a good policy to have the embrace come from a sitting rather than a standing position. Refer to what was said in Chapter IV regarding the actor's technique in embracing and kissing.

Exercises in technical details in movement

1. Build an abstract scene solely by movement.
2. Each group give in pantomime a murder scene, using a weapon.
3. Each group give in pantomime a love scene—different from the sofa example.

F. GENERAL KINDS OF MOVEMENT

1. STORY

Movement may be used to express the story of a play. As such it is usually indicated by the playwright. It covers such actions as entrances and exits of characters, hiding of objects, going to a window to look out, serving meals, fighting, and dancing. They are the obvious movements for the necessary action in the progression of the story. Movements illustrative of the lines belong to this kind of movement.

Examples: 1. Entrance of cocks in *Chantecler*.
2. Movement of Mrs. Bramson (*Night Must Fall*) in her hysterical scenes.
3. Duel in *Hamlet*.

2. BACKGROUND

These are the movements that establish locale and atmosphere. They are often supplied by the playwright, but more often than not it is up to the director to supply them when essential for a fuller realization of the scene. Scenes such as the street in *Dead End,* the deck on the boat *Excursion,* the waiting room in *Counsellor-at-law* require background movement.

3. CHARACTER

These movements portray the type of character with which we are dealing or the character's state of mind. To express the temperament of a high-strung, restless character we should give him plenty of movement: rising, sitting, rising again, moving about from one side of the stage to the other—movement on the slightest provocation, but a kind of movement that demands careful control (Tony in *Royal Family*). The sluggish type of character, on the other hand, would be portrayed with very little movement (Lennie in *Of Mice and Men*). Impatience, confusion, uncertainty, fear, torment, and the like may be expressed by proper movement (Euripides' *Elektra*).

4. TECHNICAL

We have on stage technical as well as emotional reasons for movement. By this we mean that movement may be made for the aesthetic reasons of good composition or out of sheer necessity dependent upon clearing the stage for entrances and exits.

a. Compositional

The movements for obtaining emphasis as discussed under Composition come under this class. So also do those movements for obtaining stability, sequence, or balance in the composition. "Taking" or "giving the scene" is a purely technical movement for emphasis; "stealing" for position or "dressing stage" is a purely technical movement to achieve a balanced composition—in these instances the subtle manner of execution should make the movement unobtrusive. The movements for variety, as the arbitrary breaking up of a scene; movements to stimulate the attention of the audience or to relieve tension are technical movements. In realistic plays technical movements must be motivated and must be related directly to the line.

b. Transitional

Transitional scenes are usually of entrances and exits. During them we may change the actors to effective positions for the ensuing action. In addition, such scenes demand some fill-in movement at this time (such as expectant pacing, crossing to piece of furniture or fireplace) which keeps them alive until the new scene begins.

G. MOTIVATION OF MOVEMENT

Movement used to express story, background, or character may be motivated or unmotivated, depending upon the script that is to be directed. That which is unmotivated we call arbitrary, and it is of a technical and intellectual nature, whereas the motivated or realistic type has a more emotional basis. For this reason we say that, as a general rule, the movement of comedy is more arbitrary than that of tragedy.

There are several ways in which motivation of movement on stage may be treated. The first is that related to purely arbitrary movement. The second is the fully motivated type of movement which includes realistic follow-through, psychological follow-through, and the movement that is the result of character pattern or fundamental design.

I. ARBITRARY USE

Arbitrary movement is superimposed by director or actor on a script that is inherently static or talky. For example, we enhance the play of wit in such comedies of manners as those of Oscar Wilde, Noel Coward, Philip Barry, and Somerset Maugham by movement calculated to emphasize the significance of the line. The movement may be one of ennui, sarcasm, pretended joy, overdone sorrow, mock fatigue, etc. In any event it springs from the intent of the line and the desire to increase its laugh-provoking power. Likewise, character movements may be made for the same reasons, or the movement may be made for sheer variety which is arbitrary movement at its best. The clever director who inserts movement of this kind into the performance is always careful to rehearse it over and over again so that it is smooth and definitely related to situation or character. As a result, this "arbitrarily" inserted movement, although not an intrinsic part of the script, seems to be so. The advantage of this lies, of course, in the fact that great vitality is supplied to an otherwise talky and static scene.

Arbitrary movement selects its end and proceeds to it with despatch and neatness. The result is a well-paced, clean-cut movement unhampered by minutely worked-out detail. Such movement is admirably suited to the playing of comedy.

In farce or farce comedies where geometric movements like parallel and counter- are continually introduced to enhance situations, we find still another instance of the arbitrary use of movement.

Nothing is more disconcerting than that stage movement which an audience recognizes as being completely and thoroughly unrelated to any element of the play. For this reason the director should be careful to have the arbitrary movement in some way pertinent to the line, situation, or characterization.

2. MOTIVATED

a. *Realistic follow-through*

In realistic follow-through, movement must have an objective to which it is directed. In this the motivation is obvious and thoroughly worked out. Realistic follow-through demands that an actor present every step of the movement so that there is nothing false about it. This is appropriate to the plays of Ibsen, of O'Neill, of Maxwell Anderson—plays that depend upon the richness and truth of character and situation. Many melodramas employ highly detailed realistic movement due to the exigencies of the situation.

In such plays even purely technical movement must have realistic follow-through. In other words, consistency demands that technical movements do not become purely the arbitrary sort. Let us say that for technical reasons it is important to have the character cross from one area to another. To give a realistic follow-through to the movement the director will have the character start toward the bookcase, presumably to pick out a book, but will have him stop on the way to speak, leaving the motivation unfulfilled. The director has motivated a movement executed solely for technical reasons. Actually, this is an arbitrary movement, but motivation has been supplied to blend in with the over-all realistic follow-through of the entire play. In a realistic play every movement must be motivated in some way, even though the objective of the motivation is never reached nor the motivation fulfilled. This motivation, as we have seen, may be the beginning to go somewhere, to sit down, to leave, etc. Background movements in realistic plays must also have a realistic follow-through of movement.

b. Psychological follow-through

These are the movements motivated by the emotional and intellectual content of the line or by the character expression. They have already been discussed under relation of movement to the kinds of line and under movements that portray the character's state of mind. They are the movements by which we can illustrate changes in thought of the character. These movements also illustrate changes in character relationships and as such clearly picturize in action the mental and emotional attitudes of characters toward one another.

c. Movement as a result of character pattern

Associated with and dependent upon psychological follow-through of movement are character patterns. These show graphically the interplay between two or more characters, either in one scene or during the whole play, when the story and theme rest upon such interplay. Character pattern is achieved by the combination of the changing picturization of the emotional relationships and connotative movement. The scene so worked out will have a definite pattern in the movement that is clear to the observer and can be drawn in diagrammatic form.

Demonstration

Romeo and Juliet, Act III, Scene 5—scene beginning with the entrance of Capulet and Nurse.

In this scene Juliet makes three appeals: to Capulet, to Lady Capulet, and to the Nurse. Each time her appeal is rebuffed. In the interplay of the four characters the motivation to action comes from Juliet. We immediately see that in order to project the greatest dramatic value of the scene we must interpret the action from Juliet's point of view. The pattern for the scene, then, must graphically show this play of action and reaction, or, in terms of this particular scene, appeal and rebuff. Certainly, if we have each of the three go to Juliet, we shall lose the significance of the scene. The diagram below shows the pattern for the scene that will best express the nature of the situation. Lines drawn designate the movements of Juliet.

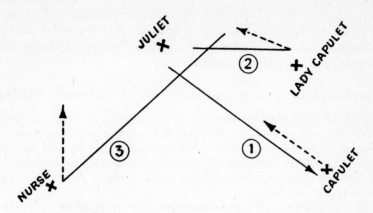

Exercise in movement as a result of character pattern

Work out without learning the lines this scene from *Romeo and Juliet*.

d. *Movement as a result of fundamental design*

Similar to character patterns is fundamental design which is usually extended to a whole act rather than restricted to a scene. Furthermore, it shows pictorially not so much the changing relationships of character to character as the relationship of a character to a group or a force. The picturization of this usually places the character in a particular location on the stage and shows by connotative movement the opposing forces coming toward or away from him, or it may show the protagonist in movement demonstrating himself in relation to the more or less static force.

In arriving at the fundamental design we first determine the meaning of the act and then interpret this meaning in terms of areas, levels, lines, emphasis, etc., so that the composition of the act is expressive of the idea. This in movement will give the design for the main action of an act or a whole play. There will be minor scenes that will deviate from the main design; but these scenes of themselves, it will be noticed, are inherently deviations from the main idea of the act. Moreover, the design must have variations so as not to make it too obvious. The blatancy, or clear-cut quality, of such a design in a play varies proportionately with the abstruseness of the

writing. Strindberg's *Dream Play,* Evreinov's *Life of Man,*
O'Casey's *Within the Gates* will be made clear to the audience
through a strong fundamental design. Fundamental design,
therefore, is a symbolic pattern.

Demonstration in movement as a result of fundamental design

Under Picturization we discussed the changing use of levels as treated
in a production of Sophocles' *Oedipus Rex* to bring out the progressive
steps of the king's downfall. The fundamental design, planned for the
entire play, shows pictorially the changing relationship of Oedipus to
the forces bearing down on him. Refer to this section in Picturization for
the treatment of the design.

In graphical form on paper demonstrate this treatment of the fundamental design for *Oedipus Rex.*

H. EFFECT OF MOVEMENT ON MOOD

Connotative movements have a picturizing value of their
own like those suggested earlier in this chapter. They are also
the movements contributive to mood expressions. For a better
appreciation of this let us consider movement as an extension
in time of line, mass, and form which in their various arrangements create a mood or arouse an emotional response in the
audience. When discussing the mood effect of line, mass, and
form in composition, we considered it from a static point of
view. A play in performance, however, is action, and the mood
effect achieved must be visualized dynamically by seeing these
lines, masses, and forms in movement. The grace portrayed
by the use of curved lines on stage exists more often in the
sweep of the real movement than in the static form. So it is
with mass in movement and form in movement. In all cases
the mood effect achieved exists in the composition, but in
actual execution on stage it becomes a composition in flux which
is movement.

I. LINE EXPRESSED IN MOVEMENT

Just as line in composition, so stage movement may be classified as horizontal, perpendicular, and diagonal, and these
movements may be treated in a straight, curved, or broken

manner to obtain the various mood effects desired. We have only to refer to Line under Composition to analyze the mood effects of these different movements with their variations and combinations, for they are nothing more than these lines in action. The perpendicular movement, however, in execution on stage can exist only as movement from level to level; movements to higher levels, which are strong movements, have the same connotative values as those discussed under Perpendicular Lines. Such movements may also be from higher to lower levels in which instances we express defeat, loss of aspiration, frustration, loss of grandeur or dignity—in other words all that is implied by weak movement.

2. MASS EXPRESSED IN MOVEMENT

The effect of mass in composition depends on the number of people used and on the handling of this group as regards the space intervals between members of the group as well as upon the body positions that they assume. In movement we have the additional factor of this mass in action. A heavy mass moving in one direction creates power and determination, in contrast to this same mass milling about in diverse directions which is connotative of restlessness, instability, or turmoil.

3. FORM EXPRESSED IN MOVEMENT

The different arrangements of form in composition can also be thought of as existing in action, which is exactly what happens with the play in performance. Stage movement may be regular or irregular in execution; it may extend through all the planes of the stage, or it may be confined more or less to a single plane; it may be spread over all the areas, or it may be restricted to one or two. Consider the stage movements in *The Lower Depths:* Characters move in irregularity of form; they extend their movements from upstage to downstage; their actions spread over most of the areas. Compare these stage movements with those in a play like *The Way of the World,* a Restoration comedy of manners. The wit, the sharp delineation of character, the artifice of situation are best captured in movements that are regular, that are confined to a few planes, and that cover definite areas of the stage. In all cases the mood effects achieved by form in movement are those which we have analyzed under Composition.

Along with the various mood effects of lines, masses, and forms in movement are the connotative values of the different ways in which movement may be executed. In the total mood expression the amount, the strength or weakness, the length, the direction, the intensity, and the rhythm of the movement are important considerations.

4. AMOUNT OF MOVEMENT

Is the movement to be constant or occasional? Plays of continual excitement, of characters requiring no detailed characterization, of dialogue lacking innuendoes, of thought, of sharp contrasts in mood—plays like melodramas, rowdy farces, or many of the propaganda plays—demand constant movement. But the play of rounded characterization, of ideas, of infrequent climactic moments, of protracted moods, etc., takes only occasional movement. We sense immediately that the amount of movement used is directly dependent on its appropriateness in expressing the mood of the play, the situation, the character, the locale, and the atmosphere.

5. STRENGTH OF MOVEMENT

Is the movement to be weak or strong? Here we must take into account the evaluation of body movement and stage movement in terms of strength and weakness which we outlined at the beginning of this chapter. Certainly the variations in these values are contributive to the mood effect and, as we found under Values of the Lines of Dialogue, are definitely related to the ultimate impression of the sentiments in the lines. In determining the over-all effect of strong and weak movement and whether a greater amount of one or the other is used, we must consider the kind of play, the nature of the situation, the characters, and the atmosphere. Chekhov's plays of futility are abundant in weak movements, since the mood of futility can be visually portrayed only by the use of weak movement. On the other hand, the over-all mood quality of plays of positive action like *Dead End* demands strong movement.

6. LENGTH OF MOVEMENT

Is the movement to be long or short? Here, again, we must go to our play, our situation, etc. You will find that long movements convey impressions of composure, deliberation, futility, languor, lack of emotional strain, etc.; whereas short movements are expressive of excitement, sharpness, irritability, impulsiveness, gayety, etc. Long movement has a legato, or smooth, quality; short movement has a staccato, or sharp, quality.

7. DIRECTION OF MOVEMENT

Shall we have the character move toward the left or toward the right? For this we refer you to what was said under Values of Movement from left stage to right stage and vice versa where the connotative effects of each were discussed.

Closely related to these are the diagonal movements from down right to up left and down left to up right and vice versa. The connotative value of these we analyzed in the demonstrations under Diagonal Movement. If we analyzed these correctly, we found that for Demonstration 2 the diagonal exit for *A, B,* and *C* is from up right, where *D* cheerfully says goodby, to down left—a movement that is not only long but also weak, as it follows the course from right to left, leaving *D* victorious and *A, B,* and *C* defeated. In the reversal of this, *A, B,* and *C* in leaving strong and victorious would start up left where *D* stands and leave by down right, thereby making not only a strong movement from a weak area but a movement that goes from left to right. As regards the mood effect of these diagonal movements we find that the movement from down right to up left is the weakest of them all and therefore a movement that implies utter defeat, uncertainty, a departure into the unknown, or a leaving forever.

8. INTENSITY OF MOVEMENT

What degree of intensity should we give the movement? This depends on the emotional content of the scene and the emotional status of the character. Heightened emotion is conveyed by greater intensity in movement as well as in voice. Highly emotional utterances coming from a character who makes ineffectual, lax movements are not convincing. Such movement often accompanies a scene for farcical or comic effects.

9. RHYTHM OF MOVEMENT

What about the rhythm of the movement? Is it to be strongly accented? Is its tempo to be slow or fast? Is it to accelerate or diminish? An answer to these questions demands a chapter in itself.

Exercises in the effect of movement on mood

1. Redo the exercises on the effect of the composition on the emotions of the audience. Describe the mood effect, and explain the method of conveyance of this mood in terms of movement of line, mass, and form.

2. In doing the following exercises use the right amount, direction, and kind of movement that will be expressive of the mood and characters:

a. Three condemned prisoners await sentence. The verdict of death is announced. The condemned are led out.

b. Four workers are trapped in a coal mine. Rescuers enter, and the miners are led out to safety.

c. Six actors are in a dressing room just before curtain time on the opening night of a premiere. They return with the play a grand success. They return with the play a "flop."

d. Four tourists are about to cross a frontier on their way to a winter carnival. Their passports are being inspected. War is declared, and the tourists are ordered back.

I. EXERCISES IN MOVEMENT

1. Take any play, and find five lines with movement dictated by the story. Execute these lines on stage with their respective movement.

2. For the following, work out the scenes giving the movements a realistic or a psychological follow-through or both, as the situation may warrant. Choose scenes from realistic plays.

a. Each group work out a scene that calls for background movement.

b. Each group work out a scene in which movement is used to portray the type of character.

c. Each group work out a scene in which movement is used to express the state of mind of the character or to illustrate changes in character relationships.

d. Each group work out a transitional scene where movement is necessary to keep the scene alive.

3. Each group work out a scene from high comedy demanding arbitrary use of movement.

4. Create a scene in which the connotative value of movement expresses a mood of grief, of joy, of loneliness, of turmoil, of oppression, of peace.

5. Exercises in character patterns.

a. Each group work out the character pattern for the scene from *The Cassilis Engagement,* by St. John Hankin, Act III, page 98 (Samuel French ed.)—see excerpt at end of this chapter.

b. Each group work out the character pattern for the scene from *Alice-Sit-by-the-Fire,* by James M. Barrie, Act II—see excerpt at end of this chapter.

c. Each member of a group work out on paper the character pattern for a scene from a play of his own choosing.

6. Exercises in fundamental design.

a. Each group work out the fundamental design for the scene from *Ambush,* by Arthur Richman, Act III—see excerpt at end of this chapter.

b. Each group work out the fundamental design for the scene from *The Truth about Blayds,* by A. A. Milne, Act I, page 24 (Samuel French ed.)—see excerpt at end of this chapter.

c. Each member of a group work out on paper the fundamental design for a scene from a play of his own choosing.

7. Each member of a group work out a short scene from a play that will demonstrate at least ten of the points discussed under Movement. The scene must be approximately five minutes long. Do not have the actors learn lines.

AMBUSH*

HARRIETT: How are things today?

WALTER: Not very good. I didn't have the heart to tell Margaret, but there are some ugly rumors going about concerning the oil supply. I put up the last thousand today.

HARRIETT: You don't suppose the rumors were true?

WALTER: Seymour says they're circulated on purpose, so people will sell and the officers of the company can buy up the stock cheap. I tried to see one of the officers, but they are all too busy. That isn't what worries me—I had a long talk with Mr. Preston just now—and I haven't got a position.

HARRIETT: You mean he discharged you? [*Walter nods.*] After all these years?

WALTER: I've been with that firm seventeen years—seventeen years—think of it.

HARRIETT: And now he discharges you—the ungrateful pig!

WALTER: Harriett—don't.

HARRIETT: Oh—it's all right for you to take these things quietly—— But I've got red blood in my veins and if I had him here I'd tell him what I think of him.

WALTER: He isn't to be blamed—not altogether. You see, I haven't been doing my work very well of late—that stock investment has been on my mind—especially these l-last three months while it's been fluctuating so much. I've made excuses to leave the office to go around to the broker's.

HARRIETT: Well, say you have? You've been with them seventeen years——

WALTER: There's no sentiment in business, Harriett—not much anyhow. I've made one or two mistakes on the books. They warned me the first time it occurred, but my mind's been so agitated, and I made another.

HARRIETT: What'll you do now?

WALTER: Look for something else. Mr. Preston offered me an excellent recommendation.

HARRIETT: That was nice of him!

WALTER: So I ought to get something before long——

*From *Ambush,* by Arthur Richman. Used by permission of Dodd, Mead & Company, Inc.

HARRIETT: Well, I hope so—I suppose you know the rent's due today?

WALTER: It's lucky Seymour bought the house, isn't it? He'll understand our position and be patient. Tell me, dear, h-has Margaret mentioned anything to you about giving up work?

HARRIETT: She's talked about it a lot lately.

WALTER: Of course you told her to keep on?

HARRIETT: No, I didn't. I don't altogether disagree with her. A girl has to think of her future.

WALTER: But—s-surely her working doesn't endanger her future? Besides, we shall need all the money we can scrape together until the Wall Street situation improves. [*The bell rings.*] I'll open. [*Enter Seymour and Mrs. Jennison.*]

SEYMOUR: Well, what'll we do now?

WALTER: Has—has anything happened?

SEYMOUR: Happened! [*To Mrs. Jennison.*] Did you hear him? He asked me if anything's happened!

WALTER: The company——?

SEYMOUR: Damn the company! They're liars and robbers! I'll bring an action against them—just you see if I don't. There must be some way of getting back what's been stolen from you!

WALTER: Then the rumors were true?

SEYMOUR: Don't you know? Good God, man, where have you been?

WALTER: The last quotation I saw was at two o'clock. When I was leaving, Mr. Preston called me to his office to—for a private talk. It filled my thoughts so, I didn't have a chance——

SEYMOUR: The last hour is the one that did it. Magnificus Oil went to Hell! I'm ruined! I'll be lucky if I get a thousand dollars out of it! You're ruined—they stole *your* money just the way they stole *mine*. [*Harriett sinks into a chair.*]

WALTER: It's all right, Harriett—don't take it so hard.

SEYMOUR: It ain't as bad for him as it is for me—*he's* got a regular job to fall back on.

WALTER: A job!

SEYMOUR: Haven't you? But look at me—I've got nothing! Of course, a proposition's been put to me—hundreds of thousands involved in it——

HARRIETT: Keep quiet, Seymour Jennison! You're not fit to talk to decent people.

WALTER: Harriett!

HARRIETT: You come around here, telling people to invest in that rotten company of yours—telling them how much money they're going to make and how safe it is. Why don't they make a law forcing people like you to keep quiet and let other folks alone? If I had anything to say——

WALTER: Harriett!

HARRIETT: Oh, you can be quiet if you want to, but I'll tell him what I think of him to his face!

MRS. JENNISON: You have no right to talk that way, Harriett. Seymour was perfectly honest and sincere, and if he made a mistake—well, he's paying for it.

HARRIETT: Does *his* losing money help *us?*

WALTER: Harriett, you must not say these things. [*To the others.*] I'm sorry Harriett spoke like that. She'll be sorry too, when her excitement subsides. You see, all this is v-very hard on us. We wanted money so badly, and a——

SEYMOUR: You were right—I'll grant you that. You didn't want to go in at first. You must'a' had an instinct about it. What made you hesitate?

WALTER: My nature, I guess. I'm—I'm inclined to be conservative in everything. But I was just going to explain why this is such a blow to us. The job Seymour was talking about—well, I haven't got it.

SEYMOUR: Haven't got it!

WALTER: I'm not so good at my work as I used to be.

SEYMOUR: Hm, that's too bad.

MRS. JENNISON: I'm awfully sorry, Walter.

SEYMOUR: Of course that won't make any difference? Between us, I mean. [*Walter is puzzled. Harriett looks up.*] Of course you know what day this is?

WALTER: December eighteenth—one week from Christmas.

SEYMOUR: Christmas!—hah!

WALTER: Wait a moment—I know what you mean.

SEYMOUR: 'Course you do. The rent on this house is due today. It'll certainly come in handy.

WALTER: I—I haven't got it, Seymour.

SEYMOUR: Haven't got it?

WALTER: I have a little, but not all of it.

SEYMOUR: But these houses are the only things I own!

WALTER: You're richer than I am.

SEYMOUR: I could get tenants at twice the rent you pay. Interest on one of the mortgages is due the first of the year. How do you expect *me* to pay if *you* don't?

WALTER: I will, Seymour. Only have patience——

SEYMOUR: I don't want to be harsh with you, Walter——

HARRIETT: I can't listen to another word from that man! Let me know when he's gone. [*Exits into kitchen. She slams the door behind her.*]

SEYMOUR: Seeing that your wife doesn't mince words, Walter, I won't either. If you don't pay as you're supposed to, I'll have to get other tenants. [*To Mrs. Jennison.*] I've got to look into that new proposition. Let's go along.

MRS. JENNISON: You go ahead, Seymour. I want just a word with Walter.

SEYMOUR: What about?

MRS. JENNISON: Oh, just neighborly talk. I won't be long.

SEYMOUR: Tell him I'm in earnest about what I said. I've lost money enough in one thing—I can't take chances on another. And remember, Julia, this new proposition might mean big money and I need your advice. [*Exit Seymour rear.*]

MRS. JENNISON: I'm awfully sorry things happened like this, Walter. I wanted to tell you not to go in with Seymour, but I was afraid it would be disloyal.

WALTER: Not to go in! Did you know anything about it?

MRS. JENNISON: Not a thing! It's only this: some people seem kind of marked to go through life without success—have you ever noticed that? I'm afraid Seymour's that kind.

WALTER: I hope not.

MRS. JENNISON: This sounds as if I was finding fault, but I'm not. Seymour means so well and I understand him and love him.

WALTER: Of course you do.

MRS. JENNISON: But sometimes——Were you ever very tired, Walter, and knew that you had to keep going? So tired that just to hold your head up hurt the back of your neck? That's how I am. I want to rest—just to stop everything and rest a long, long time. Oh, I'm not tired of keeping house and marketing and mending socks—I'm tired of having to be ambitious. I knew you were too—that's why I stopped to talk with you. I thought it might help you to know I understood, and I thought it might help *me* if *you* understood.

WALTER: How did you know it was that way with me?

MRS. JENNISON: I saw it in lots of things. I used to notice how contented you were to let things slide along, and the pride you took in simply being decent.

WALTER: You saw *that* too!

MRS. JENNISON: I'm like that. At least, I used to be. But I got so tired of having Seymour tell me I was old-fashioned that I learned to hide it.

WALTER: There's something fine about having principles, Julia.

MRS. JENNISON: If you can keep them, Walter.

WALTER: It's hard sometimes.

MRS. JENNISON: It's a curse to be born like this—we take things so hard that other people brush aside. Because sometimes you *can't* keep them. Sometimes Fate seems to close in on you from every side—to get you into ambush—and you've got to give up. Don't tell Seymour about this conversation, he'd think I was crazy. You know what's going to happen now? I'll find Seymour with a lot of papers in front of him, covered with figures, and he'll tell me about the millions of dollars he's going to make in some new scheme or other. He won't tell me about it because he wants my advice—he'll talk in order to convince *himself*. And he'll be convinced.

WALTER: An ambush!

MRS. JENNISON: Isn't that what it is? The other forces—the things we're fighting against—come in on you like this, and this, until there's no way to turn. [*Margaret comes downstairs.*]

MARGARET: Hello, Mrs. Jennison. [*To Walter, referring to the dress.*] Now you see why I couldn't travel in the tube? [*To Mrs. Jennison.*] Have you leased that apartment yet in New York?

MRS. JENNISON: I never expected to.

MARGARET: You ought to, if you can. A person's foolish to stay here if they don't have to.

MRS. JENNISON: Margaret, dear. We have had a little misfortune. Your father has suffered too.

MARGARET: The oil company?

MRS. JENNISON: The stock is practically worthless. Your father doesn't mind so much for himself, but he's unhappy on account of your mother and you. Put your arms around his neck and tell him you believe in him, anyhow.

MARGARET: What's the sense of that?

WALTER: Margaret isn't the demonstrative kind, Julia. It's all right, though.

MRS. JENNISON: Do it, then, when you're alone. I'll get Seymour to come over after supper. Good luck!

WALTER: Good luck to *you!* [*Mrs. Jennison goes out.*] A fine woman, Mrs. Jennison.

MARGARET: I suppose so. Then it's settled—about the stock?

WALTER: I'm afraid it is. How sweet you look.

MARGARET: Where's mother?

WALTER: Getting supper, I suppose. I'm sorry you're not staying home—Margaret!

MARGARET: What?

WALTER: Do you—do you despise me for—for not having good luck?

MARGARET: It's funny the way *some men* manage to succeed.

WALTER: I don't want you to despise me, dear.

MARGARET: Please don't touch me. You'll muss my clothes! [*Harriett at kitchen door.*]

HARRIETT: Has he gone?

WALTER: S-Seymour? Yes, he's gone.

HARRIETT: The loud-mouthed fool! Supper'll be ready soon. [*A ring at bell.*]

GEORGE [*outside*]: Hello! Hello! Margie!

MARGARET: That's George. [*Goes to door and opens it, sheltering herself behind it. Enter George Lithridge.*] Quick! We'll all take cold. [*He enters, and she shuts door.*] You know mother.

GEORGE: Certainly do. How's mother?

HARRIETT: Very well, thanks.

GEORGE: And father?

WALTER: How do you do?

GEORGE: I say, Margie, how far is this house from the North Pole?

WALTER: It is rather windy, isn't it?

GEORGE: I'll say it is! The chauff's nearly frozen. Lucky it's a limousine.

WALTER: Margaret tells me you're going to dine in New York.

GEORGE: Yes, got a table engaged, and all that. I say, Margie, that I've got a table engaged. Wouldn't be a bad idea to get started.

MARGARET: Do you mind if we're a few minutes late, George? We're only fifteen minutes from the ferry. There's something I want to talk to you about.

GEORGE: Before we go? It's got to be important—this trip gave me an appetite.

MARGARET: Just come into the pantry a moment.

GEORGE: The pantry! Maybe you'll give me a cookie to keep me going? [*Exeunt George and Margaret into kitchen.*]

HARRIETT: Margaret is awfully unhappy.

WALTER: About the—m-money?

HARRIETT: She counted on it so much.

WALTER: If there were only something I could do!

HARRIETT: She believes Mr. Lithridge might help you.

WALTER: Help me! You don't mean he'd lend me money? I wouldn't take it.

HARRIETT [*dryly*]: Beggars can't be choosers. Margaret's a good girl to think about it. But it isn't lending you money so much as it's a job. She just told me that maybe he'd offer you something in *his* place.

WALTER: In his business?

HARRIETT: Yes.

WALTER: How does he know of our misfortune?

HARRIETT: He doesn't. Maybe he does *now*. Margaret was going to tell him.

WALTER: But that's so—so much like asking f-for help.

HARRIETT: Did anything decent ever happen to you that you didn't find something the matter with it? [*Bell rings.*] Who is *that*, I wonder? [*She goes to the door, leaving Walter deep in thought. Enter Harry.*]

HARRY: Good evenin'. Hello, Mr. Nichols. Margaret home?

WALTER: Yes, she's home.

HARRIETT: I'll just go and see what I can do. [*Exit into kitchen.*]

HARRY: What's Margaret doing this evening?

WALTER: She's going to New York.

HARRY: That's why there's a limousine in front of the house, hey?

WALTER: Yes. Have you been drinking, Harry?

HARRY: Only one or two. Friend o' mine's got a lot of it.

WALTER: Would you think me rude, Harry, if I asked you not to stay? Something of great importance to us is happening just now.

HARRY: 'Bout Margaret?

WALTER: It concerns all of us.

HARRY: So you're like that too, now!

WALTER: I don't understand you.

HARRY: You don't want her swell friends to see me; is that it? Well, don't be afraid I'll spoil anything——

WALTER: You've been drinking more than is good for you.

HARRY: Don't worry about me—I can take care of myself. [*Laughs as door opens.*] Hah! It's too late now, anyhow.

GEORGE: Good cake this—[*Enter George and Margaret from the kitchen. George is munching a cake.*] Don't remember when I've enjoyed anything more.

MARGARET [*to Harry*]: Mother told me you were here.

HARRY: Yes, I'm here.

WALTER: This is Mr. Lithridge—Mr. Gleason.

HARRY: "Lithridge?"

GEORGE: That's it. How d'ye do?—Something funny about me?

MARGARET: He's drunk.

HARRY: I am not drunk. And don't think I'm going right away either, 'cause I'm not.

GEORGE: Evidently a relation.

MARGARET: No, he's not. Stay if you want to, but don't interfere. [*To Walter.*] Father, George and I have been talking over a certain matter and George has something to say to you.

GEORGE: Mr. Nichols, your wife and daughter tell me you've had a hard knock in the market.

WALTER: I have—rather.

GEORGE: So've I. Only, I guess I can stand it better than some people. They also tell me you've lost a job you held for a long time.

WALTER: Seventeen years.

GEORGE: Just so! Now, I've got a pretty good-sized business in New York. Don't think I'm boasting—believe me, I've got nothin' to boast *about*. The business was left to me—it ain't my fault that it's big. But most of the clerks are getting old and little by little they're being retired. I don't retire 'em—I've got people to look after all that. All I do is read letters and sign checks and say "yes" whenever anybody asks me a question. [*Laughs.*] What would you say to taking a job as clerk in my business? Mrs. Nichols just told me how much you used to get, and I'll see to it that you get twenty dollars a week more.

WALTER: Mr. Lithridge, this is more than I'd hoped for——

GEORGE: Think it over—there's no hurry. Margie can ring me up in the morning, if you like, and tell me what you've decided on. [*Margaret makes him a sign.*] What? All right. [*To Walter, laughing.*] I'm ordered out. I'll wait in the car. Don't be long. [*To Walter.*] Good night. [*Exits rear.*]

MARGARET: What are you going to do, father?

WALTER: I shall accept, of course. It seems a splendid offer.

MARGARET: That's sensible. And here, Father—here is enough money to pay the rent for the house. [*Gives him some bills.*]

WALTER: No! No! I can't take it.

MARGARET: Don't be foolish. It's a loan, and George has such heaps of money it doesn't make any difference to him.

WALTER: I can't take it.

MARGARET: I'll leave it here. You can do as you please. [*Lays money on desk.*]

HARRY: Well, I'll be damned! [*They look at him.*]

WALTER: You ought to be ashamed of yourself, coming here in this condition.

HARRY: Is that so? Well, I know what I'm doing, don't you fear. Why do you suppose that fellow is doing all this? [*Margaret is about to protest.*] Do you suppose there's nothing more between them than friendship?

WALTER: You're in no fit condition——

HARRY: Ain't I? Well, I'll leave it to anybody. Here's a married man coming to see Margaret, lending her father money, giving him a job——

WALTER: A married man!

MARGARET: Can't you see he's drunk?

HARRY: Oh! I know him! The first job I ever had, I used to see him. He's got a wife and two or three kids. Find out for yourself.

WALTER: W-what he says isn't true?

MARGARET: Well, what if it is?

WALTER: You—you knew it all the time?

MARGARET: I knew he was married before I met him!

WALTER: But only a little while ago you gave me to understand—here, in this v-very room—that you thought he might marry you!

MARGARET: Well, I had to tell you something, didn't I?

WALTER: But—I can't believe it! I won't!

MARGARET [*coolly*]: Can't believe what?

WALTER: After that other time you promised——

MARGARET: Yes, and I meant it.

WALTER: You meant it! Well, then, if you meant it——

MARGARET: Do we have to talk about this in front of him?

WALTER: I don't understand any of it! All I know is that everything—everything—is going to pieces!

MARGARET: Why shouldn't it, when a man thinks more of fine ideas than he does of supporting his family?

WALTER: Stop it! Stop it! You're just that kind of a woman! Forget that I said that—I didn't mean it! It's all that other man's fault—that Alan Kraigne——[*Remembering Harry's presence, he look at him open-mouthed.*]

MARGARET: He's heard enough to understand. You might just as well go on. But what's Alan got to do with all this, I'd like to know?

WALTER: If he hadn't deceived you—made promises and then lied about them—none of this would have happened.

MARGARET: He didn't lie to me.

WALTER: He promised to marry you.

MARGARET: He did nothing of the kind. Oh, the time has come for a showdown, and you might as well know the truth.

WALTER: The truth! The truth!

MARGARET: That I belonged to somebody else before he met me——Him! [*Walter wheels about.*]

HARRY: You're crazy!

MARGARET: Why do you suppose he was so mad when I went around with Alan? Why do you suppose he told you about George being married—though I suppose you'd have found that out if you were working for him? But I don't care any more *what* you find out—if all this makes you unhappy, it's your own fault.

WALTER: You will have to marry him.

MARGARET: Who? [*Walter is pointing at Harry.*] Harry?

WALTER: You'll have to marry him!

MARGARET: Watch me!

HARRY: If she'll do it, I'm ready.

MARGARET: Get out!

HARRY: I'll forget whatever's happened since—I'll marry her.

MARGARET: Oh, damn it, get out of here. [*Harry exits.*] We might just as well have this whole thing out. [*Harry disappears.*] Only, hurry up, because I hate to keep George waiting.

WALTER: Have you no shame?

MARGARET [*putting on her coat*]: I'm not going to discuss *that*. If I wanted to, I could leave here tonight and never come back. Don't you suppose I could live in New York if I wanted to?

WALTER: Not—not if his wife knew about it.

MARGARET: She *does* know it. Oh, not who I am—George is too much of a gentleman to let her learn my name. But they haven't lived together for a year. Now listen! I'd rather stay here—it looks better, and it'll be easier some day when I want to get married. Besides, I'm fond of mother and you. But if I do stay, I'll live as I please and I won't have questions and criticisms.

WALTER: Not so loud! We're forgetting your mother.

MARGARET: You see this coat? Well, you may as well know that I've got lots of things upstairs you've never seen. After this I'll wear them.

WALTER: From—from Mr. Lithridge?

MARGARET: You don't suppose I'd accept things from anyone else? What kind of a girl do you think I am? George is so good natured, he'd wait all night for his dinner if I wanted him to. But now I *must* go. There's the money for the house, if you want to use it. And remember about the job. [*She is almost at the door, wrapping the coat closely about her, when Walter breaks out.*]

WALTER: I won't have it! I won't! I'll go out there and threaten him! I'll make him understand! [*Walter plunges toward the door.*]

MARGARET: Mother!

WALTER: Margaret! You mustn't let *her* know.

MARGARET: Mother! [*Harriet appears.*] Father wants to make trouble with George—stop him.

HARRIETT: What were you going to do just now?

WALTER: Nothing, dear. Margaret and I had a little misunderstanding, but it's all right.

HARRIETT: Yes, it looks as if it was all right. Are you going to take the job? [*Margaret goes out while they are talking; Walter starts as the door closes.*] Are you going to take the job?

WALTER: With Mr. Lithridge? That's what I was—what I was going to talk to him about. It isn't in my line.

HARRIETT: You'd better. If you don't, things'll be very unpleasant.

WALTER: Oh, I'll find something else.

HARRIETT: And there's the rent.

WALTER: If the worst comes to the worst, we'll move.

HARRIETT: To a smaller place?

WALTER: There are some apartments going up in Bergen that would be just the thing—just the thing for us. You'd have no stairs to climb——

HARRIETT: Margaret won't move to a smaller place. If you ask her to do that she'll live in New York. And if she goes—I'll go with her.

WALTER: You'll do what?

HARRIETT: I know all about everything. I've known it all along.

WALTER: About what?

HARRIETT: About Margaret.

WALTER: You—what do you mean?

HARRIETT: I know all the things you know. If I didn't, she mightn't be living with us now. That day I came back after riding with the Jennisons, she told me how you'd acted about Alan Kraigne and it was all I could do to keep her from leaving us.

WALTER: You're a wicked woman!

HARRIETT: Why? For not driving her away? All these months I've had to fight and fight in order to keep her from leaving us.

WALTER: You knew—you knew about everything?

HARRIETT: That bracelet—do you suppose I ever thought it was imitation? Margaret showed it to me the day she got it. Oh, Walter, it isn't pleasant for a mother to know things like that are going on, but it don't do any good to quarrel all the time. I was the one who said it was imitation, because I saw there'd be trouble if I didn't.

WALTER [*momentarily relieved*]: Oh, you knew about the bracelet? Do you know that Lithridge is a married man?

HARRIETT: She never told me that. I didn't ask her. But I'm not surprised.

WALTER: You helped her lie to me! What's to become of her now?

HARRIETT: That depends upon us, I guess. If we keep her here and make the best of it, things may turn out all right. The question for us now is: what are we going to do?

WALTER: Whatever I say! And you'll both stay here and listen to *me*.

HARRIETT: How are you going to prevent Margaret from going to New York if she wants to?

WALTER: Let her go then! She'll continue her shameless life wherever she is—but you won't go.

HARRIETT: Don't you know that if she goes it's the very time she'll need me most? No, Walter, the only thing for you to do is to swallow that pride of yours and take the job Mr. Lithridge offers you.

WALTER: Accept help f-from him! I won't! No! No! I won't! [*A ring at the bell.*] Maybe she's forgotten something. Now we'll see!

HARRIETT: I warn you; I meant what I said! [*Seymour Jennison and his wife enter.*]

SEYMOUR: Julia persuaded me to come and make friends. How about it, Harriett?

HARRIETT: Shut the door.

SEYMOUR: We'll let bygones be bygones—that's my nature.

HARRIETT [*shaking his hand*]: All right, Seymour. I'd ask you two to supper, but there isn't enough in the house.

MRS. JENNISON: We've had it, thanks.

SEYMOUR: This is a terrible world. Margaret passed our house a few minutes ago in a limousine with a New York license, and do you know who the chauffeur was? Frank, the boy *I* used to have! Think of it! *He* lives in New York and *I* don't. [*Then to Walter.*] Have you decided on anything?

HARRIETT: Walter's been offered a very good job; we were talking about it when you came in.

SEYMOUR: That so? Pretty quick work, isn't it? I've got something too—looks big. If that's so, I suppose I can expect my rent before long.

WALTER: Rent?

SEYMOUR: Sure—for the house.

WALTER: Oh!——[*Takes a step toward desk.*]

SEYMOUR: What's the matter, Walter? You ain't sick, are you?

MRS. JENNISON: What is it, Walter?

WALTER: It's nothing—nothing. I—I'm all right now.

SEYMOUR: It's that damn oil company—they're responsible for it all.

WALTER: Here's—here's the money, Seymour—the exact amount——

SEYMOUR: Well! Now tell me about the job, Walter. Is it a good one?

HARRIETT: Better than the old one—more money and a chance for advancement. I've got to attend to supper. Come in the kitchen and I'll tell you more. [*Harriett goes into the kitchen.*]

SEYMOUR: Coming, Julia? [*Goes out.*]

WALTER: They come in on you like this, and this, until there's no way to turn. You and I, Julia—if we'd married, we'd 'a' done something of use in the world.

MRS. JENNISON: Hush, Walter, I don't understand you.

WALTER: Everything I stood for—everything I lived for—everything God put me on this earth for—turns out wrong. What can I do now?

MRS. JENNISON: Whatever has happened, you must go on just the same.

WALTER: Why? Why? Why?

CURTAIN

A TOAST TO OLIVER BLAYDS*

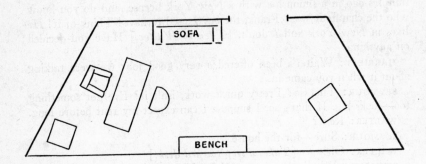

Scene: A living room.

Cast: Seven people.

[*William and Royce on stage. Enter UL, Septima with tray containing decanter and seven glasses, Marion and Oliver.*]

WILLIAM: Ah, that's right. Now, then, let me see . . . I think—Marion, will you sit here? Septima, you there, Oliver—Oliver, that's a very light pair of trousers you're wearing.

OLIVER: It's a birthday, Father, not a funeral.

WILLIAM [*with dignity*]: Yes, but whose birthday? Well, it's too late now—you sit there. Mr. Royce, you sit next to me so that I can take you up. [*Goes to bell rope behind desk.*] Now are we all ready?

SEPTIMA [*wickedly*]: Wait a moment. [*She blows her nose.*] Right.

WILLIAM: All ready? [*Oliver bangs his ankle against sofa.*]

OLIVER: Damn! Ooh! [*He rubs his ankle.*]

WILLIAM: Ssh! [*He rings bell.*] [*There is solemn silence and then Blayds, in an invalid chair, is wheeled in by Isobel. They all stand up.*]

BLAYDS: Good day to you all.

WILLIAM: Marion! [*indicating she is to come forward.*]

MARION [*going forward and kissing his forehead*]: Many happy returns of the day, Father.

BLAYDS: Thank you, Marion. Happy, I hope; many, I neither expect nor want. [*William, who is just going forward, stops for a moment to jot this down on his cuff.*]

WILLIAM: My heartiest congratulations, sir.

BLAYDS: Thank you, William. When you are ninety, I'll do as much for you.

WILLIAM [*laughing heartily*]: Ha, ha! Very good, sir. May I present Mr. A. L. Royce the well-known critic. [*Royce comes to center stage.*]

BLAYDS [*looking thoughtfully at Royce*]: We have met before, Mr. Royce?

ROYCE: At Bournemouth, sir. Eighteen years ago.

BLAYDS: Yes, I remember.

WILLIAM: Wonderful, wonderful!

BLAYDS [*holding out his hand*]: Thank you for wasting your time now on an old man. You must stay and talk to me afterwards.

ROYCE: It is very kind of you, sir. I——[*about to present book.*]

WILLIAM: Just a moment, Mr. Royce. [*He indicates Septima and Oliver.*]

ROYCE: Oh, I beg your pardon. [*He returns to his chair.*]

WILLIAM [*in a whisper*]: Septima.

SEPTIMA [*coming forward*]: Congratulations, Grandfather. [*She bends her head, and he kisses her.*]

BLAYDS: Thank you, my dear. I don't know what I've done, but thank you! [*She returns.*]

OLIVER [*coming forward*]: Congratulations, Grandfather. [*He bends down, and Blayds puts a hand on his head.*]

BLAYDS: Thank you, my boy, thank you. [*Wistfully.*] I was your age once. [*Oliver returns to his seat.*]

WILLIAM [*He holds up his glass.*]: Are we all ready? [*They all stand up.*] Blayds!

ALL: Blayds! [*They drink.*]

BLAYDS [*moved as always by this*]: Thank you, thank you. [*Recovering himself.*] Is that the Jubilee port, William?

WILLIAM: Yes, sir.

BLADYS [*looking wistfully at Isobel*]: May I?

ISOBEL: Yes, dear, if you like. William——

WILLIAM [*anxiously*]: Do you think——? [*She nods, and he pours out a glass.*] Here you are, sir.

BLAYDS [*taking it in rather a shaky hand*]: Mr. Royce, I will drink to you; and, through you, to all that eager youth which is seeking, each in his own way, for beauty! [*He raises his glass.*] May they find it at the last! [*He drinks.*]

ROYCE: Thank you very much, sir. I shall remember.

ALICE-SIT-BY-THE-FIRE*

AMY: I wonder you can touch me.

ALICE: The more you ask of your mother the more she has to give. It is my love you need, Amy; and you can draw upon it, and draw upon it.

AMY: Pray excuse me.

ALICE: How can you be so hard! My child, I am not saying one harsh word to you. I am asking you only to hide your head upon your mother's breast.

AMY: I decline.

ALICE: Take care, Amy, or I shall begin to believe that your father was right. What do you think would happen if I were to leave you to him!

AMY: Poor father.

ALICE: Poor indeed with such a daughter.

AMY: He has gone, mother; so do you really think you need keep up this pretence before me?

ALICE: Amy, what you need is a whipping.

AMY: You ought to know what I need.

ALICE: Amy, Amy, it was all Steve's fault.

AMY: You needn't expect me to believe that.

ALICE: No doubt you thought at the beginning that he was a gallant gentleman.

AMY: Not at all; I knew he was depraved from the moment I set eyes on him.

ALICE: My Amy! Then how—how——

AMY: Ginevra knew too.

ALICE: She knew!

AMY: We planned it together—to treat him in the same way as Sir Harry Paskill and Ralph Devereux.

ALICE: Amy, you are not in your senses. You don't mean that there were others?

AMY: There was Major—Major—I forget his name, but he was another.

ALICE: Wretched girl.

*From *Alice-Sit-by-the-Fire*, by James M. Barrie. Reprinted by permission of Charles Scribner's Sons.

AMY: Leave go.

ALICE: How did you get to know them?

AMY: To know them? They are characters in plays.

ALICE [*bereft*]: Characters in plays? Plays!

AMY: We went to five last week.

ALICE [*Wild hopes spring up in Alice's breast*]: Amy, tell me quickly, when did you see Steve for the first time?

AMY: When you were saying good-by to him this afternoon.

ALICE: Can it be true?

AMY: Perhaps we shouldn't have listened; but they always listen when there is a screen.

ALICE: Listened? What did you hear?

AMY: Everything, mother! We saw him kiss you and heard you make an assignation to meet him here.

ALICE: I'll whip you directly, but go on, darling.

AMY [*childishly*]: You shan't whip me. [*Then once more heroic.*] As in a flash Ginevra and I saw that there was only one way to save you. I must go to his chambers and force him to return the letters.

ALICE [*inspired*]: My letters?

AMY: Of course. He behaved at first as they all do—pretended that he did not know what I was talking about. At that moment, a visitor; I knew at once that it must be the husband; it always is, it was; I hid. Again a visitor. I knew it must be you, it was; oh, the agony to me in there. I was wondering when he would begin to suspect, for I knew the time would come, and I stood ready to emerge and sacrifice myself to save you.

ALICE: As you have done, Amy?

AMY: As I have done. [*Once more the arms go around her.*] I want none of that.

ALICE: Forgive me. [*A thought comes to Alice that enthralls her.*] Steve! Does he know what you think—about me?

AMY: I had to be open with him.

ALICE: And Steve believes it. He thinks that I—I—Alice Grey—oh, ecstasy!

AMY: You need not pretend.

ALICE: What is to be done?

AMY: Though I abhor him I must marry him for aye. Ginevra is to be my only bridesmaid. We are both to wear black.

ALICE: You are sure you don't rather like him, Amy?

AMY: Mother!

ALICE: Amy, weren't you terrified to come alone to the rooms of a man you didn't even know? Some men——

AMY: I was not afraid. I am a soldier's daughter; and Ginevra gave me this. [*She produces a tiny dagger. This is altogether too much for Alice.*]

ALICE: My darling! You do love me a little, Amy, don't you?

AMY: Yes, yes.

ALICE: You don't think I have been really bad, dear?

AMY: Oh, no, only foolish.

ALICE: Thank you, Amy.

AMY: What are we to do now, dear mother?

OTHELLO*

OTHELLO: Give me a living reason she's disloyal.

IAGO: I do not like the office:
But sith I am enter'd in this cause so far,
Prick'd to't by foolish honesty and love,
I will go on. I lay with Cassio lately,
And being troubled with a raging tooth,
I could not sleep.
There are a kind of men so loose of soul,
That in their sleeps will mutter their affairs:
One of this kind is Cassio:
In sleep I heard him say 'Sweet Desdemona,
Let us be wary, let us hide our loves';
And then, sir, would he gripe and wring my hand,
Cry 'O sweet creature!' and then . . .
. . . 'Cursed fate that gave thee to the Moor!'

OTHELLO: O monstrous! monstrous!

IAGO: Nay, this was but his dream.

OTHELLO: But this denoted a foregone conclusion:
'Tis a shrewd doubt, though it be but a dream.

IAGO: And this may help to thicken other proofs
That do demonstrate thinly.

OTHELLO: I'll tear her all to pieces.

IAGO: Nay, but be wise: yet we see nothing done;
She may be honest yet. Tell me but this,

*From *Othello, The Moor of Venice*, by William Shakespeare.

Have you not sometimes seen a handkerchief
Spotted with strawberries in your wife's hand?

OTHELLO: I gave her such a one; 'twas my first gift. . . .
Arise, black vengeance, from thy hollow cell!
Yield up, O love, thy crown and hearted throne
To tyrannous hate! Swell, bosom, with thy fraught,
For 'tis of aspics' tongues!

IAGO: Yet be content.

OTHELLO: O, blood, blood, blood!

IAGO: Patience, I say; your mind perhaps may change.

HER HUSBAND'S WIFE*

IRENE: There they go! [*Following to the French window.*] Look at them—before my very eyes, and on my birthday, too. You see he's forgotten.

UNCLE: She isn't exactly dowdy, is she?

IRENE: Dowdy, dowdy! Why—she—she's a viper, I tell you, a viper!

UNCLE: My poor Irene!

IRENE: She's clever. Yes, she's clever, but she's made one mistake. She showed me that she's clever and it's not yet too late.

UNCLE: Why, my dear girl!

IRENE: You think I'd let that woman marry my husband?

UNCLE: Eh?

IRENE: I guess not!

UNCLE: But I thought——

IRENE: But don't you see I didn't know?

UNCLE: What, that she was attractive?

IRENE: Oh, it isn't that, it isn't that, it's the deceit—the underhandedness of the creature. She came to me looking like a heartbroken little sparrow. I took her in——

UNCLE: And she took you in?

IRENE: And pitied her and now she turns out a regular bird of paradise.

UNCLE: First she was a viper and now she's a bird.

IRENE: Well, so she is. But viper—or—or——

UNCLE: Or bird——

IRENE: Or bird—she shall never, never marry my husband! [*Goes to settee and sits determinedly.*]

UNCLE: I don't see how you're going to prevent it.

IRENE: You'll see.

UNCLE: Besides, it's all arranged. You persuaded her against her own better judgment.

IRENE [*rises*]: Don't remind me of it.

UNCLE: And you just turned Richard against her.

IRENE: I?——You know very well it was you who did it.

UNCLE: I like that. When I told him she•was engaged you said, "Oh, yes, Richard, she told me so herself." And when he asked if it was some one he knew, didn't you say, "Yes, I believe so, isn't he, Uncle John?"

IRENE: *She happened to be driving by!* Yes, yes, yes, to be sure. Uncle John, you're not really set upon this—this thing, are you?

UNCLE: What thing, my dear?

IRENE: You wouldn't mind if this—this arrangement I made with Emily were broken off?

THE CASSILIS ENGAGEMENT*

[*Ethel, left alone, sits scowling furiously at the carpet and biting her nails. There is a considerable pause, during which her rage and weariness are silently expressed. Then Geoffrey and Mabel enter, quite cheerful, in riding things. They make a curious contrast to the almost tragic figure of sulkiness which meets their eyes.*]

GEOFFREY: Hullo, Ethel! There you are, are you?

ETHEL: You can see me, I suppose.

MABEL: We didn't get our ride after all.

ETHEL: Didn't you?

MABEL: No. Basil has strained one of his sinews, poor darling. He'll have to lie up for a day or two.

GEOFFREY: Isn't it hard luck? It would have been such a glorious day for a ride. We were going round by Long Winton and up to Tenterden's farm and——

ETHEL: You needn't trouble to tell me. I don't want to hear. [*There is an awkward pause after this explosion.*]

MABEL: I think I'll go up and change my habit, Geoff. [*Geoffrey nods, and Mabel goes out. Geoffrey after a moment goes up to Ethel, and lays a hand gently on her shoulder.*]

GEOFFREY: What is it, Ethel? Is anything the matter?

ETHEL: Please don't touch me.

GEOFFREY: Something has happened. What is it?

ETHEL: Nothing's happened. Nothing ever does happen *here*. [*Geoffrey tries to take her hand. She pulls it pettishly away. He slightly shrugs his shoulders. A long pause. He rises slowly and turns towards the door.*]

ETHEL: Geoff.

GEOFFREY: Yes.

ETHEL: I want to break off our engagement.

GEOFFREY: My dear girl!

ETHEL: I think it would be better. Better for both of us.

GEOFFREY: Might one ask why?

ETHEL: For many reasons. Oh, don't let us go into all that. Just say you release me and there's an end.

GEOFFREY: My dear Ethel. What *is* the matter? Aren't you well?

ETHEL: I'm perfectly well.

GEOFFREY: I don't think you are. You look quite flushed. I wish you'd take more exercise. You'd be ever so much better.

ETHEL: Geoffrey, you're simply maddening. Do please understand that I know when I'm well and when I'm ill. There's nothing whatever the matter with me. I believe you think everything in life would go right if only everyone took a cold bath every morning and spent the rest of the day shooting partridges.

GEOFFREY: Well, there's a lot in that, isn't there?

ETHEL: Rubbish!

GEOFFREY: It's not that silly business about the riding again, is it?

ETHEL: Oh no! no! *Please* believe that I'm not a child and that I know what I'm saying. *I want to break off our engagement.* I don't think we're suited to each other.

GEOFFREY: This is rather sudden, isn't it?

ETHEL: How do you know it's sudden?

GEOFFREY: But isn't it?

ETHEL: *No.* It's not.

GEOFFREY: Ethel, has my mother . . .?

ETHEL: Your mother has nothing whatever to do with it.

GEOFFREY: She hasn't said anything?

ETHEL: Your mother has been everything that's kind and good. In fact, if it hadn't been for her I think I should have broken it off before. But I didn't want to hurt her.

GEOFFREY: Ethel you mustn't come to a decision like this hastily. You must take time to consider.

ETHEL: Thank you. My mind is quite made up.

GEOFFREY: Still, you might think it over for a day or two—a week, perhaps. It—it wouldn't be fair of me to take you at your word in this way.

ETHEL: Why not?

GEOFFREY: You might—regret it afterwards.

ETHEL: You're very modest!

GEOFFREY: Oh, I'm not vain enough to imagine that you would find anything to regret in *me*. *I*'m a commonplace fellow enough. But there are other things which a girl has to consider in marriage, aren't there? Position. Money. If you broke off our engagement now, mightn't you regret these later on, however little you regret *me?*

ETHEL: Geoff, dear, I'm sorry I hurt you. I didn't mean to. You're a good fellow. Far too good for me. And I know you mean it kindly when you ask me to take time, and all that. But my mind's quite made up. Don't let's say any more about it.

GEOFFREY: You don't love me any more, then?

ETHEL: No. I don't love you any more. Perhaps I never did love you really, Geoff. I don't know.

GEOFFREY: I loved *you,* Ethel.

ETHEL: I wonder.

GEOFFREY: You know I did.

ETHEL: You thought you did. But that's not always the same thing, is it? Many a girl takes a man's fancy for a moment. Yet people say one only loves once, don't they?

GEOFFREY: Ethel . . . I don't know how to say it. . . . You'll laugh at me again. . . . But—you're sure you're not doing this on *my* account?

ETHEL: On *your* account?

GEOFFREY: Yes. To spare me. Because you think I ought to marry in my own class, as Lady Remenham would say?

ETHEL: No.

GEOFFREY: Quite sure?

ETHEL: Quite.

GEOFFREY: Then I *can't* understand it!

ETHEL: My dear Geoff, is it impossible for you to understand that I don't *want* to marry you? That if I married you I should be bored to death? That I *loathe* the life down here among your highly respectable friends? That if I had to *live* here with you I should yawn myself into my grave in six months?

GEOFFREY: Don't you *like* Deynham?

ETHEL: No. I *detest* it. Oh, it's pretty enough, I suppose, and the fields are very green, and the view from Milverton Hill is much admired. And you live all alone in a great park, and you've horses and dogs, and a butler and two footmen. But that's not enough for *me*. I want *life,* people, *lots* of people. If I lived down here I should go blue-mouldy in three weeks. I'm town-bred, a true cockney. I want streets and shops and gas lamps. I don't want your carriages and pair. Give me a penny omnibus.

GEOFFREY: Ethel!

ETHEL: Now you're shocked. It *is* vulgar, isn't it? But *I*'m vulgar. And I'm not ashamed of it. Now you know.

GEOFFREY: It's all over, then?

ETHEL: All over and done with. I surrender my claim to everything, the half of your worldly goods, of your mother's worldly goods, of your house, your park, your men-servants and maid-servants, your aristocratic relations. Don't let's forget your aristocratic relations. I surrender them all. There's my hand on it.

GEOFFREY: Don't, Ethel.

ETHEL: My dear Geoff, you don't mean to say you're *sorry!* You ought to be flinging your cap in the air at regaining your liberty. Why, I believe there are *tears* in your eyes! Actually tears! Let me look.

GEOFFREY: You don't suppose a fellow *likes* being thrown over like this, do you?

ETHEL: Vanity, my dear Geoff. Mere vanity.

GEOFFREY: It's *not!*

ETHEL: Geoff, do you *want* our engagement to go on? Do you *want* to marry me still? Do you *love* me still? No, Geoff. Think before you speak. On your honour! There, you see! Come, dear, cheer up. It's best as it is. Give me a kiss. The last one. And now I'll run upstairs and tell mother. Poor mother! Won't she make a shine!

X

Rhythm *

A. RHYTHMIC EXPERIENCE

RHYTHM IS the experience that we receive when a sequence of impressions, auditory or visual, has been ordered into a recurrence of accented groups. This experience is marked by a willingness on our part to adjust ourselves emotionally and muscularly so as to conform with the accented groups we see or hear. Dependent upon the intensity of the impressions our experience is expressed by degrees of emotional and muscular reaction ranging from pure inner feeling to bodily movement.

Two special features are common to all rhythms—vitality and power of attraction. The pulsing quality in rhythmic experience is related to two fundamental life processes in nature. One is the beating of the heart, and the other is the breathing of the lungs. Both these function in a rhythm of expansion and contraction which follow in endless sequence. Things that are rhythmic, therefore, are associated with these processes, and so we speak of their vitality.

Whatever the rhythmic experience, it is marked by an "effortlessness" and ease which are impossible to resist because they, somehow, seem to persuade us to fall in with them. The secret of our aesthetic pleasure in rhythmic experience has probably a more practical basis than we suspect, for rhythm seems to satisfy the natural longing for progressive movement which is ordered rather than chaotic and haphazard. To fall into rhythm with something represents an adjustment and an adaptation for which most of us are very grateful. Since we seem to be naturally inclined toward it, we speak of its power of attraction.

*Unfortunately, at the time of his death the author had not completed his chapter on *Rhythm*. Since it is a unique contribution, it was deemed advisable to retain it in semi-outline form as it here appears rather than to ask one of his colleagues to expand it.

When we see a rhythmic performance on stage, we become aware of a human organism in rhythm with his surroundings and performing with ease that which seems complicated. It becomes an example for us that we are willing to follow whole-heartedly, and so we find our rhythms conforming with those of the performance on stage either in the matter of feeling or in that of actual physical movement. The sensation of pleasurable surprise with which we discover this fact is one of the joys of rhythmic experience.

B. How Rhythm of a Play Is Determined

Each play has a fundamental rhythm of its own which is determined by

1. RHYTHM OF THE LINES OF THE SCRIPT ITSELF

This is the fundamental determinant. If the lines are not written within the contained rhythm of the situation, the characters, the locale, etc., the director's problem of blending the whole into that rhythm becomes great. Rhythm of comedy dialogue, for example, must be clear cut and must allow for proper pointing, timing, etc.

2. RHYTHM OF THE LOCALE AND ATMOSPHERE

Each locality and country has a distinctive rhythm. Rhythm conveys race and nationality. Every nation moves in its own individual rhythm. This should be definitely determined in studying a play in which racial or national characteristics are particularly important. Consider Negro plays, Chinese plays, Russian plays. Catching the rhythm of the race and nationality is especially important when the play is being acted by persons of another race or nationality.

Rhythm is one of the most important means of establishing atmosphere, that is, the times of day, seasons of the year, etc.

3. RHYTHM OF THE CHARACTERS

The characters in the play will contribute toward establishing the rhythm. For example, they may be slow thinking, slow moving, plodding, definite; or they may be quick, sharp, rapid thinking, gay. Each of these groups would establish a different fundamental beat.

C. Functions of Rhythm in a Play

Rhythm is primarily the factor that gives life to a play; that ties it together into a unified whole, coordinating action, actors, dialogue; creating an illusion; and carrying the audience along through the action of the play. Its special functions are

1. TO ESTABLISH MOOD (Rhythm, however, is only one of many ways of obtaining mood.)

This is established by the rhythmic pattern itself and largely by the placement of the accent. Examples of the general value of different rhythms are as follows:

 a. Three beats to a measure convey gentleness, smoothness, restfulness, quiet. The accent on the first beat gives a sense of formality and definiteness. The accent on the third gives a lift and a lilt to the rhythm.

 b. Four beats to a measure and its multiples convey regularity, heaviness, impressiveness.

 c. An odd number of beats to the measure, such as five and seven, convey irregularity, uneasiness, restlessness.

 d. Six beats to the measure may give a sense of grandeur when the accent is on the last beat or of excitement and tension when it is on the fifth.

2. TO CONVEY AN IMPRESSION OF LOCALE

3. TO ESTABLISH CHARACTERIZATION

4. TO CONVEY CHANGE OF SCENE OR CHANGE OF LOCALE THROUGH CHANGE IN RHYTHM

5. TO TIE TOGETHER THE ACTORS INTO A COORDINATED GROUP

6. TO TIE TOGETHER AND BLEND ALL PARTS OF THE PLAY

 a. Rhythm blends comedy scenes in tragic or serious plays and vice versa.

b. Rhythm bolsters up transitional and parallel scenes, holds interest, and ties them in with the whole.

c. Rhythm determines the timing of entrances and exits, of all movements, of interpolations, of pauses, of the building of accelerated scenes and scenes of low beat. It determines the timing of offstage noises, music used, and other such problems.

d. Rhythm ties together seemingly unrelated elements, as the groups in a naturalistic play in which no one pays any attention to anyone else.

D. APPLICATION OF RHYTHM TO A PLAY

The director will prefer to have rhythm come into his play through the unconscious reactions of his sensitive actors to the rhythm of the lines, the locale suggested by the script and the action of the play, and the characters that they are portraying. However, if rhythm does not come into the play of itself, the director must work to superimpose it. The use of music as an accompaniment during rehearsals is one method that may be used especially for rhythms unfamiliar to the cast.

I. PARTICULAR POINTS WHERE RHYTHM MUST BE MAINTAINED

Points at which he must watch the rhythm in all plays and definite methods of keeping up the desired rhythm are as follows:

a. In transitional scenes watch the rhythm, and keep the speed of the movement and dialogue in harmony with it.

b. Keep the rhythm the same throughout a scene, although the tempo changes. The fundamental rhythm of a play will flow through even the minor changes where the change of scene makes a change in rhythm essential.

c. Watch the length of pauses, determined by rhythm.

d. Watch pauses on entrances and exits. Gauge hubbub on exits according to rhythm.

e. Watch the rhythm of such movements as a rocking chair or recurring noises on or offstage and the speed of that movement or sound.

f. Watch the rhythm and speed of the dialogue.

g. Conserve height of increased speed for climax.

2. WAYS OF MAINTAINING THE FUNDAMENTAL RHYTHM

a. Person holding the stage from one scene to the next is the one to maintain the rhythm.

b. Re-establish it at the beginning of the scene with the entrance of a new character.

c. Carry through and re-establish it at the end of the scene.

d. Hold it by a stronger or louder beat than the variations.

e. Hold it by having it the rhythm of the majority.

E. Tempo

1. DEFINITION

Tempo is the speed of the rhythmic pattern, the pace at which it moves. It can be characterized as fast, slow, or medium. A change in tempo in no way changes the fundamental rhythmic pattern.

A play should contain as many variations of the fundamental rhythmic pattern as is practical. A production in which the fundamental beat is unvaried and continuously pounded at the audience is monotonous, tiresome, and uninteresting. Variations must not break or violate the fundamental beat, for that results only in a state of confusion; but they must all be based on it and must be multiples or divisions of it.

2. WAYS OF VARYING TEMPO

a. After the basic rhythm of a scene has been established, variations that are a multiple or fraction of the fundamental beat may be introduced. Certain characters will have relatively fast or slow tempos which will be revealed through movement, speech, and gesture.

b. Tempo may be varied by increasing or decreasing the note or beat value as determined by the emotional intensity of the scene. As the note value is decreased in length, the tempo is speeded up, and the intensity of the scene is increased. This use of tempo is absolutely dependent upon the basic rhythm, and the maximum and minimum development are set by the fundamental rhythm. A play of fundamentally slow rhythm will have a slower minimum than a play of fast rhythm, but it will never have so rapid a climax or maximum. This is very important in judging how high a scene should be built or how low it should be diminished or dropped.

Note also that the proportion that the different rhythms of the characters bear to the fundamental rhythm must be maintained during such changes in tempo. Change in characterization may alter this.

3. TYPES OF SCENES AND THEIR TEMPO

Where a scene begins and where it ends must always be determined in order to distribute correct proportion of the intensifying elements.

a. Parallel scenes

These usually occur at the beginning of the first act when the minds of the people on the stage are going along in the same direction. There is no conflict, mental or physical, in the actors' lines. They are usually scenes of love, of atmosphere, or of exposition. If a parallel scene comes late in the play, the director has to resort to a forced building up by movement; increased tempo; much breaking up; a very marked, sometimes stylized rhythm.

b. Scenes of conflict

In these scenes the minds and bodies of the actors are in direct conflict. They must be built up to a climactic result by breaking-up movements. These are scenes of exposition or other scenes that are based on conflict. They must be treated with increased tempo.

c. Transitional scenes

These are scenes void of dramatic action and movement that tie together two other scenes, those of entrance and exit. The even, steady beat of the rhythm is applied. These scenes are important in the matter of rhythm which ties them into the rest of the play and keeps up life and interest during them. In this way the audience is not conscious of the break between one scene and the next and is not dropping its interest in the play, even though the play has little drama at the time.

d. Climactic scenes

These are scenes of inherent dramatic, of accelerated, intensity—scenes in which the inherent emotions are increasing in intensity and building to a climax. They present the problem of building, which may be done by any or all of the following methods:

i. Increased in tempo, building it to the highest permissible by the rhythm.

ii. In voice:

Topping by differences in tone, increased volume, changes in pitch, increased intensity, increased speed. Pick up cues with greater and greater speed until speeches are overlapped and you have the highest part of the scene telescoped. (Watch telescoping in a serious play to see that it doesn't break rhythm and cause a comic effect.) Use telescoping when scenes are overwritten.

iii. In movement:

Conserve at the beginning of the scene; and then increase size of movement, speed of movement, number of people moving, and then numbers moving at once.

iv. Use increased sound of offstage noises, music, etc., letting them recur more and more frequently.

v. Use increased number of people on the stage.

Demonstration of building a scene

1. Have four people on the stage speaking successively, each one of them to say first five letters of the alphabet, then four, then three, then two, then one, as an example of increase in building.

2. Have four people on the stage take turns in delivering three letters of the alphabet so as to demonstrate the different forms of topping.

3. Have one individual take seven letters of the alphabet and say them with seven different speeds, beginning with the slowest and work-

ing up to the fastest, as a demonstration of increase in tempo by speaking the lines faster.

4. Take fifteen people offstage. Have the first one enter on the count of one. Two people enter five counts later; three people enter four counts later; four people enter three counts later; five people enter two counts later still. The instructor will count from one to fifteen. This is an example of the increased intensity that results from an increasing number of people in a scene.

5. Have a group of ten use the alphabet for speech, and build an imaginary scene using as many of the methods of building as possible.

e. Diminishing scenes

A diminishing scene is one in which the intensity is diminished slowly. This should be done by dropping off, in reverse order, the means that have been used one by one to build the scene. Doing this should not take more than approximately one-third the time that it took to build the scene.

f. Drop scenes

In a drop scene there is a sudden change from a point of high intensity to a much lower point. If a drop scene precedes a scene that builds to a climax, it helps to intensify that build. A drop scene may create emotion in an audience in that it comes so suddenly and in such great contrast to the high pitch of the scene that preceded it.

g. Suspense scenes

A suspense scene is one prolonged so as to include several rises and falls within it. It usually begins higher in intensity than an ordinary climactic scene, then drops, rises, drops, rises, drops, and rises. The nuances exist within the scene itself. The speeches upon which the suspense element depends need special attention in emphasis, and the drops can thereafter be considerably lower. The build of the final portion of the scene must be higher than any previous part, and its height of intensity must be determined by its relation to the main build of the play.

F. Results of Changes in Tempo in Rhythmic Pattern

The rhythmic pattern through its change in tempo produces:

I. VARIETY

Nuance is the shading resulting from the change and contrast in the tempo of the various scenes.

2. MAIN BUILD OF A PLAY

After the planting of the exposition, including the atmosphere of where, when, etc.; antecedent action; the main idea; the lining up of the two forces (what); the carry-over scene (how); the main struggle of the play begins.

The scenes that follow are minor climaxes which are alternated with transitional and lower scenes of low emotional intensity until the main climax or obligatory scene is reached which results in a denouement or catastrophe. These are usually diminished scenes. The increased build of the minor climaxes to the main or obligatory scene is the means by which tempo contributes to the main build of the play.

G. Diagram of the Main Build of a Play

The climaxes become longer and greater as they progress during the play. The low scenes become lower in proportion each time but never actually so low as at the first of the play. They become shorter as the play progresses. The diagram below shows the main build of a play together with the intermediate scenes.

(NOTE: The rising and dropping of emotional intensity make a graphic chart of the nuances.)

Diagram of main build of a play

The diagram below shows the comparison of structure of modern and the old four-act plays. The horizontal line rising and falling shows climax and the leading up to it. (Dotted lines, old four-act plays; unbroken lines, modern plays.)

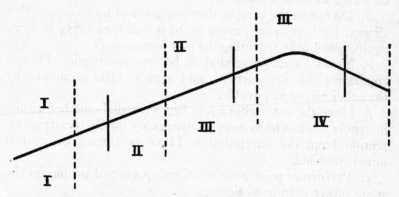

Chart showing comparison of structure between modern three-act and old fashioned four-act play

H. Methods of Treating Interpolations of Dancing and Music in a Play

1. General Principles

It is important to blend the interpolation into the rhythm of the scene so that it does not stand out as a specialty or an individual bit of entertainment. It must be part of the whole. Above all things, you must avoid applause, avoid any break between the interpolation and the play that would break the illusion and take the interpolation out of the play where it belongs.

2. Procedure

a. Accompaniment should start before the dancing or singing and continue into the dialogue. It should continue through the dialogue, through the number, and on into the dialogue again. (If music starts for dancing offstage, have it start before someone says "There's the music.") It should begin and end very quietly, trailing off unnoticed.

b. Begin song or dance quietly, smoothly, with little motion, and let it die off at the end.

c. Have the person singing or dancing or playing begin definitely in a weak area and position. Dancing should also trail off into a weakened area.

d. Do not let the song or dance or piece of music stop with a climax. If there is one, come up to it and then bring it down again, possibly by repeating the first measure.

e. Never let the interpolation become spectacular. Do not emphasize any introductions, and have as little persuasion by the other actors as possible.

f. Have the other characters begin the dialogue before the interpolation is wholly over and speak up loudly to attract attention from the interpolation. Have performer begin own lines if possible.

g. Performer must bear relationship toward people on the stage rather than to audience.

h. Watch the footwear of the dancers, and be sure that it is in character and not ballet. It should be what the character would be wearing in the scene.

i. Always motivate the source of the accompaniment.

j. Keep the interpolation as short as possible.

k. Have the actors and performer get into their positions gradually during the dialogue preceding the interpolation, being sure there is not a break or silence between the dialogue and the interpolation while they get into their positions.

l. Do not use familiar music.

m. The music must fit into the rhythm of the play, the tempo of the scene, and the rhythm of the characters in the scene.

I. Exercises

a. Exercises in rhythmic pattern and connotative value

In working out the following exercises, the people on stage are to be arranged without any emotional relationship but in arbitrary design. The tempo must be the normal tempo of life and is to be kept the same throughout the exercise. The beats of the pattern must be executed in unison.

Example: Four beats to a measure with the accent on the fourth beat. Figure *A*: Position UC facing front. Action: walk three steps forward, turn facing upstage, walk three steps forward, turn facing front, etc. The turn becomes the accent.

Figure *B*: Position at R facing front. Action: arms outstretched at beginning, then fold one arm, fold other arm, extend both arms, outstretch both arms, etc. Outstretching the arms becomes the accent.

Figure *C*: Position at L facing front. Action: clap hands on a 1-2-3-4 pattern, giving the greatest stress to the fourth beat.

Figure *D*: Position DR facing UC. Action: walk from DR to UCR to DC to UCL to DL, and return by same path. Walk on a 1-2-3-4 pattern, giving the greatest stress to the fourth beat.

The four people execute each of their actions at one time, maintaining uniformity in beat. Keep the action going for one minute. Have the class give their emotional reaction to the pattern, and then have them analyze the pattern as to the number of beats and the placement of the accent.

Execute the following exercises in fashion similar to the example given; work out the design appropriate to the pattern; have the class give their emotional reaction; have them analyze the pattern.

1. Three beats to a measure with accent on the first beat.
2. Three beats to a measure with accent on the second beat.
3. Three beats to a measure with accent on the third beat.
4. Four beats to a measure with accent on the first beat, second beat, third beat.
5. Five beats to a measure with accent on the first beat, second beat, third beat, fourth beat, fifth beat.
6. Six beats to a measure with accent on the first beat, etc.
7. Seven beats to a measure with accent on the first beat, etc.
8. Eight beats to a measure with accent on the first beat, etc.
9. A measure with irregularity in the placement of the accent.
10. A measure of your own choosing with regularity in the placement of the accent.

b. Exercises in rhythm

1. The following exercises are to be devoid of any pantomimic action. The people on stage are to be arranged without any emotional relationship but in arbitrary design. The exercise should show the basic rhythm by having the larger proportion of people carrying the fundamental beat and with the other people carrying variations of that pattern. Use as many variations as possible.
Rhythms of
   a. A small-town library.
   b. A Negro hut.
   c. A farce.

d. A comedy.

e. A tragedy.

f. A city newspaper office during a big scoop.

g. A water front during a fog.

h. A street corner in a shopping district during rush hour.

i. That same street corner on Sunday morning.

j. A picnic.

k. A revival meeting.

l. A city hotel office.

m. A country store.

n. A London drawing room.

o. London Bridge at midnight.

p. Breakfast with three of the children late for school.

Have the class analyze each rhythm.

2. Each group do an original rhythm.

3. Scenes of building: These are to be abstract in design and devoid of emotional relationship. Use as many methods as possible in building.

a. Scene built and diminished.

b. Scene built and dropped.

XI

Pantomimic Dramatization

A. DEFINITION

THE VISUAL elements that the director has used so far in dramatizing a play have consisted of composition, picturization, movement, and rhythm. Now he adds the fifth fundamental element of play directing, pantomimic dramatization.

The importance of pantomimic dramatization to the performance of a play is evidenced by the psychological fact that most people are visually minded and therefore are more deeply impressed by what they see than by what they hear. This element of directing is most valuable in giving a play distinction, warmth, richness, vitality, and an illusion of life.

To arrive at a general understanding of the term pantomimic dramatization it is best to define the word "pantomime." Pantomime is action without words. By action is meant a sequence of facial expressions, gestures, hand operations, and body positions and movements that, observed from life, is used imaginatively by the actor and the director to tell something about the elements of character, situation, locale, and atmosphere of a play. If these elements are made clear without the use of dialogue, they are dramatized by pantomime. This process is called "pantomimic dramatization." It is in this particular limited sense that the term will be used in this chapter.

A wider meaning of pantomimic dramatization is the complete visual performance of a play and, as such, includes the use of composition, picturization, movement, rhythm, and pantomime to convey, without the use of words, all the elements of a play. A solo performer may dramatize a simple story by means of pantomime, movement, rhythm, and picturizing body positions. The presence of several characters in a play demands the full use of composition and picturization as well as pantomime, movement, and rhythm to convey the complete content of story, character relationships, and theme. The exer-

cises at the end of the chapter which involve a group of characters demonstrate this wider use of pantomimic dramatization.

Before proceeding to the general characteristics, application,
and use of pantomimic dramatization, it is well to point out
two things: the relation of pantomime and business to properties and the distinction between pantomime and business.

Gestures, body positions, and movements unrelated to properties are called "pantomime," or "business." They may be
related to and involve the use of properties and still be called
pantomime, or business.

Business means going through the motions of actually opening and closing doors, wrapping bundles, dialing a telephone,
writing a letter, and making other movements, gestures, and
reactions without dialogue or in synchronization with dialogue.
The old meaning of pantomime was prolonged action without
words. Pantomimic dramatization includes both business and
pantomime. All these terms will be used interchangeably in
the discussion that follows.

(Note that a particular use of the term pantomime during
early rehearsals without properties is the direction "Pantomime the business." This means that the business is to be executed without the actual use of properties.)

B. Determination of Pantomimic Dramatization

The imaginative use of good pantomimic detail comes from
an understanding and observation of life, but the springboard
for this imagination is the play. In order that we may at the
outset give free scope to our imaginative flight, we should,
when reading the play, read no further than the general title
of a scene and disregard the detailed directions of the author
regarding actions, modes of expression, descriptions of characters, etc. Thus we allow full play to our own interpretation,
imagination, and creation. Following this unrestricted visualization comes the restriction of selecting, arranging, and controlling these things visualized in terms of situation, the kind
of scene, the pacing of the play, emphasis, and the many other
controls that will be discussed in this chapter.

The springboard for our imagination, then, is the play, and the elements of the play that give it support are story, dialogue, character, locale, and atmosphere.

1. STORY

The story or any one situation will tell us that certain business is essential in the action of the play. The playwright will usually have prescribed this, but before reading his detailed description we should visualize for ourselves the elaboration of the necessary action.

Necessary business is inherent in the action: the burial of Ophelia in *Hamlet,* the shooting in *On Borrowed Time,* the departure for the Boer War in *Cavalcade,* the incoming returns the evening of election in *Abe Lincoln in Illinois.* These are the obvious examples of business prescribed by the story or the content of the scene. There are instances, however, where business inherent in the action is the creation only of the director's imagination. For example, in the second act a character gives the summary of a book that he has just read. We have here a suggestion for business that might be given this character in the first act, that is, the reading of this book. For use of business in one act, look for suggestions in other acts through which you might create continuity.

Suggestions for business may come from actions that are happening offstage and to which the situation on stage may be directly related, though at the moment no reference to it is made in the dialogue. A murder by poisoning is being committed upstairs. We are to learn about this later on in the scene, but at the actual moment of the deed one of the characters on stage knows what is taking place. Immediately we have suggestions for pantomimic business to give this character in the run of the dialogue on stage. Such use of pantomime not only plants the seed for coming developments but adds as well a three-dimensional quality to the scene.

2. DIALOGUE

One of the greatest sources for inspiration in the creation of pantomime is the dialogue. Business suggested by the dia-

logue may be merely illustrative of the line, as the handling of
the duel scene in *Cyrano de Bergerac* where the business is suggested in the ballad that Cyrano improvises, or Hamlet's
handling of the skull in the graveyard scene, or Molière's
Mascarille showing off his costume.

We give life, clarity, and emphasis to the line by the use of
gestures or bits of business. Falstaff describing the attack on
his person will give life and humor to the description if he re-
enacts all that presumably took place. In creating such business
from dialogue we go to the imagery behind the language and
then translate this imagery in terms of action. If the language
gives no imagery, then we must seek action out of nouns and
verbs themselves.

For fuller imagination we must often create situations that
bring out or might bring out the particular dialogue. This is no
more than saying that you must picturize to the fullest the
implication of the dialogue, thereby giving that dialogue fertile
ground out of which it flowers.

3. CHARACTERS

Characters offer us an abundance of possibilities for business. Their external traits: bearing, age, mannerisms of voice
and walk, mannerisms of gestures, costumes, and make-up;
their internal traits: background, culture, nationality, race,
beliefs, morality, state of mind, etc.—all these offer us numberless suggestions for business. It is important, however, that
such business, besides being pertinent to the character, be first
of all pertinent to the action. For a more complete study of the
creation of business from character, refer to the Intellectual
Study of the Role in Chapter III.

4. LOCALE

The scene in which the action takes place is replete with suggestions for business. Here, as always, we should visualize un-
restrictedly the possibilities offered by the locale to give us an
abundance of material from which to choose when we begin to
select, arrange, and control. Consider the possibilities offered
by these locales: an amusement park (*Liliom*), a hairdressing

parlor (*The Women*), preparing a breakfast for four in a country kitchen (*Our Town*).

5. ATMOSPHERE

The strata of society; the culture of the period; the customs, social conduct, manner of living, and fashions of people; the characteristics of a place; the time of day; the season of the year—these are the many sources from which we draw for inspiration of business. Whether a play belongs to a historical period or is modern in setting, the consideration of atmosphere is inherent in each situation. When the atmosphere is that of our own time and place, we enrich our imagination through observation of life. However, to capture the atmosphere of foreign lands and periods in history we must study the general characteristics of these lands or historical periods by studying their arts, culture, modes and manners, and literature.

Exercises

Using the plays suggested above or plays of your own choosing:

1. Find instances of business inherent in the action. Write out an elaboration of the action without reference to the author's detailed description.

2. Find passages of dialogue where use of gestures and bits of business will give life, clarity, and emphasis to the lines. Act out these passages, using your own imaginative contributions.

Act out, using your own imaginative contributions:

a. Falstaff describing the attack on his person in Act II, Scene 4, of *Henry IV, Part I.*

b. Cyrano's improvised ballad in the opening duel scene.

c. Hamlet's handling of the skull in the graveyard scene.

d. Mascarille showing off his costume in Molière's *The Affected Young Ladies.*

3. Write out an elaboration of the possibilities for business of a character in a play that you have studied.

4. Find instances of locales that offer possibilities for imaginative contributions of business. Write out an elaboration of the business.

Consider the possibilities offered by these locales:

a. The amusement park in *Liliom.*

b. The hairdressing parlor in *The Women.*

c. The country kitchen in *Our Town.*

Write out in full your contributions.

5. Find instances in plays where the atmosphere—customs, society, fashions, season, time, etc.—is necessary to the complete realization of the scene. Write out in detail the business that you would use to achieve this atmosphere.

C. CONTRIBUTIONS OF PANTOMIMIC DRAMATIZATION TO THE PLAY

Once he has given full power to his interpretation, imagination, and creation of pantomime from the play, the director, in plotting the business, should keep in mind the special contributions that use of pantomime gives the play.

1. ESTABLISHMENT OF SITUATION

Obviously, pantomime establishes the situation. Just as the director is able to establish this rhythmically, so, too, through pantomime he can plant definite facts that an audience is eager to know about the play either at the opening or in the later development of each scene.

Much of the opening situation of an act or scene can be expressed through details of pantomimic business which will tend to make the exposition of the situation much more vivid.

2. ESTABLISHMENT OF CHARACTER

The first impressions of a character in the first scene in which he is revealed are most important to the audience. Drawing from the wealth of material that they have gathered from the intellectual study of the role, the director and actor should establish at the outset the delineating marks of the character.

It is important to say here that many of the internal traits of a character are revealed from the development and unraveling of the story. As suggested in the study of his role, the actor should know the appropriate time to perform such and such a bit of revealing business or such and·such a gesture or expression that will enrich and give progression to his characterization. This is most important for conservation and variety. In the handling of amateurs the director will discover that a more convincing performance results from giving them "something to do."

The working out of characteristic behavior and action cannot be overemphasized, for it is a contributing factor to the life of the production. Although the beginning director should plan on paper his positions and movements, he should not become too set in his ideas of how he wants a scene to be played, for he will often receive ideas for business and interpolation from what his actors contribute. In the course of rehearsal, good actors begin to "feel their parts" and often insert bits of detail that are exactly right. The director should keep a sharp lookout for this, especially since the actor may make the interpolation quite unconsciously. Such give and take between actor and director is an ideal relationship. In this way the richest character detail is developed, and a director should stimulate his cast to make such creative suggestions.

3. ESTABLISHMENT OF LOCALE

At the beginning of a scene, the locale should be immediately established. Pantomimic detail is one important means of achieving this. The richness of such pantomime is vital to the illusion of the play. It gives a conviction of reality, showing the people as living in a place that has the feel of life and not merely acting in front of a set to which they have no relation. This relationship should be incorporated into the action of the play.

4. ESTABLISHMENT OF ATMOSPHERE

It is impossible to establish place without qualifying it in some way with atmosphere. Let us take as an example the locale "city street." Now let us give it atmosphere. Let us qualify this street. It is nightfall in the heart of Algiers; the temperature is stifling; the streets are empty except for one or two furtive figures which scurry from one doorway to another. Now we change the facts to New York, just before Christmas, Fifth Avenue, Saturday about three in the afternoon, snow falling; we could continue to qualify this locale in terms of all that atmosphere implies regarding strata of society, historical period, etc. Or the street might be a city street in the play *Julius Caesar* or in *Dead End* or again in the Restoration tragedy *Venice Preserved*. We immediately sense here how important atmosphere is in arriving at that distinctive quality which gives our play fullness, maturity, and color.

5. AID IN ESTABLISHING KIND OF PLAY

The use of pantomime helps to establish the kind of play. This is not the place nor is it within the scope of this book to go into an analysis of the four main types of play. But a few words are necessary to distinguish the kind and quality of pantomimic business that each type, irrespective of style, demands.

a. Tragedy

Since the emotional contact between audience and play is strongest in tragedies and serious dramas, and since the characterization is at its highest development, we find that we must use business that is simple, direct, honest, and less developed than in the other kinds of play. Our attention must go to the dramatic significance of the character or dialogue, and whatever business is used must not attract attention in itself but must be used as a further means of clear delineation. We must not spend time in the details of business but must choose only the significant and essential.

b. Comedy

In comedy we have a more objective point of view; laughter needs objectivity. The amount and kind of business varies inversely with the comedy's intellectual value. In high comedy the business is apt to be small, unimportant, and arbitrary; there will be great selectivity and precision. As our comedy becomes broader, so will our business assume greater and greater and greater proportions. We must remember, however, that today situation by itself hardly ever gets a laugh, at least with the more sophisticated audiences. The laugh today comes from the meaning of the line, or it may come from a gesture if that gesture speaks as a line of dialogue. What carries today is the suggestion and not so much the actuality of doing. The basis for business must have been motivated.

c. *Melodrama*

Here we must distinguish between the old melodramas and the new. Though melodramas are more or less the externals of tragedy with emphasis in situation, today ideas and character are beginning to replace the teasers of the old melodramas, as in *Petrified Forest, Post Road, Kind Lady,* and *Night Must Fall.* Business in melodrama will be realistic, carefully executed, and deliberate. It will be used primarily to strengthen the situation rather than characterization. In mystery plays we shall find much use of "plants" to foreshadow things to happen and in the suspense scenes much use of teasers to build up the suspense and anticipation.

d. *Farce*

Farce like melodrama is based on situation. It has the externals of comedy and is emphatic in antics and not language or character. Today, however, we find that farce cannot be sheer tomfoolery; it must have a purpose, preferably satiric. The true farce like *A Full House, Murray Hill, Boy Meets Girl, A Pair of Sixes* will have business that is exaggerated, lively, and done in broad strokes. Farce is a play of situation where the timing of the business should allow no time for thought. The business is created solely from emotional reactions. Much used in farces are gags—bits of business not intrinsic to the action but put in merely for their ability to provoke laughter.

So far we have listed the specific elements of locale, character, and the like that are benefited by pantomimic detail. Now let us turn to the more general over-all contributions of pantomime.

6. CONTINUITY

This special contribution to the script comes from the fact that our pantomimic dramatization is, as we said, based on the observation of life. This makes the action of the play recognizable as truthful and akin to life. The reason for this lies in the fact that careful observation results in a natural sequence of action, and this brings continuity to the behavior of the actors throughout the playing of the various scenes. Continuity is often referred to as "follow-through." Good pantomimic business is never without this element which is dependent upon several factors:

a. Motivated movement

As indicated in a previous chapter, stage movement should be filled with the sense of "reason why." In other words, the movement must be executed with a purpose. A cross is made to look out of a window, to pick up a book, or to get away from something unpleasant. Reason for moving, whatever it may be, relates it directly to the playing of the scene, thereby giving it conviction and verisimilitude.

b. Psychological motivation

These are the relationships between the various characters responsible for movement and business. Perhaps an easy exercise will demonstrate the possibilities of follow-through: Let us send four people up on to the stage, three to remain on stage and one to go off with the following instructions: Make three entrances, the first to greet one whom you like and trust wholeheartedly; a second to greet one whom you despise; a third to greet one whom you fear and dread. After each greeting make an appropriate farewell and leave the stage. During these exercises, we in the audience must test the amount of feeling that the actor carries with him before and after he relates himself to each person. In other words he is expected to keep the psychological relationship throughout the little scene. If he grasps the person's hand and drops it immediately, he destroys the continuity and the verisimilitude of the playing. One can concentrate on maintaining the psychological motivation by entering a "sphere of influence" that extends just offstage of the entrance and the exit. This is a magic area in which the actor dares not break the contact by lapsing into indifference or lifelessness. He must carry the audience toward, right up to, and beyond the object of motivation.

c. *Tension and vitality in relaxation*

The ability to stay alert when you are not actively in a scene on stage is a delicate process but absolutely necessary to the scene's continuity. It is difficult to explain just exactly how to maintain this tension in relaxation. Most assuredly it is not a matter of "reacting all over the place." Playing with a handkerchief or a necklace, coughing, twirling mustaches, etc., during a scene belonging to someone else is an unforgivable breach of stage etiquette. Keeping alive during a scene that is not yours is more a matter of listening and breathing rhythmically to the flow of the scene around you. It is a matter of maintaining the timing of the scene so that what you do or say next is in the rhythm of what has gone before.

7. ENRICHMENT AND VITALITY

Along with continuity and truthfulness come also enrichment and vitality. A director can take a set of characters and a given locale and place them on stage with nothing further in mind than that they speak their lines clearly, move around a little, and then go offstage on cue. On the other hand he can treat these things with loving care. He can become deeply interested in the psychological behavior of his characters and in certain marked aspects of his locale and atmosphere. He searches first for the truthful facts about these things; then he turns these facts over to his imagination. There they are elaborated upon, intensified, clarified, in short, made more interesting. For example, Paul Green has written a one-act play entitled *No 'count Boy;* the locale is a Negro farmyard somewhere in the Carolinas; the play opens with a young Negro girl seated beneath a tree looking through a picture book; the time is midafternoon of summer. Most of us have an idea of what such a farmyard must be like either from actual experience or from pictures in books, on the screen, etc. Then, too, we know that all farmyards have the sound of fowl and livestock as part of their atmosphere. Now we begin to imagine a few things: It is hot; the sun is strong; the girl squints as she looks at the book; she shades her eyes, finally changes her position; flies bother her; she can dig in the dirt with a twig from the tree; she gets up to straighten her dress; maybe she begins to fall asleep in the hot summer afternoon; maybe she talks to some chickens which are fighting offstage; etc. Once we have clear in our minds the essential facts of the scene, the possibilities of pantomimic embroidery are almost infinite.

Enriching the facts this way also does much to give vitality to the script. The result is warmer, more appealing, and at the same time more significant. This point becomes especially important in the direction of the play generally referred to as "historical." In addition many of the late nineteenth century and present-day problem plays and comedy dramas have a talky, static quality which needs enlivening. In a later section we make suggestions as to how this is done.

First, however, let us examine the standards whereby we judge the pantomimic dramatization in a play.

D. Essentials of Good Business

In pantomime some easily understandable and usually fairly general fact of place, character, or situation should be given at once. The more closely characteristic it is the better. Further information should be fitted in as fast as clarity permits. Above all, there should be no false leads. Once the main point is established in the minds of the audience, subsidiary details fall into place easily; but if the audience becomes confused in the beginning, it will lose later details, and instead of entering into the play it will spend time trying to puzzle it out. We list here certain elements calculated to influence the director in his use of pantomimic dramatization.

1. APPROPRIATENESS

The matter of appropriateness is particularly important. The director must visualize the scene and be certain that his pantomimic details fit into it and to the characters and situation. Here, again, it becomes a matter of how well the director has observed life and how imaginatively he has incorporated the facts.

Suppose, for instance, that we are establishing the interior of the bunkhouse in which two of the scenes in *Of Mice and Men* take place. The locale is described as follows: walls, white-washed board and bat, floors unpainted. There is a heavy, square table and around it up-ended boxes for chairs. In addition we have these facts about character: Enter the boss. He is a stocky man, dressed in blue jeans, flannel shirt, black unbuttoned vest—ordinarily he puts his thumbs in his belt. . . . Slim enters, a tall, dark man, in blue jeans and short denim jacket—he smoothes out his crushed hat, creases it in the middle, and puts it on. . . .

All the details of this scene should be appropriate to these general indications of character, locale, atmosphere, etc. For instance, we know that these men will move and sit in a manner that is hearty, rugged, and definite. Their gestures will not be in a delicate or drawing-room vein but strong and practical. They play solitaire rather than bridge and loll about the pieces of furniture. Contrasted with these details are those which would be appropriate to the pleasant, restrained atmosphere of *Candida*.

2. NATURALNESS

This essential of good business is closely related to the degree of realism in which the play is to be expressed. In the typical modern production there is as a rule a high degree of reality, and we expect that business to be as "natural" as possible. Naturalness can be attained by consideration of the continuity and follow-through of which we spoke in the previous section. In doing the exercise we compared maintaining follow-through with keeping the spell of the sphere of influence. Another analogy might be that of the animated cartoon in which each individual picture is one tiny step further in the direction of the completed action. When this is not carefully worked out, there are disconcerting and unlifelike "jumps" in the continuity; the result is unnatural.

The importance of the furniture arrangement in affecting the naturalness of the business is discussed later.

3. RICHNESS OF DETAIL

The amount of imagination with which a director presents the facts of locale, atmosphere, and character contributes that essential of good business which is richness. We have discussed the possibilities of enriching the scene in which a girl is reading beneath a tree. Much of the detail that we can imagine may by superfluous for our special needs, since there is always the possibility of cluttering the scene. We speak a little later of controlling the imagination.

4. PRECISION

So often, and especially in the case of amateurs, there is a blurred and indecisive quality to the individual performances. This is usually due to indefinite and hurried strokes in executing pieces of business. Both the director and the actor should have a clear and concise understanding of what the business is and should then polish and refine it until the result is definite and clean cut and unvarying from performance to performance.

There is much in this chapter on pantomime that is intimately bound up with the theory of acting. Taking the subjective approach, it is possible to execute a piece of business with precision by having a definite understanding of what is to be done. Complete understanding of what is being done, however, may result (especially in the directing of amateurs) in business that is true but, as we say, too small to "carry." Part of making business precise lies in the technique of making it larger than life. This must not be confused with exaggeration of detail which begins to be unrealistic. If we recall from experience the deft but precise movements of the expert bartender or seamstress or typist, we realize that because they are so proficient in their field what they do seems unusually clear and a little larger than normal activity. This is due in part to the complete absence of unnecessary intermediate steps. The matter of rehearsing an actor in a piece of business should tend to make him an "expert" at what he does with similar results.

Another point important for the precision of business is the matter of timing the action with the lines of dialogue so that neither are blurred. Usually a piece of business, unless it is very small, comes before or after the delivery of the line unless it is intended that the line be "thrown away." Cigarettes may be lighted, books read, furniture dusted, Christmas trees trimmed, etc., during mere "Yes, sirs" or "No, ma'ams" or "I'll see" and unimportant lines of this nature. Yet the moment something is said that has to do with plot or character, that is, something that affects the advancement of the play, all business must be subordinated or stopped entirely.

5. RHYTHMIC APPROPRIATENESS

A special consideration must be given to the amount of pantomime that is appropriate to the over-all rhythm of the play, to the tempo of the individual scenes, and to the rhythms of character, locale, and situation, etc. Over-all business of the characters in a comedy will have a different rhythm from that in a tragedy, although perhaps the characters are given the identical business to do. Within the play itself, the change of tempo affects the amount and kind of business. Therefore, although much business may be found in the first fifteen minutes of a play, it diminishes rapidly as the tempo of the scenes picks up. Detailed business will invariably slow up the tempo.

6. PROPORTION

Closely related to the rhythmic appropriateness of pantomime is its proportion. Proportion of pantomime is controlled by the kind of scene. Parallel scenes, transitional scenes, and the like should be made rich and interesting with pantomime. As a scene builds, business must be diminished, for it tends to slow up a scene and defeat the climax.

7. CONTROL

"Imagination," says Stanislawski in his book *An Actor Prepares,* "creates things that can be or can happen, whereas fantasy invents things that are not in existence, which never have been or will be." As we have hinted all along, imagination works to combine all the possible memories that we have of fact—in other words, the things that can be or can happen.

The director's ability to recall and to present this recollection in a provocative manner is imagination at its best. Every actor who has to perform a stage death uses his imagination; the more vivid and realistic the death the more details or combination of details must the actor be able to recall from his memory. Many directors whose plays are laid in the South Seas or in the arctic must recall what hottest August or coldest January was like and proceed from there to the workings of the imagination. In all these cases, fact must act as the springboard for the imagination.

To speak of controlling the imagination does not contradict our emphasis on richness of detail. But definite problems arise in the unrestrained use of detail in which a play can be swamped by an overactive imagination. A certain recognizable convention, or norm, is absolutely demanded by an audience. Furthermore, every attempt should be made to avoid the fantastic, unless, of course, the play calls for such effects. Unrestrained imagination tends to go in these two directions: toward an overabundance of detail or toward the introduction of fantasy. In either case the results are confusing.

8. INTERESTING GROUND PLAN AND SETTING

Essential to good business are an interesting and practicable ground plan and setting. As in the case of the business, a director should first plan out his setting with complete freedom of the imagination, disregarding the directions of the author. Later the author's ideas about the setting added to those of the director should make possible a richer and more interesting one than if the director had slavishly followed what had been suggested. The final selection, rearrangement, and control come from a consideration of the characters living there, the kind of play, the locale, and the atmosphere.

Furthermore, the director may find that the action calls for two or three important elements that need to be stressed. These elements may be particularly expressive of the locale or the character of the people, or they may be essential in the action, but in all cases the stressed elements must be properly placed as to action.

The director should be very particular not only about the exact layout of the stage setting but about the offstage surroundings as well, for the development of business is dependent both upon the setup on stage and upon where the characters come from and where they go. From his study of climactic movements and general patterns of the important scenes, the director decides where the windows, doors, and furniture can be placed most advantageously. In this respect the arrangement of all these elements should be created for movement. Arrangements that force actors to follow complicated movements or interfere with the action or hem in the characters are definitely bad.

The play that is set outdoors or in an abstract realm of levels and platforms gives the director a certain amount of freedom in preparing a ground plan, since there is an irregularity to nature and an indefiniteness to the abstract. The instant that he goes indoors, however, he is dealing with walls and is faced with the problem of introducing variety in the well-known layout of the average home. Therefore, as a conclusion to this section devoted to the essentials of good business, let us set down certain facts that govern the arrangement of the furniture in the modern play.

a. General principles

Great care should be taken to avoid the conventional placement of a sofa on one side of the stage and a table and a few chairs on the other. For years this arrangement constituted the main form of the stage furnishings; but it was overdone and has become timeworn and conventionally unreal.

A good principle is to make your stage look as much like a real room and the placement of furniture in that room as natural as possible. Furniture should be placed in relation to the walls. If these walls happen not to be a square box set but on a triangular formation, then it must be arranged in relation to this form. This means that sofas cannot be placed casually on the right or left center of the stage but must bear relationship to a fireplace (either perpendicular or parallel to it), a table, a wall, or a window, since that is the way sofas are placed in a real house. Chairs should not be placed facing the audience but in relation to other chairs or other pieces of furniture or to the room itself. One of the best ways to arrive at a good stage setting is to draw all four sides of a room and arrange the furniture as it would be in that room. Then remove one of the walls and see if, with a slight readjustment, it is not suitable for a stage setting. This will lead to irregular and unusual form. One can take a room in a house that he knows, or one can take pictures from magazines. Remember that in the final adjustment and selection the necessities to be kept and stressed are dictated by the action of the play.

b. *Plotting the ground plan*

The furniture on a stage should be placed in groups, each one constituting an acting area. A group is made up of one main piece of furniture like a sofa and the small pieces that go with it; for example, there can be a footstool, a floor lamp, an end table or a rear table, a newspaper rack, or a smoking stand. Another group would be a large armchair with a side table or floor lamp by it or possibly a stool. Another example of an area would be a table with two or three chairs about it, with magazines, a bowl of flowers, or a lamp on it. Usually each stage set should have at least three areas of furniture. This allows for one or two areas that are clear. The groups of furniture should usually have places for at least two people. In the case of the sofa and the table, that is easy. In the case of the armchair, it is possible for someone to sit on the arm and have a scene with a person sitting in the chair or to sit on the stool and talk to a person in the chair. These three groups should also be placed so that a person can sit in one area and have a scene with a person sitting in another group or area. They should bear relation to one another.

c. *Distribution*

At least one group of furniture should be placed downstage, either on the left or on the right. If a fireplace is on the side wall downstage, a stool can usually be placed alongside it on which an actor can sit and join in the conversation with people in another area. Chairs downstage on the left or right do not face the audience but should be profile to it.

The best places for mantelpieces are along the side wall, because it is only when they are so placed that an actor can play looking into them and still be seen by the audience. If a fireplace is upstage along the back wall, it is difficult to use because the actor in facing the fire has to turn his back on the audience.

Windows take careful consideration. They had best be along the side wall, as it is easier to let the audience imagine what is outside them than it is to make the exterior convincing with the use of props. Furthermore, if the window is important in the play (that is, if a person has to look out of a window and describe what is outside), it is easier for him in this position to convey what he says to the audience than it is when he has his back to the audience (as he would if the window were on the rear wall).

The placement of doors we have already discussed under Movement. A set should never have a doorway that is not used. The more doors there are in a set—up to four—the easier it is for the director, because then it is possible for him to have a person enter at the most convenient point on the stage for his relation to the group. But few rooms have as many as four doors. As a matter of fact, most of them have but one or two, and, accordingly, the director should not have more doors in a set than would be likely in a room. The problems that arise when there are only one or two doors in a set revolve mostly around congestion at the door and the finding of a motivation for entering characters to get on the farther side of the stage.

d. Motivation

The director should establish each exit on the stage so that the audience will know where it leads; and he must see that the actors are consistent in always using the same exit when they are going to the particular place that that exit designates. He should be sure that every character who has left the stage by a certain door always returns by the same door unless it is clearly explained in the script why he does not. One of the best ways for a director to keep in his mind where the doors lead to is for him to draw a plan of the entire floor of which this particular room is a part. In that way he will see the relations of this room to the different exits.

Never use the spaces between the proscenium arch and the tormentors for an entrance or exit.

e. Miscellaneous detail

In addition to the two or three main areas of furniture, there are other pieces which we call trim. These are knicknacks, small tables and chairs against the walls and in the further corners of the room, which are not used for the big scenes of the play or may not be used at all, especially if the stage is large. If it is small, these chairs along the side walls and far corners may be used for the minor characters in a scene.

If one of the scenes of the play is laid at night, each area of furniture must have its own natural source of light; that is, there must be a lamp for each group unless a group is near a fireplace which will flood it with light or near wall brackets which will be sufficient motivation for the light on the group.

In arranging the furniture on a stage, one should be careful to have balance, although a symmetrical arrangement is bad and should be avoided, except where the style demands it. One can arrive at balance without symmetry by having the areas of furniture evenly distributed over the whole stage.

Careful consideration should be given to the set to make it look real and convincing in its reproduction of the place that it is supposed to represent. The more natural the arrangement of furniture the easier the directing and the more tasteful the effect.

Not only should an attempt be made to arrive at originality in the settings of one interior, but if the play has two or three sets, care should be taken to obtain a radically different arrangement of furniture for the remaining act or acts. If there is only one set, a certain amount of business and interest will result from the change of ground plan from one act or scene to another. This change may be motivated by passage of time, introduction of a new tenant, essentials of action, or design. This last may need explanation: It is often possible to obtain variety and interest in a one-set play by changing the angle of vision of the set from one act to the other. Where in the first act the main entrance was up center and the alcove at right, in the second the main entrance may be shifted to the left and the alcove to up center. Such shifting of the angle of vision should be used, however, only when the importance of a particular area or of a particular entrance, etc., may shift from one act to the other.

E. Application of Pantomimic Dramatization

The Italian Commedia dell'Arte shows of the late fifteenth and sixteenth centuries were enthusiastically received over all western Europe. "Because," to quote a contemporary critic, "they make a strong point of gesture and represent many things through action, even those who do not understand their language cannot fail to understand the subject of the piece."

This is precisely the point to keep in mind in applying pantomimic action to the play. We must pretend that the play is to be given before an audience that does not understand the language. Now this means that characters, locales, atmospheres, and situations will have to be accurately portrayed if there is to be no misunderstanding of what is taking place. We assume that there can be no explanation by word of these things and that everything must be conveyed by gesture, facial expression, and movement. Those of us who have sat through the stiff posturing and broad gesture of the usual operatic performance realize how possible it is to obtain absolutely nothing of a play's content from the acting. Here we have the use of pantomimic detail at its stock minimum. The result is, of course, a performance that, except for the delivery of the music, is at once bland and uninteresting. What we miss completely are the details of personality and of individuality—in short, something that reveals these people as possible living beings. Pantomimic dramatization supplies such details. Based on what is said or implied in the script, it represents in action the facts of character, locale, and atmosphere.

1. GENERAL PROCEDURE

A director with a good visual sense begins to see the play "in action" during his first readings. Rereading it creates in his mind more definite pictures, movements, positions, and business. These need not be connected and continuous at this time but merely high spots in the script. It is not advisable for him to become lost in details during these first readings; rather should he concentrate on the general over-all progress of the entire play.

His next step is to plot out this business more definitely with the script at his side and, as we mentioned earlier, disregarding the stage directions until later so as to allow free scope to his imagination. Inserting his own business in this way, the director does what he considers best for the interpretation of the play, and he judges this to the extent that the business is natural and appropriate to the characters, locale, and situation. At all times he must consider his use of pantomime as an element that will lend verisimilitude to the script. This tests a director's keenness of observation of people, places, and things.

In filling in a set of characters, a locale, or situation with pantomimic detail this fact becomes especially evident. First of all, he recalls from his own experience what he knows about these elements. His next step is to filter such detail through his imagination. In other words, he takes a fact and by rearranging, eliminating, heightening certain of its features produces what is more effective, more stageworthy for his particular use. This is, of course, the "rearrangement of nature" followed by any artist. Apropos of this someone has said that there can be nothing in art that was not first in life. We see how this applies directly to pantomimic dramatization in that it is the imaginative use of details that the director has first observed from life. This is in fact the keynote of the entire chapter. All our detail is drawn from the question "What would such and such a character do in such and such a locale and atmosphere?" and we make the first test of the pantomime that we use not its originality but its verisimilitude.

The greatest care should be taken by the director to control and blend his imaginative contributions so that the audience is unaware of any trick effects. Once it senses sheer acrobatics, an audience becomes suspicious and even antagonistic.

A steady concern for the over-all flow of his production will keep the director from losing his way in a maze of detail. Frequent and uninterrupted run-throughs help in the matter of keeping this perspective on the play.

2. SELECTION AFTER PACING OF PLAY

In the matter of pacing the play we may find that much of the business that we liked when we inserted it into the rehearsal may have to be taken out. This should be done unhesitatingly, since such detail cannot be of value if it harms the over-all progress of the play. The method of filling up the play with detail and selecting what is wanted when the show is paced is good, especially for beginning directors.

3. CONTROL OF BUSINESS AT OPENING OF PLAY

The play should not start at too high a pitch of business and general action, for an audience is easily bewildered at the beginning and may react unsympathetically as a result. A director should "ease" into his effects. This becomes especially important in directing farce or melodrama, where things happen quickly and suddenly. Just as at the rise of the curtain we allow the audience time to adjust itself to the rhythm of the play, so we must give it time to adjust itself to the opening of the play and avoid shocking it by gun firing, screaming, exaggerated movement and gesture, etc. Further, opening scenes are usually replete with exposition, and it is important that business keeps clear of these lines so that there will be no distraction from them.

At the beginning of a play the playwright will often have several characters on stage, including principals and minors. It is important to focus attention as soon as possible on the principals, if this is not done by the writing. They are emphasized by directing and relating the business of the minor characters to them. In a tea scene, for example, besides emphasis through composition, there can be a difference in both detail and timing in the way tea is served to the main characters.

Moreover, depending on the scene, the principals may be served first or last.

In a scene of this kind, the attention is at first general. Then out of this diffused attention we gradually bring our focus to the main characters. The opening scene in Rostand's *Chantecler* offers an excellent example of this treatment from diffused to specific attention.

4. CONTROL OF BUSINESS AT MIDDLE OF PLAY

Here, where conflict is under way and the drama of the situation holds by its own intensity and interest, we must be careful not to cloud such scenes of conflict with too much business. The business must be apportioned, usually not more than two incidents to a page of script. In a comedy or farce, where business is introduced for laughs, it should either be accumulative in its effect, leading up to one big laugh, or else it should be apportioned. For example, too much business for laughs in any one situation at the beginning or middle of a play will eventually hurt the play by tiring the audience or by making the end tame in contrast.

In climactic scenes as the situation builds in emotional tension the amount of pantomimic detail should be reduced, except in suspense scenes where the build depends directly on the use of teasers; but care must be taken to avoid losing the start of a suspense scene by too much emphasis on the unemphatic.

5. CONTROL OF BUSINESS AT END OF SCENES

The end of a scene should receive a finishing touch of pantomime to tie it in with the whole progression of the scene. This can be done by introducing a deft bit of appropriate business.

6. CONTROL OF BUSINESS ACCORDING TO STYLE

We mentioned earlier that the kind of play controls the kind and quality of business used. We shall not elaborate on this aspect of control any further but refer you to that section. There is, however, one other consideration that enters into the control of business, and that is style. Style in playwriting and directing is a matter of the degree of realism based on what is most real to us today. Therefore, there is a scale that begins at photographic realism or highly detailed naturalism and ends with the highly selected, more abstract forms or ideas of things. The so-called photographic realism is coincident with the style known as naturalism and appears in such plays as *Dead End, Street Scene, The Lower Depths.* Pantomime done in broad, undetailed, formalized strokes is usually identified with classicism and more recently with expressionism. Business of this kind appears in the plays of the Greek dramatists and in those of Racine and Corneille. Expressionistic drama, such as *Within the Gates* and the *Adding Machine,* tends to mechanize the business into an even more formal pattern. Somewhere in between these two styles, we find the sweep and flourish of detail that is identified with the so-called romantic style, and in this we include all the Elizabethan and a large part of the nineteenth century drama. We must defer until the last chapter a more detailed discussion of this important subject of style and its relationship to the principles of directing.

7. CONTROL OF BUSINESS FOR EMPHASIS

In our application of business to a play we must take into account the fact that business reinforces a character, a line, or a movement. A sentiment of love, a burst of anger, a threat, a curse, an expression of repentance, etc., can be accentuated by immediately following it with a characterizing and appropriate bit of business.

8. CONTROL OF BUSINESS FOR LOCALE AND ATMOSPHERE

Business to establish locale and atmosphere need not be continually pounded out. After the locale and atmosphere have been clearly fixed in the audience's mind by emphasis at the beginning, in the development of the scene or act the business for such may be gradually thinned out and re-established periodically when necessary or even dispensed with altogether, as the attention of the audience is drawn into the action of the play. When the business that establishes locale and atmosphere has been carefully emphasized and controlled, dispensing with it later will not destroy the illusion of reality.

NOTE: Sound effects can do much in establishing both locale and atmosphere. However, they must not call attention to their artificiality. Rain, wind, thunder, street noises, trains, church bells, beat of drums, etc., must remain as a background to the action of the play and must be carefully timed in the play's action so that they will not drown out the delivery of lines. Sound effects often play an important part in the action of a play, as in *Liliom* and *The Emperor Jones*.

9. CONTROL OF BUSINESS RELATED TO ENSEMBLE AND IN- DIVIDUAL BUSINESS

As a play is given more and more of ensemble, general background, or, in our words, director's business, it tends to become more naturalistic. On the other hand, if the business is such that certain actors "stand out" while others recede into the shadows, there is a trend toward the arbitrary. Either of these effects is useful, depending upon the type of play to be directed. For example, plays like *Ah, Wilderness!* and *Having Wonderful Time* should be full of the ensemble business of the director. Individual business, however, high-lights the playing of plays by Oscar Wilde or Noel Coward. Actors' business is also in evidence in the "vehicle," or star, type of play such as is written for Gertrude Lawrence or Ina Claire. Some plays such as *You Can't Take It with You* call for the use of both elements. Director's business gives it the proper naturalistic, homey quality, and actor's business is, of course, essential to the individuality of the characters.

10. CONTROL OF BUSINESS RELATED TO USE OF PROPERTIES

As long as the play is placed in a realistic setting, various kinds of props can be introduced for the purpose of giving the characters a chance to do some business. The tea routine and the mixing of drinks have long been reliable stand-bys and will probably continue to be so. As for the everlasting "cigarette business," it has been said of some directors that their only ground plan is a generous distribution of cigarette boxes, matches, and ash trays. The use of properties presents again the problem of getting the director and the actor to use imagination. One is reminded of the artistry of Miss Gertrude

Lawrence and her performance in a recent play *Susan and God*.
It would be difficult to list completely the variety of means by
which she made her many scenes vital and alive—a fervid
and seemingly endless examination of the contents of her
handbag; arranging flowers, selecting one and waving it in the
breeze as the conversation progressed, finally in order to bring
the scene to a close disposing of the flower by eating part of it;
arranging and rearranging pieces of furniture; tying and un-
tying the sash of a negligee; sitting, lying, standing on the
chairs and sofas; planning a variety of coiffures in the mirror
while arguing and pleading with another character. Such business effectively executed with the lines redeems an otherwise
talky and static play.

F. Developing Business in the Historical Production and in the "Static" Play

It was stated earlier in this chapter that a director should
postpone looking at his author's suggestions for business and
detail until he has used his own imagination. Therefore, the
information in this section pertains to the directing of all plays.
There are, however, two general groups of plays that afford
him an excellent challenge in the matter of introducing business. These are the historical play and the modern static, or
"talky," play in which all the pantomimic dramatization is, in
a sense, superimposed, since there is little or no indication of it
in the script itself. Let us examine each group in order.

1. THE HISTORICAL PRODUCTION

The absence of detailed reference and stage direction in the
Elizabethan drama is often misconstrued to mean that all pantomimic business was lacking in these plays. It is difficult to believe that their popularity could have resided solely in the delivery of the language. That mere declamation would have
been criticized is evident in the remarks of a contemporary who
compared the Commedia dell'Arte performances with the
French theater in this fashion:

"There is always a happy blend of gesture and inflection with
the discourse . . . and the actors come and go, speak and act

as informally as in ordinary life. Their acting gives a far different effect of naturalness and truth from what one sees in the French theater, where four or five actors stand in line like a bas-relief at the front of the stage and each declaims his discourse in turn."

It is generally believed that business was not indicated by the Elizabethan playwright because he wrote his parts with definite actors in mind who had their individual pieces of business for which they had achieved a certain fame. This is a practice not unlike that used in the Commedia.

One of the great helps in directing a historical play is to determine whether or not there are any places where characters may sit down. This is important not only from a standpoint of composition and picturization but also because it gives to the play a note of verisimilitude. This is a familiar and human piece of business.

We have insisted all along that our pantomime is based upon an observation of life. In the historical we are faced with the problem of presenting a life that we must observe through report and document. But because these historical figures are of an age more remote than our own, they need not be the pale, wooden, impossible personalities that so often repeat their lines from the stage. It seems necessary to remind a director and actor constantly that the people that they are portraying were of flesh and blood with all the passions, faults, and virtues of present-day characters. So even though details of costume, manner, custom, even speech separate us from a Greek king or a Danish prince, still we are interested only in their similarities to us as human beings, in their character and personality, and in their response to given situations. Furthermore, they must move in a locale and atmosphere vivid and possible to conceive. Even in the types that appear in the comedies we want to know that if there is exaggeration it is the exaggeration of an actual human quality and not of something freak and impossible. The following suggestions indicate the possibilities of developing detail in the historical play which is not only rich and imaginative but human, real, plausible, and therefore lifelike.

a. Locale

The scene of action no matter how distant in time or space should have certain definite characteristics that convince an audience of its existence. Pantomimic detail will help to establish these. There are long passages in the historical play that describe accurately the setting. Pantomime can make this description more convincing. If scenery is used, as is usually the case in the modern production, then many of these passages can be deleted. In any event the interpolation of detail is important to the vividness of the surroundings. Consider, for example, *Romeo and Juliet* (Act I, Scene 1: Verona, a public place. Enter Sampson and Gregory). Without making a huge spectacle of the piece, it is important to introduce something of the activity of a public place before Sampson and Gregory begin their speeches. There may be one or two venders; one or two purchasers; a fop with his lady; groups of soldiers marching, singing, laughing; lords and ladies from court, etc.

Consider Ben Jonson's *The Silent Woman* (Act I, Scene 1: A Room in Clerimont's house. Enter Clerimont making himself ready, followed by his Page). This comedy of London manners permits the introduction of much miscellaneous detail. Here we can have servants fussing about the room, Clerimont himself viewing his person in various mirrors, etc.

In the tragedies the detail of locale is never so great as in comedy. However, even in opening a play like *Oedipus Rex* there ought to be a moment or two before Oedipus enters in which the priest and his suppliants gather about the altar. Their business will not be minutely detailed, but the effect of the locale will be enhanced if by their actions they give evidence of being before an important palace and in a holy spot which they deeply respect. Consider, for example, the possibilities of introducing a formalized dance around the altar, a gesture of blessing by the priest, an attitude of reverence toward the door through which Oedipus is about to step.

Act II, Scene 1, of *Othello* is played with the seaport of Cyprus for a locale. Much can be done in the attitude of waiting attendants to suggest such a place. A strong wind is blowing; gunfire is heard; there are shouts offstage and on. The scene builds to the arrival of Desdemona, Emilia, Iago, etc., so that as well as establishing locale, pantomime contributes to the excitement of the situation. This anticipates what we have to say in the next section. For pure locale, however, there can be business of shading the eyes, looking out to sea, wrapping cloaks firmly about the body, sitting on bales of goods, etc. In Act I, Scene 3, of *Hamlet* we are introduced into Polonius' house. Laertes and Ophelia are directed to enter. Since Ophelia is the housekeeper, it is much more interesting to discover her at a household duty and then have Laertes come in. She may be tidying up the room, watering a plant or two, perhaps mending an article of clothing.

b. Atmosphere and situation

Just as appropriate business is introduced into modern plays as reactions to murkiness, clear sunshine of a winter day, tenseness, excitement, relaxation, etc., so, too, the characters in the historical play are expected to react to conditions about them. Modern conveniences of scenery and lighting do suggest a great deal of the atmosphere and the situation, but a director must not count on these elements for emotional effects. No matter how magnificent the scenery or how significant the lighting, a performance that is bland and uninteresting puts its stamp on the whole production. Experiments have been made at the drama departments of Yale and Carnegie Institute of Technology in which true Elizabethan stages have been constructed and performances given to resemble those of Shakespeare's time. This means no change of setting for the various locales and atmospheres and requires, of course, broad, flat lighting to suggest the daylight of the courtyard theater. Effects of damp, murky dungeons; night on a battlefield; ghosts in the still of the night; splendid banquet halls, and so on depended for their atmosphere on how well the poet painted them with his words and how convincingly the actor conveyed his reactions to such places under such circumstances. These experiments provide a challenge to the imagination of both director and actor in the matter of suiting with action the words of the playwright so that an audience believes in the existence of what is so well described.

The following scenes from *A Midsummer Night's Dream* require atmospheric detail:

Act I, Scene 1: Athens. The palace of Theseus.
Act I, Scene 2: Athens. Quince's house.
Act II, Scene 1: A wood near Athens.

The atmosphere surrounding each of these scenes can be suggested by appropriate business. For instance, the attendants who usher in Theseus and his train will do so in dignified, majestic, formal manner. The company that enters Quince's house will sit, move, stumble, shout in the manner of workmen without much breeding. The woods near Athens, on the other hand, should convey the feeling of another world, and the business of the fairies and elves will be tiny, wispy, fleeting, exaggerated in detail, etc.

c. Character

We differentiated earlier between ensemble and individual business. Detail of locale, atmosphere, and situation is usually a matter of ensemble business. In other words the director inserts effects that are to suggest the background and milieu, and the actors confirm this. Of course, individual actors may put in their own suggestions, but on the whole it is a matter of ensemble effect. Individual business is important to the enrichment of character. The director should make suggestions, but he will often prefer to let an actor give what he can at first and then, only if the results are not satisfactory, inject his own ideas. With most amateurs it is almost necessary for the director to contrive something for them to do, or else they "go dead." Although individual business is important to the enrichment of character, the director must always blend the result into the script. As we mentioned earlier, some scripts demand less blending than others, for they gain their strength only from the "flash" performances of one or two of the characters.

We can get almost all our facts for character delineation by a careful examination of their descriptions in the texts themselves. For example:

Richard III: Here in the very first speech, delivered by Richard himself, we learn all that we need know about him and his relations with other people. We expect to see people recoil from him; we expect Richard's resentment of this; if we introduce a citizen or two before Clarence's entrance at the beginning of the play, we have the opportunity of setting these facts immediately. They can shrink from him, giggle at his deformity, make gibes at him when they think they are out of his hearing, etc. All this gives Richard a chance to present through action as well as word what he is like.

The Way of the World: Mirabelle's description of Mrs. Millamant in Act II, Scene II, gives an excellent suggestion of detail appropriate to this character:

"Here she comes i'faith full sail, with her fan spread and her streamers out, and a shoal of fools for tenders. . . ."

It is perfectly possible to use this as the model upon which we might base the character detail of all Restoration women. Furthermore, it suggests not only the flippancy and coquetry of these women but their costume and walk and the kind of people with whom they surrounded themselves.

d. Dramatic action from the lines themselves

Much that is rich and imaginative in detail can be obtained from close examination of the language of the play. Whenever there is opportunity to accompany the lines with appropriate pantomime, we have again that "double richness" which pantomimic dramatization brings to the production. For example, these lines indicate the possibility of action accompanying the word.

Marlowe's *Edward II:* Act I, Scene I:

EDWARD: "Throw off his golden mitre, rend his stole,
And in the channel [gutter] christen him anew."

Edward addresses these lines in derision of the hated Bishop of Coventry. Taking his cue for action from the *verbs* themselves, he can tear a part of the bishop's garment, hurl it on the floor, and give him a violent shove at the same time.

Ben Jonson's *The Silent Woman:* Act II, Scene 1:

TRUEWIT [*to Morose*]: All that is very true, sir. And then her going in disguise to that conjurer, and this cunning woman: where the first question is, how soon you shall die? [*He makes the motions of an alchemist pouring liquids from one test tube to another. Morose watches in fascination. Truewit sees this and hisses in his ear.*] Next, if her present servant love? Next, if she shall have a new servant? And how many? [*All during this Truewit acts out looking into a crystal.*]

In this example we have taken the words "conjurer" and "cunning woman" as cues for the business injected.

So much for the means of developing business in the historical play. Note how in every case we have depended upon the script to give inspiration to our imagination. This is especially so in the last mentioned procedure of seeking action in the nouns and verbs of the lines themselves. Actually we have at all times been putting into effect what Hamlet so wisely advises the Players when he says: "Suit the action to the word. . . ."

2. THE STATIC PLAY

Many plays written during the late nineteenth century are of an introspective nature. Introspection may have a talky quality such as one finds in the contemplations of Chekhov and of Shaw, or it may take the form of "mood" as in the writings of Lenormand and Maeterlinck. Those which are not introspective present a problem that was vital once but must today be treated in the interest of the characters. This being so, details of personality and situation are important. To this class belong the plays of Ibsen, Pinero, Brieux, etc.

The contemporary plays that stem from these must be treated in the same way. Examples are found in the more philosophical writings of Philip Barry such as *Hotel Universe* and *Here Come the Clowns;* the social problems of Clifford Odets; and the drawing-room problems of Rachel Crothers, Somerset Maugham, Samson Raphaelson, S. N. Behrman, and others. Very often these writers have themselves indicated elaborate bits of business, for they are aware of the necessity of supporting their characters and situations with enriching detail.

Plays of these types in which it is important to introduce business to maintain the sense of rhythmic flow and progress we call static. By this we do not mean that they are without dramatic content but that the action is of a mental and psychological nature in which the builds are gentle, far between, and not obvious. In the first place, in directing such plays, every effort is made to bring as much intensity into the builds as possible. But as we have observed by now, business drops off as a scene builds. It is rather in the scenes of exposition and transition that we take the opportunity of enlivening the script by superimposing business and bringing action to an otherwise talky or mood play. We give these scenes physical attributes or, as we said at the beginning of this chapter, an external personality.

If a play is full of mood and atmosphere, we make every effort to heighten and capitalize on all the everyday action and detail that the script will allow. For example, in Lenormand's play *Time Is a Dream* the locale is the Holland of mists and vapors. As the play proceeds, we are made to see how such an atmosphere triumphs over the happiness of the characters; the dampness and fog permeate their being; they are unable to get away; they are miserable where they are. Every line is filled with this moodiness. It is important to keep the play from becoming entirely a thin, ethereal mist. Wherever possible, everyday details of housekeeping, having tea, arranging bright flowers, making plans for a party, etc., should be emphasized so as to anchor it on this earth and give the audience a sense of relief from the everlasting mood and atmosphere.

In a play like Ibsen's *A Doll's House* it is no longer possible to emphasize the idea that a woman has a right to freedom and equality of thinking with a man. What does interest us is the kind of woman Nora is. Above all, in directing this play now, it becomes important to make her as rich and as interesting as possible. Details of her treatment of her children; of managing the household; of how she reacts to flattery, to resistance, etc., are all important to the establishment of the character. The business of locale is important, since it is Nora's world, the house in which she lives. Furthermore, Nora must set the atmosphere of each scene, since her character predominates— the way she tidies up, the greeting that she gives Mrs. Linden, and, of course, the manner in which she dances the tarantella. In all this we are emphasizing the importance of detail in order to compensate for the overabundance of idea and problem that fills the writing.

Exercises in pantomimic dramatization

These exercises are to employ a group of six to ten people. They are to be the group's idea with a leader (not a director) appointed to be in charge. Be certain that the locale and time of day are clear. The pantomimes may have a simple story, or they may be a few disconnected incidents or an atmospheric study. They should not run longer than eight minutes. The action, constantly keep in mind, which will take less than eight minutes in the pantomime, will have sufficient business to cover a forty-five-minute act. In other words, it will be much more concentrated in these exercises than it will be in a play. Do not hesitate, therefore, to overdo the amount of business. Those who comprise the audience can act as judges in suggesting what is to be eliminated.

Be sure to consider also the arrangement of the furniture as well as all the five fundamental principles of directing which must be used to convey the complete content of plot and character. If the pantomime has a story, be certain that all important characters and facts are clear and emphatic and that the story has development, proportion, build, and conclusion.

The following are intended as suggestions:

a. College boy's room.

b. Girl's boarding school after lights are supposed to be out.

c. Negro hut.

d. Overworked country housewife in a scene with her family.

e. Ship's saloon.

f. Country post office.

g. Country newspaper office.

h. City newspaper office.

i. Art exhibit.

j. Men telling after-dinner stories.

k. A tea party.

l. A dance.

m. A train.

n. A sewing party.

o. A drawing-room scene without tea, cards, or cocktails.

p. On board ship.

q. Before a funeral.

r. An informal concert.

s. Porch of a summer hotel.

t. Sitting up with the dead.

u. Getting ready for a guest.

v. A trial.

w. A rehearsal.

x. Arrival of family with flowers at a grave.

y. An automobile accident.

z. A carnival.

aa. A New York street.

bb. A country-town street.

cc. A picnic.

dd. A barbershop.

ee. Main street of a small town—noon, Sunday morning, Saturday 9 P.M.

ff. Children playing in the back yard.

gg. Lunch counter—1 P.M., 5 P.M.

hh. Hotel lobby.

ii. Sunday-school picnic.

jj. A wharf.

kk. A line waiting to get into a movie.

Each person in each group do one original pantomime. It may be a story or a bit of atmosphere. It must contain all the elements of atmosphere and locale, the correct emphasis, build, rhythm, and conclusion.

Part IV

PRODUCTION PROCEDURE

XII

Tryouts and Casting

A. TRYOUT PROCEDURE

AFTER THE play has been chosen and announced, copies of the script should be made available. When the actors have had sufficient time to read it, the director may hold either private interviews or general tryouts or a combination of both methods for casting.

1. PERSONAL-INTERVIEW METHOD

In using the personal-interview method the director should try to be as informal as possible and to do everything that he can to put the actor at ease. At first, the interview may consist of talk about the play in general, the plot, the characters, and the theme. The actor should be urged to discuss freely. Then he should be asked to read for a certain role. After a first reading, the director should make suggestions to help his interpretation. By all means, the director should hold the interview in a place that will allow the actor absolute freedom of movement and emotional expression. During the entire interview he should, without making it too obvious, study the actor and try to see him as the character in the play. This method of tryout is useful in casting a small number of parts, or it can be used after a general tryout when eliminations have been made and the number of prospective actors greatly reduced. The professional director uses the personal-interview method of casting almost exclusively.

2. GENERAL TRYOUT METHOD

The little theater or college director may find it more expedient, for the sake of impartiality and a variety of other reasons, to hold a general tryout, open to all interested. Here he first makes sure that all have read the play. If, for some reason, the script has not been made available, he may, by asking everyone to read, have the group read the play. (No one should be allowed to think that he is reading for a particular part.) In the first reading of a play it is essential that all prospective members of the cast have the opportunity to give spontaneous and uninhibited reactions to the play as a whole.

After the play has been read, the director should clear up any questions regarding the plot, theme, or style. Then he should give thumbnail sketches of the characters and answer any questions about them. Sketches or models of the scene and costume designs and ground plans may be shown to indicate the scheme of production. This creates interest and enthusiasm and helps the actors to get into the spirit of the play. An effective method of helping them capture the emotional qualities may consist in having them, as a group, sing songs in the mood of the play, listen to music in the mood of the play and move to that music, or work out pantomimic improvisations. This procedure has been used successfully in tryouts and rehearsals for folk plays. It also aids the actors to achieve physical and emotional relaxation and freedom, absolute essentials for the best results in tryouts.

In this informal and relaxed atmosphere actors are asked to read for certain parts. It is not necessary to begin with the first line of dialogue in the play and read to the end. It is best instead to pick out certain scenes. The reading of crucial scenes which will outline the character patterns is the most advisable procedure. When the director has allowed everybody to read (and, to avoid any hard feelings, everyone should be given a chance), he can then reduce the number to those who are definite cast possibilities.

B. Casting the Individual Actor

As a basis of elimination from the general tryout, the director, keeping each character in his mind's eye, should consider the actor's (1) physical appearance in general, (2) age, (3) voice quality and diction, and (4) sense of movement and rhythm.

In further determining the suitability of an actor for a part, the director must carefully consider his (1) sense of theater and background, (2) sensitivity and imagination, (3) "audience appeal" and power of "projection," (4) acting experience, (5) personal "tonality," and (6) playing ability for kind and style of play.

1. SENSE OF THEATER AND BACKGROUND

The director has various means of arriving at an estimate of an actor's mental facility and general sense of theater. Educational and social backgrounds are definite indications. Ability to understand the play and respond to suggestions for character interpretation demonstrates both sense and general intelligence of theater.

2. SENSITIVITY AND IMAGINATION

An actor's reading and his sense of movement and rhythm indicate his sensitivity and imagination. In making suggestions and generally coaching him, the director can arrive at a further appraisal by setting up for him pantomimic improvisations, with or without music. Interesting the actor in a given set of circumstances and inducing him to concentrate forces a demonstration of his imaginative ability.

3. AUDIENCE APPEAL AND POWER OF PROJECTION

To judge an actor's audience appeal and his ability to project this appeal, the director best considers general appearance, voice quality and diction, grace and precision of movement and pantomime, and general personal magnetism from the spatial and aesthetic distance of auditorium to stage. The director sits in the auditorium of the theater, tries to imagine himself a representative of the audience, and determines whether or not the actor "gets across" his personality and commands audience attention and interest. (The use of at least general distribution of light on the stage makes the task easier.) This consideration is important, for it must be realized that an actor always creates character out of his personality.

4. ACTING EXPERIENCE

If the director has seen the actor on the stage in various roles and knows of his acting experience, he will be aided in imagining him as a particular character. Besides, experience and actual technique often weigh heavier than personal, physical, and emotional qualities.

5. PERSONAL TONALITY

As a final check in casting, the director must consider an actor in terms of personal, physical, and emotional tonality in relationship to other characters in the play and the actor's rightness for the particular kind of play and its style. The actor's suitability in this respect is most important in the conveyance of the play's dramatic values. His personal "tonality" means his inherent degree of softness, hardness, lightness, heaviness, genuineness, artificiality, etc., irrespective of his use of technique to achieve a particular tonality of character. The director must be ever mindful of this personal tonality.

6. PLAYING ABILITY FOR KIND AND STYLE OF PLAY

Personal tonality may make an actor right for a particular kind of play, but he may not be able to use the special technique of playing demanded by the play. An actor's ability to use the particular technique necessary for tragedy, drama, melodrama, comedy, and farce is an important consideration. It involves his quality of voice, his use of it, his physical flexibility, and his general emotional and intellectual adaptability. For example, tragedy in all styles usually demands a rich, vibrant voice, capable of beautiful and varied reading, and a physical appearance and grace that can obtain audience sympathy. Comedy, on the other hand, usually demands a dryness and comparative hardness in voice, which is able to provoke laughter, and a physical appearance that may be in itself amusing.

The actor's ability to play in the style demanded by the play presents another question that the director must answer. Different styles of playing depend upon the actor's ability to create different degrees of lifelikeness in voice and body to convey the various kinds and degrees of roundness of character. Playing in particular styles, as well as playing in particular kinds, of plays requires a special suitability, experience, and training.

C. CASTING THE ENSEMBLE

Before definitely setting the cast individually, the director should see the entire group on stage. He should then go into the auditorium and look at them as the audience might.

I. NECESSITY OF CONTRASTS

First of all he must visualize the actors as the ensemble of characters demanded by the script. Then he must so place them on stage as to relate them to one another individually, to one another as groups and to one another as representatives of conflicting forces. He can thus see contrasts in physical appearance; and on having them read, he can hear the voices in contrast and in concert. The emotional tonalities of characters will also be evident. Remembering that the basis of the dramatic lies in contrasts that create variety and conflict, the director will sense the need to try to cast for contrast in physical appearance, voice, and emotional tonality.

2. UNITY

However, the director in casting for contrasts must not lose sight of the necessity of casting for those degrees in contrasts which will create unity. For example, naturally highly comic appearances and voices are obviously out of place in serious plays.

3. INDIVIDUAL COOPERATION

In addition to an actor's apparent ability to play a part and make the right tonal contribution to the ensemble, the director must consider his ability to work with the group in rehearsal. This depends upon a willingness and an ability to work as a unit which is only a part of the whole. Many excellent solo performers are absolutely incapable of subordinating themselves and molding themselves into an ensemble. A sense of emotional, mental, and physical cooperation and adjustment is essential. This qualification of the actor must be duly weighed when the director considers the desired ensemble effect.

XIII

Rehearsals

A. ORGANIZATION

ONLY CAREFULLY planned and organized rehearsal schedules and intelligently administered individual rehearsals can lead to finished productions. Not all the exigencies of rehearsals can be anticipated and forestalled; but certain pitfalls are characteristic of all, and these can be expected and guarded against.

1. PROPORTION OF REHEARSALS TO PARTS OF PLAY

For one thing, an organized period of rehearsals can help the director avoid the mistake of spending a disproportionate amount of time rehearsing the first part of the play and neglecting the middle and end. Paradoxically enough, the first act, which is often overrehearsed, is usually the simplest in the play and needs less rehearsing than the other two. It merely presents the characters and their *status quo* and points the direction that the play is to take, but the second and third acts consist of the development of character and situation and the denouement. Actually most of the drama in a play lies in the last two acts. It is true that there should be a good beginning to make the audience come back after the first intermission, but it must be remembered that the audience is more likely to overlook deficiencies in playwriting, acting, and directing at the beginning of a performance than it is later on in the evening when the theater seats seem harder and fatigue has set in. A good beginning may create impetus, but the good ending is what brings satisfaction.

Thoughtful planning and an intelligent division of rehearsal time according to the demands of the play, act by act and scene by scene, will safeguard the director against one of the gravest errors of rehearsal procedure.

2. TOTAL NUMBER OF REHEARSALS

To plan the total number of rehearsals necessary for the production of a play, the director must consider, first of all, the characteristics of the play itself in terms of act and scene division, number of characters, dramatic values, style, and general stageworthiness. Plays of many scenes, large numbers of characters, complex structure, and unconventional form require long rehearsal periods. "Period" and stylized plays need more rehearsals than the average realistic kind. Rehearsals for the original script which is subject to constant revision must exceed in number those necessary for the tried play.

The schedule of rehearsals may be affected by the total number of plays to be presented in a season and the consequent time allotment. If all the plays are selected in advance for the season, the director can analyze the rehearsal demands of each play and can thus apportion the rehearsal periods of each. The amateur director must consider the school calendar of events and the schedule of community activities and map out his rehearsal schedule accordingly.

The training and experience of the actors and the time that they can devote to rehearsals will obviously affect the rehearsal-time period. Inexperienced actors who can rehearse only part time necessarily require more rehearsals than do professional actors. The director must meet the demands of the particular conditions.

Although it is hazardous to lay down any rule, most plays require an over-all rehearsal period of four to six weeks, six days a week. It is seldom advisable to try to do the average play in less than four weeks with an amateur cast. More than six weeks of rehearsal may succeed in wearying a cast and may cause it to lose interest. Even though the director may be inventive and generally brilliant in his direction and extremely stimulating to his cast, a long rehearsal period can gradually dim the enthusiasm of his actors. Amateurs, especially, are under too much of a strain physically and emotionally to make long rehearsal periods advisable. Short, concentrated ones achieve the best results.

3. TIME PERIOD FOR EACH REHEARSAL

The time period for each rehearsal with the actor group can be longer than a concentrated period for coaching the individual actor. Coaching may be effective in periods of thirty minutes to an hour. After an hour's work the actor needs a rest. For the actor group, the two- or three-hour rehearsal period is more productive than a shorter or longer period. Little can be accomplished in less than two hours. After three hours of rehearsal actors, both professional and amateur, because of general fatigue begin to show less and less responsiveness to direction. Overlong rehearsals may be necessary to coordinate the scenery, lighting, costumes, and sound effects with the action of the play, but the director cannot expect anything but strained, mechanical, or hysterical performances from the actors.

4. COSTUME REVIEW

In addition to the play rehearsals, the director must plan reviews and rehearsals for the productional elements. A costume review is usually helpful. This is particularly advisable for costumes that are not modern. All the actors should wear their complete costumes and appear on the stage individually, then together with related characters, and then finally together with the entire cast. Thus the designer and the director are able to study the effect of each costume on each actor in these various static situations. The next step in the costume review is to direct the actors to go through the crucial movements and bits of business of the play, making entrances, exits, and long crosses, opening and closing doors, etc. A separate costume rehearsal simplifies the director's problems when the dress rehearsals arrive.

5. TECHNICAL REHEARSAL

At this rehearsal the actors should make all entrances and exits and learn the proper use of doors, windows, and other "practical" parts of the settings. They should also go through all business and learn to handle the actual properties to be used in the performance. They need not go through all speeches but should merely give the cues necessary for movement and business. The director must warn them, in making entrances, to keep out of "sight lines" and keep away from lighting instruments that may cast shadows; in exiting, to close doors for masking purposes and go offstage in the proper direction; and, while in the acting areas, to keep within the focus of the lighting instruments. A preliminary checkup on the distribution, intensity, and general mood of the lighting of each scene or act is another job for the director. He must also see that the sound effects are convincing and that their cues are properly timed. Although the supervision of the details of the productional elements is usually left to the technical director, the play director must make sure that these elements are quickly and smoothly coordinated. (The routine of the shifts is explained in Appendix B.)

The technical rehearsal is the first attempt to blend acting and the purely technical elements of scenery, properties, lighting, and sound effects. The greater the coordination achieved at this rehearsal and at the costume review the smoother and the more finished will be the first dress rehearsal.

6. FIRST DRESS REHEARSAL

The first dress rehearsal is a complete run-through at which all sound cues, light cues, costume changes, entrances, exits, important movement, and business should be coordinated. Costumes and make-ups must be adjusted to the lighting and to the actors' characterizations. After each scene or act, the position of the furniture should be adjusted and then painted on the floor cloth. Dialogue offstage and behind scenery should be checked for audibility. Each "curtain" must be timed exactly with the dialogue and business. At the end of the performance, "curtain calls" should be coordinated with the last curtain.

During this rehearsal, corrections should be made only at the end of scenes or acts. There should be absolute continuity within each scene and act. This is necessary to maintain the rhythm and unity of the production. Because of the necessary interruptions the actors will not be able to give emotionally consistent and unified performances; they are merely to help tie in the productional elements with the action of the play.

7. SECOND DRESS REHEARSAL

The second dress rehearsal should be a "tryout" performance before an invited and selected audience. Friends and the backstage crews, except the light and sound-effects crews who are needed backstage during the running of the performance, can make up this audience. They will stimulate the actors and help them to get the "feel" of playing to a house. If the play is a comedy, it is essential to have an audience. A comedy often loses its spirit and spontaneity in rehearsal and can be brought to life only through the stimulation of audience response. The director often loses his perspective on a play in the course of the rehearsal period, and an audience helps him to check the laughs and determine the comic dialogue that may fail to click. He can also gauge the effect of each scene and the effect of the play as a whole.

In order to allow the crews to shift scenery and properties and also see the show it is necessary to go through the following procedure:

a. The stage manager takes up the curtain on each scene or act and has the actors play for two or three minutes.

b. He calls: "Cut. Crews out front."

c. He calls: "Curtain." The actors then begin the scene over again and play to the end of the scene or act.

d. On cue, he calls: "Curtain."

e. Then he calls: "Crews on stage and in position for the shift."

f. He gives the actors a line near the end of the scene or act, and they play to the curtain which is brought down on cue.

g. After the "strike" and setup, the stage manager takes up the curtain on the next scene or act and repeats the procedure *b, c, d, e,* and *f* until the play has ended and the actors have taken their curtain calls.

If there are to be pictures of the production, they should be taken at this rehearsal. For the sake of the performance it is better to take them at the end of the show. This means taking pictures of the last act or scene first and working toward the first act or scene. If the shifts are complicated and difficult, the pictures may be taken at the end of each scene or act as the rehearsal progresses from the beginning to the end. This second procedure is harder on the actors and the continuity of the play and easier on the crews.

During the second dress rehearsal, corrections and adjustments are made by the various production departments at the end of scenes or acts while the crews are getting into position for the following scene. All changes should be made quickly and expeditiously to avoid long breaks in the rhythm of the performance. In spite of the interruptions necessary to allow the crews to see the show and also carry out their duties, and in spite of the necessity of taking pictures, everything should be done to effect continuity and unity.

8. THIRD DRESS REHEARSAL

The third dress rehearsal should be in the nature of a performance rehearsal. It is wise to have an invited audience for this performance. The play is presented, without any interruptions or stops whatsoever, from the beginning to the end. Then follow the curtains calls. This should be a performance complete in every detail. The director and the technical staff make corrections and give instructions only at the end of the performance.

At least three dress rehearsals are necessary to achieve a smoothly running production. The "preview" system recently developed in New York merely telescopes dress rehearsals with tryout showings for plays that are not toured prior to the New York opening. The amateur theater, if it is to set worth-while standards for itself, will see the necessity of holding more than one dress rehearsal, for any attempt at coordination requires sufficient time for corrections, adjustments, and trials. Play production depends upon a large number of different workers, each responsible for different artistic activity, and dramatic effectiveness depends upon the unification of all efforts.

B. Rehearsal Schedule

No schedule of rehearsals can be considered set and inviolable. The director may find it necessary to make changes from day to day to meet contingencies that may arise. The following is only a general working schedule for the average three-act play with a cast of not more than fifteen.

Rehearsal	*Procedure*
1	Reading and study of whole play
2	Reading and study of whole play
3	Reading and detailed study of Act I
4	Blocking out of Act I
5	Adjustments and addition of simple business for Act I
6	Study of Act II
7	Blocking out of Act II
8	Adjustments and addition of simple business for Act II
9	Run-through of Acts I and II
10	Study of Act III
11	Blocking out of Act III
12	Adjustments and addition of simple business for Act III
13	Study of characterization and memorization of lines for Act I
14	Run-through of Acts I, II, and III
15	Study of characterization and memorization of lines for Act II
16	Run-through of Acts I and II
17	Study of characterization and memorization of lines for Act III
18	Run-through of Acts I, II, and III
19	Detailed work on Act I for characterization, line reading, additional business, rhythm
20	Detailed work on Act II for characterization, line reading, additional business, rhythm
21	Detailed work on Act III for characterization, line reading, additional business, rhythm
22	Run-through of Acts I, II, and III
23	Rehearsal of special scenes for business, line pointing, and transitions
24	Run-through of Acts I, II, and III
25	Rehearsal of climactic scenes for tempo and ensemble playing
26	Run-through of Acts I, II, and III. Evening: costume review
27	Run-through of Acts I, II, and III for rhythm, unity

Rehearsal	Procedure
28	First dress rehearsal
29	Second dress rehearsal
30	Third dress rehearsal

It will be seen from this schedule that the actors will learn the play as a whole first and afterward will learn the parts of the whole. Thus they approach their characterizations through a knowledge of each character's relationship to the play as a whole. They also see the relationship of each situation to the rest of the situations in the play. Only through emphasis on the whole play can the director achieve a sense of proportion and relativity. Frequent run-throughs give the play continuity and unity.

Current with this schedule are coaching periods arranged with each member of the cast.

Roughly speaking, the rehearsal schedule is divided into four parts: (1) study period, (2) blocking-out period, (3) enrichment period, and (4) refinement and coordination period.

1. STUDY PERIOD

During the study period, the director, first of all, should help the actors to grasp the plot of the play—the general outline. Each member of the cast should be able to tell, not in detail but in general, the sequence of the plot development. If the actors will underscore the plot lines in the script, they will be able to memorize the plot more easily, and they will also realize the need of emphasizing these lines through line reading and pointing. The next step is to make them understand the character relationships. Then, each member of the cast should ask questions about the character that he is to play and round out a thumbnail sketch of the character. The theme, or idea, of the play must be made clear. After this preliminary discussion and study, the director should explain his general purpose, scheme, and style in producing the play.

A further study of character to learn the "spine of action" of each is the next step for the cast. A detailed study will reveal the smaller units of action, the motivations, and the subsequent sequence of stimuli and responses in terms of mental images and physical action. In this study of character the director will aid the actors in line reading, emphasis, and inflection and in pantomime and movement.

2. BLOCKING-OUT PERIOD

The blocking-out period of rehearsals consists of finding the general pattern of movement and large bits of business necessary for a revelation of the plot and the character relationships. This over-all physical pattern results from the director's clear understanding of each character, his relationship to other characters and situations. This is the dramatization by visual means, mainly by the use of composition, picturization, and movement.

3. ENRICHMENT PERIOD

The enrichment period of rehearsal is devoted to the invention of pantomime and business, action and reaction, variety and shading of line reading. During this period the director works with the individual actor, and, by dividing the actors into groups according to scene, he works with the actor group. Together with the actors he makes a further and more detailed study of the script. He tries to squeeze every last drop of drama out of each word, line, piece of business, movement, or grouping. He and the actors add to and build up each character and situation. No detail is too minute to add.

4. REFINEMENT AND COORDINATION PERIOD

The refinement and coordination period of rehearsal involves the selection of the significant, the elimination of the unnecessary, and the unification of all aspects of the performance. During this time the director tries to shape his production according to its style. He must sense and determine the kind and amount of the various elements of performance necessary for consistency, harmony, and unity. This process will involve throwing out certain business that may be out of key, eliminating distracting or inessential movement, changing line readings, and sharpening visual and aural emphasis. After these refinements and attempts at articulation, the director focuses his attention on the tempo of the various scenes and the over-all rhythm of the play. He works for timing in pauses, picking up cues, building speeches and scenes, and the blending of scenes to obtain a rhythmic flow. In "building" scenes great attention must be paid to the pitch of each in relation to that of the other scenes in the play; that is, the extent to which each scene is built must be made relative to the intensity and key of the other scenes. Thus the performance may become refined, rhythmic, and synchronized.

XIV

*Directing the Play**

WITH A thorough knowledge of the five fundamental elements of play directing and the technique essential in directing the average play, we are ready to consider an approach to directing.

A. EMOTIONAL VALUES OF THE PLAY

Since play directing, like orchestral conducting, is an inter-pretative art, the producer, like the conductor, must vary his manner so that the script conveys its own individual qualities. Musical criticism will suggest to us the first step in our approach which from the very beginning will aid us in obtaining variety in the tonal results. We know that great musicians perform Bach differently from Wagner, Beethoven from Respighi. We know that the opera star sings the music of *The Magic Flute* differently from the way he sings *Il Trovatore*. What specifically are the basic differences in musical treatment, and what are the corresponding elements on the stage?

Although there is, of course, no standardized formula for directing a play, repeated productions have taught us not to work out the particular detail of a scene—its composition, picturization, movement, rhythm, or business—but to consider the general tonal and emotional values of the play and how they may be sensed by an audience. Only by the actor's conveying these qualities in a performance will the director be able to direct six or seven plays a season before practically the same audience year in and year out and not mark each production with the same rubber stamp.

*This chapter was originally published as an article in *Theatre Arts Monthly*, October, 1937, and permission to reprint is hereby gratefully acknowledged.

1. MOOD AND ITS CONVEYANCE BY MOVEMENT AND RHYTHM

The mood of the script, therefore, is the first element to consider, because it is the most difficult to recapture after one becomes involved in the technical aspects of acting and the production. Accordingly, after the first reading it is necessary to pause to let the mood penetrate, to feel the play as if it were music, and then to decide how this emotional quality may best be translated into rhythm and movement. We determine the basic rhythm, the predominant timing of the production; we sense the intensity and number of emotional climaxes and whether these are to be based on character or on theatric effect. However, mood is not conveyed by timing alone. The amount and kind of movement contribute to the emotional tone as well. Here, as we have seen, the director can learn much from recent developments in the dance, especially in the modern ballet. Is the mood to be expressed by constant or little movement? Do we want to add as much as possible or to eliminate all but the absolutely necessary action? Is the movement to be long or short, rapid or slow, vibrant or relaxed?

Take, for instance, an exciting, devastating, many-scened drama of big-city crookedness, as pictured in *Five-star Final* or *Merry-go-round*. The author recalls vividly his mood impression of the latter when he first read it for production. It had a dominant constant basic rhythm as rapid and driving as a steel riveter and a movement that was constant, short, quick, and divergent. In directing it, no time could be taken for detailed characterization, no pauses for innuendo or for picturized effect. It must have continuous rises and tense drops in tempo. It must have bold, broad, and contrasting moving about. Compare this mood quality and its execution with that of *Russet Mantle*. This play had a light, quickened rhythm with only occasional climactic moments. The movement was easy, long-flowing, and occasional.

Two entirely different dance patterns. With all lines cut and the actors going through the play in pantomime, the mood qualities would come over the footlights as if each had been a ballet.

Here is where any written analysis of an approach fails.

Already the skeptic has said, "But every play does not have a predominant mood quality to be expressed by the director." True, and few plays have all points of consideration. When a play does not, certain of the considerations are eliminated. But if the director is not concerned with mood, what "kind of play" it is demands as much analysis.

2. KIND OF PLAY AND TREATMENT

Tragedy, melodrama, farce, comedy, and the various combinations of these which the freedom of modern playwriting allows us have distinctive qualities which must be considered. How farcical in this comedy may the actors become? How much melodramatic effect can be allowed in this tragedy? How much characterization may be developed in this melodrama? Are the comic possibilities to be emphasized as much as or more than the serious thematic scenes? How can two opposite qualities be blended? There are a hundred general questions that need to be answered. The specific treatment is easily executed later.

3. EMOTIONAL VALUES AND CASTING

Whether the play's emotional quality rests in the determination of its mood or of its type, a general consideration of its casting arises at this time. Versatility in characterization is found in actors both professional and amateur, but almost never is it possible to find versatility in mood and tonal quality. So, at this stage of studying the script, one should determine what qualities of voice, body, and personality the actors must have in order to convey the musical tone of the play.

4. STYLE

The next major problem is the style. This will determine the manner of the direction, which perhaps more than any other factor leads to variety in the productions of a single director. No other subject connected with the theater is so difficult to express in a few words, because, although terminology has been given to a few of the major schools of writing

—classic, romantic, realistic, naturalistic, expressionistic—a modern play seldom has a pure style, and there are almost as many styles as plays.

To the author, style is the degree and kind of lifelikeness that a playwright has used in his writing, the degree of his selectivity in dramatic form and structure. The purely realistic play is perhaps the easiest to direct, but within the scope of reality there is a wide range—from the arbitrariness of Shaw's *Getting Married* to the seeming actuality of O'Neill's *Ah, Wilderness!* from the picturesque reality of *Victoria Regina* to the life illusion of *Dead End*. Polonius' combinations of tragedy, comedy, history, pastoral are sheer baby talk in comparison to the combinations of styles from classical to expressionistic realism in plays today.

5. TREATMENT

The determination of style will tell the degree, kind, and amount of composition, the simplicity or complexity of form to be used in the groupings. It will settle the actors' body relationship to the audience, the use of area and levels. For instance, are the stage pictures to be "closed in," as if the fourth wall had been removed; or are they to be flat and open to an audience to connote a more artificial form? Are only the front areas to be used for the most part, or is every inch of the stage to be utilized? Are the actors standing about on a stage or moving around in an actual place? Is the setting to be a mere pictorial background, or is it to be used by the characters as part of their actions? Is the movement to be arbitrary or highly motivated? Is the business to be scant or rich in its inventiveness and "follow-through"? Answers to these questions and many more of the same kind determine the definite style or manner that the play is to acquire from the direction.

B. MEANING OF THE PLAY

At this point we work on the meaning of the play. We should work as if we were the dramatist, analyzing the theme and the way that it is to be expressed, the meaning of each scene in relation to the whole play. It is now that we want to go over each scene with the author to gauge its length, its purpose, and its achievement; whether or not it accomplishes logically what it should do, whether or not the psychological states of the character in each scene are clear. For the past ten years the author has worked almost entirely on original scripts. With them there is always considerable rewriting to supervise, in order to eliminate repetition, to accomplish progression, and to insure consistency of characterization. Too often the beginning writer confuses his issues, and there is always much work in clarifying and emphasizing the important parts and adjusting the proportions of the play. Although many errors in writing are bound to turn up at rehearsals, many more can be detected from the written script than is ordinarily supposed.

C. Procedure in Directing

1. PRECONCEIVED DIRECTIONS

The author strongly advocates for the beginning director the procedure of planning positions and movements on paper. When the latter has had considerable experience and his ideas come more quickly than the actors can absorb them, then it is safe to discard premeditated directions. No director, on the other hand, should become too set in his ideas of how he wants a scene to be played, for he will often receive ideas for business and interpretation from the actors themselves. This is perhaps the ideal relationship, and it will work except when he is dealing with professionals who automatically want to rush to the "downstage center" or amateurs who always "feel" like sitting down.

2. DESIGNING THE GROUND PLAN AND THE FURNITURE ARRANGEMENT

After the intensive work on the script with the author, the director knows the play thoroughly. Rereading and reworking it will create in his mind definite pictures, movements, positions, and business. These need not be connected and continuous but high spots in the script. The climactic movements and general patterns of the important scenes will tell him where the windows, doors, and furniture can be placed most advantageously. He can then make his ground plan and discuss it with the designer. He should be very particular not only about the exact layout for the stage setting but about the offstage surroundings, for the visual-minded type of director must know where his characters come from and where they are to go. The arrangement of the stage, especially when the play is different in style from the last production, is a constant assistance to the director. As interesting and novel arrangements as can be should be devised unless the style is very arbitrary.

3. WORKING OUT BEHAVIOR OF CHARACTERS

With the ground plan of the set made, we are ready to meet the cast and to begin actual stage movement. "What do you do with your actors when you get them on the stage?" The direct answer is, "I try to keep them from thinking that they are on a stage." They enter through the door of a room, and they do what they would do if they were coming into that room. For these early rehearsals it is expedient for the director very often to sit on the stage and work out with each one his characteristic behavior and action. The lines are read slowly and simply for an understanding of their meaning, and business is evolved in relation to them. This results in placing on the stage as nearly as possible a reproduction of actual life.

4. TECHNICAL ADJUSTMENTS

While the director is urging the actors to concentrate on themselves as characters in a real situation and in a certain place, he should at the same time be injecting a slight modification and rearrangement of positions for such technical considerations as variety in area, emphasis, asymmetrical balance, third-dimensional effect, sight lines, and other considerations in composition. The movement that was static as an imitation of real life is now varied by arbitrary breaking up, by the changes in character relationship, or by the demands of the mood and kind of play.

5. LINE READING AND PLAYING

After the play is blocked out in positions and movements and there have been several run-throughs, intensive work begins on the actual reading of lines. This has been constantly improving as the actors and the director have planned positions and movements. Now the playing becomes of major importance.

6. RHYTHM AND TEMPO OF WHOLE PLAY

The rhythm and tempo of the whole play are the last elements to rehearse. Only when the actors are entirely familiar with their lines and movements, only when he himself has finished watching details, can the director sit back and, in perspective, pull the loose scenes together and watch the timing with its changing, its shading, its building and diminishing.

Such an analysis as this on the approach to directing the play necessarily places the stress on the purely intellectual and technical aspects of directing. In no way is it intended to lessen the value of pure imagination or intuitive creation. All arts, as we have seen, must have both the technique of conveying a feeling and the purely creative impulse itself. Any experienced artist blends these two parts so that he creates in form. It is the same with the director or actor.

Appendix A

These photographs demonstrate composition and picturization in actual productions, the analyses bringing out the predominant principles employed. To avoid repetition, complete analysis is not made in each instance.

Permission to reprint these photographs, with the single exception of Plate III, *Russet Mantle,* has been granted by the Yale University Theater, whose generosity is gratefully acknowledged. For permission to reprint Plate III, the author is indebted to the White Studio, Inc., New York City.

PLATE I

She Stoops to Compromise

by J. Wong-Quincy

EMPHASIS: Full-front body position, C area.

BALANCE: Symmetrical.

VARIETY: Irregular body positions, different areas and planes.

MOOD: Predominance of perpendicular straight line with form regular, deep, and scattered, expressing coldness, formality, indifference, and individuality.

REMARKS: Note relationship of furniture to angularity of walls.

PLATE II

The God Innis

by HELEN R. WILLIAMS and GEORGE DOWELL

YALE UNIVERSITY THEATER

EMPHASIS: Level, expansive distance, full-front body position, UC area, visual line.

BALANCE: Symmetrical with emphatic figure at fulcrum and stabilized by mass downstage.

VARIETY: Different treatments of grouping, different levels of sitting positions, counterfocus.

MOOD: Predominance of mass with mainly concentrated groupings expressing heaviness and severity.

REMARKS: Note use of most of the considerations discussed under Emphasis in a Crowd Scene; note also richness of detail in the treatment of the crowd and the irregular groups of figures in the downstage plane; stability of composition.

PLATE III

Russet Mantle

by LYNN RIGGS

EMPHASIS: Contrast in body position, visual focus.

PLATE IV

Taken from Life

by ARMAND ZIMMERMAN

YALE UNIVERSITY THEATER

EMPHASIS: Contrast in level, position in middle of semicircular formation, visual line.

BALANCE: Asymmetrical (if no figure were at DL, the grouping at the right half of stage would be balanced in itself).

VARIETY: Levels, counterfocus of the two figures sitting on floor and figure sitting DR.

MOOD: Compact, irregular form with broken line in curved formation expressing intimacy, informality, and warmth.

REMARKS: Note how the varying levels give vitality to the composition by creating a vertical triangular form.

PLATE V
Done Got Over
by RICHARD OLIVER

YALE UNIVERSITY THEATER

EMPHASIS: Space, contrast of horizontal line, visual focus.

BALANCE: Aesthetic (weight of mass against one emphatic figure).

MOOD: Compact mass effect expressing gravity.

PLATE VI

Crabapple

by THEODORE PACKARD

YALE UNIVERSITY THEATER

EMPHASIS: Repetition of perpendicular line given by archway, UC area, space.

BALANCE: Asymmetrical (visual line relates emphatic figure to group at L; in the full-stage composition the group at R balances this unity).

PLATE VII

Decade

by MARION HAZARD

YALE UNIVERSITY THEATER

EMPHASIS: Space, downstage plane, contrasting horizontal line of sofa.

BALANCE: Asymmetrical and aesthetic (added weight through visual line).

VARIETY: Indirect focus given by center figure at table; counter-focus given by maid.

REMARKS: Note the several acting areas achieved by the different units in the furniture arrangement; note also the opened-up position of the chairs in relation to the round table.

PLATE VIII

One Shall Be

by LUTHER KENNETT

YALE UNIVERSITY THEATER

EMPHASIS: Actual line, visual line.

SEQUENCE: Full-stage composition tied together by rhythmic spacing.

VARIETY: Levels, indirect focus given by figure at C.

PLATE IX

The King's Coat

by FREDERICK KLEIBACKER

YALE UNIVERSITY THEATER

EMPHASIS: Visual line.

SEQUENCE: Rhythmic spacing in an irregular formation with progressive use of space at right stage.

REMARKS: Note how the positions in the DR and DL areas can become emphatic in a crowd scene.

PLATE X

The God Innis

by HELEN R. WILLIAMS AND GEORGE DOWELL

YALE UNIVERSITY THEATER

EMPHASIS: Visual line, space; variety of body positions.

BALANCE: Asymmetrical large mass groups versus scattered group.

SEQUENCE: Spatial relationship from central figure to group leaning doorway R.

PLATE XI

This Fallow Ground

by Arnold Sundgaard

YALE UNIVERSITY THEATER

EMPHASIS: Center area, visual line.

VARIETY: Counterfocus of figure at L.

REMARKS: The placement of several figures is such that the emphasis can be easily shifted to any one of them by slight movements, making it basically a composition with diversified emphasis.

PLATE XII

Murder in the Cathedral
by T. S. Eliot

YALE UNIVERSITY THEATER

EMPHASIS: Apex of triangle, actual line, visual line, UC area.

VARIETY: Spacing and level of figures in triangle irregular, lines of legs of triangle irregular, added figures to basic triangle; body positions, levels.

MOOD: Predominance of broken diagonal line in a large mass with scattered form expressing action, unreality, turmoil, and austerity.

REMARKS: Note that the emphasis is created by the impression of two triangles—the larger one beginning at the downstage plane, and the smaller created by the two figures midway on the flight of steps. Note also how the figures at the downstage plane stabilize the entire composition.

PLATE XIII
A Rogue in Bed
by RONALD MITCHELL

YALE UNIVERSITY THEATER

EMPHASIS: Visual line, actual line, apex of triangle.

COUNTER-
FOCUS: Group UL (softens overemphasis).

REMARKS: Note position of bed, permitting scenes to be played in opened-up positions.

PLATE XIV

Venice Preserved

by THOMAS OTWAY

YALE UNIVERSITY THEATER

DUO-
EMPHASIS: Standing figure receiving emphasis through UC area,
body position, level, repetition, actual line, visual line,
apex of triangle; lying figure receiving emphasis through
contrast of level, contrast of line, UC area, visual line.

BALANCE: Symmetrical.

MOOD: Large mass in regular, shallow, compact form with
diagonal line expressing force, excitement, and artificiality.

PLATE XV

Uncle Harry

by THOMAS JOB

YALE UNIVERSITY THEATER

EMPHASIS: Note emphasis of figure at piano through space.

BALANCE: Example of balanced stage when only half of it is in use

VARIETY: Note variety in positions around table.

PLATE XVI

The God Innis

by HELEN R. WILLIAMS AND GEORGE DOWELL

YALE UNIVERSITY THEATER

DUO-EMPHASIS:	Figure pointing receiving emphasis through C area, full-front body position, visual line. Figure standing below table receiving emphasis through downstage plane, visual line, actual line, contrast of horizontal line.
VARIETY:	Levels, body positions, counterfocus, indirect focus, areas, planes.
MOOD:	Irregular, deep, scattered form giving reality and richness to the composition in a scene of conflict.
REMARKS:	Note the placement of the figures around the table at C; note also the interest given the composition by the creation of several vertical triangles.

PLATE XVII

Venice Preserved

by Thomas Otway

YALE UNIVERSITY THEATER

EMPHASIS: Three emphatic figures: Figure UC: level, apex of triangle, area, full-front body position, repetition. Figure LC: area, repetition, visual line. Figure RC: area, repetition, visual line.

BALANCE: Symmetrical.

STABILITY: Groups DR and DL.

MOOD: Predominance of straight perpendicular line with regularity of form expressing regal impressiveness, formality, and severity.

PLATE XVIII
Chantecler
by EDMOND ROSTAND

YALE UNIVERSITY THEATER

DIVERSIFIED EMPHASIS: Attention carries from one group or figure to the other.

VARIETY: All factors of emphasis used in creating the different points of attention.

PLATE XIX

The King's Coat

by FREDERICK KLEIBACKER

YALE UNIVERSITY THEATER

EMPHASIS
with
SECONDARY
EMPHASIS: Primary emphasis: UC area, full-front body position, apex of triangle, visual line, repetition.

Secondary emphasis: Actual line and visual line coming from the primary emphasis: actual and visual line from figures DR.

VARIETY: Irregularity in spacing of figures in legs of triangle; added figure to basic form.

PLATE XX

Passée

by MARION MORGAN

YALE UNIVERSITY THEATER

EMPHASIS: Level, full-front body positions, apex of triangle, actual line, visual line.

SEQUENCE: Space used progressively.

VARIETY: Counterfocus, indirect focus, areas, levels.

REMARKS: Note the several acting areas.

PLATE XXI

Chantecler

by EDMOND ROSTAND

YALE UNIVERSITY THEATER

EMPHASIS: C area, visual line, space, actual line.

SEQUENCE: Spacing of figures to show sequence from crowd to emphatic figure.

BALANCE: Aesthetic.

PLATE XXII

Spring of the Year

by WILLIAM ROBERTSON

YALE UNIVERSITY THEATER

BALANCE: Asymmetrical with visual line creating equal points of emphasis on group R and group CL.

SEQUENCE: Each group tied together through space relationship.

PLATE XXIII

Merry-Go-Round

by ALBERT MALTZ AND GEORGE SKLAR

YALE UNIVERSITY THEATER

MULTIPLE
COMPOSITION: Four points of emphasis with upper composition having emphasis on the speaker through C area, full-front body position, contrast of horizontal line, visual line.

REMARKS: In an evenly lighted, full-stage picture three points of emphasis would be established by the vertical triangle with secondary emphasis falling on the hanging figure.

PLATE XXIV
The King's Coat
by FREDERICK KLEIBACKER

YALE UNIVERSITY THEATER

EMPHASIS: Visual line.

BALANCE: Asymmetrical; masses stage R; individual spread-out figures stage L.

STABILITY: Figures DL and DR. Notice division of crowd into individual groups across stage.

Appendix B

THE STAGE, SETTING, AND STAGE MANAGEMENT

Listed in this appendix are a glossary of terms for the stage and its equipment, detailed information about sets and lighting, back-stage terminology, a description of the duties of both the technical staff and the stage manager and his assistants—essential information for everyone connected with the theater.

A. Equipment from Auditorium to Backstage

Pit. Originally this referred to the entire lower floor, or what is now known in America as the orchestra and in England as the stalls. Today it refers solely to a sunken pit before the stage in which the orchestra plays.

Proscenium, or Proscenium Arch. The open frame in the solid wall of the auditorium which discloses the stage.
    a. Proscenium width. The horizontal distance of the opening from wall to wall.
    b. Proscenium height. The vertical distance of this opening from the stage floor to the uppermost part.

Apron. That portion of the stage extending out into the auditorium beyond the line of the proscenium arch.

Footlights, or Foots. The row of low-wattage colored lights in a metal trough which is usually sunk in the stage floor at the front of the apron. A metal reflector prevents the light from striking the eyes of the people in the house and sends it back on to the stage. Footlights are usually wired in three circuits, one color for each. This row of lights should not extend the full width of the stage. When it does, the end bulbs cast an unfortunate shadow on the downstage end of the setting. If the stage manager finds in his theater that the footlights do extend too far, he should loosen, or "black-out," the end bulbs up to the point where the light no longer shows on the end flats.

Asbestos. The fireproof curtain, directly behind the proscenium, usually made of asbestos, occasionally of steel. When it is raised, it goes completely out of sight. The law in some states requires every theater with a seating capacity of over 299 to be equipped with one. It must be lowered before the theater is opened for a performance and the audience admitted. Generally it is raised (by the stage carpenter at the stage manager's signal) in full view of the audience five minutes before the performance starts. Actors would do well to know, and stage managers must know, where the rope is for the lowering of this curtain. The law requires that a knife be fastened to the stage wall near the emergency rope which, when cut, will lower the asbestos. The emergency rope is at either side of the proscenium.

Grand Drapery. Seldom used in our theaters of today except in revivals, this is still found in old theaters and opera houses on the road. It is painted canvas hung permanently in the upper part of the proscenium arch just behind the asbestos curtain. It consists of a crosspiece which fills in the proscenium when it is any shape but rectangular and has two side pieces dropping to the stage floor. Usually it is painted to represent folds of rich velvet with many tassels, hung profusely around painted marble columns.

Act Curtain. The curtain directly behind the grand drapery. It is used when necessary to conceal the stage from the audience before, during, or after the play. It is either drawn up and let down vertically, a fly curtain; or parted in the center and drawn horizontally one-half to each side, a draw curtain.

Curtain Line. The location at which the act curtain strikes the stage floor when lowered or slides along the stage floor when drawn.

Tormentors. Directly behind the act curtain is another framework which cuts down the size of the proscenium opening to the exact proportion that the scene designer desires for his setting. The height of this inner framework varies in different theaters and is used with flats from eight or nine to twenty feet in height. In the old theaters the tormentors were the side pieces of this inner framework.

They are the first flats behind the act curtain. There is one on each side, coming out on to the stage and parallel to the footlights. Their position is adjustable in that they are made to be placed farther on stage or drawn off according to the width of the set.

Teaser. This is the very first crosspiece of canvas between the two tormentors. In design and color it matches the tormentors and with them forms an inner picture frame. In the older theaters it cut down the proscenium to a smaller opening than the "grand drapery." The teaser is fastened to ropes above so that it can be raised and lowered to varying heights.

Box Teaser. Another form of the teaser is the one in the shape of an L, with the vertical side facing the audience and the bottom part serving as support for light equipment.

Inner Proscenium. Today the grand drapery and the old teaser and tormentors have for the most part disappeared. In their place, a framework covered with canvas and painted in a neutral color cuts down the plaster proscenium arch to the size that the designer plans. It is not solid, for the upper part which corresponds to the old teaser can be raised and lowered, and, like the tormentors, the side pieces can be moved on and off stage. Although the inner proscenium is a single unit, its sides are still referred to as tormentors, and the upper crosspiece as a teaser.

Tormentor and Teaser Draperies of the same color and material as the act curtain are sometimes hung at the top and sides of this inner proscenium, not entirely but partially covering it. In this manner there is a definite blending of color and material from the act curtain to the neutral color of the inner proscenium.

Set Width, or Opening refers to the distance between the sides or tormentors of the inner proscenium rather than to the actual proscenium width, since it is this width alone which is considered in relation to the set and the acting areas. The set width varies in different theaters; in the little theaters it is as narrow as eighteen to twenty feet; in the larger professional ones as wide as thirty to forty feet.

Set Line. The outline of the entire set in relation to the stage floor. The front set line is the location of the downstage extremities of the set and playing areas demarcated by the tormentors of the inner proscenium. In the realistic theater the actor always stays within the front set line.

Teaser Height, Teaser Trim, or Trimming Height refers to the distance from the stage floor to the lower edge of the upper crosspiece, or teaser. This, too, varies from eight or nine feet in the amateur to greater heights in the professional theater.

A Return. A flat, or a drapery, placed between the inner proscenium or the tormentors and the downstage end of the box set in order to mask the opening made when the set is narrower than the space ordinarily allowed between the tormentors.

Special Inner, or False, Proscenium. A frame covered with canvas taking the place of the regular inner proscenium or set behind the inner proscenium opening in order to cut down the proscenium opening still more. In its special design and color it ties and blends into the set. It is not permanent equipment, being used most often in musical productions and frequently in elaborate productions of plays. It usually has its own front drop which again ties into the particular scene design. In a musical production there is a space between it and the act curtain deep enough so that actors may perform before this special proscenium and its curtain.

Taking first the floor of the stage, we find:

Stage Floor. This is necessarily made of soft wood so that tacks and screws may be easily driven into it. The wood is often covered with linoleum.

Trap. A good-sized opening, roughly six feet parallel to the foots and three feet deep, cut in the stage floor with a ladder, a ramp, or a rising and lowering platform through which an actor can ascend or be raised or descend or be lowered. Every professional theater has provisions whereby a trap may be opened in practically any portion of the stage.

Stage-floor Pocket. Sunk just below the level of the stage floor are metal receptacles that contain several outlets for electric current from the switchboard. They are usually located around the stage just outside the average set lines and are used to supply current to lights used in entrances and fixtures in the set itself. There are one or two on each side and three or four along the rear.

The next series of definitions describes the physical equipment over the stage and its use in a production.

Gridiron. This is the most important piece of stage machinery, as it is used to manipulate the hanging of scenery. It is a slatted or grated frame of metal or wooden beams high up over the stage, built a few feet below the roof of the stage. In the best of the modern theaters there is just space enough between it and the roof for a man to stand erect. The gridiron should be forty to eighty feet above the stage floor if the sets are to be raised out of sight of the first rows of the auditorium.

Rope-line Rigging. Along the center of the gridiron, on a line at a right angle to the footlights, is set a row of blocks with pulleys of a special type for stage use. Equidistant from the part of the stage within the proscenium, right and left of this center row, are other rows. Sometimes this space is divided into four rows. Over these block pulleys, ropes are passed. Accordingly, there are sets of rope, three or four in a row and in rows parallel to the footlights. The number of these sets varies in theaters. A well-equipped professional theater will have as many as twenty-five to fifty.

Lines. The lines are the ropes attached to the top of a curtain or series of flats or to the pipe, or batten, on which electrical equipment or parts of the scenery is attached. These lines go through pulleys attached to the gridiron and are counterbalanced. By manipulating them the scenery is raised or lowered. Lines should be made of the best hemp rope, one-half inch or larger, and should be carefully examined at definite periods.

Short Line is the one that is attached to the side of the stage where the ropes are to be fastened.

Long Line is the rope attached to the farthest end of the gridiron. The two in the center are known as the *short-center* and the *long-center* lines. If there are only three lines in a set, the middle line is called the *center line*. In lowering a drop it is essential that its batten be perfectly horizontal. When the drop comes down from above, it is often necessary to have these different lines pulled separately. The stage manager frequently is required to call to the stagehand in charge of the lines which line needs tightening in order to make the drop hang evenly.

Set of Lines. The lines, either three or four, are the short, center, or long lines, in one horizontal row or plane, that will hang the drop or set of flats.

Pin Rail. The ends of the lines, after they have passed through the pulleys on the gridiron, are brought down at one side of the stage as a set of three to be operated as one. These are attached then to the pin rail, a long beam of wood or steel firmly built into the walls of the building and running the full depth of the playing part of the stage, with crosspieces, or "pins," to which the lines may be more easily fastened.

Counterweight System is the second type of rigging. Compared to the "rope-line" system, it is a permanent setup; steel cables are used in place of rope; these cables are attached to iron-pipe battens which run horizontal to the footlights the length of the playing area. Whatever is to be raised or lowered is attached to these pipe battens. The battens are counterweighted by steel weights placed in carriages that run along the side wall from the gridiron to the stage floor. The control ropes for the carriages are locked at the pin rail. Professional houses have one or the other of these two systems of rigging. A few of them have both.

Fly Gallery. The pin rail was originally built on a platform, raised at least twenty feet from the stage and known as the fly gallery. Today it is usually lowered to within about three feet from the stage floor, but the space above it is still known as the fly gallery.

Counterweight. Weights attached to the end of a set of lines or weights used in carriages to balance the weight of the scenery hung so that it may be raised and lowered with ease without being hauled up as dead weight.

Sandbag. A strongly made canvas bag which when filled with sand is used on the stage ends of the lines when not in use, so that their weight will bring down the line from the gridiron when that line is wanted for hanging a piece of scenery or drop.

Large Sandbags are often attached to the fly-gallery end of lines to serve as a counterweight for scenery hung on those lines to facilitate raising and lowering.

Pipe Batten. A length of iron pipe about three inches in diameter attached to the steel cables. Drops, borders, scenery, or lighting equipment are attached to it in order to be raised and lowered on to the stage.

Wooden Batten. A strip of wood of almost any length and generally three inches wide and one inch thick. As border battens they are the length of the stage opening. On to these are tacked and glued the canvas of the teaser and other borders and drop curtains, and then another batten is screwed to the first so that the cloth material is held between the two battens.

Flies. The space above the stage where scenery is hung by lines from the gridiron. To be of any value the flies must be high enough to hang the scenery so that it flies well above the ceiling of a standing set. "To fly," or "to raise," means to hang anything in this space.

    a. Flyman. The stagehand who operates the rigging that controls the scenery hung in the flies is called the flyman.

       i. To Trim. Hanging a drop so that its lower edge is in proper juxtaposition to the floor—usually parallel though not always. Unusual scenery sometimes is not hung parallel. If a drop is lowered from the flies and it is not properly hung, it is trimmed by drawing, tightening, or loosening the long, center, or short line. Drops and other parts of scenery attached to the pipe battens of the counterweight system are permanently trimmed when first attached to the batten.

       ii. Make Fast. This refers to tying a set of lines to a piece of scenery and also tying the lines firmly to the pin rail.

       iii. To Foul. Scenery "fouls" when it or its lines tangle up and catch in other pieces of scenery in the flies, as "the back wall is fouled with a drop."

Other parts of the full stage contain the following:

Stage Manager's Desk. This is usually directly to the right or left of the proscenium arch, depending upon the placement of the fly gallery and the switchboard. It may or may not be on the same side of the stage with them. It is a small shelf, large enough to hold a script and a pad of paper for notes and cue sheets. Above the shelf are the signals to the flyman; to the electrician at the switchboard; to the curtain man; to the lobby and lounge so that he may signal the audience at the beginning of the acts two minutes before the curtain; and in some theaters to the greenroom and dressing rooms. For expediency, accuracy, and silence, the stage manager should always signal warnings and cues, even though he is near enough to speak them. He *rings up* and *rings down* the curtain, even though his signals are given by lights. By the stage manager's desk is also frequently a telephone to the front of the house or box office.

Switchboard. This is the center of all the distribution of electric current to the lighting instruments on the stage and to the auditorium. Without going into the full description of the construction and mounting of the switchboard, let us consider a few of the requisites. Switches for each branch circuit open and close the current for each light on the stage. Each light unit on the stage should be separately controlled from the board. It should be possible to control groups of like units, classed by location or color, such as all the X-ray units or all the blue footlights as opposed to the red. The switchboard is often on the floor level, but frequently it is raised from the floor, like the fly gallery. It may be in front of and below the stage.

Portable Switchboard. A board mounted in a box that is equipped with casters so that it can be moved from place to place. Most productions use their own portable switchboards and attach them to the company switch for current. The house switchboard usually handles the auditorium or house lights with sometimes the foots and overhead lights.

Dimmer. The mechanical object that controls the flow of current and thereby varies the intensity of light coming from a light instrument. Theoretically there should be a dimmer for each switch on the board, but usually there is only a limited number. In this case the electrician can connect those lights which require dimming and leave others constant.

Master Control. This is the handle that controls the series of individual light switches or dimmers which have been interlocked so as to act as one unit.

Grand Master. The dimmer control handle, or switch, that controls the entire set of lights in the switchboard. It is used for fade-outs and black-outs.

　　a. Terminology.

　　　　i. Fade-outs. The gradual elimination of all light on the stage by means of dimmers. It differs from "black-out," in that it is gradual.

　　　　ii. Black-out. An immediate switching off of all lights. It is used mostly in revues, but it may also be used in plays when all the lights in a room are switched out by an actor.

House Lights. All lights in the auditorium except the "exit" lights. House lights should always be in control from the switchboard and not from anywhere else. They should be on dimmers.

Work Lights. Lights used solely for illuminating the stage when it is not being watched by an audience, as at rehearsals and when scenery is being shifted. They are also lights behind the setting used for making working conditions possible for the stagehands who otherwise would have to work in the dark. Work lights should be a special light equipment; but if the stage is not equipped with them, then border lights are used for work lights.

Emergency Lights. All lights used to light the stage and auditorium as well as at exits in case of an emergency such as fire or failure of the regular service. Usually they have their own generating power, separate from the general source. They should not be all attached to the switchboard but be near it to be controlled by the electrician. The stage manager should see that the electrician tests them before every performance.

Dock. The place where odd scenery is stored and often painted. Frequently it is just a far corner of the stage. In winter and summer stock and repertory theaters it is usually in a separate shed or addition to the main stage.

Paint Frame. A frame into which scenery is fastened for painting. It may be stationary and require ladders for the scene painter to mount in order to reach the various heights, or it may itself be movable up and down through a slot in the floor, thus allowing the painter to remain on the floor. Its placement is similar to the scene dock.

Loading Door. The large double door through which scenery is brought on to the stage from the outside. It always opens directly from the stage on to an alley usually large enough to admit large trucks or vans.

Stage Exit. There will always be a door leading from the stage to the outside corridor and to the stairs leading up to the dressing rooms and to the back outside door of the theater known as the stage door. It is used by the actors and the crew and all people dealing with these two groups. By this door there should always be an emergency light which is lit during performances.

Call Board. A bulletin board located backstage and near the stage door, on which are posted important notices for actors, including rehearsal calls, rules of the company, the next booking date, time and place of departure, hotels and rates, etc.

Stage Dressing Room. Many stage fire laws prohibit the opening of the dressing rooms on to the stage, because in case of fire the actors would be trapped and unable to escape. Accordingly, actors must go out into the corridor to get to the dressing rooms. However, there is likely to be one dressing room (especially if there is a second door for escape and if it can have a fire door) leading directly from the stage. If these two conditions are not possible, there is certain to be one dressing room at the entrance to the corridor. In either case this is the stage dressing room, and it is not used regularly by any one member of the cast, but by whoever during the course of the action of the play has to change his costume quickly. It is fully equipped. If nobody has a quick change, it may be used by the star, although often the star's dressing room is equally convenient.

Quick-change Room. If there is not a stage dressing room leading off-stage where an actor may change his costume in less time than it takes for him to go to his own, the crew will erect a small one with flats. Props will place chair, table, mirror, and clothes hanger in it.

B. THE SETTING

Beginning with an imaginary interior set, we shall list its parts and their positions on stage.

Plot. This is a layout and schedule of sequence of particular objects, occurrences, or specifications in connection with a performance—for example, scene plot, property plot, light plot, and sound plot. The stage manager prepares these plots for the different heads of departments.

Floor Cloth. A canvas cloth is used to cover the wooden surface of the stage floor in order to deaden the sound of leather heels on wood between the places where rugs are placed and in exterior scenes. The traveling companies carry their own cloth, and the first thing done in erecting the stage set is to put it in place. It is tacked down and should be stretched very tight. It is usually a light tan in color, but for special productions it is painted to represent grass, cobblestones, etc.

Sometimes such a cloth is not used in one- or two-set living-room productions, but in its place a soft carpeting covers the entire floor space within the set and a few feet beyond it offstage.

The floor cloth or carpet should not be so large as to cover the floor pockets offstage. The floor cloth is often called the ground cloth, or stage cloth.

Set. The complete arrangement of the scenery with its accompanying properties and lights. "To set" is to place the scenery, properties, and lighting equipment in position on the stage, as "the stage is to be set up," or "the stage is set."

Set Height. The average living-room set has a height of twelve to fourteen feet.

R1, R2, and R3. The lettering in chalk on the back of the flats for those which are being set up on the right side of the stage. R1 is the one set farthest downstage and next to the tormentor.

L1, L2, and L3. This is the lettering on those flats on the stage left.

C1, C2, and C3. The markings on the flats to be set up along the rear forming the rear wall. C1 is the first flat on the stage right. The lettering of flats varies somewhat according to the specifications that a particular designer or stage carpentry shops may prefer.

Flat. The basic unit of scene construction is a wooden frame, reinforced and covered with canvas or muslin. The canvas is glued and tacked to the width of the frame, not over the edges. The height varies from nine feet in small theaters to fourteen or sixteen feet in regular professional theaters to twenty or twenty-two feet for special productions. The average width is five feet nine inches, because this just allows a flat to be loaded into a box car for road travel.

Door Flat. A flat containing an opening into which the door frame with the door is inserted.

Fireplace Flat. A flat containing a low opening for the recess of a fireplace.

Fireproofing. A chemical compound component that makes scenery, curtains, drops, etc., uninflammable. Materials fireproofed will burn when brought into direct contact with flame, but the flame will not travel along the fireproofed surfaces by itself. Fireproofing is required by law of all scenery, curtains, etc.

Corner Blocks. A triangle of three layers of wood, glued together with the grains placed alternately at right angles to each other. They are used to reinforce the corners and joints of flats.

Loose-pin Hinge. A hinge whose pin is not permanently inserted but from which it may be removed in order to separate the two parts. It is used almost exclusively on the stage, not only for doors but when flats are hinged together.

Lash Lines. The sash cord attached near the top on the right-hand side on the back of the flats which allows them to be lashed together. The *lash-line cleat* is an iron attached to the flat about three feet from the floor on both the right and the left sides. There is also a third cleat on each flat on the left side, just below where the sash cord is attached on the right. The cord of one flat is hooked over this upper cleat of another flat and laced tightly to the lower ones alternately so that when tied the two flats will be firmly held together.

Battening Flats. Nearly always the flats along the rear wall are not only lashed tightly together, supported by stage braces, but also battened together. They are laid face down side by side on the stage floor, and one batten laid across the top and one along the bottom and nailed. Each flat then is firmly fixed to the batten, making the rear wall steady and lessening the possibility of cracks between the flats. Then the whole rear wall may be flown as a single unit.

Stiffeners. The wooden battens to steady a section of flats. They are nailed as mentioned above or are held in place by hooks designed for the purpose.

Dutchman. A strip of canvas tacked and glued across the crack between two flats on their front surface and painted the color of the set. This makes the rear wall look solid and prevents the outline of the flats from being evident to the audience. It is also a strip of black or dark cloth tacked across the crack between two flats in the back or behind the crack of an opened door so as not to allow light to "spill" through.

Stage-brace Cleat. A metal cleat having an eye in one end in which the hook of a stage brace can be caught. It is attached to the frame of the back side of the flat just above the middle.

Stage Brace. A hardwood brace of adjustable length with a hook on one end for fastening to the eye in the stage-brace cleat on the back of a flat, and an iron with a hole in it at the other. Through this a stage screw is put and screwed into the stage floor. Thus door frames are steadied so as not to shake when the door is closed. High flats which are joined by lash lines are supported by stage braces.

Stage Screw. A sharp screw fitted with a handle is used as a means of fastening the stage brace into the stage floor.

Thickness Piece. A term used to designate that portion of a window, door, or arch frame which recedes in or back and becomes, thereby, the thickness of the wall. It is also a one-foot-wide flat which is used to project on stage.

Jog. A term also used for this one-foot flat. Also it is used as a verb to denote such a treatment of setting up scenery as when one flat of any size juts out at approximate right angle to the perpendicular flat going upstage. Jogging the set includes a series of such setting up.

Rake. A convention of long standing, now frequently discarded, allows the side walls of a set to slant slightly in toward the center of the stage. This enables the upstage entrances to be in better view from the sides of the auditorium. The rake is the angle at which the side walls come on stage from the tormentor, or proscenium arch.

Backing. A drop, or flat, is used behind an opening in the set as in a door, an arch, or a window. It also is called a window backing, door backing, sky backing, or hall backing. Sometimes it is very elaborate as in the case of a full drop when seen through French windows. More often it consists of two small flats, hinged together and painted a neutral color, which are placed for backing behind a door.

    a. Masking and *"To Mask Off."* A masking is a backing or other piece of scenery set in such a way as to prevent the audience's seeing backstage through an opening. Its meaning is made clear in this statement: "The backing doesn't mask." It is used in connection with door backings as well as drops.

Drop. A piece of scenery made of canvas or muslin fastened to battens at top and bottom, hung in the flies so as to be lowered or "dropped" into position for a scene. It is painted with perspective or a plain sky color. In the older theaters scenes were played before a drop. Today drops are used almost solely as backdrops, hung far upstage usually on the last set of lines, and have the distant landscape painted on them. They are the backing seen through French windows, over a wall or balcony in an exterior set, etc.

Ceiling. The scenery unit of wooden frame and painted canvas that rests upon the side and rear flats of a box set to represent the ceiling of the room. This unit should be painted light neutral gray or tan. The ceiling is hung on two sets of lines, one back and one forward. It must be hung so that the downstage edge is close to the teaser and so that the people in the front row in the audience do not see up into the flies. When a ceiling is hung in the flies, the front row of lines is detached. The ceiling is usually the first piece of scenery rigged; in a setup, however, it is the last piece of scenery to be lowered into position.

Sight Lines. The line of sight from the sides of the auditorium and from the top of the balcony will determine the size and playing area of the stage visible from all parts of the auditorium.

Fourth Wall. This is the imaginary side of the room toward the audience which has theoretically been removed so that the spectators may look in.

C. Lighting

We have roughly explained the setting, and now we shall take up a simple sketch of the lighting. Already we have placed the footlights. In addition to these, the most important light equipment and terminology are:

Layout. The distribution of the various pieces of electrical equipment for a particular production laid out in working drawings and specifications.

Light Area. Generally speaking this is the spot on the stage that will be covered by one large spotlight. The imaginary interior set that we have been discussing will have approximately six light areas—three downstage and three up. They are usually numbered as follows: 1 is DL; 2 is DC; 3 is DR; 4 is UL; 5 is UC; 6 is UR. On a large full set, especially an exterior, there will be nine areas. Each of these should have a spotlight covering it.

Spotlight. The general terminology for all single lights that direct a ray of light to a designated spot or area. They contain high-powered bulbs of 500, 1,000, and 1,500 watts in a metal hood which can be tilted at any angle.

Baby Spot. A small spotlight containing a 250-watt bulb and having the other equipment of a spotlight. Baby spots are used ordinarily to cover special small areas on the stage.

Hood. The large metal receptacle of the light instrument housing the lamp.

Lamp. A general term used for a single electric light bulb. Lamps vary from 50 watts for the footlights to 1,500 watts in the larger spotlights.

Lens. An optical glass that is used to gather or disperse by refraction rays of light that pass through it. It is an essential element of a spotlight.

Gelatin. The color medium for lighting equipment such as flood and spotlights. It is a thin sheet of glutinous substance and colored with aniline dye.

Shutter. Shutters are metal flippers, mats, irises, or any other means of cutting off entirely or in part the light from an electrical instrument. They are mounted on the outside of the instrument in front of the lens. The stage areas covered from a spotlight will approximately be a sixth of the average playing space. By means of shutters it can be narrowed from a full spread down to the area the size of a face.

Cable. Rubber- or fiber-insulated wires carrying electric current from the switchboard or from the floor pockets to the fixtures to a given source. Actors should be careful to avoid tripping on them both off and on stage. By having a small rug put over it stage managers should see to it that the cable to a lamp on stage is not exposed.

Tormentor Lights. The electrical equipment, either a stand with a spotlight or a strip of lights, placed directly behind the tormentors. Usually the flats of a set are lashed to the tormentor which obviously eliminates the use of these lights. Frequently, however, they are not, but the downstage end is placed directly back of the tormentors to allow for these lights. In exterior scenes these lights are almost always used.

X-ray Border. A row of lamps in reflector sections usually suspended from a border batten on the first lines downstage, to light the acting areas. There are usually from six to twelve units in a section, and each section is wired for two, three, or four colors. The metal hood in which the reflector units are mounted is equipped with color frame slides for each compartment.

Balcony, Booth Spotlight, or Front Lighting. Several large spotlights covering the stage areas and placed in front of the balcony or in the projection booth in the auditorium. Together with spots placed in the box-teaser light bridge or near the X-ray border they cover all stage areas. X-rays and foots blend and tone these area lights into an evenly lighted stage. Sometimes, but rarely, there are openings in the ceilings of auditoriums that allow for additional front lighting. These are called *beam lights,* or *ceiling lights.*

Backing Strip. A small portable strip of light equipment hung by doors or in front of all backings. It contains low-wattage lamps and furnishes a diffused light for the backing. Actors should be careful not to stand in front of these, thereby casting a shadow while they are waiting to enter.

Floodlight, or a Flood. A lighting instrument composed of a metal hood and contains several low-wattage lamps or one large one. It is shaped to throw a strong flood of light on to broad surfaces like backdrops or entrances from close range. Sometimes it is hung and sometimes used on a stand.

Special. A spotlight focused so that it covers a special person or a special area in which important or emphatic action takes place. It may be referred to as "door special," "chair special," "throne special," etc. It gives special and added illumination to the important and much used area.

Light Bridge. A long, narrow platform suspended, by adjustable lines, directly over the inner proscenium opening or any other portion of the stage. On this are placed the spotlights for the upstage areas, special spots, etc. One or two operators adjust the focus of the spots and change gelatins for the different acts. Because of the steady rise in salaries of union labor, it is common practice to use more lamps previously set and angled for successive scenes.

Follow Spot. A spotlight mounted with special equipment so that an operator can direct the beam of light in any direction and thereby follow an actor in his various movements over the stage. Used in musical comedy mostly but also in productions of certain other plays.

D. Backstage Terminology

We now come to terminology used for cues, calls and the removal of one set and setting up of another.

Cue. Any word, speech, move, sound, or light that is a predetermined signal to an actor or stagehand to perform a subsequent function in connection with the performance.

Cue Sheet. A tabulation of all the stage manager's responsibilities for noises, entrances of actor, change in lights, etc. Often this is not a separate sheet but is simply represented by blue-penciling in the prompt copy. Every actual cue should have a warning cue.

Stand-by. A term meaning to be ready to perform an act as soon as the cue comes. A stage crew stands by to strike. An actor stands by to take a curtain call.

Tag Line. An actor's line of speech at the close of a particular climax or situation, that succinctly points up or comments on the preceding speech or situation.

Curtain Line. The last line of a scene or act spoken by an actor before the curtain comes down.

Take a Call. This term is used when an actor comes before the audience and bows.

Act Call. The signal given by the stage manager to summon the actors to the stage to begin an act. It is the signal in the foyers, lobbies, lounges, etc., of the theater announcing that an act is about to begin. It is rung by the stage manager, generally two minutes before the rise of the curtain.

Clear Stage. A command given by stage managers to all stagehands and actors, not including those who begin or open the scene, to leave the stage and to take with them all tools and appurtenances that do not belong on stage at opening of scene.

Heads Up. A warning phrase that an object is falling or being lowered from above. When called, each person on the stage should stop and look up to see whether or not he is the one in danger. The lowering of a drop or any object or piece of scenery from the flies demands this call.

Strike. "Strike" is the call that the stage manager gives for the stage crew to clear the set already standing. If it is between acts, it includes the setting up of the next set. If it is the end of the play, it means to strike and clear the stage. It includes the striking of all scenery, properties, and lights. The call "strike" is also used for the removal of a single object; for example, "Strike that chair."

Shift. The process of striking and setting up the scenery, properties, and lighting equipment. The procedure for the shift is given in full later. "Shift" is also used to change the position of a single object; for example, "Shift the sofa."

Run. A synonym for sliding, as running a flat across the floor to its setup place or its pack; also to run a piano off the stage.

Kill. To eliminate a piece of scenery or property from a set; sometimes in dress rehearsals to take it permanently from the set, other times to remove it only from the immediate setting. In reference to light instruments, it means to "turn the light off" either permanently or temporarily.

Pack, or Scene Pack. Flats stacked face to face or back to back against the wall of the stage. The tilt of a flat should be as slight as possible to keep it from falling back, because stacking it at a decided angle with the weight of the others on it warps and bends it permanently. Great care should be taken in stacking the scenery of the second and third acts before the performance begins, so that the center flat of the rear wall is at the bottom of the stack nearest to the wall. Next to these are the flats on the right and left of the center, then the flats on the upstage right and left, until the top flats, or the first ones that the carriers come to, are those which are to be lashed to the left and right tormentors.

Live Pack is that set which is yet to be used even though it has already been used once in the performance.

Dead. Scenery and properties that are of no further use in a performance. Those appurtenances which are not to be used after an act that is over are said to be "dead." The pile of scenery that is stacked and not used again is known as the "dead pack," or "stack."

E. Equipment in an Exterior Set

We shall now define those parts of stage equipment which occur more often in an exterior set.

Wing. A flat set at either side of the stage parallel to footlights at intervals approximately seven feet back of each other so that backstage is not disclosed to the audience. For interiors wings are no longer used, but for exteriors they still remain the most satisfactory way to mask off the sides of the stage. Wings are marked R1, R2, etc.; L1, L2, etc. with "one" being the downstage, or first, wing. Most stages do not require more than three wings to mask the sides. They formerly were set in grooves. Today they have a return on the offstage end that allows them to stand by themselves. This helps to mask the open spaces between them from the front seats of the auditorium.

Spot- and floodlights are usually placed behind the wings.

Wood wings have an irregular outer edge of profile board to simulate tree trunks. Occasionally there will be an opening in them to represent further the realism of the space between the trees or its branches.

Border. A painted stretch of canvas attached to the batten lowered from the flies, usually about three to four feet deep and running the entire width of the stage. Today no first-class theater uses such a thing for a ceiling, although originally this was the accepted convention. In exteriors, however, borders are necessarily used to mask the flies from the first rows. The sky border is painted blue. Borders are placed directly in front of the wings, and three flown at seven-foot intervals are usually sufficient to mask.

Foliage Border, or Cut Border. A border made of canvas or similar material, the lower parts of which are cut, following an irregular design, generally to represent tree branches or foliage. Theatrical net is attached to the cut edges to keep the irregular cut parts in position.

Border Light, or Strip. A long trough of low-wattage lights, almost as long as the acting stage is wide. It is suspended by lines from the gridiron. Placed usually behind each border, it lights the upstage areas. The average number for a stage is four.

Strip Lights. A general term applied to a row of low-wattage bulbs, mounted in a long metal hood. They are used in many places, as for border or tormentor and sometimes ground row.

Spotlight Strip. A row of baby spotlights mounted on a frame and hung on a batten. Some productions use it instead of X-rays. It also takes the place in exterior scenes of the strip light in the borders.

Set Piece. Door frames, arch frames, mantelpieces, stairs, platforms, windows, and other heavy architecturally built objects are known as set pieces. They fit into scenery and are often used with draperies or a cyc for a set.

Exterior sets use the exterior cyc and wings and then add fences, walls, pumps, mounds, trees, ramps, steps, etc., for their set pieces.

Leg Drop. Is made of one or more vertical strips of canvas, with battens at top and bottom. It is used for cutouts and tree trunks.

Grass Mats. A canvas or burlap backing to which is sewed or glued artificial material that poorly resembles grass and is painted green. Grass mats are often used just offstage by the exterior door of an interior set and almost always in exterior sets, especially around the foot of trees so as to cover the break between the tree and the stage floor.

Ramp. The sloping part of a platform that gradually rises from the stage floor to a level. A mound or walk up a cliff is technically referred to as a ramp rather than by the name of the object that it represents.

Levels. Platforms designated by one, two, or three steps, constructed of a hinged framework which closes up flat and has a flat, detachable top.

Practical. Anything that is used for its true functional purpose—as opposed to "ornamental"—for example, scenery built solidly so that it can stand the weight of the actors and be used by them to sit or stand on. *Unpractical* is the reverse of this in so far as a flight of steps or rocks or tree stump or mound may look solid but is constructed so that it may not hold average weights. Sometimes a set piece will be partially practical and partially unpractical; for instance, a hillside ramp will have parts on which an actor can walk or sit and some parts that must be avoided. The same is true of rocks on a stage.

Ground row. A piece of scenery, usually long and low, representing the distant perspective of mountains, hills, etc., placed in front of the backdrop or cyclorama in order to complete the exterior set and to mask the horizon cyc lights—practically another name for cutout.

Cutout. A piece of flat scenery having an irregular outside edge, usually made of profile board, representing distant objects. Cutouts are usually larger than ground rows, as they often represent nearer objects like houses, wharves, trees. They serve the same purpose in exterior scenes and are often used as backings for windows in interior sets.

Ground-row Strips. These strips of lighting equipment are placed in front of the ground row to help give a greater sense of distance and perspective. Accordingly, low-wattage lights are used.

Cyclorama, or Cyc. A smooth curved surface of canvas or other material, generally used as a sky backing for the scenery. In the best theaters in recent years it has taken the place of the original backdrop. Cyclorama may also mean any set of curtains or draperies enclosing the scene on three sides.

Cyclorama, or Cyc, Lights. Those strips or rows of lights which illumine the cyc. Those at the bottom are designated as horizon lights; those at the top, as cyc overheads.

Linnebach Projector. A large lantern for projecting the image from a slide on to a large drop, cyc, or set. This image becomes part of the setting.

Effect Machine. An electrical instrument, with a clock or motor mechanism, which reflects images in movement on the backdrop or gauze drop. Snow, rain, clouds, rippling water, and fire can be represented.

    All offstage or on stage sound machines, etc., are also called "effect machines." Of these we commonly have a

    a. Thunder Sheet. A four-by-eight-foot sheet of common or galvanized iron from sixteen to twenty gauge or a sheet of laminated profile board of the same size. The depth of tone depends on the size of the sheet. It is hung up and either shaken by hand or beaten with a padded hammer.

b. *Wind Machine.* A wooden drum or cylinder revolved by a crank under a tightened layer of canvas.

c. *Glass Crash.* A wooden box or a bag filled with odds and ends of broken glass and bottles, to represent the offstage noise of broken glass.

Tower. A high stand or platform of wood or steel with one or more levels on which to place powerful spotlights. It is upstage right or up left or behind the tormentors, according to its use, and it will contain instruments to simulate sunrise, sunset, moonlight, etc.

Gauze. A large, seamless mesh curtain, generally stretched tight between top and bottom battens. It is used for "visions," etc., when lights are slowly dimmed behind it; and sometimes it is used in back of stage and in front of cutouts and painted drops in order to make them seem more distant, more blended, and more real.

F. The Tab Curtain and Other Old Terms

Now and then one will hear in the theater a few terms and descriptions of former days.

Tab. The tab curtain was way downstage next to the act drop. It was used as a background in burlesque and vaudeville houses for a single or duo act performed on the apron while the next setting was being prepared. Today it is made of the same material as the act curtain and furnishes a backing when the latter is drawn aside for the actors to take a bow. It allows for a change of scenery the moment the act curtain is lowered. The Metropolitan Opera Company uses a tab curtain for curtain calls. In the theater an actor who portrays a character who has died in the last act will use one, choosing to appear for a call as an individual separate and distinct from the part and setting.

"In One," "In Two," "In Three." These phrases are used to design the hanging of a drop. They refer to the distance back from the act drop and coincide with the placement of the wings. "In one" would mean a drop on lines directly in front of the first wing; "in two," the second wing; etc.

Olio. Except in vaudeville houses this term is seldom used. It is the backing, flown halfway between "in one and in two," giving a greater space for the actor to perform than "in one" and yet not enough to prevent the setting of the next scene.

Front Scene. In the old drama a front scene was played before a painted drop; a full stage set was followed by a front with the drop as background. This was called "played as a front scene" or "played in one."

Today this refers to a small box set in front of a full stage set, to which a later set returns.

Different treatments of scenery and productions are constantly appearing in our theater. The structural arrangement and handling of scenery are constantly widening in scope and possibilities. The more common ones should be recognized and known by the beginning directors and actors.

G. Forms of Scenery

Winged Set. As the term implies, the winged set is composed of wings, borders, and backdrop, or cyc. It is the oldest form of scenery, developing as the stage did from the classical, formal, or permanent structure.

Box Set. The walls on three sides are filled in solidly with flats of one kind or another, with framed ceiling. Originally borders were used for the ceiling, but today a framed ceiling is in common practice.

Portal Set. The original portal entrances were two permanent side doors or arches, one on each side of the downstage areas. They were used from the very beginning of the theater down to the nineteenth century. In the modern theater the portal set is one that has its downstage flats the same throughout all settings of a production. By a change of the rear wall flats and the two upstage side-wall flats, the set takes on a wholly new aspect for the new scene.

Permanent Set. This is used in plays requiring settings in many different places. It consists of the main, practically constant, arrangement of flats and the insertion of various additional pieces, such as different-colored and architecturally constructed door frames, fireplaces, windows, and furniture, to change the locale of the setting.

Unit Set. The unit set is very similar to the permanent set in so far as many of the flats stand throughout an entire performance. The change in place is made by rearranging the flats and set pieces and by adding new pieces and "killing" others.

Sliding, or Wagon, Stage Set. A low platform mounted on rollers, running on tracks, as wide as the proscenium opening, and large enough to contain a set. It rolls to either side of the stage so that with two sliding stages one may be used while the other is being set up, and a quick change of scene will follow. Sometimes three wagons are used, the third coming in from the rear.

Revolving Stage Set. A large circular part of the stage floor which in its initial construction is equipped with machinery and propelled by a windlass below so that it may be revolved. Three and sometimes four sets can be erected on a revolving stage which can revolve from one setting to another in a few seconds. The settings must be erected on it, before the play begins, in rotation like the segments of a pie.

Recently, revolving stages have been set up in a regular stage floor, thereby slightly raising the floor of the revolving stage and becoming a circular platform on rollers. In this and in the sliding stage, the proscenium opening must have a slightly raised ramp to the floor of the platform so as to mask the rollers.

Sometimes the act curtain is lowered for the changes; at other times the change is made in darkness with music or stage noises to fill in the thirty odd seconds that it takes to make the shift.

H. Technical Staff

House Crew. Theaters have a staff, or crew, of workers that consists of a stage carpenter, a property man, and an electrician. In addition to these chiefs there are a varying number of "grips," or stagehands, who handle the scenery and the properties. Their number depends upon the stage union's decree as to how many "hands" it will take "to work" the show. Each of these chiefs has assistants. The number for different shows varies from ten to thirty odd.

Company Crew. Each production that goes on the road has a crew of three: a stage carpenter, a "props," and an electrician. These must be union members. The carpenter is in charge of the whole production. He has the layout of the set and works with the house carpenter in the rigging and setting up of the production. The props attends to the hand props (those objects which are used by the actors during the course of the play) and also organizes the grips who are to handle the furniture, all set pieces, rugs, floor cloth, levels, ramps, curtains, etc. The electrician, or "lights," attends to all lighting setup, electrical machines, and water machines. The props also attends to the trunks of the company, both personal (those collected and delivered to the hotels) and theater (those collected and delivered to the dressing rooms).

A New York production may have a company crew in addition or supplementary in part to the house crew.

I. Stage Management

Stage Manager and Duties. As his title implies, the stage manager is the person who is in complete charge of all the backstage, including the actors and the crews. Sometimes he may take a small part in the show. He is at all times associated with the crews in the setting up of the production and in the running of a performance. He knows the entire production and possesses all layouts, plots, and cue sheets.

Since he has such responsibilities, it is difficult to enumerate completely all his duties, especially as in all emergencies he is the one to act.

Before rehearsals he assists the director in casting; he helps get the manuscript into condition; he obtains all records of the cast (telephone numbers, addresses, etc.); he checks with the Equity representative to see that all members of the cast are or will become Equity members; with the business manager he arranges for rehearsal halls, getting permits, etc., to use them.

The stage manager should be present at all rehearsals. His duty is to lay out the floor plan of the set on the floor of the rehearsal hall; to arrange the rehearsal furniture for the director; to attend to the posting of all notices and calls for rehearsals, etc.; to keep the record of rehearsal time and of cost of heat, light, doorman, etc., of the rehearsal hall; to arrange for costume fittings with costume designer; to help the director plot rehearsals so that no time is lost during costume fittings; to make out these plots as rehearsal progresses; to spot properties, etc.; to keep a complete list of appointments, rehearsals, etc., for the cast, director, technicians, etc.; to follow closely all the business and instructions given by the director and to be able to take charge of rehearsals if he is called away; to keep prompt script up to date in duplicate (this requires a lot of night work). If there are children in the cast, he obtains their permits; if fire or guns are used, he obtains permits. For radio and publicity stunts he arranges scenes that may be used.

Assistant Stage Manager and Duties. The stage manager may have an assistant even though the production is a simple one. If it is elaborate scenically, he should have two. The duties of these assistants vary as the division of work varies with each particular production. Each accordingly should know all the duties of the stage manager, as he can never be certain what particular work is going to be his charge. During rehearsals he may "hold the book" instead of the stage manager's holding it. He may arrange the furniture. He may even work out noises that are required during the course of the play. He must be ready to take care of the hundred and one details and to run errands which are always necessary during rehearsals. He should be alert and quick to anticipate the opportunities of being useful to the stage manager and to the director.

Holding the Book. With a new play in rehearsal this is a highly responsible duty. During the early stages it consists of following carefully the script of the play; crossing out all lines that are cut; adding any new ones; writing in all business and positions on the stage that the director gives the actors. For these directions the abbreviations that have been given and used in the exercises under Stage Positions should be used. In addition to the directions the stage manager will also draw, on the right-hand margin of the script, small ground plans, signifying the positions of the characters on the stage. Further involved crosses and movements will be diagrammed. The book holder should check in some way the pauses in or between the speeches so that he will not prompt when the actor is pausing deliberately. The sign "——" is suggested for this use.

When the business has been set and the actors know their lines, prompting begins. A good prompter is quick to give the cue, often sensing the hesitation even before the actor actually "goes up" in his lines. This is especially demanded of the prompter during a performance. At rehearsals actors vary as to whether or not they wish to have a moment to think. Usually at the first rehearsals, during which they go without their parts, they do; but in the later rehearsals they will want the cue quickly. A prompter will do well to find out the actors' desires in this matter.

A prompter should never leave the book while the actors are rehearsing but take his rest while the actors and director are taking theirs.

The book holder will, during the first rehearsals, sit at a table downstage on the apron beside the director. As the play progresses in the rehearsal period and the business is set and the director is back in the house getting his "perspective" on the performance, the prompter will sit on stage right just above the tormentor. During the performance his position will vary as the set varies. He is usually at any downstage opening, behind the fireplace, a window, or a doorway. If possible, he should be downstage so that in prompting his voice will go upstage and not out into the audience.

The position from which the assistant stage manager is to prompt is known as the prompt side. It will vary between the acts of the same play, usually being placed on the side of the stage on which the longest scenes are to be played and in which there is the best opening. An actor should always know which the prompt side is, as it is not always coincident with the placing of the stage manager's box. The assistant stage manager usually prompts in a regular production during the first week of playing. If changes of script are being made, of course the prompting is continued until the play is set. Then it is unnecessary to hold the book except for noise and light cues. Occasionally a company will have an old actor who never is certain of his lines and who is likely to "go up," or "blow up," at a different place at any performance. When such is the case, the assistant stage manager should always stand with the script ready to prompt every scene in which that actor appears. The prompt book should be marked in such a way that scenes can be found quickly.

Technical Rehearsal. Before technical rehearsal the stage manager should arrange with the business manager the number of grips needed. Depending on arrangements made with the house, part of the technical staff may be furnished by the house; the remainder, by the production. The stage manager must keep a record of the number of hours that each man works.

Before technical rehearsal the stage manager should, with the assistance of the prop man, mark the positions of furniture on the ground cloth. These positions, of course, will already have been established by the director and scene designer. A different color or mark should be used for each new setup of furniture.

The stage manager supervises the technical rehearsal held exclusively for the crews to work out the routine of shifts, to work out sound effects, to set cues, and to perform other technical features of the production. He should be able to rely on the stage carpenter for working out the routine, but he must be able to suggest tactfully short cuts, time-saving moves, better routines, etc. This also holds true for the property man and electrician.

Shift Routine. Following is a suggested routine for shifting from one interior to another:

The stage manager calls "Strike," claps hands, or makes some other predetermined signal for the shift to begin. At his signal the flyman should raise the ceiling and then the backdrop. The stage crew should come on the stage and remove the rear backing. Next, they should begin to strike the scenery, beginning at the center of the rear wall of the set, unlashing it and taking it over to a part of the stage that has been cleared for the purpose of stacking it. If it is battened, after the grips have unlashed each end the flyman will raise it into the flies. Then the grips will strike the sides of the set. At the call to strike, two of the props should begin to take the furniture away from the rear wall and draw it to the middle of the stage. Then they go to the side walls and draw that furniture offstage only when the grips have removed the rear wall. They should be sure to have a place backstage cleared for receiving this furniture, and it is best to have it on the opposite side of the stage from where the scenery is being stacked.

An important factor in the quick changing of properties is to have second act furniture placed near the space where the first act furniture is to be stored, so that when the props carry the furniture from the stage to the clear space ready to receive it they can quickly take a piece from the place allotted for the second act and bring it downstage center with them as they return. They continue this process until all the furniture is cleared from the first set and all the furniture for the second set is on the stage.

The props who is handling the small props, or "trim," as soon as the call of strike is given, goes to the rear wall and removes anything on it that is to come off. He takes out, often in a basket specially provided for the purpose, the small, breakable knicknacks. When he has finished with the rear wall, he goes to the side walls for the same purpose, being careful to keep ahead of the grips in the shift. He carries these properties offstage and brings on the small properties for the second act. The props also shifts the rugs, set pieces, and levels. The light crew should remove lamps and fire logs as well as changing gelatins and refocusing the lights. The stage manager should always remain downstage center through the entire shift.

When the crews have finished striking the side walls, they begin building up the second act set. They start at the tormentors and work toward the center of the rear wall. They can begin to build up the side walls almost immediately after they have struck the first act, but they must not put in the back wall until they make sure that all the large properties are on the stage. From experience, however, we learn that they will seldom have to wait, because if the property people are taking off the old furniture and bringing on the new at the same time, they will have it all placed before the stage crew gets to the rear wall.

The grips, after they have completed the rear walls, put into place the backings for the doors and windows of the second act.

The props, as soon as the grips have put in the side walls, begins placing the furniture along those walls and dresses them with trim while other props set the mantels, doors, or windows.

As soon as the lights are set, the electrician reports to the stage manager.

As soon as the walls of the set, ceiling, and backings are in place, the stage carpenter reports to the stage manager.

As soon as the properties are in place, the props makes his report to the stage manager. When the rear wall is finished, the props can put into place the properties that go on near it. The furniture in the middle of the room can be arranged at any convenient time during the shift. The flyman lowers the ceiling and then the backdrop.

Then the assistant stage manager checks up on all the hand props on stage and the exact placement of furniture on their markings. To save time the assistant should check on these as they are being put in place.

When the set is an exterior, either to be set up or to be struck, the routine is similar although usually much simpler. The exterior set is usually made up of a cyclorama, or backdrop.

The prop crew removes the furniture and set pieces through the back. They bring on through the rear the properties for the next act.

The grips remove the side wings.

The reversal of this process is used if the shift goes into another exterior. If the next scene is an interior, the process of setting it up as given above holds good.

Dress Rehearsal. Before dress rehearsal and after he has consulted the producer or the company manager, the stage manager should post a list of the actors and the dressing rooms they are to use. The assignments he makes will depend on the "importance" of the actors and on their sex and age as well as on the position of the dressing rooms.

The stage manager should advise actors when they may bring their costumes and make-up to the theater. He should advise the business manager which actors want trunks sent to the theater.

The successful running of a dress rehearsal depends to a large degree on the stage manager. Careful organization, control, and a thorough knowledge of the production will do much in smoothing over the numberless problems that will arise.

The number of dress rehearsals will depend on the size of the production. The final dress rehearsal should function as a performance.

Performance Routine. The opening night is naturally filled with excitement and tension. If the backstage routine has been well organized during technical and dress rehearsals, much will have been done toward achieving a smoothly running technical production. This is conducive to a good performance by the actors. A carefully organized and smoothly running stage not only saves long waits between acts and unfortunate mishaps during the course of the play but also has an excellent effect on the actors. It puts confidence and stability into them, whereas confusion behind the scenes makes them more nervous, excitable, and uncertain.

The routine on the stage during a performance is highly involved. Let us suppose that the performance begins at eight-thirty.

a. At seven-thirty, or at a time specified by the stage manager depending on the complexity of make-up, all the actors in the first act should be in their dressing rooms.

b. The crews are setting the scenery for the first act. This may be true even if the production has but one set, since the fire laws of some states require the scenery to be struck between performances. No lights should be on except the work lights. The stage manager or his assistant should see that all people are kept off the stage.

c. At eight o'clock the assistant stage manager calls, "Half hour." At eight fifteen, he calls, "Fifteen minutes." Then he should check up on all the properties on the stage. At eight twenty-five, he calls, "Act I," at which time all the actors should come down to the stage and make a definite report to the assistant stage manager that they are there. On this trip from the dressing rooms, he should see that the entire cast are present, no matter how late their entrance is in the play. The stage manager should signal the lobby and lounge bells that Act I is to begin.

d. The stage manager should give the cue to the electrician to light the stage.

e. The production is ready to begin. In many theaters, however, the stage manager has to await word from the house manager as to when he is to begin, because people may be coming in in such numbers that it would be unwise to ring up the curtain at that moment. However, the wait here should not be long, for it is bad for the actors and establishes a bad principle for the audience. The maximum time of waiting should be seven minutes after the scheduled time.

f. Word has now come back for the play to begin.

g. The stage manager calls, "Places."

h. The actors go on stage, and the prompter to his place.

i. The stage manager signals to the light man, who brings up his footlights and front lights, if any, and lowers his house lights.

j. The stage manager then signals to the flyman to raise the curtain.

k. The play begins. On his time sheet the stage manager records the actual curtain time.

This is a printed form that the stage manager keeps in his box on which he records the actual time of the raising and lowering of the curtain for each act and scene. It gives, accordingly, the playing time of each act, and he and the producers can tell whether or not the company is dragging the performance. On this sheet is also a place to note the weather, a rough estimation of the size of the audience, its reaction to the performance, and the number of curtain calls. Also there is a space in which to make any report to the management, as, for instance, lateness of an actor or a stagehand in arriving at the theater or for a cue, other behavior out of the normal, complaints, etc.

This report is sent daily to the producer's office, whether the company is playing in New York or on the road.

l. During the course of the act, the stage manager and his assistant must see that there is absolute silence backstage and that other actors do not stand around talking and making noise when they are not in the scene. One or the other must then get from the cue sheet or prompt book the noises for which he is responsible and be waiting for his cue. He must further check up with the electrician any cues that he may have and see that everything is done correctly on cue.

m. The assistant stage manager should see that the actors are ready for each of their entrance cues.

n. The prop man must be near his prop table to see that each person has his hand properties before he goes on stage.

o. Two minutes before the act is over, the stage manager should give a signal to the stage crew to stand by.

p. About eight speeches before the end of the first act, the stage manager should give a warning cue to the curtain man, the light man, and all others concerned. He records in his time sheet the time that the curtain falls. When the cue for the curtain comes, he gives the signal for its lowering.

Every curtain takes some time to lower. The director and stage manager should have gauged this carefully so that the cue for the curtain will produce the right dramatic effect. This avoids the actors' having to hold a forced position for any length of time after the last word while the curtain is being lowered. If the last words of an act are vitally important and the whole meaning of a part of the play depends upon the audience's getting them, the director should have planned business to follow these last words so that the actors can be following through as the curtain falls. In this case the curtain has the final word for its cue.

Even though curtain calls do not come at the end of our first act, the light man should be careful not to kill the applause by bringing on the house lights too soon. He should wait until it begins to die down before bringing them on and should do so on cue from the stage manager.

q. The stage manager calls strike whether or not there is to be a change of scenery and goes to the down center of the stage near the act curtain. The actors, as soon as they are through with this act, even those who do not have any change of costume, must leave the stage.

r. If it is a one-set play, the intermission is comparatively simple, as the props merely checks on the new properties on the stage for the second act, and the lights make whatever changes they have for gelatins and readjust the focus of any instruments.

If there is a change, as soon as the curtain is lowered the stage manager calls strike, and all workers go into the regular shift routine, striking the first act and setting up the second. If the set is an interior, the procedure of the shift will be very similar to the one that we outlined under Technical Rehearsal.

s. The assistant stage manager two minutes before the end of the time alloted for the intermission calls the actors who come at once and directly to the stage. The stage manager signals the lobby and lounge.

t. The actors get their hand props.

u. When the stage manager has received reports from the three technical heads, he calls, "Clear stage." All but the actors who are to open the scene leave the set at once, taking with them all tools and working materials.

v. The stage manager goes to his position, signaling the lights to bring up the footlights and lower the house lights.

w. The stage manager records the time.

x. He gives the signal for the curtain.

y. The second act has begun.

For the shift from second to third act, the same routine is followed.

The stage manager, usually in conjunction with the director or producer, decides the number of curtain calls and who is to take them. There will usually be two lists: curtain calls for the opening night and those for the entire run. These he will post on the call board. In stock companies a new order must go up each week.

After the performance the stage manager must mail his report to the producer's office.

After the show has opened, the stage manager on a designated morning each week must rehearse the understudies, going through the entire play. He himself and his assistant are usually understudies, besides other members of the company staff. Understudies must be present at each performance a half hour before curtain time and should stay until at least half through the performance. Some stage managers will require them to remain during the whole performance.

On long runs, the stage manager will periodically hold company rehearsals to keep up the playing of the cast, the timing, and actions or business that members of the cast may blur during a long run. The frequency of these company rehearsals depends on how well the cast keeps up the performance.

When a show closes or moves from one location to another, the stage manager must be present to supervise the work.

On the Road. When a company travels, the stage manager should know the rigging and handling of the sets, properties, and lights, although the company carpenter actually superintends the rigging with the house carpenter, the props with the house props, and lights with the house lights. However, the stage manager will find that most of this whole first day of each stand on the road will be spent in the theater.

The advance man will already have arranged for the orchestra, the numbers, etc., but the stage manager will arrange with the leader of the orchestra for the cues, volume, etc.

The stage manager will check all material that arrives at the theater and will post dressing-room assignments.

He also holds understudy and company rehearsals when on the road.

Index

415